A Life for the Tsar:
Triumph and Tragedy at the Coronation of Emperor Nicholas II

By Greg King & Janet Ashton

ISBN: 978-1-944207-04-5

EUROHISTORY.COM

6300 Kensington Avenue
East Richmond Heights, CA 94805 USA
Phone: (510) 236-1730 — Email: books@eurohistory.com

A Life for the Tsar:
Triumph and Tragedy at the
Coronation of Emperor Nicholas II

© 2016 Greg King & Janet Ashton

ISBN: 978-1-944207-04-5

Artistic Design ©Arturo Beéche & David W. Higdon
Cover Design ©David W. Higdon

All rights reserved. No part of this book covered by the copyrights herein may be reproduced or used in any form or by any means without prior consent of the publisher, except for brief passages covered by reviewers or fair use by other authors. Reproducing passages from this book by any means, including mimeographic, photocopying, scanning, recording, or by any information retrieval system is an infringement of copyright law.

We would like to express our appreciation to:

Annet Bakker at Hoogstraten English Bookstore, Nicolas Fouint
at Librairie Galignani, Joe Little and Jeannie Pittard-Whitmarsh at MAJESTY,
Maria Smith and Denise Kilpatrick, Ian Shapiro, Judith Grant, Hilde Vieveen,
Mary Houck, Geoff Teeter, Katrina Warne, Seth Leonard, Henry Wong, Ian Shapiro,
the late Jacques Ferrand, and the late William Mead Lalor.

Special appreciation to Princess Elizabeth of Yugoslavia and Count Hans-Veit zu Toerring-Jettenbach for allowing use of some of their photos.

List of Contents

Author's Note	i
Acknowledgements	iii
Cast of Characters	v
Introduction	xi
Chapter I	1
Chapter II	18
Chapter III	35
Chapter IV	46
Chapter V	59
Chapter VI	68
Chapter VII	79
Chapter VIII	90
Chapter IX	107
Chapter X	128
Chapter XI	140
Chapter XII	161
Epilogue	176
Family Tree	190
End Notes	192
Bibliography	204
Index	212

To the victims of Khodynka ...

Author's Note

It is a truism of books about Russia that Western readers find the long names confusing and hard on the eye. This is because a Russian has two first names: a Christian name and a patronymic derived from his or her father. The masculine form takes the father's first name and adds *"o/evich"* to the ending, indicating "son of." Thus Emperor Nicholas II was Nikolai Alexandrovich, son of Alexander. For daughters, *"o/evna"* is added to the end of the father's name: Maria Pavlovna, daughter of Grand Duke Paul, for example. Surnames take a masculine or feminine ending as well: Nikolai Alexandrovich Romanov and Maria Pavlovna Romanova. During the reign of Nicholas II, the Imperial Family included some sixty individuals, who often shared Christian names but who, in common with most royalty, did not generally use their surname. To distinguish between them, we have therefore frequently used their patronymics in the text, as was also the contemporary custom, with the hope that this will make the complex relationships in the Imperial Family easier for readers to follow. However, for the sake of brevity, we have eschewed normal Russian custom and have not given patronymics for ministers, court officials and others who customarily used surnames and who are therefore unlikely to be confused with each other.

Tsar Nicholas II and his only son Tsesarevich Alexei Nikolaievich.

We have also tried not to overuse formalities, but in a book about a coronation, readers will inevitably encounter a variety of titles. Until 1721, as we explain in the Introduction, all Romanov rulers were called tsar, which was commonly believed to have derived from the Latin word caesar but was actually adapted from the Greek translation of the Byzantine title basileus, signifying a Christian emperor. Peter the Great officially adopted the title Gosudar Imperator, or Sovereign Emperor; until the end of the Empire, this was the correct form of address. Despite this, the Emperor was still often referred to as Tsar, particularly in more nationalist circles, and his wife, bearing the title Imperatritsa, or Empress, was commonly called Tsaritsa. *"Tsarina,"* familiar to some readers, is a westernization that never existed in Russian. As a Slavophile who proclaimed his love for all things traditional, Nicholas II preferred the older title of Tsar; conversely, his wife Alexandra preferred Empress. In this book, which focuses on the moment in his reign when titles needed to be most precise, we have chosen Emperor and Empress, leaving Tsar and Tsaritsa in place only for direct quotations.

Peter the Great also altered the title of the heir to the throne from Tsarevich, meaning *"son of the tsar,"* to Tsesarevich, a higher distinction derived from Byzantine models. Nicholas I refined the title to Gosudar Naslednik: *"sovereign heir."* Nicholas II had no son until 1904, so the title is rarely mentioned here, except occasionally in reference to Nicholas himself before his own accession. It was actually assigned on his accession to his eldest surviving brother, Grand Duke George Alexandrovich, but erroneously so since George was not Heir Apparent but rather Heir Presumptive. As he was living in the Caucasus with advanced tuberculosis, George did not take part in the Coronation. He died in 1899.

Paul I established a number of rules governing the Imperial Family, which also spelled out the distinctions in their titles. A male was a *Velikii Kniaz*, translated by the Imperial Court, which used French as its official language, as *"Grand Duc,"* or Grand Duke in English; a female was a *Velikaia Kniazhna*, or Grand Duchess. Married women were marked with a subtle difference, *Velikaia Kniaginia*, although there was no change to their designation in translation as Grand Duchesses. In 1886, Alexander III restricted the use of Grand Duke and Grand Duchess to the children and the male-line grandsons of an Emperor; lesser members of the Imperial Family were thereafter titled a Prince or a Princess of the Imperial Blood.

Titles used by the imperial court present their own unique difficulties. Court offices followed Peter the Great's Table of Ranks, or Chin, a system he introduced that established sixteen categories of officials, arranged according to their hierarchy. Although French was the official language of the Court, its officials largely bore titles originally drawn from German models but transliterated into their own, peculiar Russian form: Ober-Tseremoniimeister (Grand Master of Ceremonies), Kammer-Junker (Gentleman of the Chamber), and Fligel-Adjutant (Aide-de-Camp). An additional corruption stems from the fact that in the Russian language, there is no letter *"h."* Titles copied from German models, such as Hof-Marschall (Master of the Court) and Hof-Meisterina (Mistress of the Court) therefore become, in Russian, Gof-Marschal and Gof-Meisterina. This led to a mixture of German and English, such Freilina (Maid of Honor). As such, they stand as curiosities, and often their English translations are awkward. We have given English translations as the Russian versions of these titles appear in the text, though we have moved freely between these three languages throughout, in an effort to not only maintain the flavor of Nicholas II's court but also ease the task for readers.

In transliterating all these Russian words, we have largely followed the Library of Congress method. This allows Christian names – and those names familiar to English-speaking readers – to be rendered in a *"conventional form"* in English: thus, we have *"Nicholas"* instead of *"Nikolai,"* *"Alexandra"* for *"Aleksandra,"* *"Marie"* rather than *"Mariia,"* *"Xenia"* for *"Ksenia,"* and *"Tchaikovsky"* in place of the unfamiliar *"Chaikovskii."* We have done the same for some patronymics, choosing the form *"Alexandrovich"* – a patronymic shared by many of the Grand Dukes – over the strict transliteration *"Aleksandrovich."* We also vary spellings on a few other occasions, mainly in respect of place or other proper names which we feel look strange in transliteration to English-speakers, or which have a conventional form commonly used in English. Hence, we call Moscow's main street the *"Tverskaya,"* although a literal transliteration would be *"Tverskaia;"* the elite regiment whose uniform Nicholas wore for the ceremony is *"Preobrazhensky"* rather than the literal *"Preobrazhenskii."*

For Chinese names we use the Wade Giles system, which is no longer the scholarly preference, but which reflects the spellings commonly chosen in our Nineteenth Century sources. Hence, the Chinese ambassador to Nicholas's Coronation is Li-Hung Chang here, rather than Li Hongzhang, as he might be spelled today. For Japanese and Korean names, we have followed current academic conventions.

An icon of Emperor Nicholas II in Coronation regalia.

Until spring 1918, Russia used the Julian calendar rather than the Gregorian one that is used in the West. As a result, dates in the Nineteenth Century were twelve days behind those in the West. We have elected to render dates in the Julian calendar, in keeping with the Coronation setting. Where important for the readers' understanding, or when events took place in Western Europe, we have given dates according to both calendars or to the Gregorian calendar.

When discussing issues of finance, we have used a calculation based on an 1895 valuation of the ruble, dollar, franc and pound sterling. In giving 2014 equivalents, we start with the original currency and then render it separately into each of the others – we do not, for example, put rubles into dollars and then dollars into pound sterling, as the relationships between the foreign currencies are inevitably different from each of their own relationships to the ruble. Sources do not agree on exact relative values (it can depend whether one is speaking of real estate, food, labor or so on), so it goes without saying that there is some considerable degree of flexibility in these figures. We have given them as rough indictors only to provide context to the expenditures.

Acknowledgements

This book is the result of a long, organic evolution. Fascinated as we both are with the Romanov Dynasty and interested in pursuing unique and exciting aspects of its history, we stumbled upon the Coronation of Nicholas II as a potential subject quite by accident. The ceremony itself formed an integral part of Greg's 2005 work *The Court of the Last Tsar: Pomp, Power, and Pageantry in the Reign of Nicholas II*. In the research and writing process, Janet discovered a wealth of previously neglected materials on the subject that helped bring the event to dramatic life: so much material, in fact, that it was impossible to include more than a tantalizing hint in a single chapter.

In these years, we collaborated and exchanged ideas. There were articles for *Atlantis Magazine: In the Courts of Memory*, which Greg founded and edited with Penny Wilson, as well as *Royalty Digest*, but the idea of a book on the events of 1896 always lingered as a future possibility. A range of experiences – from members of the Imperial Family and their royal cousins to foreign tourists and factory workers – existed about the coronation but had largely escaped notice. A few works had included extracts of various accounts, but not one attempted to draw all of the disparate strands together into a cogent narrative while analyzing the event's impact on Russian society. The Coronation, as this book's subtitle suggests, exemplified Nicholas II's reign as whole: a time of triumphs alongside tragedies; in addition, we both realized that the pivotal nature of these events had been largely overlooked. What happened in Moscow helped establish perceptions about Russia's new sovereign and actually damaged the monarchy in ways few had yet perceived. There was the allure of grand ceremony alongside a very human story of disaster that has often been ignored. Realizing this gap, a book on the subject seemed in order. After more than a decade of research and writing, we were finally able to compose a mosaic of these events that included not only pageantry but also pathos.

Over those years we worked – actively or otherwise – on collecting material and developing thoughts, and many people have contributed suggestions or answered questions that have led us to sources or ideas. We owe a particular debt to one historian with whom neither of us has any direct contact: Dr. Richard Wortman, author of many seminal works on ceremony and myth at the Russian Court. We also have the pleasure of being able to thank our friends, influential Russian history colleagues Joseph Fuhrmann and Dave Schimmelpenninck van der Oye.

In working on the book itself, we have prevailed on the time and goodwill of many friends, colleagues, archivists, curators and librarians who have assisted in hunting down sources or replying to queries. For their time and helpful input, we would like to thank Father David Cole; Richard Davies; Milan Grba; Coryne Hall; Michael Jones of the John A. Logan Museum; the staff of the Maryhill Museum of Art at Goldendale, Washington; Katya Rogatshevskaia; Prince Nicholas Romanoff; Niall Slater; Elena Tsvetkova; Debbie Usher; Katrina Warne; Christopher Warwick; Frances Wood; and the late John Wimbles. Damon Smith's first offer to publish gave us the impetus to start writing, and Dr. Barry Taylor, editor of the British Library's electronic *Journal*, enthusiastically accepted an article based on some of the research we had done for this book, which meant a lot when we were at a low point and despaired of ever seeing it in print. Ian Shapiro shared some invaluable photographs from the collection if Princess Irene of Prussia. For support ranging from conference invitations to kind messages to floors to sleep on, we would like to thank Dominic Albanese; Lisa Davidson; Mark Grassick; Gretchen Haskin; Gary Holtzman; Emma Lambert; Mathieu Martyn; the late Richard Thornton; Marion Wynn; and all present at the *Royalty Digest Weekend* in Ticehurst in April 2009, and *European Royal History Journal* conference in San Francisco, October 2010. Of course, Arturo Beéche, publisher of the *European Royal History Journal* (*Eurohistory*) and organizer of its conferences (San

Francisco, London and The Hague), has been an enthusiastic supporter of this book and we are delighted to have him as our publisher.

Ten people have read the manuscript in whole or in part, as their own lives and schedules have allowed. For the gift of their time, honesty and knowledge, providing helpful comments to correct information and confirm or query style and direction, we owe gratitude to Ilana Miller; Sarah Miller; Helen Rappaport; Salome Samii; Penny Wilson; and Sue Woolmans. William Lee not only read one of the several "final" versions at short notice but also contributed translations from his own research. Griff Henninger drew our attention to some sources of especial interest, responding with great generosity of spirit to a manuscript that articulates a perspective on Nicholas II very different to his own. And Simon Donoghue and Mike Pyles both read the manuscript twice, their ideas and responses proving of particular value at a conceptual level in helping us to focus on what we wanted the book to achieve.

As always, we thank our families and friends for their enthusiastic support and devotion. Christophe Martyn has put the hours taken from his personal life to equally good use, building a success internet music business during the same period that this book was in gestation!

Greg King and Janet Ashton
April 2016

Cast of Characters

The House of Romanov

Nicholas II (1868–1918), last Russian Emperor, reigned 1894–1917.
Alexandra Feodorovna (1872–1918), Empress and consort of Nicholas II, born Princess Alix of Hesse and by Rhine.
Olga Nikolaievna (1895–1918), Grand Duchess and eldest daughter of Nicholas and Alexandra.
Marie Feodorovna (1847–1928), Dowager Empress of Russia, widow of Alexander III, and mother of Nicholas II; born Princess Dagmar, daughter of King Christian IX of Denmark.
George Alexandrovich (1871-1899), Grand Duke and younger brother of Nicholas II.
Xenia Alexandrovna (1875–1960), Grand Duchess, eldest sister of Nicholas II, wife of Grand Duke Alexander Mikhailovich.
Michael Alexandrovich (1878-1918) ("Misha"), Grand Duke and youngest brother of Nicholas II.
Olga Alexandrovna (1882–1960), Grand Duchess, youngest sister of Nicholas II.
Vladimir Alexandrovich (1847-1909), Grand Duke, third son of Alexander II, younger brother of Alexander III, uncle to Nicholas II, Infantry General of the Russian Army and Commander of the Imperial Guard and of the Moscow Garrison during the Coronation.
Marie Pavlovna (1854-1920) ("Miechen"), Grand Duchess, wife of Grand Duke Vladimir Alexandrovich, daughter of Grand Duke Friedrich Franz II of Mecklenburg-Schwerin.
Kirill Vladimirovich (1876–1938), Grand Duke, eldest son of Grand Duke Vladimir Alexandrovich and first cousin to Nicholas II; married (1905) Princess Victoria Melita ("Ducky"), divorced wife of Grand Duke Ernst Ludwig of Hesse and by Rhine.
Alexei Alexandrovich (1850-1908), Grand Duke, fourth son of Alexander II, younger brother of Alexander III, uncle to Nicholas II, General-Admiral of the Russian Navy and Commander of the Imperial Fleet.
Sergei Alexandrovich (1857-1905), Grand Duke, fifth son of Alexander II, younger brother of Alexander III, uncle and brother-in-law to Nicholas II, Governor-General of Moscow.
Elisabeth Feodorovna (1864-1918) ("Ella"), Grand Duchess, former Princess of Hesse and by Rhine, elder sister to Empress Alexandra, married (1884) to Nicholas II's uncle Grand Duke Sergei Alexandrovich.
Paul Alexandrovich (1860-1919), Grand Duke, sixth son of Alexander II, youngest brother of Alexander III, uncle to Nicholas II, Commander of the Imperial Guards Cavalry Division.
Alexandra Iosifovna (1830-1911) ("Aunt Sanny"), Grand Duchess, widow of Nicholas I's son Grand Duke Konstantin Nikolaievich.
Konstantin Konstantinovich (1858-1915), Grand Duke, son of Grand Duchess Alexandra Iosifiovna, brother of Queen Olga of Greece.
Michael Nikolaievich (1832-1909), Grand Duke and fourth son of Nicholas I.
Nicholas Mikhailovich (1859-1919) ("Bimbo"), Grand Duke, eldest son of Grand Duke Michael Nikolaievich, historian, first cousin once removed to Nicholas II.
Alexander Mikhailovich (1866-1932) ("Sandro"), Grand Duke, son of Grand Duke Michael Nikolaievich, cousin once removed and brother-in-law to Nicholas II.

Royal Relations

Ernst Ludwig (1868–1937) ("Ernie"), Grand Duke of Hesse and by Rhine, brother of Empress Alexandra, married their first cousin Princess Victoria Melita of Great Britain ("Ducky") 1894 (divorced 1901).
Victoria Melita (1876-1936) ("Ducky"), Grand Duchess of Hesse and by Rhine, born Princess of Great Britain

Empress Marie Feodorovna and her eldest son, then Tsesarevich Nicholas Alexandrovich.

and Edinburgh (later of Saxe-Coburg and Gotha), daughter of Queen Victoria's second son Prince Alfred and his wife Grand Duchess Marie Alexandrovna; first cousin to both Nicholas II and Empress Alexandra Feodorovna; sister to Crown Princess Marie of Romania ("Missy"); married (1894) her first cousin Grand Duke Ernst Ludwig of Hesse and by Rhine ("Ernie") (divorced 1901); married (1905) her first cousin Grand Duke Kirill Vladimirovich.

Louis (1854-1921), Prince of Battenberg (later Marquess of Milford Haven), morganatic son of Prince Alexander of Hesse and by Rhine, brother of Empress Marie Alexandrovna, and of Princess Julie of Battenberg (née von Hauke); brother-in-law of Nicholas II and Alexandra Feodorovna.

Victoria (1863-1950), Princess Louis of Battenberg (later Marchioness of Milford Haven), born Princess Victoria of Hesse and by Rhine, eldest sister to Empress Alexandra Feodorovna; married (1884) Prince Louis of Battenberg (later Marquess of Milford Haven).

Heinrich (1862-1929) ("Henry"), Prince of Prussia, younger brother of Kaiser Wilhelm II, first cousin to Empress Alexandra, married (1888) her sister Princess Irene of Hesse and by Rhine (1866–1953).

Irene (1866-1953) ("Irene"), Princess Henry of Prussia, former Princess of Hesse and by Rhine, elder sister to Empress Alexandra, married (1888) to Prince Henry of Prussia.

Marie (1875-1938) ("Missy"), Crown Princess of Romania, born Princess of Great Britain and Edinburgh (and later of Saxe-Coburg and Gotha), daughter of Queen Victoria's second son Prince Alfred and his wife Grand Duchess Marie Alexandrovna; first cousin to both Nicholas II and Empress Alexandra Feodorovna; sister to Victoria Melita ("Ducky"), Grand Duchess of Hesse and by Rhine; married (1893) Crown Prince Ferdinand of Romania (the future King Ferdinand I of Romania); later Queen of Romania 1914-1927 (as consort).

Olga Konstantinovna (1851-1926), Queen of Greece, granddaughter of Emperor Nicholas I, daughter of Grand Duke Konstantin Nikolaievich and Alexandra Iosifovna, first cousin to Alexander III; married King George I of the Hellenes (former Prince Wilhelm of Denmark), brother of Dowager Empress Marie Feodorovna; aunt to Nicholas II.

Frederick (1843-1912), Crown Prince of Denmark (King Frederick VIII 1906-1912), eldest son of King Christian IX of Denmark, brother to Dowager Empress Marie Feodorovna, uncle to Nicholas II.

Alfred (1844-1900) ("Affie"), Prince of Great Britain, Duke of Edinburgh, (from 1893) Duke of Saxe-Coburg and Gotha; second son of Queen Victoria; uncle to Empress Alexandra Feodorovna; married (1874) Grand Duchess Marie Alexandrovna, only daughter of Alexander II and aunt to Nicholas II; father of both Grand Duchess Victoria Melita of Hesse and by Rhine ("Ducky") and Crown Princess Marie of Romania ("Missy"); inherited the throne of the German Duchy of Saxe-Coburg and Gotha 1893 from his paternal uncle Duke Ernst II.

Marie Alexandrovna (1853-1920), Grand Duchess, Duchess of Edinburgh, (from 1893) Duchess of Saxe-Coburg and Gotha; only daughter of Alexander II; married (1874) Prince Alfred, Duke of Edinburgh ("Affie"), second son of Queen Victoria; mother to both Grand Duchess Victoria Melita of Hesse and by Rhine ("Ducky") and Crown Princess Marie of Romania ("Missy"); aunt to Nicholas II.

Arthur (1850-1942), Prince of Great Britain, Duke of Connaught; third son of Queen Victoria; uncle to Empress Alexandra Feodorovna; attended Coronation with his wife Louise Margaret, formerly Princess of Prussia.

Diplomatic Representatives

Agliardi, Cardinal Antonio (1832-1915), Papal Nuncio, represented Pope Leo XIII in Moscow; during stay elevated from Archbishop of Caesarea to the rank of Cardinal.

Breckinridge, Clifton R. (1846-1932), American Minister to Russia; married to Katherine Carson Breckinridge (1853-1921).

Creighton, Dr. Mandell (1843-1901), Bishop of Peterborough; represented the Church of England at the Coronation in Moscow.

Grenfell, Major-General Sir Francis (1841-1925), Inspector-General of the British Army Auxiliary Forces; attended Coronation as part of the official British delegation; author of Coronation memoir.

Li-Hung Chang (Li Hongzhang) (1823-1901), Grand Chancellor and Extraordinary Ambassador from China to the Coronation.

Logan, Captain John A. (born Manning Alexander Logan) (1865-1899), son of U. S. Senator John A. Logan and his wife Mary Cunningham Logan; Army attaché in official American delegation at the Coronation; author of Coronation memoir.

Malcolm, Ian (1868-1944), diplomat, Member of Parliament; attended Coronation as part of the official British

delegation.
*****Montebello, Count Louis Gustave de***** (1838-1907), French Ambassador to Russia; married (1873) Madeleine Guillemin (1853-1930).
*****O'Conor, Sir Nicholas***** (1843-1908), British Ambassador to Russia.
*****von Radolin, Prince Hugo***** (1841-1917), German Ambassador to Russia.
*****Sayed Abd al-Ahad Bakhadur-Khan***** (1859-1910), Emir of Bokhara.

Interested Parties

*****Hickley, Mary***** (1856-1932), British missionary; witnessed Coronation proceedings as guest of the Golitsyn family; author of Coronation memoir.
*****Kanatchikov, Semen***** (1879-1940), young apprentice at the Gustav List Factory in Moscow during the Coronation; later Communist Party official.
*****Koon, Katherine***** ("Kate") (1874-1964), daughter of Minneapolis judge Martin Buren Koon; attended Coronation with her sister Louise in the care of Mrs. Mary Cunningham Logan of Washington, D.C.; author of Coronation memoir.
*****Koon, Marilla Louise***** ("Lou") (1876-1962), daughter of Minneapolis judge Martin Buren Koon; attended Coronation with her sister Katherine ("Kate") in the care of Mrs. Mary Cunningham Logan of Washington D.C.
*****Kschessinska, Mathilde***** (later Princess Romanovsky-Krassinsky) (1872-1971), prima ballerina, former mistress to Nicholas II; later married his first cousin Grand Duke Andrei Vladimirovich, son of Grand Duke Vladimir Alexandrovich.
*****Logan, Mary Cunningham***** (1838-1923), widow of U. S. Senator John Logan, mother of Captain John A. Logan who attended the Coronation as part of the official American delegation; came to Moscow from Washington, D.C. as chaperone to Katherine and Louise Koon.
*****Moisson, Charles, and François Doublier,***** cinematographers from the Lumiere Company in Lyon; filmed Coronation processions and scenes at Khodynka Field.
*****Palmer, Bertha Honoré***** (1849-1918), Chicago gilded age hostess; attended the Coronation with her husband real estate developer Potter Palmer.
*****Roebling, Emily Warren***** (1843-1903), American tourist at the Coronation, supervised completion of New York's Brooklyn Bridge.

Journalists

*****Davis, Richard Harding***** (1864-1916), American journalist; reported on the Coronation for Harper's Magazine and the New York Journal.
*****LaPauze, Henry,***** French art critic and writer; wrote memoirs of the Coronation.
*****Maude, Aylmer***** (1858-1938), British-born translator and journalist in Moscow; wrote critical memoir of the Coronation.
*****Nemirovich-Danchenko, Vladimir***** (1858-1943), journalist in Moscow representing the popular illustrated journal Niva.
*****Stanhope, Aubrey,***** American journalist; reported on the Coronation in Moscow for The New York Herald.
*****Suvorin, Alexei***** (1834-1912), prominent journalist, owner of conservative newspaper Novoe Vremia.
*****Sykes, Arthur Alkin,***** British journalist; wrote memoir of the Coronation.
*****Vianzone, Therese,***** French religious writer; wrote memoir of the Coronation.
*****Wallace, Sir Donald Mackenzie***** (1841-1919), British journalist, writer and diplomat; reported on the Coronation for The Times of London.

Officials in Moscow

*****Berr, General N. N.,***** Moscow Chairman of the Special Commission for the Arrangement of the Coronation Popular Spectacles and Festivals; responsible for planning the People's Feast on Khodynka Field.

Princess Alix of Hesse and by Rhine with her father, Grand Duke Ludwig IV.

***Ioannakius**, Metropolitan of Kiev 1891-1900 (born Rudnev), Russian Orthodox cleric, assisted at the Coronation.
***Izvolsky, Alexander** (1856-1919), Court Chamberlain during the Coronation; future Minister of Foreign Affairs; cousin to Minister of Justice Nicholas Muraviev; married to niece of Count Konstantin von der Pahlen.
***Muraviev, Nicholas** (1850-1908), Minister of Justice; protégé of Grand Duke Sergei Alexandrovich; conducted investigation into the Khodynka tragedy.
***Palladius**, Metropolitan of St. Petersburg 1892-1898 (born Paul Raev-Pisarev) (1827-1898), Russian Orthodox cleric, assisted at the Coronation.
***Pobedonostsev, Konstantin** (1827-1907), prominent statesman, former tutor to Nicholas II; Ober-Procurator of the Holy Synod (Minister of Religion).
***Sergei**, Metropolitan of Moscow, Russian Orthodox cleric, officiated at the Coronation.
***Trubetskoy, Prince Peter**, Head of the Moscow Nobility.
***Vlassovsky, Colonel A. A.**, formerly Chief of Police in Riga; Chief of the Moscow Police.
***Witte, Sergei** (1849-1915), prominent statesman, Minister of Finance to Alexander III and Nicholas II; later Prime Minister to Nicholas II.
***Yanishev, Father Ioann** (1826-1910), Russian Orthodox cleric, Personal Confessor to Nicholas II and Empress Alexandra.

Courtiers

***Dolgoruky, Prince Alexander Sergeievich**, Chief Grand Master of Ceremonies.
***de Freedericksz, Baron (later Count) Vladimir*, Deputy Minister of the Imperial Court; Minister of the Imperial Court from 1897-1917.
***Krivenko, Vassili**, Chief of the Imperial Chancellery; head of the official Correspondents' Bureau in Moscow; later edited the official Coronation Album published by the Ministry of the Imperial Court.
***Naryshkina-Kurakina, Princess Elizabeth**, Lady-in-Waiting to the Empress; acted as her Chief Lady-in-Waiting and Mistress of the Robes during the Coronation.
***von der Pahlen, Count Konstantin*, former Minister of the Imperial Court; Chief Grand Marshal of the Imperial Court; later conducted private investigation into the Khodynka tragedy.
***Shuvalov, Count Paul** (1859-1905), adjutant to Grand Duke Sergei Alexandrovich; married (1890) to Alexandra, daughter of Minister of the Imperial Court Count Hilarion Vorontsov-Dashkov.
***Volkov, Alexei** (1868–1929), valet to Grand Duke Paul Alexandrovich; later valet de chambre to Empress Alexandra Feodorovna.
***Vorontsov-Dashkov, General Count Hilarion** (1837-1916), Minister of the Imperial Court; planned the Coronation ceremonies; father-in-law to Count Paul Shuvalov, adjutant to Grand Duke Sergei Alexandrovich; relieved of his post in 1897 in the wake of the Khodynka tragedy; later Viceroy of the Caucasus.

Members of the Imperial Corps des Pages

***Keller, General Count Feodor** (1850-1904), officer in the Imperial Army; Director of the Imperial Corps des Pages in St. Petersburg in 1896.
***Apraxin**, Kammer Page assigned to Empress Alexandra Feodorovna.
***Cherkesov, Sergei**, Kammer Page assigned to Crown Princess Marie of Romania; killed in the Russo-Japanese War.
***Deruzhinsky**, Kammer Page assigned to Dowager Empress Marie Feodorovna.
***Engelhardt, Boris**, Kammer Page assigned to Dowager Empress Marie Feodorovna.
***Ignatiev, Alexei**, Kammer Page assigned to Empress Alexandra Feodorovna.
***Mandryk, Alexander**, Kammer Page assigned to Nicholas II.
***Roop, Sergei**, Kammer Page during the Coronation.

Introduction

*I*t was beautiful, opulent, and almost surreal. Wispy clouds of incense drifted upwards through golden shafts of sunshine, while the *"high, clear voices of the boys mingled with the deeper bass notes of the men"* intoning sonorous hymns as Russia unknowingly celebrated the coronation of its last emperor. Flickering flames of a thousand votive candles shimmered over gowns of silver brocade, flashed across gilded icons, sparkled against diamonds, and glanced on medals. This intoxicating pageant of sounds and colors, scents and sensations left onlookers *"dazed."*[1]

Nicholas II's Coronation in Moscow's Cathedral of the Assumption that May of 1896 was a carefully crafted piece of stagecraft, meant to transport the densely packed congregation to a realm of intense spiritual power fused to unyielding autocracy. The scene was not without irony: the imperial splendor and religious rituals of the Russian Orthodox Church celebrated a monarch who scarcely carried a drop of Russian blood in his veins. The young Nicholas stood before the congregation, his face pale. It was not just the emotion of the moment: the heavy crown atop his head and the golden mantle enveloping his shoulders – the very symbols of majestic power – nearly subsumed him. He looked small, trapped, almost overwhelmed by the opulent surroundings at the ceremonial pinnacle of his reign.

No one gathered in the cathedral that day suspected that Russia would never again witness such a lavish political and religious pageant. The moment of triumph was short. Four days later, over a thousand people were crushed to death during a popular coronation festival on Moscow's Khodynka Meadow. In the years that followed Russia witnessed political unrest, assassinations, and military defeats. Alongside Nicholas II's personal tragedies of a hemophiliac heir, a distraught wife under the spell of the infamous peasant Gregory Rasputin, and an erosion of loyalty, these brought Revolution and carried the Imperial Family to their deaths in a dingy Siberian cellar in 1918. Yet it was the Khodynka disaster that set the fateful pattern and defined the Emperor's and his peoples' reactions to each other. More than hemophilia, more than Rasputin, more than the revolution of 1905, the loss of life on that crowded, dusty field shattered the imperial mythology of a benevolent tsar paternally tending to the needs of his people. Caught between archaic autocracy and a world of modern expectations, Nicholas II fell at the first hurdle, destroying the work of generations.

Tsar Nicholas II of Russia.

On the surface, the coronation ceremonies in Moscow offered visible demonstrations of the Imperial Court's brilliance and the Russian Empire's greatness, meant to enforce the monarch's power and prestige.[2] Yet the dazzling pomp and imposing ceremonial were merely a bewitching façade concealing what was, at heart, a marriage of spiritual grace and temporal power in a single man, unlike anything else in Europe.

By 1896, grand ceremonial coronations of autocratic monarchs were a thing of the past. Civil War in England had brought Charles I to an executioner in Whitehall when his conception of autocracy placed him at odds with parliament, and years of taxation and discontent with Bourbon rule took Louis XVI and

Marie Antoinette to a guillotine in Paris. Reform and modern expectation led the rulers of Sweden, Spain, Italy, Greece, Denmark, Germany, Austria, Romania, Portugal, and the Netherlands to forego the elaborate, ritualized coronations of their ancestors in favor of simple oaths. Nicholas and Alexandra's British relatives were notable exceptions, though they had abandoned any claim to divine rule.

Russians, though, viewed the ceremonies through a deeper, transcendent lens. The celebrations reinforced not only their menial positions in the Empire and the sanctity of their ruling family, but also the validity of the autocracy itself. There were, or so went the popular national formula, three Romes in history. The first, insisting on the primacy of Catholic theology, had fallen into the heresy that brought about the 1054 schism between the Roman and Eastern churches. The second Rome, Constantinople, had guarded the True Faith in its Byzantine Empire, but in 1453 – and in a clear sign of divine judgment – it had fallen to the invading Turks. Into the void stepped Moscow, proclaiming itself to be the "Third Rome," rightful successor to the Byzantine Empire, defender of the one True Faith, and its ruler the spiritual inheritor of autocratic, Christian sovereignty.[3]

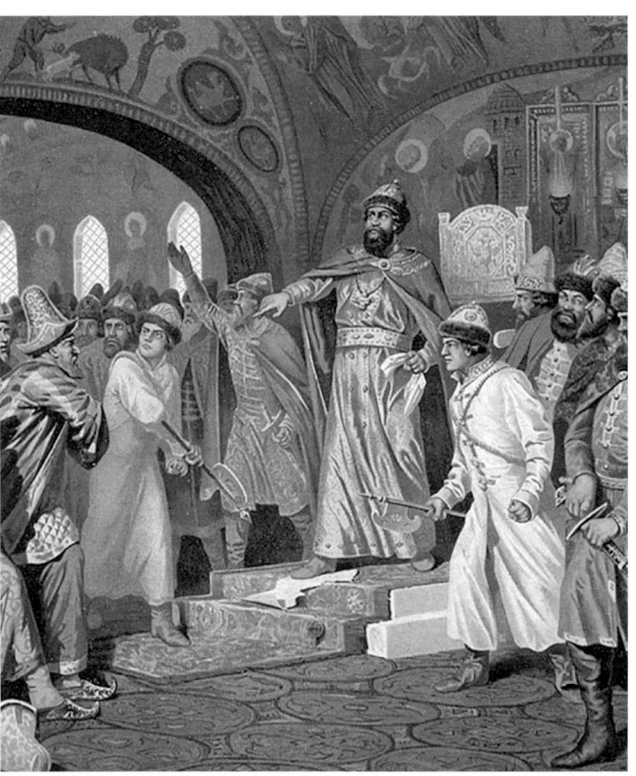
Ivan III, Grand Prince of Moscow.

Religion shrouded every aspect of the coronation: parades and processions, reviews and banquets – all, noted a journalist in amazement, were *"solemn"* according to proclamations by the Russian Government.[4] It was not merely the physical crowning of a ruler: it was the anointing, at the hands of priests, bishops, and metropolitans of the Orthodox Church, of the monarch as God's Representative on earth, *Batiushka*-Tsar, Father of the Russian People. *"In the Christian world,"* declared a Russian historian, *"Autocracy is the highest level of power. It is the last link between the power of man and the power of God."*[5] Nicholas II shared these views, even if he regarded the crown as a burden; in his diary, he referred to his coronation festivities as *"the difficult days ahead."*[6]

No one could escape the overarching message: in advance of Nicholas II's coronation, his government provided foreign journalists with a helpful explanation. Printed in four languages (Russian, English, German, and French), it declared that Imperial power *"forms the heart of the nation. All Russia prays for the Tsar, as for her father; from Him descends grace and benevolence upon His subjects; in Him all good finds support and protection, and evil merited punishment."* Nicholas II himself, imbued with *"the affection of the Lord,"* was guided by *"the right hand of the Almighty"* in all he did. The autocracy, it insisted, was nothing less than God's *"manifestation of His affection for the Russian people."*[7]

These people, official Russia was sure, were absolute in their loyalty. *"To a man,"* one diplomat insisted, *"they all believe in the divine origin of the Imperial dignity….To our simple-minded peasants, the Tsar comes immediately after the Holy Trinity; it is God Himself who has given him his power and commands them to obey. To the pious minds of these humble folk, such radiance thus emanates from his sacred person that he appears to be the image of Christ on Earth."*[8]

The Emperor was *"supreme defender and protector of the dogmas of the established Russian Orthodox Faith,"* charged with *"protecting the purity"* of the church.[9] Nicholas II codified such beliefs into law. The crime of sacrilege extended to any offense *"against God"* as *"represented by Our Most Holy Sovereign,"* while treason, *"punishable by death,"* included such offenses as any effort to restrict the Emperor's *"Supreme Authority"* or any changes to the form of autocratic government.[10] Sanction by the Russian Orthodox Church, as one journal commented, merely confirmed Nicholas's exceptional position and blessed him as he embarked on his *"heroic struggle"* to *"avoid the ills of the West."*[11]

Muscovite and Imperial monarchs had developed and cemented these beliefs. In 1474, Ivan III, Grand Prince of Moscow, wed Zoe Paleologue, niece of the last Byzantine emperor. Ivan promptly wrapped his Rurik Dynasty in a patina of divine rule borrowed from his wife's heritage, claiming God ordained him with extraordinary autocratic powers. The rights of nobles and humble subjects alike were suppressed as Ivan imposed an unforgiving concept of power actually learned from the ferocious Tartars. The Byzantine double-headed eagle, stolen from his wife's ancestors, now became an iconic emblem of absolute authority legitimized by the Orthodox Church.[12]

Religious despotism reached new heights in 1547 when the unstable Ivan IV proclaimed himself Tsar of All Russia. Claiming spiritual and temporal descent from Byzantium, he even brought printing to Russia in an attempt to disseminate his agenda and his new state and church laws. In a coronation ceremony full of purloined ritual he was crowned with the Cap of Monomakh, given – according to legend – to Grand Prince Vladimir of Kiev by Byzantine Emperor Basil II when he converted to Orthodoxy and married the latter's sister. Russians viewed the little crown of chased gold rimmed with sable as a harbinger of good, visible evidence of their link with Byzantium. In fact – and despite the legend – the Cap was almost certainly of Tartar origin, like the autocracy itself.[13] Certainly it conferred no grace on the luckless Ivan. The premature death of his wife Anastasia (a Romanov by birth) drove him mad, and he spent his days killing courtiers and even his own heir, alternately repenting then returning to the barbaric ways that earned him the epithet of Ivan the Terrible.

Nor did the Cap's legendary qualities aid Ivan's successors, as his House of Rurik staggered to its end. The regency and rule of Boris Godunov gave way to three successive pretenders, each insisting that he was Ivan's youngest son Dimitri. The young Dimitri was said to have died under mysterious circumstances while living in a small town outside of Moscow. Few believed it, and uncertainty over the succession led to invading foreign armies and palace coups. Then in 1613, at the height of what became known as Russia's Time of Troubles, a national assembly of nobles, the *Zemsky Sobor*, voted to offer the vacant throne to Ivan the Terrible's sixteen-year-old grandnephew Michael Romanov, who was then hiding in a monastery at remote Kostroma. Polish forces bent on seizing the boy marched off but never reached him: according to legend, a local peasant named Ivan Susanin led them deep into a forest, sacrificing his life so that Michael might take the throne. It was a piece of questionable mythology, but one deeply ingrained in the Russian psyche, later celebrated in Michael Glinka's great patriotic opera *A Life for the Tsar*.

The Cap of Monomakh.

With the most tenuous of claims to Russia's throne, early members of the Romanov Dynasty repeated Byzantine coronation rituals to justify their power, a power that Michael's grandson Peter I finally solidified into totalitarian autocracy. Sweeping reforms, modernization of the army, creation of a navy, the founding of a new capital on the Baltic, and relentless Westernization earned him the name Peter the Great. Yet he greatly altered the relationship between crown and people. Peter claimed the right to control every aspect of his country's life. An almost feudal sense of duty, imposed equally on nameless Serfs laboring for landowners and aristocratic courtiers clad in their new European clothing, marked the end of any benevolent patriarchy.

Peter attempted to bridge the uneasy relationship between medieval Russia and modern Europe when, in 1724, he broke with precedent and had his second wife Catherine crowned in Moscow. Gone was the traditional title of Tsar: Peter declared himself Emperor, and the crowning of his Empress, in a ceremony that grafted Byzantine rituals on to a distinctly Western pageant, spoke more of Vienna than of Moscow. A new, European-style crown replaced the Cap of Monomakh and a mantle edged with ermine supplanted golden priestly vestments. Catherine's coronation also marked a new chapter in the country's religious life. The Patriarch had previously crowned sovereigns, signifying that divine sanction to rule came through the intervening grace of the Russian Orthodox Church. In 1721, though, Peter had abolished the Patriarchate and replaced it with a Holy Synod headed by an Ober-Procurator who became, in effect, State Minister of Religion. This sublimated the church to the throne, a change made clear when Catherine became the first sovereign crowned without the Precept, the prayer through which the Church had traditionally invested the ruler with authority.[14] The meaning was clear: the sovereign's providential grace and power came not through the intervening acts of the Church but instead existed from the moment of birth.

With large-scale military reviews and parades, a feast for the people of Moscow, and a display of fireworks, Catherine's coronation was the first to reach beyond the walls of the Kremlin's Cathedral of the Assumption and involve her husband's subjects in the surrounding ceremonies.[15] Recognition of the people, though, did not imply democratic principles, as Peter's daughter Empress Elisabeth demonstrated at her 1742 coronation. She traveled from St. Petersburg to Moscow with a retinue of 24,000 courtiers and aristocrats to surround her with worshipful glory, and would remain in the former capital for eight months. During the service, Elizabeth also became the first Russian ruler to place the crown upon her own head in imitation of Byzantine emperors, declaring that her power came *"not from Earth but from Heaven."*[16] It was a belief to which her successors clung until the Revolution in 1917.

Catherine the Great, like the first Romanov Tsars, used her 1762 coronation to legitimize her rule. Five months after the coup that brought her to the throne, she entered Moscow in a procession full of military pomp and imperial pageantry, hoping to impress her new subjects and win their support.[17] For all her talk of enlightened rule, the new, diamond-encrusted crown she placed atop her head during the ceremony offered visible proof that Catherine meant to remain a privileged autocrat.

Thirty-five-years later, Catherine's unfortunate son followed her to the throne as Emperor Paul. Never quite certain of his paternity, he hated his mother and blamed her – probably correctly – for his father's assassination. Ostentatiously religious, he accepted without question the national myth of a divine autocracy, but Paul went further than any previous ruler. At his coronation in 1797, he proclaimed himself Head of the Russian Orthodox Church; believing himself to be an actual priest of the church, he wore a golden dalmatic and even took communion at the altar – something forbidden to members of the laity.[18] Divine intervention, though, failed to save him from that most pernicious of all Russian traditions, the palace coup, and in 1801 a group of aristocrats murdered him as he cowered in his bedroom.

Empress Catherine II of Russia.

Paul's son, the new Alexander I, had endorsed the conspirators, if not their regicide, and he took the throne racked with guilt. Catherine the Great had carefully trained him to be a liberal ruler, but Napoleon's invasion of Russia swept away any such tendencies. Although he turned into a suspicious reactionary, Alexander I did leave one indelible mark on the throne. In place of plotting siblings and palace coups, the Romanovs emerged as a united Imperial Family, objects of personal identification and adoration for the nation, moral models for their subjects and bastions of Nineteenth Century respectability – at least on the surface.[19]

Alexander's brother Nicholas I made this clear in his reign. He came to the throne amid another attempted coup, an aristocratic push for reforms known as the Decembrist Rebellion. Faced with thousands of mutinous soldiers in St. Petersburg's Senate Square, the Emperor attempted mediation; only after the rebels killed an elderly general did Nicholas reluctantly order his troops to return fire. *"I saw that either I had to take on the spilling of the blood of a few and save nearly all or, being merciful to myself, to sacrifice the state,"* Nicholas commented sadly.[20] Peace was restored, but the episode drove the Emperor into radically reactionary policies. Exposure to democratic, Western ideas, he was sure, had corrupted the aristocratic minds behind the Decembrist Rebellion. And so Nicholas I turned his back on Europe, embracing a chauvinistic nationalism that elaborated and celebrated the country's past glories. Russia answered the French Revolution's unsettling slogan, *"Liberty, Equality, and Fraternity,"* with its own tripartite formula, *"Autocracy, Orthodoxy, and Nationality,"* emotional words used to justify oppressive rule.[21]

Nicholas I's Coronation emphasized a new imperial vision, with vivid accounts and detailed sketches in newspapers and magazines celebrating an idealized Imperial Family dedicated to Russia's service. Supposedly ancient antecedents now linked the throne more directly with its Muscovite origins, emphasizing autocracy's *"consensual subordination"* that kept the people firmly in the background.[22] This was, paradoxically, displayed during a moment of ostensible humility. Following their crowning, Nicholas I and his consort Empress Alexandra climbed to the top of the Kremlin's historic Red Staircase, turned to the thousands gathered below in Cathedral Square, and bowed three times. Never before had a sovereign so acknowledged the people; the gesture, complained a critic, was beneath the Emperor's *"godlike person,"* suggesting that he was *"beholden to mere mortals."* But the triple bow was less a nod to the people as it was an opportunity to bask in popular acclaim, to read into the cheers *"historical justification for absolute monarchy."*[23]

Russia had feared Nicholas I's iron rule, but his son Alexander II went to his own coronation weakened in the wake of the humiliating Crimean War. The Empire was restless, plagued by growing discontent as modern aspirations clashed with an archaic government and social system. Unfortunate omens during the coronation seemed to presage the troubles ahead. An officer dropped the cushion holding the Emperor's Diamond Collar of the Order of St. Andrei, and the crown atop Empress Marie Alexandrovna's head nearly crashed to the floor.[24] The Cathedral was hot and crowded: openly complaining of discomfort and their inability to see the goings on, members of the congregation loudly ate and drank throughout the solemn prayers.[25]

Alexander II freed Russia's serfs, but his attempts to slowly transform the autocracy through social, judicial, and military reform brought discontent, not stability. It was the era of Dostoyevsky and Turgenev, when the dispossessed embraced the revolutionary ideas of Michael Bakunin calling for anarchic vengeance against the Imperial system. An increasingly radicalized generation of university students and determined Nihilists arose across Russia, determined to wrest change from a reluctant sovereign. This desire finally burst forth in a terrorist bomb tossed at Alexander II in 1881. The Emperor was killed, and the autocracy itself was mortally wounded.

Tsar Nicholas I of Russia.

The familiar pattern now repeated itself: hints of liberalism, followed by repression as Alexander III took the throne. Convinced that the late Emperor's dangerous adventures in concessions had led to his death, Alexander III eschewed his father's Western tastes and manners and returned to the rigid nationalism of Nicholas I. Throughout his thirteen-year reign, oppression kept a lid on the cauldron of revolutionary discontent. The autocracy became the central focus of national life, the Emperor the embodiment of God's divine plan for Russia.

Under Nicholas II, Imperial mythology rewrote

Russian history to expand notions of a divinely mandated emperor. Not only did Nicholas present himself as the spiritual descendant of Byzantium but he also erased the role of the people, in the form of the *Zemsky Sobor*, from having had any decisive role in the 1613 election of Michael Romanov as Tsar. Michael's election to the throne, it was now declared, was merely an expression of the will of God: *"Not the people,"* insisted one narrative, *"but God made him Tsar; the people only fulfilled the Divine Will."*[26]

This conception of semi-divine monarch stood in stark contrast with the popular image Nicholas II carefully cultivated. Many of the thousand Westerners flocking to Moscow that May of 1896 seemed enraptured with the new Imperial couple. Nicholas I had presented his family to the nation as symbols of moral duty; under Nicholas II, this shifted to the domestic, centered on a thoroughly idealized love. Souvenir postcards and popular periodicals celebrated Nicholas and Alexandra's romance and their happy family life, explicitly inviting identification with the personal, not the political. It was an expression of reconciling medieval rule to modern desire, attempting to meld a heroic Russian past to personal idolization of Nicholas and Alexandra, as the Imperial court sought to shield the anachronistic realities of autocracy behind a humanizing veneer of sentimental appeal. Nicholas II imagined that this would ensure loyalty; in fact, it merely opened up his private life to public scrutiny. Autocratic propaganda magnified ordinary domestic behaviors and virtues to exaggerated saintliness in service of the crown, at the expense of political reality.[27] It was grimly ironic: Nicholas II wanted his subjects and the world to view him in recognizable terms as a man, a loving husband, and a devoted father, while he jealousy clung to a belief that he stood above all men as God's anointed.

Naively hopeful, entranced by the handsome Nicholas and his statuesque bride, many Western visitors took the Imperial couple's youth and pleasing appearance as evidence of open minds and liberal intentions. Russia, after all, could hardly go on with repression forever, and in marrying Queen Victoria's granddaughter, or so the reasoning went, surely Nicholas would fall under the influence of democratic ideas. *"Nicholas II begins his reign with the good wishes of the entire world,"* declared one American visitor to Moscow. *"Monarchies, empires, and republics alike united to wish him bon voyage on his momentous journey."* In the Emperor's *"kindly, smiling face,"* he foresaw *"the promise of a reign beneficent and just,"* center of *"the highest hopes and prayers of all the myriad hearts turned toward him."*[28] Journalist W. T. Stead offered a more personal call for identification. He thought that *"to bury a father, to marry a wife, and to receive into his arms his first born,"* and all within twelve months, was an oppressive, emotional burden on Nicholas II.[29]

Nicholas II and his wife Alexandra Feodorovna.

The million people who poured into Moscow that May of 1896 faced confounding contrasts. Princes and potentates, ambassadors and emissaries, aristocrats and socialites came face to face with Nicholas II's common subjects. Ukrainian farmers stood with humble Balts, exotically dressed Central Asians with turbaned Tartars from the Crimea, factory workers and struggling merchants fusing into the nameless, anonymous narod, the people who, according to the Imperial vision, burned with undying passion for the throne. No group was more demonstrative than the peasants, *moujiks*, *"in their rugged, picturesque national costume,"* recorded a credulous western journalist, who *"fell on their knees and pressed their foreheads on the stone pavement"* in honor of their Emperor.[30]

For many Western visitors, everything was exciting. *"Beautiful, barbaric Moscow,"* sighed a visitor, shimmered beneath fresh paint, fluttered with flags, and sparkled with strands of electric lights awaiting the darkness of night.[31] Waves of enthusiastic cheers, cannon thunder, and strains of the national anthem followed Nicholas II as he crossed the city on May 9, in a State Entrance that swept him toward his date with destiny. This *"panorama of majesty and wealth,"* said an American journalist, flashed by in glittering splendor: *"tall Cossacks in long scarlet tunics," "Tartars in furs and Mongolians in silver robes,"* and *"Chevalier Guards in coats of ivory-white with silver breastplates."*[32] Nicholas rode a white horse and, reported *The New York Times*, *"looked every inch the Caesar."*[33] Behind him came his mother and then his wife, each riding in ornately carved and gilded carriages beneath a cloudless blue sky. *"Our eyes were dazzled,"* gasped one witness, *"with one continuous passing spectacle of extraordinary pomp and magnificence."*[34]

Five days later, standing in the Cathedral of the Assumption and watched by a thousand privileged guests, the Emperor placed Catherine the Great's Imperial State Crown atop his head. *"It looked a simple enough gesture,"* said his sister Grand Duchess Olga Alexandrovna, *"but from that very moment Nicky's responsibility was to God only."* It was *"a most solemn and binding contract between God and the sovereign, His servant."*[35] The pageantry, the rituals, the clouds of incense, and the choir chanting Slavonic hymns in *"the dim Byzantine interior with its faded frescoes"* wrapped the ceremonies in a mantle of evocative symbolism and religious ecstasy.[36] Crowning enshrined Nicholas II with temporal power; anointing by the clergy recognized and sealed the extraordinary divine gifts he was said to possess; and communion within the sanctuary, a privilege granted to an Emperor only at his coronation, raised him to an autocratic priesthood, where he alone mediated with God on behalf of his country.

Those in the Cathedral were effusive in their enthusiasm. The coronation, recalled Queen Marie of Romania, a first cousin to both Nicholas II and Empress Alexandra, was *"more like a dream than reality,"* a pageant of *"stupendous magnificence"* that she likened to *"suddenly stepping from the dark into dazzling sunshine."*[37]

Grand Duchess Olga Alexandrovna.

The staid *Times of London* sadly noted, *"Western Europe has nothing to show at all comparable to the sustained splendor and long-drawn magnificence of the Coronation of the Tsar. Splendid and lavish ceremonial has a significance and a value in Russia."*[38] Even proudly democratic Americans witnessing the scene were moved to flights of fancy. *"The most gorgeous ceremonies the world has ever seen,"* The New York Times reported to its readers.[39] *"As grand a display and as touching a sight as this generation or indeed any other is likely to look upon,"* declared a military attaché from Washington D.C.[40] Clifton Breckinridge, American Minister in Russia, was in awe. *"It is not simply that the old ceremonials were preserved out of affection for the past and kept in company with the historic structures of the Kremlin and Moscow,"* he wrote, *"but they are still used as a positive force, of great effect as governing the majority of the peoples of the Empire, and along with them come abundantly the ideas and appliances of modern civilization and government."*[41]

The moment of triumph, though, was short-lived. *"I remember talking to someone,"* wrote Prince Sergei Volkonsky, *"who shared my feeling that this coronation would be the last. In the midst of this carefree climax I thought, we have to be vigilant, because what if the people have had enough of shouting 'Hurrah,' and what will they do when they no longer get any pleasure out of a piece of theatre?"*[42]

The "hurrahs" stopped on a dusty Moscow field four days after the crowning, in what Nicholas II's mother called a *"dreadful accident"* that *"draped a black veil over all the splendor and glory."*[43] A half-million workers, peasants, pilgrims, and tourists gathered on Khodynka Meadow for a popular feast watched in horror as the surging crowd stumbled into ravines and wells, trampled to death in waves of panic. *"A very grave sin,"* wrote Nicholas II, a *"ghastly"* accident that left him *"with the most appalling impression."* At two that afternoon, Emperor and Empress appeared at Khodynka Meadow as scheduled; the remaining crowd sang *God Save the Tsar* as husbands, wives, fathers and mothers were still pulling the bloodied corpses of relatives from the pits.

Nicholas made no mention of the tragedy, offered no prayers, asked for no moment of silence for the victims – the festive program went on, he wrote without a hint of irony, *"like nothing had happened."*[44] That night, as thousands lay dead or dying in the city's hospitals, Nicholas and Alexandra attended a magnificent ball given by the French Ambassador, dancing into the early morning hours.

"The people," ran the official account of the Coronation festivities, *"understood the suffering and emotion of their Emperor, and showed sympathy for his sorrows."*[45] This idea, that Nicholas II was the real victim of the tragedy, exposed the gap between rulers and ruled, between Court and Country that only widened throughout his reign. One American visitor to Moscow, completely bewitched by three weeks of Imperial pomp and pageantry, even insisted that the disaster proved to the Empire *"that their new ruler has a kind, a brave, a manly heart."* Nicholas, he erroneously declared, *"showed the greatest grief over what had happened"* during his appearance at Khodynka Meadow. The tragedy, he asserted, *"laid the foundations of a sympathy between the great under class of the Russian people and the Throne."*[46]

Reality was different. No one doubted that the tragedy horrified Nicholas and Alexandra, at least in the abstract. They visited the wounded in Moscow's hospitals, and Nicholas announced that he would compensate the victims – all the correct displays of sorrow, the outward signs of painful remorse. Yet the visits were mechanical and the pledge of financial aid went largely unfulfilled. It was as if the Russian autocrat, claiming patrimony over his nation, could not be bothered with the deaths of these nameless, faceless souls, as if what happened on Khodynka Meadow had been a manifestation of Fate, to be accepted and just as quickly forgotten.

Nicholas *could* have altered the schedule of remaining coronation events as a mark of personal grief and unity with his subjects. He *could* have honored his public pledges to provide the victims with financial compensation. He *could* have held those responsible for the breakdown in planning and security arrangements accountable. That he did none of these things ensured that his coronation was forever associated with the deaths on Khodynka Meadow. As the May sun beat down upon Moscow, wreaking havoc with piles of still unburied victims, the festive atmosphere turned into a nightmare. The city became a hothouse tinged with the sickly smell of death as the Emperor and his family went through the motions of celebration, walking on one occasion almost literally on the bodies of the dead.

Russia and its rulers had lurched through many disasters before Khodynka, but never before had high and low alike viewed a sovereign as both incompetent and heartless, and so early in his reign. Young, religious, and well intentioned though they may have been, Nicholas and Alexandra's response to Khodynka revealed a couple incapable of learning from mistakes. A narrative began that lasted to the end of the dynasty: a deeply disordered autocratic system lay in the naïve hands of a man unfit for the challenges of governance. Creating an unlikely unity of opinion between ordinary Russian and privileged aristocrat, the tragedy revealed an all too human Nicholas at odds with the exalted myth of an all-knowing, divinely-guided autocrat celebrated at his crowning. The misfortunes that followed – from the disastrous Russo-Japanese War to the 1905 Revolution, the Imperial Family's retreat from public life to the shadow of Rasputin – all of these fell on an Imperial couple already discredited by events in Moscow. It was easier for people to believe the worst of Nicholas and Alexandra, to seize upon rumor as truth, and to dismiss the Emperor as incompetent precisely because he had been negligent in his response to Khodynka.

Three weeks in Moscow, begun in triumphant celebration of God's anointed representative on earth, ended in a tragedy that shattered centuries of carefully crafted Russian mythology. Imperial splendor faded with the passing years of Nicholas II's disastrous reign, until revolution condemned the old order to oblivion. Soviet Russia replaced Tsarist pageantry with militaristic parades on Moscow's Red Square, Imperial banners with enormous portraits of Lenin, Marx, and Stalin. Ironically the intent was the same: loyalty through intimidation, awe through artifice, evolving state ceremonial designed to conceal the fatal weaknesses of two very different empires destined for the dustbins of history.

Eleven months after the ceremonies, Nicholas II presented his wife with an elaborate Imperial Easter Egg by celebrated Russian jeweler Peter Karl Fabergé. A sphere of translucent gold enamel ornamented with black double-headed eagles set with diamonds replicated their coronation mantles; within perched a gold replica of the coach in which Alexandra had made her State Entrance into Moscow.[47] Today, visitors to the Kremlin Armory can view the thrones and the crowns, the Imperial mantles, and even the Preobrazhensky uniform and silver brocade gown worn by Nicholas and Alexandra on that distant day. In pallid, ghostly images, faded sepia photographs, flickering newsreels, and boldly colored menus, hints of the magnificence remain frozen in the amber of time.

The Russian Court commemorated the event in typically lavish fashion. Three years after the Moscow ceremonies, the Ministry of the Imperial Court published *Koronationnyi Sbornik* to mark the occasion. The enormous, magnificently bound and illuminated two-volume set was not only the largest coronation album ever produced but was also the most expensive, with a staggering cost of some 166,000 rubles (approximately $2.4 million or £1.7 million in 2014) for a mere 1,650 copies. The text, in Russian and in French, spread over pages adorned with Slavonic lettering, medieval illuminations, colored lithographs, and, for the first time, photographs, providing a fusion of modern technology with Byzantine rituals. The narrative was exultant, the tone reverential, and the message unambiguous in its praise of Nicholas II.[48]

This was the perspective of official Russia. A world of experiences, though, lay beyond the pages of *Koronationnyi Sbornik*, prismatic glimpses of visitors and journalists, diplomats and guests who came to Moscow with eager eyes and flowing pens. Photographs and films, memoirs and magazines, letters and long-forgotten newspapers also chronicled the coronation. These accounts, ranging from the commonplace to the comical, the transcendent to the tragic, capture the human story of those three weeks in ways beyond the scope of officialdom. Though unaware that this would be the last ceremony of its kind ever held, most understood that they were witness to an event of historic importance. Nicholas II, his relatives, royal guests, diplomats, courtiers, dignitaries, journalists, and tourists alike recorded impressions. There was the future Queen Marie of Romania, loquacious and condemnatory by turns; British General Sir Francis Grenfell, keenly examining the Russian military; Chinese diplomat Li-Hung Chang, charged with secret negotiations in Moscow; missionary Mary Hickley, visiting from England as a guest of an aristocratic family; and Kate Koon, a young American debutante awed by the splendor. Correspondents came from across the world, including the effusive American Richard Harding Davis and Sir Donald Mackenzie Wallace from Great Britain. British expatriate Aylmer Maude provided an important critical contrast: his scornful eye and sharp pen cut through official treacle, exposing an Imperial system he believed utterly wastrel in its extravagance and incompetent in its symbolic functions. This book draws on this wide array of voices and experiences, weaving together tales to paint a kaleidoscopic picture capturing both the coronation's majestic pomp and the unspeakable tragedy of the Khodynka disaster.

Marie of Romania on her wedding day.

"*It is said,*" Kate Koon recorded on her last day in Moscow, "*that never again will Russia have such coronation festivities, for the people cannot stand the expense, and surely nowhere else in the world could there be a greater magnificence.*"[49] She and a million others gathered in the city witnessed the parades and pageantry, the ceremonies and celebrations. Their accounts offer an important view as an empire symbolically collected to echo the patriotic sacrifice magnificently rendered in Glinka's *A Life for the Tsar*. No one knew that the incessant symphonic overtures were actually a prescient funeral dirge soon to burst forth in unspeakable tragedy.

Tsar Alexander III.

Chapter I

Telephone and telegraph brought the news to Moscow: Alexander III, Emperor of Russia, was dead. Bells of the city's *"forty times forty"* churches tolled a relentless dirge that washed like the October rain across the city's cobbled streets and broad avenues, over colored roofs and gilded onion domes looming through the dankness of the autumn afternoon. Though Peter the Great had abandoned the city in favor of St. Petersburg, his new capital on the Baltic, Moscow remained the "Third Rome," citadel of the Orthodox Church, center of Russia's spiritual and national conscience.

Alexander III had been like Moscow: apparently uncorrupted by Western thought, polished enough to impress visitors but rough around the edges. Tall and bear-like, proudly bearded in repudiation of two centuries of Romanov tradition, he had shuffled ungracefully into rooms, shouted at his officials, and awed his family with manly shows of strength. Determinedly Russian in appearance and manner, he resembled a *bogatyr*, the powerful hero of peasant folk tales.

No city in Russia should have mourned Alexander III's 1894 passing more than nationalistic Moscow. Endless ribbons of black bunting hung miserably across building façades as priests sang solemn requiems in the churches. Yet Moscow, said an official, *"seemed indifferent to the change of sovereigns. The people in the streets were the ordinary, everyday business crowd, with everyone hurrying about his own affairs, showing no concern for the future."*[1]

Moscow glimpsed its new Emperor when Nicholas II, clad in an officer's greatcoat and bearded face taut with emotion, walked behind an elaborate plumed hearse to the Kremlin, where his father lay in state before burial in St. Petersburg. *"It didn't register in my head that the young, rather short man before us was our ruler,"* recalled one man.[2] Many noted the contrast between the *"large, tall, fine-looking men"* of the Imperial Family and the diminutive Nicholas, whose short stature conflicted with *"the idea of majesty."*[3] Yet there was also sympathy: at twenty-six, Nicholas seemed too young to shoulder the heavy burdens of the Imperial crown.[4]

No one knew quite what to expect: the new Nicholas II was a mystery to most of his 140 million subjects. Eighteenth sovereign of the Romanov Dynasty, successor of such legendary figures as Ivan the Terrible, Peter the Great, and Catherine the Great, he ruled a Russian Empire stretching over one-sixth of the globe. Reaction had flourished under Alexander III: peace prevailed and the economy modernized, but at the expense of individual liberty, press censorship, and pervasive suspicion. After years of oppression, a weary Russia yearned for change: even conservative voices talked of it.[5] *"Liberal reforms,"* said a diplomat, *"were spoken of on all sides. The nation impatiently awaited these reforms and centered its hopes on the young Sovereign."*[6]

An official more attuned to the inner workings of the new Emperor's mind, though, warned that such things were unlikely. Nicholas, he declared, *"has never displayed an opinion contrary to that of his father, and it may be pretty positively affirmed that he will tread in his footsteps."*[7] This was prescient: citing his faith in *"the wisdom of Providence,"* Nicholas warned his subjects that in transferring their allegiance to him, they must *"not forget that the strength and stability of Holy Russia lie in her Unity with Us, and in her unbounded devotion to Us."*[8] The Emperor was Russia: loyalty to the throne would ensure the Empire's greatness.

***

"I have a presentiment – more than a presentiment, a secret conviction – that I am destined for terrible trials," Nicholas II once declared. "But I shall not receive my reward on this earth. How often have I not applied to myself the words of Job: 'Hardly have I entertained a fear than it comes to pass, and all the evils I foresee descend upon my head.'"[9] Even his birth, on May 6, 1868, seemed ominous. In the Orthodox Church's liturgical calendar, it was the feast day commemorating the unlucky St. Job. Fate, Nicholas was sure, not only selected him to rule but had also marked him for misfortune. Superstitious and suspicious, he passively ascribed the turmoil of his life and reign to *"God's Will."*

Tsesarevich Alexander and Marie Feodorovna brought up Nicholas and his siblings – George, born in 1871, Xenia, 1875, Michael, 1878, and Olga, born in 1882 – in an idealized Victorian atmosphere of doting attentions coupled with studied privations. Romanov family custom dictated a Spartan regime, with army camp beds, cold baths, and plain food.[10] Most people agreed that the children, though charming, were immature and wild in their behavior. One courtier likened their manners to those *"of the children of petty provincial nobles."*[11] Outlandish pranks and questionable humor reigned. *"I don't like watching while people throw pellets of bread across the table!"* complained their great-aunt Queen Olga of Württemberg.[12]

Sentimental by nature, the future Alexander III adored his children and shared their games, yet his relationship with Nicholas was uneasy. Alexander might laugh and joke, but he was also an intimidating man and *"a stern father," "ruthless even with his children,"* recalled a courtier.[13] The family feared his unpredictable outbursts,

Marie Feodorovna with some of her children. From the left: George, Nicholas, Xenia, Marie Feodorovna and Michael.

and the children were *"uneasy and constrained in his presence."*[14] Alexander *"loathed anything that savored of weakness,"* said one intimate, and Nicholas shrank away in his father's imposing presence.[15] Nicholas was short, unlike his hulking father; he was quiet and soft-spoken, unlike the loud, impulsive Alexander. The young boy had an almost feminine air of delicacy, in contrast to the father who liked to rip apart packs of playing cards and bend iron pokers to show his strength.[16] At times, Alexander seemed to deliberately undermine his eldest son's confidence. He made no secret of the fact that Michael, and not his heir, was his favorite son.[17] Taking Nicholas's reserve for timidity, Alexander tried to toughen him up, but ended by simply bullying and browbeating the boy into fearful submission. He made fun of him in front of others, ridiculed him as unworthy of the Romanov name, and threatened to tell his grandfather that he was a disappointment. *"You are a little girlie!"* he once taunted Nicholas in front of a playmate.[18]

This emotional abuse proved fatal. Nicholas wanted to please his father but he knew he was a disappointment. Uncertain of himself, he withdrew, into an equally unfortunate world created by his mother. Witty and vivacious, Marie Feodorovna – a former Danish princess – was extremely popular in Russia, a welcome contrast to her somewhat grim and intimidating husband. Yet as a mother, her influence over Nicholas was equally damaging. Intensely selfish and afraid of losing control of her children to outside influences, she treated them as treasured possessions, was by turns indulgent and oppressive, and smothered them to the point of immaturity. An *"unquestioning reverence for the principal of the family"* became her guiding rule.[19] Obedience was esteemed, and independent thought suppressed. Even when Nicholas was a married man, his mother treated him as a child, trying to control and influence her son in an effort to ensure the continued devotion she demanded.

A shocking event in 1881 abruptly ended the twelve-year-old Nicholas's childhood. One March afternoon, an explosion thundered across St. Petersburg; Nicholas and his tutor raced to the Winter Palace, following a trail of blood to the shattered body of his grandfather Alexander II, victim of a Nihilist bomb.[20] *"No one spoke,"* Nicholas remembered later. *"My grandfather was lying on the narrow camp bed he always slept in, covered by the military cloak he used as a dressing gown. His face was deadly pale. There were small wounds all over it."* Nicholas's father pulled him toward this bleeding figure, whispering, *"Papa, your sunshine is here."* In a moment, Nicholas saw *"the flicker of an eye. Grandfather's blue eyes opened, and he tried to smile."*[21] It was a horrifying scene: the bomb had eviscerated the stomach, shattered the left leg, torn off the right beneath the knee, and driven shards of Alexander II's wedding ring into his crushed hand.[22] Doctors hovered uselessly; three-quarters of an hour later, Alexander II's bloody hand fell to the floor with a thud. For the new Alexander III and his eldest son, now Tsesarevich Nicholas, the terrible scene was all the evidence needed of the horrible uncertainty surrounding the Throne.

Tsesarevich Nicholas Alexandrovich and his brother Grand Duke Duke George Alexandrovich.

A family gathering at Bernstorff Palace (1892): Back row, from left: Prince George of Greece and Prince Valdemar of Denmark, King Christian IX of Denmark, Empress Marie Feodorovna, the Princess of Wales, Queen Louise of Denmark, Queen Olga of Greece, Prince Nicholas of Greece, Princess Maud of Wales, Tsesarevich Nicholas Alexandrovich, Tsar Alexander III. On the steps, in the same order: the Duchess of Cumberland with her children Prince Ernst August and Princess Alexandra, Prince Christopher of Greece (standing in front of Queen Louise), Princess Olga, Prince Christian and Prince Georg of Cumberland, Grand Duchess Olga Alexandrovna, Princess Victoria of Wales and Grand Duke Michael Alexandrovich.

Political concessions and liberal flirtations, Alexander III believed, had led to his father's assassination. He was reluctant to even stage a coronation in Moscow, to parade himself and his family before thousands of potentially disaffected citizens who might hurl bombs. Twenty-six months – the longest interval in Russian history – passed before he finally went to his crowning.[23] The American Minister's wife feared that Nihilists would *"take advantage of that crowd to blow up everybody,"* and Imperial security made no pretense over notions of unity between Throne and People.[24] Windows along parade routes were sealed and guarded; a triple line of armed soldiers flanked the Emperor and his family in public; people were forbidden to throw hats in the air to celebrate; canes, umbrellas, and parasols were banned for fear that they concealed guns, and Cossacks charged crowds deemed too enthusiastic.[25] So vital to national legend, the people were *"not the least excited or enthusiastic"* at this treatment, said an onlooker, and watched the spectacle almost blankly.[26]

Fifteen at the time, Nicholas rode behind his father through the potentially dangerous streets of Moscow, for the first time exposed to the clash between autocratic myth and modern reality. His mother, admitting that she felt *"like a sacrificial lamb,"* followed in a gilded carriage, looking *"grave and very pale,"* as if expecting the worst.[27] After the chaotic end of his father's reign, Alexander III used his own rough simplicity – so unlike the refined and Westernized Alexander II – to emphasize anachronistic themes of an invisible, spiritual bond between Autocracy and Church.[28]

Tsar Alexander II.

This was how Alexander III presented himself in Moscow, and how he reigned. Russia, he believed, stood apart from Europe: its past and its people, its culture and its church, were beyond the understanding of the West. Nationalism thrived and moderate voices were silenced.[29] His was a repressive autocracy that inspired more fear than loyalty. Dogmatic in his views and fearful of mankind, Alexander abandoned reforms. Anti-Semitism ran rampant, police arrested thousands branded *"suspicious,"* ethnic minorities were suppressed in the name of the state, and newspapers were even forbidden to print the word, *"Constitution."*[30] Discontent, though, remained: in 1887 a group of revolutionary students bungled an attempt on the Emperor's life. Five of the naïve conspirators were hanged, among them a young man named Alexander Ulyanov, older brother of the future Vladimir Lenin. The noose around Ulyanov's neck tightened around the country as well.

Fear of a fate similar to his father drove Alexander III and his family into the closely guarded Gatchina Palace outside of St. Petersburg, where they lived like prisoners in a vast, gilded cage. There was, said a courtier, a *"feeling of unrest"* in the air, worry *"of another murderous attempt."*[31] Seclusion at Gatchina set a dangerous precedent: members of the extended Romanov Family were no longer welcomed except by rare invitation, and court entertainments became rare.[32] Ceremonial duties fell victim to personal desire – a fatal pattern that Nicholas repeated and expanded upon when he came to the throne.

A handful of Alexander III's trusted friends were admitted to the inner circle at Gatchina, playing boisterous games of cards and drinking. Marie Feodorovna tried to intervene, asking servants halt the alcohol; Alexander responded by concealing flasks in his boots.[33] Some of the more lurid tales of Alexander III's drinking have likely been exaggerated, but it is impossible to entirely dismiss them. These gatherings clearly affected Nicholas: he later expressed a hatred of card games as unwelcome reminders of his father's evenings.[34]

Nicholas's education might have alleviated some of these conflicting childhood influences by developing his self-esteem and introducing him to critical thinking. His general education was not, as is often said, inadequate. Yet it was carried out along idiosyncratic lines: tutors who lectured Nicholas in history, Russian literature, the classics, geography, arithmetic, science, languages, and religion were forbidden to question him or even grade his work, leaving his opinions unchallenged and his analytical faculties undeveloped.[35] He was a good pupil, with a quick mind, though the way his lessons were conducted left him disengaged and often uninterested. One tutor complained that the regime had turned Nicholas into *"a restrained, careful old man and not a sprightly youth."*[36]

Nicholas enjoyed history, but it was a myopic history filtered through a highly nationalistic prism: the romanticized works of Nicholas Karamzin, evoking a heroic Russian past, sang to the boy as they had to his great-grandfather Nicholas I, emphasizing the Empire as Orthodox kingdom and appealing to the idea of religious mission. That mission, Nicholas learned, now lay in the Far East. Great Britain had India and territories across the globe, but Russia, according to lectures by Vassili Klyuchevsky, was meant to colonize Asia. Spreading beyond Siberia to Central Asia, China, and Korea would ensure Russia's future and fulfill her destinies on the international stage. Such views eventually led Nicholas II to a disastrous war with Japan in 1904.

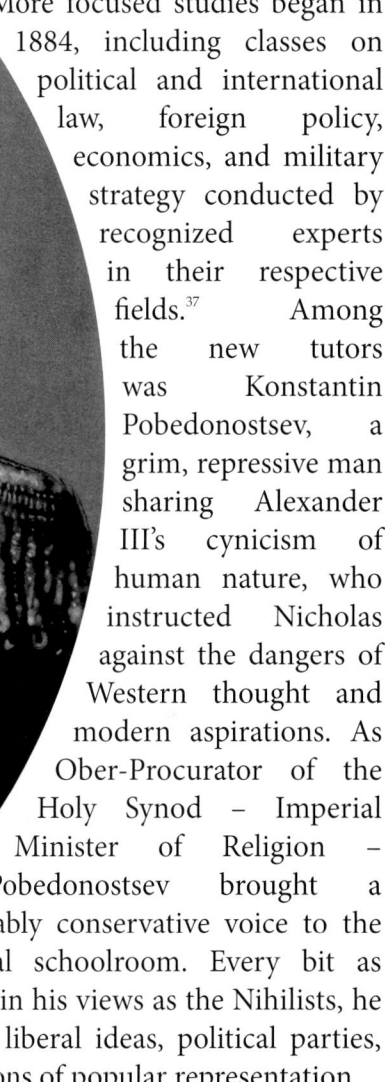

Tsar Alexander III.

More focused studies began in 1884, including classes on political and international law, foreign policy, economics, and military strategy conducted by recognized experts in their respective fields.[37] Among the new tutors was Konstantin Pobedonostsev, a grim, repressive man sharing Alexander III's cynicism of human nature, who instructed Nicholas against the dangers of Western thought and modern aspirations. As Ober-Procurator of the Holy Synod – Imperial Minister of Religion – Pobedonostsev brought a reliably conservative voice to the imperial schoolroom. Every bit as fanatical in his views as the Nihilists, he despised liberal ideas, political parties, and notions of popular representation.

For Pobedonostsev, Russia was divided between two groups, the *narod* and the bureaucracy. The *narod*, a term encompassing the great mass of the country's subjects, exemplified all that was good in Russia: simple, loyal to the church, subservient to authority, and bound to the throne in an unseen, mystical union. The bureaucracy occupied the opposite side of the spectrum: aristocrats, government ministers, ambitious military officers, merchants, students, and the press. These broad definitions thus embodied Russia's conflict: on one side stood traditional elements like church and throne, on the other, those whose self-interest made it necessary to treat them with suspicion. Pobedonostsev invoked this presumed struggle when he wrote from St. Petersburg: *"Oh, what a cursed city I live in! And what an abyss there is between it and Russia, whose destiny it directs!"*38

Pobedonostsev argued that those who wanted reform constantly threatened the peace. *"The very word reform,"* he wrote, *"is now so common that we have confused it with improvement."*39 He made no distinction between moderate voices and radicalized revolutionaries. In this, Pobedonostsev simply embodied the extremes that had always characterized the country. To him, the university student was just as potentially perilous, just as likely to be lethal, as a dedicated anarchist. A little education was good; too much, Pobedonostsev taught, was a dangerous thing.40

Tsesarevich Nicholas Alexandrovich and his cousin the Duke of York (George V).

Russia, Pobedonostsev contended, was *"mighty thanks to autocracy, thanks to the unlimited mutual trust and the close ties between the people and the Emperor. These ties are an invaluable blessing."*41 When Nicholas came to the throne, he should ignore unwelcome advice of squabbling, self-interested bureaucrats and rule by instinct. *"The absolute power of the sovereign is not only necessary for Russia,"* Pobedonostsev insisted, *"it is not only the guarantee of domestic peace but it is the essential condition of national unity and the political power of the state."*42

From birth, Nicholas learned that the Emperor was God's anointed on earth, endowed with spiritual gifts that elevated him above all other men and made him answerable only to his own conscience. Other monarchies had abandoned overt public declarations of celestial intervention; personal belief was sublimated to working within an established framework and with an existing political apparatus. Previous Russian Emperors had recognized this political fabric, presenting themselves as divinely inspired autocrats in the service of the state. Pobedonostsev introduced a new conception: the Emperor was the state, and everything he did was not only inspired by God but was also predestined.

Imperial rule was, under this theory, a sacrificial office ordained by God. Nicholas fully embraced this vision because it accorded with Orthodox notions of submission to divine will. He was less fatalistic – the word most commonly used to describe his outlook – than he was certain that his life and rule lay in God's hands, that every occurrence good and bad was the manifestation of divine providence. For Nicholas, frequent attribution of disaster to "God's Will" merely echoed the larger Russian belief in *sudba*, pervasive, inescapable Fate. It bore generations of peasants through famine, soldiers through hardship, factory workers through misery, and the future Nicholas II through his own trials. To question events was to question the will of God, to challenge the divine order – ideas anathema to the Russian soul. He had, as one courtier put it, *"an unshakable faith in the providential nature of his high office. His mission emanated from God. For his actions he was responsible only to his conscience and to God."*43

This educational regime did little to bolster Nicholas's self-confidence or equip him with the tools of mature reason. Alexander III regarded his heir as something of a physical and intellectual non-entity. When Finance Minister Sergei Witte suggested that Nicholas be given a responsible official appointment, the Emperor professed himself stunned. *"Have you ever had a serious conversation with him?"* he asked Witte, before condemning his son as *"nothing but a boy whose judgments are utterly childish."* Witte thought that this remark was somewhat unfair, and that Nicholas was *"far superior to his father in intellect and ability as well as in education."*[44] Indeed, it is possible that Alexander's comment may have stemmed from bitterness. As a second son, he had been denied the comprehensive education that his son had received, and he may have harbored some resentment at the disparity and at Nicholas's apparent failure to capitalize on the advantages offered him.

Yet there is something unnerving about a father and Emperor so openly complaining of his heir's abilities to an official. Alexander may have simply been speaking with despairing frankness, or seeking support for himself and his son, but such talk left official Russia and members of the Dynasty prepared to disregard Nicholas from the first, to treat him, as his father treated him, as a weakling, to be ordered around, ignored, or dictated to as whim demanded. This sense did not escape Nicholas, and in fact accounted for some of his later, otherwise inexplicable behavior in refusing to listen to the counsel of others and gradually pulling away from government and Imperial responsibilities into private life.

Nicholas would bemoan his lack of practical experience. *"I don't know anything,"* he said to a minister after his father's death. *"The late Sovereign did not foresee his end and did initiate me into anything."*[45] He complained to a cousin that Alexander III *"had never once mentioned the responsibilities that awaited him."*[46] Even Nicholas's sister Olga later said: *"It was my father's fault. I know my father disliked the mere idea of state matters encroaching on our family life but, after all, Nicky was his heir."*[47]

Reality, though, was somewhat different. For all of his faults, Alexander III did initiate practical training with his heir. Starting in 1889, he asked Nicholas to sit with him while ministers were received and made their reports. On his orders, Nicholas was appointed to the State Council and to the Council of Ministers, as well as to several governmental committees. He also began receiving state papers for his review.[48] The results proved negligible. Nicholas hated the

Konstantin Pobedonostsev.

Count Sergei Witte.

Tsar Nicholas II while visiting Scotland (Balmoral, September 1896).

laborious ritual of reading state papers. "*I simply do not understand,*" he wrote in 1891, "*how one can manage to read such a mass of papers in one week. I constantly limit myself to one or two of the most interesting matters but the rest go straight to the fireplace.*"[49] The lengthy bureaucratic council meetings left him frequently and obviously bored, and his interest in their proceedings was never consistent. Most, he frankly confessed to his diary, were a bore, and he did little to disguise his lack of enthusiasm.[50] Pobedonostsev summed up his former pupil's character in a few devastating sentences: "*He has a naturally bright mind, is shrewd, quickly grasps the meaning of what he hears, but only understands the significance of some isolated fact, without connection with the rest, without appreciating the interrelation of all other pertinent facts, events, trends, occurrences. He sticks to his insignificant, petty point of view.*"[51] It was little wonder, then, that many officials readily dismissed him. Nicholas, complained N. M. Chikhachev, Minister of the Imperial Navy, was "*a mere child, without experience, training, or even an inclination to study great problems of state. His interests are still those of a child.*"[52]

Quiet and sentimental, pious and suspicious, Nicholas emerged from his education as a genial young man, handsome and polite, with his mother's short stature and expressive blue eyes. On the surface he was invariably pleasant and passively calm, but the placid exterior concealed inner turmoil. Years of aggressive taunts and treatment by his father had eroded his self-confidence, while his mother's obsessive control had left him dependent and immature. With the innate dislike of confrontation bred into him since childhood, he loathed emotional scenes and let others dictate to him: passive acceptance was better than troublesome arguments. He learned to dissimilate and agree. A veneer of unflappable amiability ruled his life. Nicholas was invariably pleasant, charming, and agreeable to all those whom he met. This affable façade concealed his personal conflicts: the years of pacifying and pleasing cloaked a character at once headstrong and plagued with doubt.

In keeping with tradition, Nicholas joined the Imperial Army, enjoying military life and for the first time regular – albeit aristocratic - companions his own age. His mother worried that Nicholas would forget himself in this convivial atmosphere. "*Never forget,*" she warned him, "*that everyone's eyes are turned on you now, waiting to see what your first independent steps in life will be. Always be polite and courteous with everybody so that you get along with all your comrades without discrimination, although without too much familiarity or intimacy, and never listen to flatterers.*" To this rather insulting advice, Nicholas politely replied: "*I will always try to follow your advice, my dearest, darling Mama. One has to be cautious with everyone at first.*"[53] The message continued to be the same: Nicholas must obey his parents, follow his mother's wishes, and avoid any independent steps.

Nicholas did well in the army, rising through several regiments until he was made Colonel of the Horse Guards Artillery. He enjoyed the cautious camaraderie of life at camp: the regulated existence appealed to his sense of order, and he was happy to have all of his decisions made for him. Gradually, his natural reserve dissipated and Nicholas joined his fellow aristocratic officers in evenings at the ballet and theatre, or carousing through the night until he passed out drunk. It was a side of life he carefully concealed from his mother; only the entries in his diary

– *"we got stewed," "tasted six sorts of port and got a bit soused," "wallowed in the grass and drank"* – offered a candid account of his nocturnal pursuits.[54]

An extended tour of Egypt, India, and the Far East came in 1890, meant to complete his formal education and introduce the Tsesarevich to his future ceremonial duties. Reluctant to let him go, his possessive mother took comfort in their emotional parting: *"Your tears made me happy and soothed my suffering heart,"* she wrote. *"For some reason I had imagined you were not sorry to leave us, so that seeing your deep and acute grief I was almost pleased, for this at least reassured me and was as a balm to my heart."*[55] The journey took Nicholas and a select group of companions to Egypt, India, and Asia, followed all the way by his mother's domineering advice. Marie Feodorovna treated her eldest son like a wayward schoolboy: *"I quite see that the balls and other official doings are not very amusing,"* she wrote, *"especially in that heat, but you must understand that your position brings this with it. You have to set your personal comfort aside, be doubly polite, and amiable, and above all never show you are bored."*[56] Throughout the journey, minders pointed out sites and whispered of Russia's mystical mission in the Far East; Asian piety and reverence for royalty greatly impressed Nicholas. Not even a narrow escape in Japan, when a fanatic attacked him with a sword and left the Tsesarevich with a painful scar on his head, dampened Nicholas's enthusiastic view of these exotic monarchies, though he had a prejudice against most Japanese officials, whom he derisively called *"monkeys."*[57]

Mathilde Kschessinska.

Nicholas returned to St. Petersburg and slipped back into his undemanding life in the army, where military drills by day alternated with drunken parties by night. Following Romanov tradition, he took a mistress, ballerina Mathilde Kschessinska, one of the rising stars in the Imperial theatre. Pretty, vivacious, and exceptionally ambitious, Kschessinska wove a web of sexual intrigue that had the capital abuzz. Nicholas bought her a house and frequently spent the night with her: *"I dashed off to see my K.,"* he wrote in his diary, *"and spent the best night yet with her. I am still under her spell – my pen is trembling in my hand!"*[58]

Kschessinska offered amorous diversion, but Nicholas was also thinking ahead. *"I've noticed something very strange within myself,"* he wrote in his diary in 1892. *"I never thought that two identical feelings, two loves could co-exist within the heart. I have loved Alix H. for three years already and constantly cherish the hope that, God willing, one day I will marry her!"*[59]

Queen Victoria and her Hessian grandchildren. From the left: Princess Victoria and Hereditary Grand Duke Ernst Ludwig, Queen Victoria, Grand Duke Ludwig IV of Hesse and by Rhine, Princess Irene, Princess Elisabeth and Princess Alix.

Nicholas had first met Princess Alix of Hesse and by Rhine, the *"Alix H"* of his diary, in 1884, when she came to Russia for the marriage of her sister Elisabeth, known as Ella, to his uncle Grand Duke Sergei Alexandrovich. Alexander III's own mother Empress Marie Alexandrovna had been a Hessian Princess, and the 1862 marriage of the future Grand Duke Ludwig IV to Princess Alice, Queen Victoria's second daughter, brought further prestige to the German dynasty in Darmstadt. Tragedy soon overshadowed Alix's birth in 1872: her hemophiliac brother Friedrich died in 1873, and Alice never ceased to mourn his loss. Intelligent but depressive, mystical, and full of ruminations on sacrifice and the afterlife, Alice – along with a young daughter – fell victim to diphtheria five years later.

For Alix and the siblings who survived – blunt Victoria, beautiful Elisabeth, gentle Irene, and artistic, highly-strung Ernst Ludwig – their grandmother Queen Victoria provided endless talk of heaven and admonitions about the magnitude of their loss. Persistent tales of a grim, repressive childhood clouded by perpetual mourning, though, have been highly exaggerated. Alix had few memories of her mother and at first seemed almost unaffected by the loss.[60] Yet she was a most peculiar princess. Unlike her siblings, she kept to herself, indulging in introspection to the point of alienation. Shyness and social unease crippled her around both strangers and family, and Alix always felt that others were judging her. Distrustful, she closed herself off and concealed emotions behind an icy demeanor. She *"seldom smiled,"* said her cousin Crown Princess Marie of Romania, *"and when she did it was grudging, as though making a concession. No warmth emanated from her, and her ways were strangely cold."*[61]

Grand Duke Ludwig IV and Grand Duchess Alice of Hesse and by Rhine.

Queen Victoria took charge of her Hessian granddaughter's education, and in many ways her influence proved more damaging than bereavement. Alix was the Queen's granddaughter in many ways, not all of them positive. She copied the Queen's insistent belief in the superiority of her own opinions, her refusal to listen to contrary voices, her fascination with ill-health, and her desire for seclusion. The young Princess was widely read, but her preference for philosophy and comparative religious studies only emphasized her tendency to introspection. While clinging to notions of a sweeping intellect, Alix relied on emotion, not reason, to guide her in life.

That summer of 1884, though, sixteen-year-old Tsesarevich Nicholas saw none of this. He lavished twelve-year-old Alix with attentions. By week's end, he was writing, *"Alix and I wrote our names on the back window of the little Italian house (we love each other)."*[62] They met again in 1889, when Alix spent the winter with her sister in the Russian capital. More mature, the couple danced, skated, and dined together as St. Petersburg society watched the apparent attraction develop. Aristocrats noted her beauty, her golden red hair, and her imposing manner, but the Princess, they whispered, rarely smiled, danced badly, and wore unfashionable clothes.[63] *"Very awkward,"* agreed Marie Feodorovna after observing Alix that winter.[64] Since her father had lost Danish territories to Germany, Marie Feodorovna disliked all Germans, and Alix was German. The Princess, she thought, lacked the social graces necessary in a future Empress of Russia. The mystical atmosphere of the Orthodox Church, she worried, would unduly influence a mind already inclined to excessive religiosity.[65] More to the point, the Empress resented Alix because she threatened to come between herself and Nicholas, to destroy the web of emotional dependence and break apart Marie Feodorovna's ideal family. When Alix joined Nicholas's sister Xenia for tea at the palace, Marie Feodorovna was so upset that she summoned Elisabeth, warning that Alix was not to come again.[66]

Nicholas, though, was not so easily swayed. Alix was young and beautiful, a princess who shared his religious intensity and idealized, bourgeois notions of family life. During his Far Eastern tour, despite his burgeoning affair with Mathilde Kschessinska and the distractions of geishas and dancing girls, it was a framed photograph of Alix that stood on his bedside table.[67] He faced one seemingly insurmountable difficulty: the wife of the future Emperor had to be Orthodox, and Alix was Lutheran. Religion, to her, was all seriousness, meant to introspective analysis and self-improvement, but not necessarily personal comfort or joy: to abandon her church for romantic happiness was anathema.

Letters flew back and forth between the Tsesarevich and the Hessian Princess, each explaining, imploring, and begging the other to reconsider entrenched attitudes. *"I have tried to look at it in every light possible,"* Alix wrote to Nicholas in 1893, *"but I always return to one thing. I cannot do it against my conscience. You, dear Nicky, who also have such a strong belief will understand me that I think it is a sin to change my belief, and I should be miserable all the days of my life, knowing that I had done a wrongful thing."*[68]

In a life defined by moments of personal weakness, pursuit of Alix was one instance when Nicholas showed that, if he wished, he could be just as stubbornly autocratic as any of his Muscovite predecessors. He acted like a petulant schoolboy, insisting that if he could not marry Alix, he would renounce the throne and become a monk. *"I knew from the beginning what an obstacle there rose between us,"* he wrote Alix, suggesting that her reluctance stemmed from lack of true knowledge about the Russian Orthodox Church. *"How am I to change my feelings after waiting and wishing for so long, even now after that sad letter you sent me?…Do not say 'no' directly, my dearest Alix, do not ruin my life already! Do you think there can exist any happiness in the whole world without you?"*[69]

Conversions happened all the time: Alix's sister Elisabeth adopted Orthodoxy in 1892, after eight years of marriage to Sergei, and she now used her new faith as a weapon. If Alix married the future Emperor of Russia, both Elisabeth and Sergei envisioned wielding enormous power and influence over the throne. Hoping to facilitate the match, Elisabeth manipulated and lied. To Alexander III and Marie Feodorovna, she insisted that Alix would never change her faith while secretly encouraging Nicholas to persevere in his quest. She even assured Alix that no doctrinal differences existed between the two churches. In April 1894, convinced by Elisabeth that Alix would never convert, Alexander III and Marie Feodorovna finally agreed that Nicholas could make what they believed would be a futile proposal.

Grand Duchess Alice surrounded by her children. From the left: Elisabeth, Alix, Grand Duchess Alice holding Marie, Victoria, Ernst Ludwig and Irene. One son, Friedrich, had died in 1873 after falling from a window.

His chance came at the wedding of her brother Ernst Ludwig to their mutual cousin Victoria Melita ("Ducky") in Coburg. Alix's resistance was low: ceding her place in Darmstadt, sharing her brother's affections, and welcoming her new sister-in-law into her childhood home, Nicholas wrote, were the final drops in her *"cup of suffering and hesitation."*[70] After rejecting a first proposal,

Standing, from left: King George I of the Hellenes, Empress Marie Feodorovna, Queen Olga with her children Prince Nicholas and Princess Alexandra of Greece, Grand Duchess Xenia Alexandrovna, and Crown Prince Constantine of Greece with his sister Princess Marie. At front, same order: Grand Duchess Olga Alexandrovna, Tsar Alexander III and Grand Duke Michael Alexandrovich.

Grand Duchess Elisabeth Feodorovna with her husband Grand Duke Serge Alexandrovich and his brother Grand Duke Paul Alexandrovich (1892).

Alix suddenly agreed. It was, Nicholas wrote, a *"wonderful, unforgettable day."*[71] Nicholas had a princess who shared his values and sense of duty; Alix had the promise of a union imbued with spiritual significance that, according to Russia's national myth, offered her service in the divine plan that she now believed lay in store for them both. The press celebrated this *"triumph of love,"* and hopefully speculated that Alix, as granddaughter of the world's most powerful constitutional monarch, would influence her husband to make liberal concessions in Russia.

Nicholas won this victory as his father's health crumbled alarmingly. Years of stress and kidney failure left Alexander III a shrunken, hollow shell of his former self. In October, a terrified Nicholas hastily summoned Alix to Livadia, the Crimean estate where the Emperor now lay dying. Arriving amid the chaos and emotional confusion of a family watching its patriarch perish, Alix felt ignored and alone, though she made her presence known by turning to her fiancé's diary, imploring Nicholas to assert himself with doctors and officials, setting what would become a lifelong precedent of advising, lecturing, and even bullying her husband into submission.

Alexander III's death on October 20, Nicholas admitted, threw the twenty-six-year-old man into a role he had "dreaded" all of his life.[72] A mere week passed between solemn funeral rites for the late Emperor and the subdued ceremony uniting Nicholas and the newly-converted Alix – now christened Alexandra Feodorovna – in marriage as his widowed mother sobbed openly. Russia had seen its new sovereign come to the throne and wed amid a chorus of sympathy. Still, critical voices called out in the wilderness, warning that the new reign was unlikely to break with the repressive past. As for Alexandra, only censorious St. Petersburg had yet formed an opinion: watching as her carriage passed in the late Emperor's funeral procession, women crossed themselves, muttering sadly, *"A bad omen…she has come to us behind a coffin."*[73]

From the left: Princess Alix, her brother Ernst Ludwig and their sister Elisabeth.

***

"The beginning of a new reign!" enthused a foreign visitor to Russia in 1896. *"What possibilities it contains in this country, Russia, above all, where its ruler is an autocrat, and his sovereign will supreme….The hope and belief possesses everyone that Tsar Nicholas II…will do his best to fulfill his tremendous duties, and that the unwritten page of Russian history now opened may hold the record of a happy and beneficent reign, making for the good of his great country, and for the peace of the world."*[74]

Foreign opinions were almost universally positive. In retrospect, the views seem staggering naïve. Emile Flourens, Foreign Minister of Russia's only European ally, France, declared that Nicholas had *"a serious and deeply reflective spirit, showing a tact and maturity of judgment typical of one who has been on the throne for many years."*[75] *"I am convinced he will cut a great figure in history,"* insisted another journalist. *"Europe can look upon him with the greatest confidence, trusting every word he utters."*[76] Journalists described Nicholas as *"a noble, generous character, opposed to every kind of persecution, and especially to religious fanaticism."*[77] Another suggested that Nicholas, imbued with *"the progressive ideas of the younger generation,"* would break with Russia's repressive autocratic past.[78]

Few who actually knew Nicholas II shared such optimistic ideas. Aristocrats, ministers, courtiers and Romanovs saw him grow from shy, sequestered, undisciplined boy to frivolous youth and finally immature, indecisive monarch. One cousin worried over Nicholas's *"tendency to agree with the last opinion voiced."*[79] Well-intentioned he might be, said a former tutor, but the new Emperor was *"easily influenced and without personal reactions."*[80] Doubts about his ability to cope with the political demands simmering beneath the Empire's temporarily calm surface were widespread. Exacerbating the problem, Nicholas and his fiercely supportive bride knew the dismissive attitudes, aware that he was viewed as a weak non-entity incapable of filling his father's decisive and commanding shoes.

Before he came to the Throne, once upon it, and even after – as he stepped into the pages of history – Nicholas

A royal gathering at Schloß Rosenau, April 1894. Standing from left: Prince Henry of Battenberg, Prince Philipp of Saxe-Coburg and Gotha, Crown Prince Ferdinand of Romania, Prince Heinrich of Prussia, Duke Alfred of Saxe-Coburg and Gotha, Grand Duke Paul Alexandrovich, Tsesarevich Nicholas Alexandrovich, Kaiser Wilhelm II, Grand Duke Vladimir Alexandrovich, the Duke of Connaught, Prince Louis of Battenberg, Princess Alexandra of Saxe-Coburg and Gotha, the Prince of Wales (Edward VII). Seated, same order: Princess Victoria of Battenberg, Princess Louise of Saxe-Coburg and Gotha, Princess Beatrice of Battenberg, the Duchess of Connaught, Grand Duchess Marie Alexandrovna, Crown Princess Marie of Romania, Princess Alix of Hesse and by Rhine, Grand Duchess Marie Pavlovna, and Hereditary Princess Charlotte of Saxe-Meiningen. On the floor, same order: Princess Irene of Prussia, Princess Beatrice of Saxe-Coburg and Gotha, Grand Duke Sergei Alexandrovich, Princess Feodora of Saxe-Meiningen, Grand Duchess Elisabeth Feodorovna and Hereditary Prince Alfred of Saxe-Coburg and Gotha.

II was an enigma. Guarded in his behavior and emotions, he ruled as he lived, pleasant and polite to those he encountered. *"He truly desired happiness and a peaceful life for Russia,"* said his Finance Minister Sergei Witte, who was convinced that he had *"a thoroughly good, kind heart."*[81] On this nearly everyone agreed: he was personally kind, gentle, amiable, and charming.[82] Yet he always remained aloof and reserved. *"I found him invariably pleasant and gracious,"* noted one courtier, *"yet inscrutable. As I was soon to learn even with persons of his immediate Entourage he seldom revealed what he thought or how he felt except in trivial matters, never showed like or dislike, and never made his position known on any subject."*[83]

Order and discipline ruled Nicholas's life. Each pen and book in his study was carefully placed and no one was allowed to move any object: Nicholas said he wanted to be able to enter in the dark and immediately know where everything was located. A misplaced drop of glue when pasting photographs into albums sent him into a panic; he took hours to compose a simple letter.[84] Every night, he habitually wrote in his diary, recording the weather, how he had spent his day, how many animals he had shot, and what he had read. Only rarely did personal thoughts intrude. *"The reason I am writing so briefly,"* Nicholas jotted in his diary in 1891, *"is because I have to get up so early tomorrow morning, although I know, too, that it will be boring later to read these lines again."*[85] Yet he found comfort in the routine.

Nicholas, it has often been said, would have made an ideal British gentleman, or a model constitutional monarch. He loved his family, life in the country, and had thoroughly bourgeois inclinations. He spoke English with a perfectly clipped aristocratic accent (it was the language used by the Imperial couple in private), and even looked enough like his British cousin the future King George V to have passed for his brother. Appearances, though, were deceptive: beneath the benign façade of Victorian respectability and polished manner lurked the heart of a true Russian autocrat, deeply superstitious, mistrustful of nearly everyone, jealous of his power, and infused with certainty that as Emperor he stood apart from mankind as God's anointed. He evinced a preference for Peter the Great's father Tsar Alexei, extolling his virtues as a gentle, thoughtful ruler, even though he had littered his reign with the tortured and executed bodies of perceived enemies.[86] It was the era that Nicholas found so appealing, a time when the country was allegedly uncorrupted by foreign influences and Western ideas, when no bureaucracy stood between throne and a compliantly loyal populace. *"He thought he was a second Tsar Alexei Mikhailovich,"* said an aristocrat, noting that Nicholas II believed his country *"needed anointed ones, synods, and gendarmes, when what Russia needed were quick steps through a parliamentary system and capitalism to planning, new taxes, freedom of speech and the press, and 20th Century technology."*[87]

Autocratic mythology surrounded Nicholas with religious conceits that he wholeheartedly embraced. There was no parliament to help govern, no trusted advisor to encourage, no respected diplomat to lead the Emperor through his onerous tasks. It was, Nicholas commented, a *"terrible responsibility"* that he alone bore.[88] Yet the autocracy taught by Pobedonostsev and enacted by his father allowed for no concessions. *"I shall never, under any circumstances,"* Nicholas once declared, *"agree to a representative form of government, because I consider it harmful to the people God has entrusted to my care."*[89] The people, according to this reasoning, played little role: Nicholas resented members of his own government, and viewed his subjects both high and low as mere servants of the crown, valued not for their wisdom but for their presumed loyalty.[90] Nicholas ruled by resignation, unable to adapt to changing times and circumstances, arbitrarily

Tsesarevich Nicholas Alexandrovich and Princess Alix of Hesse on the day they became engaged, Schloß Rosenau, April 1894.

accepting or rejecting opinion according to his mood. *"Once inspired by the will of God he became adamant,"* recalled a diplomat, *"to the surprise and despair of his ministers, who vainly tried to oppose what they considered weak and unfounded opinions."*[91] He never recognized the need for urgent reforms or the wisdom in acknowledging the aspirations of his subjects. He could not, as one historian wrote, *"understand why people would not be content with the lot which destiny had assigned them, as he was: after all, he carried on even though he derived no enjoyment from his difficult and often tedious responsibilities."*[92]

Evidence of this belief came soon enough. In January 1895, Nicholas received representatives of provincial assemblies of local officials, workers, and peasants from across the Empire. In his address, the deputy from Tver suggested that the new Emperor move the country along a liberal path and listen to the voices of his subjects.[93] Receiving the delegates in the Winter Palace, Nicholas quickly disabused them of such ideas. He derided them for indulging *"in senseless dreams of representative participation in the affairs of internal administration."*[94] Official tongues clucked over this naïve and tactless phrasing.[95] It was, thought one diplomat, *"prompted by weakness, an attempt to resent the suggestion that he himself was insufficient for all the needs of Russia."*[96] Nicholas compounded the error with a bit of autocratic petulance. So incensed was he by this perceived threat to his own prerogatives that he had the offending Tver deputy stripped of all of his civil rights for a year.[97] The words and actions rang across Russia, signaling that hopes for an enlightened and progressive era of reform were stillborn.

***

Nicholas and Alexandra passed their first year of married life quietly, sheltered from public duties by mourning for Alexander III. They first lived with the widowed Dowager Empress Marie Feodorovna at St. Petersburg's Anickhov Palace, sharing six cramped rooms that Nicholas had used as a child. It was intimate and pleasant but for one thing: the tension that arose between Alexandra and her mother-in-law. According to etiquette, Marie Feodorovna took precedence over her daughter-in-law, and there were arguments over patronage of the Russian Red Cross; whose name should come first in prayers for the Imperial Family; and possession of certain pieces of jewelry.[98] Patronage, prayers, and precious stones symbolized a larger problem: both women, proud, stubborn, and plunged into difficult new lives, fought for Nicholas II's limited time and attentions, and resentments soured the already uneasy relationship between the two Empresses.

Empress Alexandra Feodorovna.

Society expected much of Alexandra. She was, people thought, *"kind, humane, cultivated in the extreme, and imbued with all the humanitarian ideas for which the children and grandchildren of Queen Victoria had been so remarkable."*[99] Yet from the first the shy and serious young woman was terrified by her role as Empress. *"I am dying of fright,"* she confessed before a ball. *"Fancy, I* shall have to make a cercle in a room with 55 Mamas and more daughters – it is cruel, & I don't know how I shall ever manage it."[100] She never understood that, in marrying Nicholas, she had to put ceremonial obligations above private desires. Even more fatally, she expected Russia to accommodate her values and tastes, rather than adapt and learn how to become a Russian Empress. When she appeared at court receptions, Alexandra remained cold and grim, an unbecoming blush hinting at her discomfort. She quickly alienated aristocratic ladies by gazing down reception lines to see how much longer she had to stay. Alexandra exacerbated the situation by openly criticizing her new contemporaries. Russian aristocrats, she said, were too frivolous, too hedonistic, and too immoral.[101] And society was equally judgmental: the new Empress, they said, rarely smiled, seemed acutely uncomfortable, and lacked her mother-in-law's famous charm.[102]

Alienation set in and Alexandra soon receded into the background, leading Nicholas into the shadows of a prized but fatally secluded private life. The ruling couple disappeared behind the walls of the Alexander Palace at Tsarskoye Selo south of St. Petersburg, into a series of pastel-hued rooms crowded with chintz-covered sofas, built-in cozy-corners, and a thoroughly middle class profusion of Victorian bric-a-brac. They walked in the park, he read English novels and Russian classics to her, and they pasted hundreds of photographs into leather-bound albums as their personal romantic fantasy played out. In November Alexandra gave birth to a daughter they named Olga, and nursed and bathed the child herself.

This narrow universe of domestic concerns and humble pleasures dominated their lives. Traditional ceremonies and imperial entertainments gradually ebbed, as the Imperial couple's confused philosophy, mingling the domestic with the political to express a new vision, placed their family at the heart of national life.

Immaturity and personal inclination drove the Imperial couple into self-imposed exile from the Russian Court, yet in 1896 this enigmatic pair prepared for the most evocative and meaningful moment of Nicholas II's life, his coronation. Nicholas cast himself as a martyr to the Imperial cause, and viewed his coronation as an inescapable burden. It would be, he wrote, *"a great ordeal, sent by God,"* where *"every step"* would evoke memories of his late father's crowning.[103]

Yet Nicholas also approached the coronation in an atmosphere of religious ecstasy. In Moscow, he would be bound to Orthodox Russia in a spiritual contract that sanctified his place above all others; anointing and crowning would elevate Nicholas into an earthly pantheon where divine wisdom would guide his rule. For Nicholas, the ceremony promised benediction and transformation, confirming personal beliefs and signifying his role as Batiushka-Tsar, benevolent father of the Russian people. Prayers and fragrant clouds of incense, though, could not conceal a different reality that loomed in Moscow. It, too, would envelope Nicholas, shattering forever the old and treasured national myths.

Tsar Nicholas II with his wife Alexandra Feodorovna and her sister Elisabeth Feodorovna standing behind him.

Chapter II

Winter gave way to a rainy spring in 1896 as Moscow readied itself for the coming coronation. Since its birth, sophisticated St. Petersburg had always looked down on the former capital: it was thought backward, its streets squalid, and its people narrow-minded and superstitious. Yet for all of its Western niceties and emphasis on European etiquette, tradition deemed Peter the Great's city on the Baltic too new, too morally corrupt, to witness the sacred and solemn coronation.

The ceremonies in Moscow took eighteen months to plan. In earlier reigns, particularly when a sovereign had come to the throne amidst court intrigues and political chaos, coronations often occurred soon after accession. Catherine the Great was crowned just a few weeks after she took the throne from her husband, while Alexander I held his coronation a month after the coup that had killed his father Emperor Paul.[1] In the more stable modern era, however, practical considerations prevailed. Court mourning for Alexander III, along with worry over the weather and restrictions in the Orthodox Liturgical Calendar influenced the schedule for Nicholas II's coronation. Convention demanded a full year's mourning for the late Emperor, precluding any coronation before October 1895, but no one wanted to hold parades and public spectacles in a rainy Moscow autumn. Snow would come with the New Year; not until the great Easter celebrations had ended could the coronation take place. For sentimental reasons Nicholas may have wished to be crowned on May 15, the anniversary of his father's coronation. Marie Feodorovna, however, was already agonized at having to see her son crowned, and watching him do so on such an evocative date would have been more than she could bear. Speculation finally ended on March 8, 1895, when the Ministry of the Imperial Court issued a magnificently illuminated decree that Nicholas II's Coronation would take place on May 14, 1896.[2]

From parades and processions, reviews and receptions, every aspect of the coronation was carefully choreographed as this imposing piece of religious and political theatre took form. Nothing was left to chance. Details for every parade and banquet were laid out in precise, expansive detail, with tables to chart precedence for Romanovs, foreign royalties, and visiting diplomats, and rehearsals to time their every movement. Meanwhile, advisors poured over menu suggestions and seating arrangements for banquets and musical selections for balls.[3] The Coronation Committee published elaborately designed, colorfully illuminated proclamations and programs, histories of the Romanov Dynasty, character sketches of Nicholas and Alexandra, explanations of the coronation rituals, and timetables for the events.[4]

Moscow's rarely used palaces needed remodeling, its cathedrals renovation, its theatres refurbishment, and its official buildings electrical wiring. The city had no power station to support the galaxy of new electric lights that themselves became coronation attractions. One was hastily and almost secretively constructed within the walls of the Kremlin, supplying the palaces and strings of twinkling decorations while public streets remained gas lit. Thousands of carpenters, florists, and electricians decorated the city, and craftsmen built pavilions and tribunes to hold spectators. The Ministry of the Imperial Court established a temporary Chancellery in Moscow, dispatching 1,300 officials and servants from St. Petersburg and taking on another 1,200 temporary workers to oversee the ceremonies. Some 800 coachmen, equerries, and grooms from the Imperial Stables joined 600 horses sent to Moscow, and another 800 men and animals twere hired in the former capital to drive visiting dignitaries.[5] The cost was enormous: 6,971,000 rubles (approximately $93 million, or £69,710,000 in 2014 figures), making it the single most expensive Russian coronation ceremony ever held. Nicholas contributed 995,000 rubles from his annual civil list; the Imperial Treasury paid the remaining sum.[6] *"We have placed no limit on the expense,"* one Muscovite

Chapter II

The Moscow Kremlin. This is a view from the West and dates from the time as coronation preparations were going on in earnest.

declared proudly. *"We are rich enough to pay the bill whatever it is and are more than willing."*⁷

The city seized opportunities to enrich itself. The Imperial Court commandeered nearly every respectable hotel in the city. A temporary Imperial Chancellery with hundreds of courtiers took over the immense Bolshaya Moskovskaya Hotel; foreign princes, emissaries, and diplomats without private accommodation were housed at the Slavyansky Bazaar and the Kontinental Hotels, and aristocrats and military officials were directed to rooms at the Metropol Hotel.⁸ Beds were at a premium. *"Many people,"* reported a British resident, *"let their houses for May and June, at more than a usual year's rent."*⁹ Apartments rented for as much as 2,500 rubles a month ($33,750, or £25,000 in 2014 figures); a single room or balcony overlooking Tverskaya Boulevard down which the Emperor would make his State Entrance into Moscow, went for upwards of 500 rubles ($6,750, or £5,000). Those who found this too expensive could pay 15 rubles ($200, or £150) for the privilege of crowding into a window with others hoping to peer out at the scene.¹⁰ The usual monthly rate of 75 rubles ($1010 or £750) for a horse and carriage swelled tenfold, sometimes to as much as 900 rubles ($12,000 or £9,000) in May, with another 300 rubles ($4,000, or £3,000) if a driver was needed. Even fashionable clothing was not immune. Moscow couturier Korday's sold gowns for 2,000 rubles ($27,000 or £20,000), asking – and receiving – another 400 rubles ($5,400, or £4,000) for the necessary court trains appended to them.¹¹

"If it be, as some people suppose, always a good thing to provide employment for the common people," wrote a critic, *"then assuredly the Coronation was a blessing to the world, for hundreds of thousands of people were called on to expend much labor on many things, both for the Coronation itself and for the feasting and adorning of people who attended it, with the embellishment of the houses they temporarily occupied and the fine coaches in which they traveled by rail or through the streets. It is a pity that most of these things were quite useless, and that the money to pay for them had to be taken from other poor people, who would rather their industry had provided wealth for themselves."*¹²

Outrageous prices were not the only thing different in Moscow that spring. The Government ordered the city purged of potentially troublesome elements.¹³ Forever suspicious to authorities because of their interest in new ideas, students suddenly found people lingering outside their lodgings; they pretended to be bystanders or innocent cab drivers, but were actually spies. Some 500 students preparing for examinations at Moscow University were temporarily exiled to the provinces; with them went hundreds of others – middle class business people, factory workers, even members of the police – whose loyalty to the throne seemed questionable.¹⁴ A woman found with dynamite was arrested, tried, and condemned to Siberian exile in the space of a few hours.¹⁵ A hundred thousand troops arrived to keep order; 5,000 extra police from St. Petersburg joined 3,000 of their Muscovite colleagues, and another 92,000 ordinary citizens were paid to act as undercover agents – Moscow, said a reporter, *"swarmed with spies."*¹⁶

In poorer lodgings, janitors frequently checked rooms, asked for papers, examined registration forms, and searched for undesirable elements planning to disrupt the celebrations. *"Spies and stool-pigeons of all kinds made their way stealthily through the city's outlying neighborhoods,"* said one resident, *"through the working class quarters, listening attentively for talk that might sound excessive."*¹⁷ Doormen, carriage drivers, and shop owners pointed accusatory fingers at anyone deemed suspicious: even commenting negatively on the street decorations could lead to arrest.[18] Agents infiltrated factories and bars, pretended to be drunk, and made deliberately provocative comments hoping to entrap would-be anarchists.[19] An *"atmosphere of suspicion and pursuit,"* said a worker, suffused the entire city.[20]

The Government's indulgent treatment of journalists stood in stark contrast to such repression. State censorship muzzled the Russian press, but foreign journalists were flattered and fawned over to ensure favorable reports. National and international press had been used since the reign of Nicholas I to portray the desired themes and disseminate them to the world. In 1883, forty-nine accredited foreign correspondents covered Alexander III's coronation; more than 300 reporters descended on Moscow in 1896. They spoke *"eleven different languages,"* and advanced their *"individual claims and the claims of the periodical represented with a pertinacity and vigor worthy of a great cause."* Princes, ambassadors, merchants, bankers, and bureaucrats had their favorites, lobbying, bribing, and pleading with officials for accreditation.[21]

W. T. Stead.

The unusual courtesies extended to these reporters, historian Richard Wortman has noted, revealed *"the monarchy adapting to contemporary forms of mass publicity and consumption"* in its efforts to win popular support.[22] For Alexander III, for his *eminence gris* Pobedonostsev, and now for Nicholas II, the press formed a vital part of the Autocracy's propaganda strategy. Alexander III had done the previously unthinkable when he granted British Russophile and press magnate W. T. Stead an interview. No other Emperor had made such a play for popular appeal, and Stead's gushing tribute to an unrepentant autocrat left many aghast. Liberal colleagues accused Stead of selling out his principles to bask in temporary Imperial favor. *"To secure a few minutes conversation with a celebrity is a privilege which entitles* [Stead] *to speak of 'My friend, the High Muck-a-Muck,'"* sneered one writer.[23]

Nicholas II was somewhat more suspicious of modern media. The press, and especially a free press without the restraining hand of the state, Pobedonostsev had taught, was especially dangerous. *"Who are the representatives of that dreadful power that calls itself public opinion?"* Pobedonostsev asked. *"Who confers on them the rights and the authority to rule in the name of society? Who nominates them to subvert the existing order and to proclaim new ideas of moral and positive law?"* He deemed the press filled with *"the most contemptible persons, retired usurpers, Yid merchants, louts, cads and card sharps."*[24]

Vladimir Nemirovich-Danchenko.

"Control of those irresponsible people who compose the newspapers is one of the most difficult questions of the present time," Nicholas II once confided to a diplomat.[25] Like his father, though, he knew the value of cultivating the burgeoning media. He, too, sat with Stead, and wasted no opportunity to publish photographs of his attractive family to create favorable impressions of his rule.[26]

Alexei Suvorin.

Russians formed the largest contingent of reporters in Moscow. Michael Zaguliaev filed dispatches for *Journal de Petersbourg*, read by the capital's fashionable society; Vladimir Nemirovich-Danchenko, correspondent for the popular illustrated journal *Niva*, offered detailed commentaries; and Vladimir Giliarovsky put pen to paper for *Russkiye Vedomosti*. Most influential was sixty-one-year-old Alexei Suvorin, owner of the conservative newspaper *Novoe Vremya*. Born a peasant, Suvorin began his career as a teacher but switched to writing to support Alexander II's liberal reforms. His touch seemed golden: businesses, newspapers, art, the theatre, and politics all flourished under Suvorin's guidance. When a young liberal officer murdered his wife, with whom he was having an affair, Suvorin turned his back on reforms. His *Novoe Vremya* became the conservative, often anti-Semitic organ of the far right, espousing Alexander III's repressive policies and urging the new Nicholas II to follow the nationalistic tradition of *"Autocracy, Orthodoxy, and Nationality."*[27]

Wealthy and well-connected, Suvorin suffered few of the uncertainties or discomforts experienced by his fellow correspondents: he took a room in Moscow's Dresden Hotel at 450 rubles ($6,075, or £4,500 in 2014) – a rate inflated by the demands of the coronation. He confessed himself bored by the celebrations. *"I love noise, movement, crowds,"* he wrote perceptively, *"but the thought that I would have to write about it spoiled the pleasure. What to say? A profound topic like this can't just be covered by producing an effect. All processions are surely very lovely, but they still give an impression of constraint, and all, or most, who take part in them always seem a bit worried."*[28]

The Russian press was reverential in tone, infused with exalted notions of Orthodoxy and Autocracy. Many foreign journalists, though, adopted similar views. Reporters from Republican France, Imperial Russia's European ally, seemed to forget their egalitarian leanings on arriving in Moscow. Religious writer Therese Vianzone regarded Nicholas with a breathless adoration approaching worship. Pierre d'Alheim of *Le Temps* offered similarly florid accounts. Emphasizing the special relationship between Russia and France, he carefully portrayed the Imperial couple that would visit Paris later that autumn as the very models of enlightened rule. Only French art critic Henry LaPauze's narrative of his Russian adventures escaped his colleagues' tendency to hyperbole.

French correspondents delighted in signs of Russian favoritism and were quick to point out the military alliance between the two countries. *"This evidence,"* reported *Le Siecle*, *"is obviously not pleasing to the Wilhelmstrasse and St. James's Palace."* Ominously, it hinted that other European countries *"should ask themselves if there's a situation in which Russia's interests would not oblige her to join France in a war against a country, which just might happen to be Germany?"*[29]

From Britain, veteran correspondent Edwin Arnold, a poet and

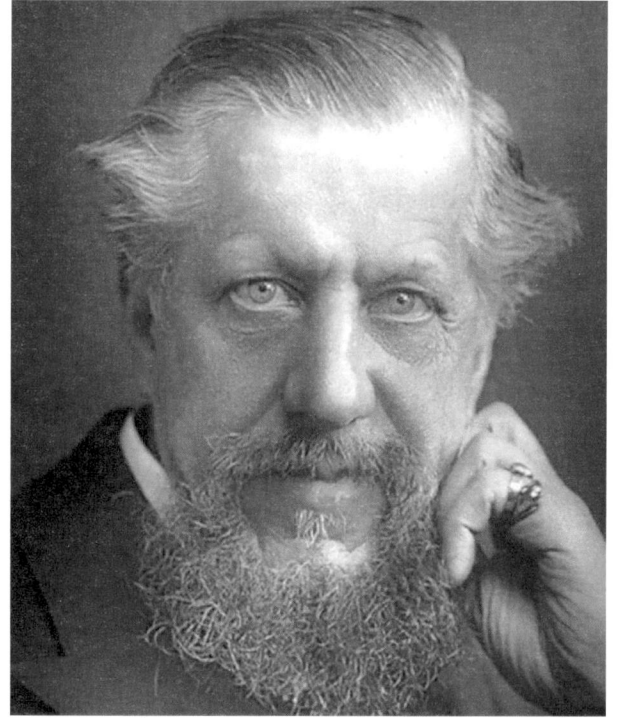
Edwin Arnold.

editor of the *Telegraph*, came to Moscow armed with £25,000 (the equivalent of £2,500,000 or $3,375,000 in 2014) to pay expenses, bribe officials, and facilitate access.³⁰ Though British as well, Aubrey Stanhope received credentials as a reporter for *The New York Herald*.³¹ He was an odd man of flexible patriotism, later destined for infamy as a German propagandist in World War I. Sir Donald Mackenzie Wallace, writing for *The Times of London*, was the most prominent British journalist covering the coronation. Wallace had met the then-Tsesarevich during Nicholas's Far Eastern tour, accompanying him through British India and steering the young man away from dubious political contacts with disaffected colonials. According to W. T. Stead, Wallace's company had so bored one of Nicholas's companions that it had turned the young man into an Anglophobe.³² Wallace received the Russian Order of St. Stanislav for his services: his fluency with the language and work in Russia as both a diplomat and a journalist made him a natural to report on the coronation. But despite many years there, Wallace's familiarity with the country, at least according to Sergei Witte, was limited. Nicholas II's Finance Minister complained that Wallace was *"always misinformed"* about the empire, and merely adopted the conservative views of aristocrat friends whose favor he snobbishly cultivated.³³

Full of boyish lark at the unfolding pageantry and exotic sights was Arthur Alkin Sykes, who had translated several of Gogol's works and occasionally

Sir Donald Mackenzie Wallace.

Aylmer Maude.

wrote for the satirical *Punch*. Lacking privileged social connections, Sykes was content to soak up the unfolding adventures in Moscow. He and his colleagues arrived early at their lodgings in the Paris Furnished Apartments, much to the horror of their new landlady who hurriedly *"sent out in all directions for linen, towels, forks and spoons."* Sykes took it all in his stride. *"The furniture of our apartments,"* he wrote, *"was limited, consisting principally of a squirt-washstand which worked with a pedal, and had no plug. The bottom of the first, in which we inserted a cork, gave way under such unwonted treatment. For bedding we had to be content with a single sheet apiece, and we generally had all things in common, but, on the whole, we were as comfortable as could be expected under the circumstances."* There was even a manservant named Peter; as a joke, Sykes and his colleagues taught the young man to crow when asking if they wanted eggs for breakfast.³⁴

Aylmer Maude was the one thorn in the side of all of this British joviality. Son of an Ipswich clergyman, Maude came to Russia in 1874, studying at the Moscow Lyceum and working as an English-language tutor before marrying the daughter of a British jeweler. Early business success allowed him to retire before he was forty, and Maude took up issues of social justice. A friend and translator of Leo Tolstoy, a Fabian, and a true radical, Maude quickly became a dedicated enemy of the Imperial regime. Nicholas, he complained, was an average man of twenty-eight; he differed from

Richard Harding Davis.

other young men only by his lack of concern with "the actual business of life, the task of wringing from nature food, clothes, and shelter." Yet his exalted birth demanded that Nicholas be crowned for the *"deception"* of his humble subjects.[35] Under the pseudonym *"de Monte Alto,"* Maude penned a scathing account of the Coronation that recorded matters other, less politically inclined writers ignored. Maude saw excess and incompetence everywhere he looked in Moscow, even among his own colleagues. Journalist though he was in effect, Maude decried his fellow correspondents *"telegraphing nonsense all over Europe and to the Republican United States of America"* as well as those *"foolish children"* who *"wasted"* time reading the glowing accounts.[36]

Republican America, like Republican France, wanted in on the journalistic game. Correspondents from the Associated Press and the United Press fought fellow American reporter Richard Harding Davis for access in Moscow. A pushy, resourceful man of thirty-two, Davis wrote with great style and wit, later achieving renown as a war reporter. He had just published *Princess Aline*, a frothy romance novel about an American man stalking the coolly beautiful title character across Europe. What made it fascinating was that Davis plainly modeled his literary hero on himself, and his Aline was really the former Princess Alix of Hesse, the new Empress of Russia whose husband's coronation he now covered. Davis must have kept his enthusiasm in check, as his devotion to Alexandra caused no international incidents, though he made himself a thorough pest in Moscow in other ways. A fellow visiting American, who met him over dinner, recorded in obvious surprise that Davis was *"a very nice sort of fellow, and we didn't see any signs of the egotism about which we had heard so much."*[37] Representing *Harper's Magazine* and the *New York Journal*, Davis stuck his foot into the most coveted doorways in the city, using any means necessary.[38]

Davis was determined to obtain one of the two seats reserved for American correspondents in the Cathedral of the Assumption during the actual coronation. *"Five are trying for it,"* he noted; those journalists not selected – including all of the women correspondents – would have to make do with places outside the church, where they could see the processions but would miss the actual crowning.[39] A plea before the Russian Government's press liaison proved disastrous when Davis relied on a friend named Augustus Trowbridge to translate. Unfortunately, as Davis wrote, Trowbridge's Russian was *"limited to a single phrase, which reflected on the ancestors of the person to whom it was addressed,"* scarcely the vocabulary needed to influence officials.[40] Not surprisingly, Davis complained, no one *"gave me the least encouragement as to getting in at the Coronation."* In despair, he finally turned to Clifton R. Breckinridge, the American Minister to Russia, explaining rather disingenuously that he had already *"advertised"* his articles about the coronation in advance and therefore *had* to obtain a ticket to the Cathedral. Breckinridge intervened, and Davis won the coveted seat.[41]

William Randolph Hearst.

Obtaining the seat solved one problem, but for Davis there remained the important matter of getting his reports onto the telegraph wires and back to the United States. *"That, I am happy to say, we are as assured of as I could hope to be,"* he gloated, after more cajoling and wheeler-dealing. *"I own the head of the telegraph bureau soul, body, and mind. He sent out my first cable today, ahead of twelve others; he has also given us entrée to a private door to his office, all the other correspondents having to go to the press rooms and undergo a sort of press censorship, which entails on each man the cutting up of his story into three parts, so as to give all a chance."* Davis happily used all manner of underhanded tactics, instructing Trowbridge that *"we did not want a fair chance – we wanted an unfair advantage over every one else."* The pair, Davis said, managed to *"flatter, lie, threaten and bribe with a skill and assurance that is simply beautiful.… There is not a wire we have not pulled, nor a leg, either, and we go dashing about all day in a bath-chair, with a driver in a bell hat and blue nightgown, leaving cards and writing notes and giving drinks and having secretaries to lunch and buying flowers for wives and cigar boxes for husbands."* And it all had to be done on a meager budget. Newspaper tycoon William Randolph Hearst, Davis complained, *"never sent me a cent for the cables until it was so late that I could not get it out of the bank, and we have spent and borrowed every penny we have. Imagine trying to write a story, and to fight to be allowed the chance to write it, and at the same time be pressed for money for expenses and tolls so that you were worn out by that alone!"*[42]

Albert Nikolaievich Benois.

The Coronation rituals recorded by these journalists harkened back to a medieval Russian past, and the Government also commissioned traditional artists to capture the ceremonies. The Imperial Academy of Art in St. Petersburg dispatched a number of noted painters, including Viktor Vasnetsov, Michael Nesterov, Andrei Ryabushkin, Albert Benois, Ilya Repin, and Valentin Serov, to record the parades and processions.[43] Their work, published in the official coronation album, *"introduced a sensibility sometimes at odds with the solemn spirituality of the ceremonies,"*[43] as historian Richard Wortman noted. *"The watercolors, reproduced in chromolithography, dissolved the masses of the Kremlin buildings into iridescent and translucent forms caught in a play of light, expressing the pictorial brilliance rather than the gravity of the occasion."* The resulting images *"transformed the event into personal visual statements that betray the influence of contemporary Paris more than that of Seventeenth Century Moscow."*[44]

Laurits Regner Tuxen.

Henri Gerveux came from France, one of two foreign artists commissioned to paint the scene in the Cathedral of the Assumption. He joined Laurits Regner Tuxen, a Danish court painter who had succeeded the celebrated Winterhalter as the era's most fashionable chronicler of royal personages. Both men produced monumental canvases depicting the moment of Nicholas II's crowning; Tuxen's work was so detailed and enormous that it was not completed until 1899.[45]

Paul Jakovlevich Piasetsky's magnificent panoramic painting of the coronation festivities. It took the artist four years (1896-1900) to complete this masterpiece.

The single most impressive artistic accomplishment, though, belonged to Paul Piasetsky, a doctor, geographical explorer, and talented watercolorist who had been made an Honorary Member of the Imperial Academy of Fine Arts. Piasetsky specialized in immense, panoramic views, and had previously recorded events in the Russo-Turkish War and provincial scenes from across the Empire and in the Far East.[46] In December of 1895, he asked the Minister of the Imperial Court for permission to create a new panorama commemorating the coronation in Moscow. *"If I do indeed get leave to do this,"* he explained, *"then I feel obligated to request that you show me the best vantage points for the depiction of the materials. Part of this can be done some time in advance, as for instance the costumes, the architecture of the buildings, and the streets from special angles. I will also need to know the program of the ceremonial by which the events will occur."* The request was duly granted, and Piasetsky took four years to complete the nearly 200-foot-long canvas, depicting events in Moscow from the arrival of Nicholas and Alexandra through all of the ceremonies until their departure, capturing the chronological flow of the coronation festivities in a single, unique work that drew on the similar, progressive illustrations used to record previous significant royal occasions from the Sixteenth to the Eighteenth Centuries.[47]

While relying on the written word and artistic depictions, the Government also embraced the modern era's fascination with the newest popular medium of all, cinematography. Camille Cerf, occasional correspondent for *Le Figaro* and an investor in the burgeoning Lumiere Brothers Cinema, used his influence to win the company accreditation in Moscow. It was the first time the Russian Government had granted a film concession, and even Nicholas II was uncertain. Although he later admired the medium as entertainment, in these years Nicholas sniffed at it from on high as *"an empty, useless and even pernicious diversion,"* a *"sideshow business"* that *"only an abnormal person"* could call *"art."*[48] Lumiere dispatched Charles Moisson, chief cine engineer at their Lyon studios, along with his seventeen-year-old assistant François Doublier, to Russia, armed with sixty-foot-long rolls of celluloid and a new Kinematophone camera to film the processions to and from the Cathedral on Coronation day.[49]

To accommodate and coddle these gathered journalists, the Ministry of the Imperial Court established a

Correspondents' Bureau in Moscow under the direction of Vassili Krivenko, Chief of the Imperial Chancellery.[50] Temporarily quartered in the Kristii House, a palatial mansion on Moscow's Rakhmanovsky Boulevard, the Correspondents' Bureau resembled an exclusive private club, where journalists gathered day and night to exchange stories over lengthy dinners and expensive cigars. Entering into this restrictive world, though, was not easy, as many foreign correspondents discovered. Those seeking accreditation had to deposit five photographs in various bureaus before March 31, along with requests and credentials to be scrutinized by officials. Applicants approved had one of the photographs returned, with a seal, label, and details stamped on the front and back showing that they had received the Court's sanction; these photographs had to be carried at all times, along with credentials issued by the Correspondents' Bureau requesting *"authorities of the Government and public institutions to withhold no possible assistance"* from the reporter in question. Those recognized by the Government, remembered Arthur Sykes, were assisted *"in every possible way,"* receiving tickets to observe the State Entrance, passes for receptions, and even invitations to a gala performance at the Bolshoi.[51] Journalists quickly became a familiar sight in Moscow, proudly wearing special bronze badges with the Imperial couple's initials in blue enamel, inscribed with the date, an Orthodox cross, and a tiny raised pen and scroll to signify their status as reporters.[52] These badges allowed reporters through police lines and entitled them to free use of city cabs.[53] Thus armed, crowed a correspondent, *"all difficulties were smoothed away."*[54]

The Government helpfully provided journalists with copious official literature and Tsarist propaganda describing the ceremonies and Nicholas II to guide them in their tasks. These not only offered information but also carried, as the historian Richard Wortman notes, a deeper significance. They *"disseminated the image of the ruler"* to his subjects; wrapped the autocracy in an exotic *"otherness"* that set it and Nicholas II quite apart from the rest of mankind; and offered a symbolic interpretation of events meant to elicit the appropriate responses of loyal servitude and religious piety.[55] Looking over one such document, Richard Harding Davis was struck by two things. The information was printed in Russian, French, German, and English, an indication of international interest in the ceremony. Still, this was not as remarkable as the style of the text itself: filled with references to the Romanovs and to God, he noted how the capital letters used for names seemed *"equally divided"* between Emperor and deity,

Grand Duke Sergei Alexandrovich.
(1858-1905)

as if the two were interchangeable.⁵⁶

Government publications and papers stumbled over themselves praising Nicholas II and the national myths about the Autocracy to elicit loyal servitude and religious piety.⁵⁷ The coronation, insisted one periodical, *"sealed the unbreakable union of the Russian Autocrat with the Orthodox Church,"* cementing bonds that made the people *"inseparable from their Tsar."*⁵⁸ Another, *Moskovskie Vedomosti*, linked the idea of a religiously ordained autocracy to the Empire's greatness: the direct intervention of God in selecting Russia's rulers, the paper declared, relieved the country of political strife. The faithful prayers of his loyal subjects strengthened the Emperor in his rule, which the paper characterized not in political terms but as a heroic, spiritual struggle against the evils of the modern world.⁵⁹

One man in Moscow was engaged in his own struggle that spring of 1896. Behind the coldly neoclassical walls of his palace on Tverskaya Boulevard, Grand Duke Sergei Alexandrovich fumed with rage. As Governor-General of Moscow, he would welcome his nephew and brother-in-law Nicholas II into the city and occupy a place of primacy during the coronation. A lean, pale man with frozen blue eyes, Sergei had an image so satanic it approached caricature. *"Snobbish and unapproachable,"* went one opinion; *"frightening"* and *"menacing"* ran another; *"there was a tyrant within him, ready at any moment to burst forth"* – and these were comments from his own family.⁶⁰ A general deemed Sergei *"obstinate, stupid, arrogant, hard, cold, and extremely susceptible to take offense, although he had an extremely high opinion of himself."*⁶¹ Rumors about his private life kept Muscovite tongues wagging for years: a sadist, it was said, a pedophile, the practitioner of *"unmentionable vices"* best left unspecified.⁶² Yet his would be the official face of Moscow throughout the three weeks of ceremonies.

From his appointment as Governor-General in 1891, Sergei treated Moscow as his personal fiefdom. Defending Alexander III's reactionary policy, the Grand Duke despised liberals, university students, workers, and an independent press, condemning them as elements *"dangerous to the state."*[63] Furiously anti-Semitic – *"Jews ought to be crucified!"* Sergei once declared – he expelled some 20,000 Jews from Moscow to the infamous Pale of Settlement and delighted in enacting new humiliations on those who remained.[64] If, as government minister Vladimir Lambsdorff said, his elder brothers had *"contempt for humanity,"* Sergei was *"fully held in humanity's contempt."*[65] The Grand Duke was not in the least perturbed by this: "*The general hatred he thus aroused,*" claimed a foreign diplomat, *"filled him with pride."*[66]

Sergei was full of evocative attentions as the ceremonies approached, appealing to Nicholas II's vanity with flattery and to his conservative views with exhortations about the Emperor's religious mission.[67] With his wife Elisabeth, it was Sergei who so carefully – and disastrously – extolled the mystical nature of the Russian autocracy to his sister-in-law Alexandra. It was his voice, not the Empress's democratic and Western European roots, that spilled forth when she declared her belief that *"real"* Russia existed only beyond St. Petersburg; that the aristocracy and middle classes were *"rotten;"* and that within the hearts of peasants scattered across the Empire lay loyalty to the Throne so profound as to be inherent in the national character.[68]

The Grand Duke envisioned a great starring role for himself on the Coronation stage. There was no room in his autocratic nature for diplomacy: Sergei, complained his cousin Grand Duke Konstantin Konstantinovich, *"does not like anyone to disagree with him; he gets irritated and loses the ability to think with logical coolness."*[69] Nor did he possess the skills demanded of the task. Another cousin, Grand Duke Alexander Mikhailovich – who admittedly disliked him and was fond of a dramatic phrase – termed Sergei *"a complete ignoramus in administrative affairs."*[70]

Sergei fumed that spring because, for all of his self-importance and expectant hope, he had learned that reality was quite different, and his teacher was Count Hilarion Vorontsov-Dashkov, the powerful Minister of the Imperial Court. Born

Grand Duchess Elisabeth Feodorovna.
(1864-1918)

in 1837, scion of one of the Empire's most illustrious aristocratic families, Vorontsov-Dashkov was *"a typical Russian noble of the old school,"* said Minister of Finance Sergei Witte, *"a worthy official."* Princess Catherine Radziwill was more specific, extolling his *"perfect tact"* and his *"delicacy"* in dealing with the Imperial Family. She considered him *"a perfect gentleman and great nobleman in the fullest sense of the word."* Even the suspicious Alexander III was impressed by his loyalty, making Vorontsov-Dashkov Minister of the Imperial Court in 1881. Alexander ignored the Count's *"somewhat liberal"* political views, embracing him as an intimate, and Marie Feodorovna was especially fond of the distinguished courtier.[71] Polished as he was, Vorontsov-Dashkov conveyed an air of sophisticated hauteur that alienated some. *"Never have I seen such a swell!"* American reporter Richard Harding Davis declared. *"He made us feel like dudes from Patterson, New Jersey. He had three diamond eagles in an astrakhan cap, a white cloak, a gray uniform, and three rows of medals. He spoke English perfectly, with the most politely insolent manner that I have ever had to listen to."*[72]

Count Hilarion Ivanovich Vorontsov-Dashkov, Minister of the Imperial Court.

Vorontsov-Dashkov's relationship with Nicholas II was complex. His was a protective, almost paternal attitude toward the young man he had watched grow up; his feelings may have been tempered by doubts about the Emperor's maturity and judgment.[73] When Nicholas wished to marry immediately after his father's death, Vorontsov-Dashkov warned that superstitious Russians would take it as an unfortunate omen, but the Emperor refused to wait until mourning ended.[74] Though he held the Minister in high regard, Nicholas apparently took Vorontsov-Dashkov's frank speech as unwelcome familiarity and his manner as condescending, feelings Alexandra fully shared.[75]

By tradition, the Ministry of the Imperial Court always arranged and produced coronations as the principal ritual of any reign. In 1896, though, and ignoring precedent, Sergei attempted to take over the ceremonies in Moscow, a move that brought him into direct conflict with Vorontsov-Dashkov. Theirs was a contentious history: Alexander III had kept all of his relatives, even his trusted brother Sergei, under authoritarian control; Vorontsov-Dashkov had reported on their activities and reproved them in the Emperor's name. As a result, Sergei (and probably his brothers, too) nursed an intense personal dislike when it came to the Minister of the Court.[76] From the beginning of Nicholas's reign, the late Emperor's brothers seemed locked in a battle to wrest control of their nephew from Alexander III's favored advisers, who were equally determined to keep a hold on him.

Nearly everyone felt that Vorontsov-Dashkov was *"honorable,"* and *"incapable of a mean action or of petty revenge."*[77] But Sergei complained that the Minister thoughtlessly brushed him aside when planning the coronation and relegated him to a humiliatingly minor role. Was Catherine Radziwill referring to Sergei when she wrote that Vorontsov-Dashkov was accused of being *"very personal in his likes and dislikes"* and singularly un-obliging towards those who fell foul of him?[78] Declaring himself insulted by Vorontsov-Dashkov's plans, the Grand Duke did everything in his power to cause difficulties. The Ministry of the Imperial Court, he announced in a fit of pique, could arrange the coronation without his assistance or cooperation: he wanted no responsibilities at all, not even those that legally belonged to the Governor-General. Since his opinion mattered so little, he huffed, he would leave Moscow, absenting himself during the entire three weeks of the coronation ceremonies.[79]

This petulant move would have caused an immense scandal, and it did not take long for word of the *"grave dissension"* between the Imperial Court and the Governor-General to reach the public.[80] A *"greatly embarrassed"* Nicholas II had to intervene as mediator, trying to bring about some détente between his Minister of the Imperial Court and his uncle and brother-in-law. In an Empire filled with problems, facing the most significant moment of his ceremonial life, Nicholas was reduced to negotiating the honor of squabbling courtiers and relatives. An eventual agreement, dividing authority between Vorontsov-Dashkov and Sergei, temporarily maintained the peace but weakened supervision, setting Throne and People on a fatal collision course.[81]

The looming problem was the People's Feast, the only overt acknowledgment of the Emperor's common subjects during the three weeks of ceremonies. Thousands of hours went into choreographing elaborate parades and glittering pageantry, but when it came to the People's Feast, authorities behaved with an almost willful negligence. Over the centuries, orderly meals of roast oxen and mead for a select few in the Kremlin's Cathedral Square gave way to immense throngs dazzled with sweets, breads, beer, and free souvenirs.[82] In 1826, Nicholas I expanded the event, with 240 tables laid with meat and bread, sweets and fruit. Thousands more than expected actually turned up and the event rapidly devolved into chaos, as guests fought each other for food and beer; angry and frustrated, they smashed the tables apart, seeking some tangible souvenir of the event.[83]

Count Vladimir Nikolaievich Lambsdorff.
(1845-1907)

Alexander II moved the festivities to Khodynka Meadow some five miles northwest of the city center, whose vast, empty expanse could better accommodate the 200,000-strong crowd that appeared. The scale was colossal: *"Fifteen hundred cows, four thousand sheep, a hundred thousand ducks, and a hundred thousand chickens,"* a foreign guest wrote in amazement, *"had lost their lives in order to furnish the epic repast."*[84] It all went disastrously wrong: food arrived early and rotted for two days, the stench attracting stray dogs fighting for their share. Torrential rain greeted the feast; cold and miserable, the crowd hastily consumed everything in sight, and those denied took out their anger on the site itself, uprooting trees, smashing tables and booths, and draining barrels of free beer before tearing them apart. Alexander II gazed on this scene for a mere fifteen minutes before riding off the field in disgust.[85] Cossacks armed with whips struggled to restore order in the traditional Imperial manner, leaving remnants of the drunken mob *"resting on their laurels"* across the meadow, as a diplomat wryly observed, *"there in the very field of conflict."*[86]

"How is it possible to take precautions with such a crowd of people?" the wife of an American diplomat quizzed an official at Alexander III's coronation feast in 1883. It was, came the *"rather optimistic"* reply, the *"People's Day,"* and authorities *"anticipated no danger."*[87] But the sheer luck that had prevented any loss of life during past feasts ran out in 1883. Some 200,000 more people than expected actually arrived at Khodynka; the 400,000 souvenir mugs filled with figs, cookies and candy

quickly disappeared. Few saw the Emperor during his brief appearance on the field, and scuffles broke out over the gifts; by day's end, thirty-two people lay dead – and ominous turn authorities dismissed authorities as an unforeseeable tragedy.⁸⁸

The pattern was disturbingly clear: crowds at the popular feast were always larger than expected; Imperial souvenirs and food always ran short; the free flow of alcohol always fueled tempers; and violence seemed inevitable. Yet authorities in 1896 learned no lessons from the past. Responsibility for the welfare of this seething mass of humanity fell to the grandly titled Special Commission for the Arrangement of the Coronation Popular Spectacles and Festivals. Vorontsov-Dashkov received their reports in distant St. Petersburg, but officials in Moscow actually planned the 1896 fete. Chairman General N. N. Berr, civil engineer and architect Vladimir Nikolia, and two bureaucratic assistants named Ivanov and Petrov, a group later condemned as *"odious and ignoble…absolute nothings,"* worked out the details.⁸⁹ All four reported directly to Grand Duke Sergei who, as Governor-General, was charged with implementing the arrangements.⁹⁰ Sergei, though, still smarting over his reduced role in the festivities and consumed with upholding his prestige at the expense of working with Vorontsov-Dashkov's officials, simply abdicated responsibility, refusing to address numerous problems that arose as the plans for Khodynka progressed.

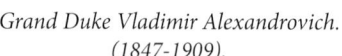

Grand Duke Vladimir Alexandrovich. (1847-1909).

Chief of Police Colonel A. A. Vlassovsky, who reported to the Governor-General, adopted his intransigent attitudes. A former police official from Riga, described by Sergei Witte as *"a sly, pushy man"* and *"a lout,"* Vlassovsky had been recommended *"as an energetic official, capable of maintaining order in the city"* when he first took up his post, and he maintained power with an *"ingratiating"* manner that appealed the Grand Duke's vanity.⁹¹ Neither the Grand Duke nor Vlassovsky set foot on Khodynka Field before the festivities, determined to avoid the appearance that they were following orders from Vorontsov-Dashkov.⁹²

Given the hundreds of thousands at previous public fetes, it was suggested that in 1896 the People's Feast actually be held at five different sites scattered around the city. This would disperse the crowd and reduced any potential problems. Berr refused on the grounds that such division would be an organizational nightmare. He vetoed wider distribution of Imperial souvenirs across Khodynka Meadow, preferring to concentrate all attention on a line of wooden stalls at one end of the field. Although 600,000 people had come to the fete in 1883, Berr insisted that the crowd in 1896 would number no more than 200,000 – despite the fact that the Government ordered 400,000 souvenir bundles.⁹³

Little was done to prepare the wind-swept expanse of Khodynka Meadow, where the plain gave way to sandy furrows and uneven ground. Year after year, soldiers had practiced military engineering here, their trenches, redoubts, and excavated wells crossing the meadow like scars. Abandoned, gaping foundations marked the remains of an 1891 French exhibition on the site.[94] In April 1896, workers cast a few shovels-full of earth into some of the holes; many more were simply ignored.[95] Planks and sheets of wood, thrown over pits and wells, rotted in the miserable spring rain, concealing the perils lurking beneath the surface.[96]

A view of Khodynka Field and the Imperial Pavillion during the Coronation celebrations.

Even less was done to ensure proper policing for the event. Security for the People's Feast always fell to the Governor-General.[97] Sergei, though, refused to fulfill his obligations, and encouraged Vlassovsky to do the same. When Vorontsov-Dashkov asked what measures were being put in place, Sergei replied that the matter did not concern him; following this lead, Chief of Police Vlassovsky insisted that he had no jurisdiction over Khodynka Meadow.[98] Berr, Petrov, and Ivanov appealed to Vlassovsky on three separate occasions for help, only to be told that he had no responsibility for the fete.[99]

This situation festered throughout the spring of 1896. Vorontsov-Dashkov eventually reminded Sergei that, as Minister of the Imperial Court, he had no police force of his own to guard the field and need the Governor-General's cooperation.[100] Sergei ignored him. The Count tried again, urging the Grand Duke to organize security for the People's Feast; again Sergei refused. A third request went to both Sergei and to his brother Grand Duke Vladimir, in charge of the Moscow Garrison during the Coronation. And for a third time Vorontsov-Dashkov was rebuffed, bluntly informed that the Governor-General did not *"recognize the authority"* of St. Petersburg's Minister of the Imperial Court over matters in Moscow.[101]

Security for the people's Feast was left to chance. When Moscow Police Colonel Budberg warned of potential problems, both Sergei and Vlassovsky pointedly ignored him.[102] Pleas to Vlassovsky brought a testy reply, *"That's my business!"*[103] General Berr asked for urgent meetings with the Governor-General and the Chief of Police; both men brushed him aside. Vlassovsky even took his telephone off the hook at one point to enjoy a gypsy orchestra, at a time when Berr was desperately trying to discuss the issue.[104]

As the feast rapidly approached, though, even Vlassovsky worried that his own forces would prove inadequate to the demands of the crowd on Khodynka. At one point, he refused to take responsibility for security if he had only the men from his own police force to deploy. When he dared request additional men, Sergei refused him. No extra troops were needed, the Grand Duke declared, when Alexander III's funeral procession had passed through Moscow in 1894. That crowd's exemplary behavior meant that there was no need to worry about potential disorders on Khodynka.[105] Jealousies, jurisdictional squabbles, and a bureaucracy that proved itself tragically inept were a lethal combination when it came to protecting the lives of the Emperor's ordinary subjects. Incompetence and wounded egos thus steered the People's Feast doggedly toward disaster.

Chapter III

On April 27, 1896, a forty-year-old woman stood on the deck of a passenger steamer, watching the harbor at Hull recede across the gray-green span of water. Full of *"high spirits,"* Mary Hickley was one of the thousands on their way to Russia to see the Coronation of Nicholas II. It was an unlikely adventure for a British vicar's daughter devoted to missionary work, but Mary had privileged entrée. The aristocratic Golitsyns, one of Russia's most illustrious families, employed her sister as governess; hearing of Mary's interest, they asked her to join them in Moscow as their guest.

After six days amid snow and Baltic wind *"that smelt of icebergs,"* her liner docked in St. Petersburg, where Mary had her first taste of Russian bureaucracy. *"Furious-looking"* officials boarded the ship, examining passports, papers, and luggage. *"Unable to find anything wrong with us,"* she wrote, *"they left-visibly disappointed."* More trouble followed. *"It is evident one is no longer in a free country,"* she noted after completing lengthy questionnaires and police documents. Finally waved through customs, she was sent on her way with a warning that she was subject to arrest if at any time she behaved suspiciously.[1]

Mary was fortunate that her compartment on the night train to Moscow had already been booked. Those arriving in St. Petersburg without reservations had to negotiate the horrors of a transportation system overwhelmed with activity and manned by workers who rarely spoke English. Aylmer Maude noted with disgust that trains were late and overcrowded, and tickets to Moscow in short supply. *"The convenience of the public,"* he complained, was ignored whenever an *"important personage"* traveled by rail. Vital post trains were delayed, and passenger trains shunted onto sidings so that dignitaries could pass without interruption.[2] Safely ensconced in her train compartment, Mary watched as the discouraging countryside – *"flat, dismal, waterlogged country, forest and swamp, swamp and forest, some of it still snow-sprinkled"* – sped by her window. All along the route, she saw, stood ranks of soldiers, thousands of armed men a few feet apart to ensure that no anarchist caused trouble.[3]

Bureaucratic incompetence and linguistic struggles also characterized the journey made by a group of Americans. A woman of formidable ambition, Mary Cunningham Logan was accustomed to privileged indulgence. Her late husband John A. Logan had been a Major General in the Civil War, a Senator representing Illinois, and a one-time Vice Presidential candidate. The couple had been influential figures on the Washington, D.C. social scene, and President Benjamin Harrison had appointed Mary the city's official representative at the World Columbian Exposition of 1893 in Chicago.[4] Her husband's death left Mary dependent on the generosity of friends to maintain her extravagant style of life: from necessity she developed a new career, providing society introductions and chaperoning daughters of wealthy Americans to Europe in exchange for financial considerations.[5] Early in 1896, Mary's thirty-one-year-old son Army Captain John A. Logan Jr., a distinguished graduate of West Point, was appointed military attaché to the American delegation traveling to Moscow. Leaving his wife Edith and three young children behind, he eagerly embarked on his Russian adventure, and his mother was determined to join him. She paid for her expensive journey to Moscow by escorting two young women to the ceremonies. Daughters of millionaire Minneapolis judge Martin Buren Koon, twenty-one-year-old Katherine Koon and her nineteen-year-old sister Louise – called Kate and Lou – were engaging, beautiful, and excited. Having recently made their American society debuts, they were eager to experience the world, and their father's money paved their way to Russia.[6]

Traveling with the three of them was another society *grande dame*, Emily Warren Roebling. Born into a family of respectable wealth and position, Emily pursued an interest in mathematics and science, later obtaining a law degree. With her husband Washington Roebling, she researched engineering standards for her father-in-law's planned bridge across the East River between New York's boroughs of Brooklyn and Manhattan, and later assumed control of the project. In 1883, when the new Brooklyn Bridge finally opened, Emily proudly inaugurated the structure, riding in a carriage at the side of President Chester A. Arthur.[7]

Despite his democratic heritage, John Logan, known as Jack, was completely enraptured by his experiences with Russia. He viewed the country through *"amazed, enchanted eyes,"* his admiration cemented as a courtier waved him through customs and escorted him to a lavish compartment aboard a special train *"as complete as it was comfortable."* As the countryside sped by, Logan noted in astonishment, liveried porters offered cigars, cigarettes, and an endless supply of food and drink.[8] *"We were welcomed royally,"* he admitted, as if all Russia *"had conspired as a man to do honor to its master by honoring his bidden guests."*[9]

Mary Logan's experiences, though, were not as smooth as her son's. Crossing the Russian border as mere tourists, Mary, Emily Roebling, and the two Koon girls soon learned, was an adventure in itself. Customs agents flung unintelligible papers at them and searched their steamer trunks as though suspecting that they carried bombs. Emily Roebling, surprised that no one spoke English or French, finally found *"a very nice-looking"* young Russian officer who understood her German and shepherded the party through their uncertainties. By the time their train reached Moscow, though, she was hoarse from having to speak for her entire group of fellow tourists.[10]

Senator John A. Logan.

Mrs. Mary Logan.

The journey by overnight train from St. Petersburg to Moscow, said a visitor, was like being *"transported into a different world."* After the cool, *"soulless"* splendor of St. Petersburg, after the miles of barren swamp and endless forests of birch trees, travelers looking out of compartment windows saw *"a multitude of spires…thousands of pointed steeples, star-spangled belfries, airy turrets, strangely shaped towers, palaces, and old convents."*[11] Leafy foliage filled trees, flowers scented the air, and sunshine sparkled over gilded domes and twisted, barley-sugar-striped cupolas to enchanting effect.[12] Here, at last, was the Russia of fabled history, of evocative dreams, the *"pulsation of her heart."*[13]

Train stations bustled with hundreds of people, pushing through the crowd, toting bags, shouting instructions in a confusing Babel of languages – *"a pandemonium of noise and confusion,"* Mary Hickley said.[14] Backed by the influential Golitsyn name, she passed through the intense security relatively unscathed, but most were not as fortunate. *"Heavy luggage was detained for days,"* remembered another traveler, *"first to be examined, and then to be consigned to its owner who, having in many cases arrived weary and travel-stained with two or three days' journey, was not prepossessed in favor of the traffic manager's arrangements."*[15] Valises, cases, and steamer trunks often went missing, never to be seen again. When – and if – luggage was returned to its owners, they often found their belongings in disarray, garments turned inside out, and linings inspected in a search for explosives or weapons. Following the orders of Government censors, police inspected newspapers, magazines, and books, looking for troublesome ideas and seditious thought. Political tracts and pamphlets always caused problems, but so did certain works by the great Leo Tolstoy, as well as seemingly innocuous articles on the coming coronation. An entirely sympathetic biographical sketch of Nicholas II by W. T. Stead – the pet journalist who had interviewed Alexander III – appeared in the May 1896 issue of his *Review of Reviews*. Although uncritically vague, the article apparently seemed too familiar or insufficiently positive, for if found a censor's scissors relieved the journal of the offending fourteen pages.[16]

Having successfully navigated the horrors of the Moscow train station, Mary Hickley followed a Golitsyn servant to a hired carriage, a *"comic little spring-less conveyance,"* she said, that rumbled and jostled over the uneven cobblestones and rutted roadways "in a way to shake the very teeth out of your head!" After an hour's drive, during which she was sure she caught sight of a wolf disappearing into a copse of trees, they reached the outskirts of the city. Here a private carriage waited, attended by a driver *"quaintly attired in a wadded blue dressing gown, a red sash round his large waist, and a turban hat encircled with peacock feathers."* The second leg of the journey took her deeper into the country. *"We splashed through mud past belief,"* she remembered; *"the squalid village street of log huts was plumped down in it – mud-stained peasants waded barefoot in it,"* before finally arriving at the Golitsyns' country house to spend the following three weeks. Much to her delight, the Golitsyns made no social distinction between her and their own aristocratic friends; the Imperial Court, however, was not so egalitarian. Though she enjoyed access to some of the coronation events, more often Mary had to make do with watching the parties and processions from afar, gathering mementoes and memories to share with her family.[17]

A postcard printed and sold to the public at the time of the coronation. The Russian government printed countless items like this one. They were to be used as propaganda, not only extolling Russian patriotism, but also in an effort to project to the outside world the greatness and might of the Tsarist Regime.

Disembarking from their train in Moscow, the adventurous American ladies met two additions to their party. Like Emily Roebling, Harriet Alexander, daughter of San Francisco railroad magnate Charles Crocker, came from Gilded Age New York, while the formidable Bertha Honoré Palmer made the journey from Chicago with her husband. Mrs. Palmer was, next to New York City's famous *the* Mrs. Astor, the grandest of all America's *grande dames*. Born in Louisville, Kentucky in 1849, she married wealthy and successful real estate tycoon Potter Palmer and quickly became acknowledged queen of Chicago society. From her lavish, half-Gothic, half-Romanesque castle on North Lake Shore Drive, Bertha Palmer ruled the city with an iron fist every bit as autocratic as those of the Romanovs, yet her interests were artistic and philanthropic. She sponsored painters and sculptors, caused endless trouble by championing the rights of workers, and was a major force behind Chicago's highly successful World Columbian Exposition.[18] Armed with an international reputation and an ease with royalty (she had entertained several Romanov relations), the stately Bertha Palmer came to Moscow complete with

Mr. Potter Palmer.

Mrs. Bertha Palmer.

immense diamond collars and glittering tiaras, determined to show that America, too, possessed a proudly refined society.[19]

Emily Roebling, Harriet Alexander, and the Potter Palmers all took rooms at the Hotel Dresden, whose windows overlooked the Tverskaya down which Nicholas II would make his State Entrance into Moscow; an American official rented the Schlippe House on Gagarin Lane for Mrs. Logan, her son John, and the two Koon girls.[20] Kate Koon was surprised by the mud along the streets, *"and when we reached a certain wooden gate, which was pushed open for us to enter a courtyard, we thought we were going into some kind of pigpen."*[21] But the brick house beyond this morass seemed large and even luxurious: parquet floors were inlaid with exotic woods, French paintings hung on the walls, *"and on the ceilings quite an army of bowed and arrowed Cupids waged their pretty warfare,"* recorded John Logan. *"There was a bit of gilt everywhere on ceiling and wall; there were dainty gilt ornamentations on the crystal candelabras; and delicate threads of gold woven in the rose brocade that hung at the windows."*[22] Kate and Lou Koon had a bedroom and a sitting room, and everyone seemed quite content with the accommodations until they went looking for the bathroom. They found a questionable sink and toilet, but no tub, and knew that they would be forced to make do with washing in portable tin baths brought into their rooms.[23]

The house came with several servants. There was a porter, *"the most solemn man I ever met,"* said John Logan, along with a footman whose manner of dress disappointed the Army Captain, a cook named Anushka, and Yertza, *"a pretty young girl with a Gypsy face"* as maid.[24] American officials hired a closed carriage, a landau, and *"beautiful chestnut horses"* for the guests at the hugely inflated rate of $20 ($540, or £400 in 2014 figures) a day, and paid even more for the drivers.[25] The coachmen, Kate saw, were exactly as Emily Roebling – who had previously visited Moscow – described: men of immense girth, wrapped in long buttoned coats tied with colorful sashes. Coachmen, Emily had explained, were judged by their weight – the bigger the better – and many smaller men padded themselves with pillows to justify higher rates. Ever cagey, Emily rather gruesomely liked to test their honesty, silently plunging her hairpins into unsuspecting drivers to see if she hit fat or filler.[26]

Most of these tourists were surprisingly naïve about the country and its young ruler. Russia, the world thought, was a fearful, barbaric, backward place where anarchists armed with bombs lurked on every street corner and brutal police sent untold thousands to Siberian exile. Yet here was Moscow, exotic and dignified, the streets full of apparently loyal and contented subjects eager to cheer their new sovereign. This was the Russia promoted by the Government, propagated by myth, and advanced to visitors: starving peasants and disgruntled factory workers were realities carefully concealed from public view. Infatuated by outward appearances and Victorian sentiment, these Westerners generally saw the country and coronation through an uncritical, romanticized lens.

Visitors flooded through Moscow, exploring the city. Richard Harding Davis sounded a rare sour note: he thought the buildings *"ugly"* and painted *"in hideous colors except the churches, which are like mosques and painted every color."*[27] There were grand palaces and monumental squares, but he thought that much of Moscow had the *"undecorated, uncared-for look of Constantinople,*

A view of the Senate Square in the Moscow Kremlin.

or any other half-barbaric capital where the city seems not have been built with design but to have grown up of itself and to have spread as it pleased."[28] Most others, though, were taken with *"beautiful, barbaric Moscow,"* as John Logan called it, with *"roofs of blue, of green, of red," "walls of yellow and of purple,"* and green parks and gardens offering relief to eyes *"wearied by their first gloating over this mad carnival of color."*[29]

The very streets themselves were radically different from the broad, symmetrical boulevards of St. Petersburg. Moscow's streets were *"winding, irregular,"* and full of mysteries.[30] *"They have no distinctive features to guide even the observant traveler,"* complained British delegate Ian Malcolm. *"In fact, the town seems built as a maze, and its mystifications are enhanced for most of the strangers by a complete incapacity to decipher the names of the streets, or to gather anything from the gendarme except a vague conception of his desire to be of use."*[31] Wide new roadways sliced through ancient quarters, disappearing into winding streets and alleys edged by arcs of leafy trees and lined by crumbling churches and houses. Whereas the St. Petersburg poor lived in squalid basements in the center of town, or migrated to the depressing outskirts of the city, Moscow's streets offered a shocking social mix of wealth and poverty, a hodge-podge of the privileged and the dispossessed crammed next to one another. *"Close to a large house, occupied by a noble, you find a wooden cottage,"* marveled another British visitor. *"In fact, it is a city of cottages, the large stone houses being the exception. When leaving a large thoroughfare and passing into a cross street, you find yourself among quiet, peaceful country retreats, with laburnum and acacia, cocks and hens, and often a cow. This is the charm of Moscow, these quiet streets lying close to the big thoroughfares."*[32]

The crowds in these streets were enormous, providing a constantly shifting spectacle as people from all parts of the Empire and all classes of Russian society rubbed shoulders with foreign guests, royalty, diplomats, special envoys, journalists, tourists, soldiers, and the ubiquitous security forces. *"There were,"* said Richard Harding Davis,

Princes in gold and plate-glass carriages of state; Russian generals seated behind black horses, driven three abreast, that never went at a slower pace than a gallop, so that the common people fell over one another to get out of danger; there were Ambassadors and governors of provinces, and all their wonderfully costumed suites; bare-kneed highlanders and bare-kneed Serbians; Mongolians in wrappers of fur and green brocade, with monster muffs for hats; proud little

Japanese soldiers in smart French uniforms; Germans with spiked helmets; English diplomats in top hats and frock coats as though they were in Piccadilly; Italian officers with five-pointed stars on their collars and green cocks' feathers in their patent-leather sombreros; Hungarian nobles in fur-trimmed satin; maharajas from the Punjab and southern India in tall turbans of silk; and masters of ceremonies and dignitaries of the Russian court in golden uniforms and ostrich feathers in their top hats.[33]

"*I imagine such a collection of men and costumes one never saw before*," marveled Kate Koon. "*Long and short coats, great and small hats, rags and velvets, furs and lace, jewels and paste, princes and paupers, babies and octogenarians, all kinds and conditions of people standing together.*"[34] Moscow's public gardens swarmed with townspeople, artisans, and workers in a constant hubbub of conversation and flirtatious encounters. The unusual profusion of smartly dressed officers turned the heads of Moscow's young ladies. Maids, cooks, seamstresses, and shop girls put on Sunday finery and haunted the lanes, smiling and flirting when the men from St. Petersburg appeared. One factory worker recorded how the "*tall, handsome Hussars and Cuirassiers in picturesque costumes, their sparkling swords dragging along the ground,*" would circle "*proudly and pompously*" with eager ladies on their arms. "*There isn't any nourishment left for the working man!*" growled Moscow's rough factory lotharios, resenting the intrusion of this polished elite into their usual romantic hunting ground.[35]

An image of the Kremlin's cathedrals. (Courtesy of Ian Shapiro)

The Moscow of May 1896 was transformed into a place of bewitching beauty, its buildings painted, whitewashed, and crowned with new roofs, its sidewalks repaved, its streets bedecked in anticipation of the coronation.[36] The entire city, declared Kate Koon, smelled of "*fresh paint.*"[37] Carpenters, painters, and electricians struggled to transform it into a sparkling jewel. The government appetite for timber was so great, said Aylmer Maude, that it was impossible for a private individual to purchase a single plank without paying "*an abnormal*" sum.[38] John Logan saw carpenters everywhere he looked: "*I noticed that they did all their work on the spot, not bringing their poles hewn and painted and ready to pop into holes already dug. They hewed and planed them on the spot, and erected them one by one.*"[39]

Triumphal arches, adorned with Imperial monograms and heraldic shields, spanned roadways; flags and bunting were so thickly strung over avenues that they hid "*the sky as completely as do the clothes that swing on lines from the back windows of New York tenements.*"[40] Tall black and gold Venetian masts, topped with crowns and hung with gold and silver tassels, marked street corners; banners fluttered from obelisks; and evergreen boughs bedecked buildings.[41] There were, said Mary Hickley, "*miles of green garlands, possible only in a country of cheap labor,*" festooning every conceivable space.[42] Most visitors were entranced: Aylmer Maude, though, sternly lamented "*such frivolous misdirection of men's minds and such costly waste of men's labor.*"[43]

Visitors fought their ways across the city as best as they could, on foot or by carriage. Tverskaya Boulevard seemed constantly alive with a sea of humanity: it was, thought a British official, *"one of the noisiest towns in Europe."*⁴⁴ *"You had to wait hours on end to cross from one side to the other,"* said one writer. *"Hundreds of splendid carriages, coaches, landaus, and other conveyances stretched the length of the boulevard."*⁴⁵ Mary Hickley found the rush of traffic *"bewildering,"* with *"every size and shape of vehicle"* driven *"at a tearing pace by shouting coachmen."*⁴⁶ A British general bemoaned the questionable skills of his own driver, a *"particularly stupid"* man who *"professes to know the way about Moscow, but having come from St. Petersburg he knows nothing, and when I am without a Russian officer, I come to dreadful grief."*⁴⁷ Even a competent coachman brought little comfort. *"The driving in Moscow,"* wrote another Englishman, *"being at full speed, and with little regard for the general traffic, it makes anxious going for the uninitiated traveler. Foot passengers cross the street with apparently no particular desire to reach the other side."*⁴⁸

Pointing symbolically west, toward the new capital of St Petersburg, the broad Tverskaya was lined with grand hotels, colorful shops, and classical palaces in which Russia's nobility lived during infrequent visits to Moscow. Fires in centuries past led to constant rebuilding, the new architecture replacing the muddled, medieval character that so charmed visitors to smaller streets. The shops all hoped for *"great things from the sightseer from afar who has pitched his tent in their midst for the next three weeks."*⁴⁹ Windows proudly displayed all of their best goods as helpful visual guides since the exotic Cyrillic alphabet bewildered most Western visitors. Maude was dismayed

Moscow streets were colorfully decorated for the Coronation.

A view of fashionable Tverskaya Boulevard, Moscow.

A view of the Kremlin from the Moskva Embankment. (Courtesy of Ian Shapiro)

The Fabergé shop on Moscow's Kuznetsky Most.

to find a foreign jewelry shop, run by an English manager, "*conspicuously, brilliantly decorated,*" complaining, "*The more completely demented people become, the better the chance for such business. If you take the greed and mendacity of mortals as your clue, you may thread your way truly through the chaos of the Coronation; but if you hope to explain what is done on any reasonable or righteous principles, you will be completely baffled.*"[50]

Language was a major difficulty. Consular officials hired an English woman, Mrs. Lehr, to guide the Americans through the city, but she could not be everywhere at once.[51] No interpreter was available for hire at the crowded Hotel Dresden, leaving Harriet Alexander, Emily Roebling, and the Potter Palmers to fend for themselves. "*Not for love or money,*" Emily complained, "*could we find a servant who could speak English and Russian.*" Eventually they procured a German-speaking footman from another American expatriate, but this, unfortunately, meant no relief from Emily's translating duties. Whenever anyone in the party went out, she was obliged to accompany them, to give directions and tell the footman what they needed him to do.[52] Those who spoke no Russian found their expeditions guided by a variety of hanging signs or painted pictures above shops advertising their wares.[53] A pork butcher spied by one visitor had a picture of a pig's head over the door; the undertaker displayed a ghoulish miniature coffin. Easier to decipher were the shop windows filled with souvenirs of Moscow and of the Coronation, along with traditional Russian folk crafts prominently displayed to appeal to sentimental visitors. Photographic studios and bookstores offered lithographs and postcards of the Imperial couple, while more expensive wares – buttons, medals, tankards, and coins – could be found at goldsmiths. Wandering into the Moscow shop of famed Court jeweler Peter Karl Fabergé on Kuznetsky Most, one young man found a selection of their finest wares that almost – but not quite – tempted him to part with his money.[54]

For those not provided meals with their lodgings, dining in the city became a necessity. The Hermitage, Moscow's most exclusive restaurant, lured in customers by assuring them that their "*French cooking was second only to Paris.*"[55] Ian Malcolm, a young military attaché in the British delegation, favored the famous Slavyansky Bazaar. Like most establishments, it had raised its ordinary prices in honor of the coronation. He found the dining hall, "*an enormous and lofty room, round which runs the hotel gallery,*" filled with "*quantities of tables of all sorts and sizes,*" and crowded with "*visitors from every land, speaking every language at the top of their voices, and eating every conceivable kind of strange meat.*" He sampled birch and rowan vodkas, followed by dinner with Crimean wine. Most of the "*first-rate*" waiters were Tartars, from the Crimea; because they were Muslim and never drank, Malcolm believed they offered better service than the occasionally suspiciously tipsy Russians. "*At the Slavyansky Bazaar they are dressed in western garb,*" he noted, "*at the Hermitage in white linen coats and trousers with scarlet girdles.*" He was disconcerted, however, by the sheer noise of cutlery and plates and glasses all clinking and clattering together; Russian restaurants, with their gypsy choirs and musicians, offered an exuberant, if at times distracting, way of dining. Gypsy women wandered from table to table, receiving champagne in exchange for songs, while young officers noisily threw their comrades into the air without any apparent care where they landed.⁵⁶

Wandering farther, John Logan sought out the famous Yar, a Moscow nightspot renowned for its expensive food and Gypsy entertainments. *"I had heard much of these exotic singers,"* he wrote, *"and was determined to see them myself."* He took a seat in the large dining room, beneath a wall draped in oleander and fringed with potted palms, eating and downing vodka as inconspicuously as possible, for he seemed to be the only foreigner in the place. At a signal the music swelled and the singers took the stage, dark women in *"short skirts and jackets of bright colors, knee boots of red, yellow, green, or bronze, and brightly-colored handkerchiefs about their heads and necks."* He found the performance intoxicating: *"They sing and dance to wild Tartar music, swaying their bodies as they do so, with complete abandon."* Only at four in the morning, when the audience of Russian officers finally retreated to their barracks, did Logan reluctantly abandon the exotic spectacle.⁵⁷

Beautiful and tempting though they were, Moscow's shops and restaurants, streets and stations, were a mere sideshow for average visitors on their way to the holy of holies. Everyone wanted to see Red Square, the Kremlin, and its cathedrals, setting for the coronation and symbolic heart of spiritual and temporal power in Russia. They traced the path that Nicholas II would follow, down the Tverskaya and through the heart of the city, past the Governor-General's Palace, the Riding School, and the great Bolshoi Theatre as they approached their goal. Day and night, an enormous crowd of pilgrims swirled around the Iversky Gate, its two towers crowning an arch opening to Red Square; here, in a small chapel adorned with malachite, marble, and gilded bronze, hung the Iversky (Iberian) Virgin, copy of an icon at Mount Athos in Greece. Brought to Russia in the Sixteenth Century and believed to possess extraordinary powers, the icon – adorned with twenty-eight pounds of gold – was greatly revered: no Russians ever passed the ornate little chapel, built by Catherine the Great, without making the sign of the cross and removing their hats, having *"put themselves to rights with heaven."*⁵⁸

Foreigners, too, passed the chapel with growing wonder as the Iversky Gate's arches revealed the vast expanse of Red Square. To one side rose the tall, battlemented walls of the Kremlin, offering a vertical contrast to the seemingly endless stretch of cobbles; to the west and south glowered the rust-colored hulk of the Imperial Historical Museum, a curious mélange of gothic and medieval architecture, and an immense, glass-roofed shopping arcade; and, a thousand feet to the north, bursting from the cobbles like some *"grotesquely beautiful"* bit of theatre, was the Cathedral of the Intercession of Theotokos on the Moat, the famed St. Basil's.⁵⁹ Built on the orders of Ivan the Terrible who, according to legend, had the architects blinded so that they could never duplicate this bizarre masterpiece, the Cathedral's asymmetrical riot of chapels and arcades, twisting stairways and tent roofs, said John Logan, were *"most perplexing"* to his American eyes, *"strange and weird"* in its *"startling, irregular beauty."*⁶⁰ It exerted an enormous fascination for visitors, the seeming embodiment of the refinement and cruelty, the grandeur and despotism of Russia's tortured past.

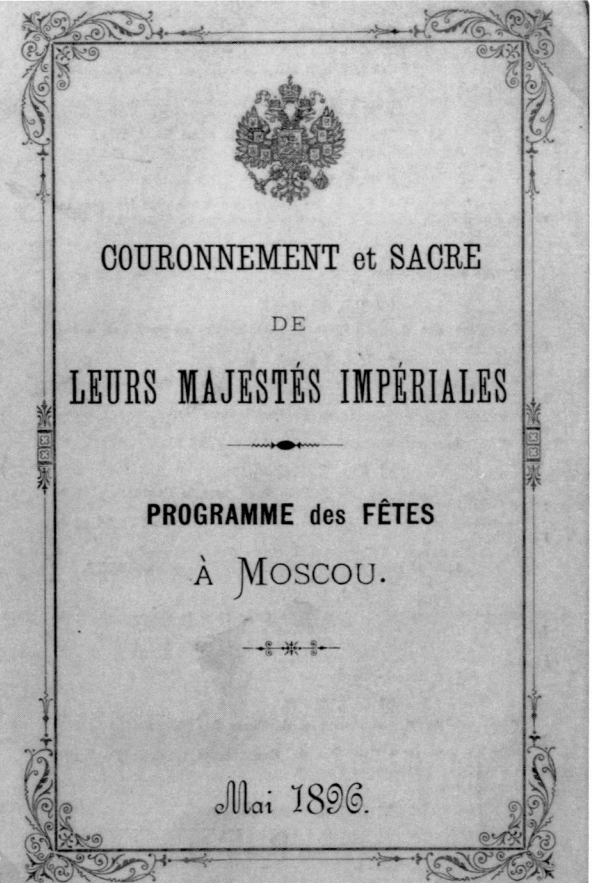

Coronation Program (from Princess Irene of Prussia's collection).

And then, heads and eyes inevitably turned east, where sixty-foot-high, red brick walls, dotted by twenty tent and conical-roofed towers bristling with gables and double-headed eagles, ringed the sixty-nine acres of the Kremlin. Crowning Borovitsky Hill above the Moskva River, the Kremlin, this mixture of ancient and modern,

The Cathedral of the Assumption.

this seat of spiritual and temporal authority, this bastion of the autocracy, spoke to visitors in powerful, evocative whispers. "*It is a thing alone,*" declared Richard Harding Davis, "*unlike the rest of Moscow; nor, indeed, is it like any other city in the world. Its great, jagged walls encompass churches, arsenals, palaces, and convents of an architecture borrowed from India and Asia and Europe of the middle ages; it is as though the Tower of London, the Houses of Parliament, Westminster Abbey, St. Paul's, and the Knightsbridge Barracks are all huddled together on the Thames Embankment and shut in with monster walls.*"[61]

It was endlessly fascinating, this jumble of palaces and churches, museums and monasteries. Past the white and yellow Arsenal Building, with its rows of captured French cannon left by Napoleon after his invasion of Moscow in 1812, the curious explored the Armory, with its impressive collection of weaponry and regalia, carriages and clothing. They marveled at the famous, 200-ton Tsar Bell, cast for Boris Godunov and believed to be the largest in the world, so heavy that it could never be properly hung, and the equally massive Tsar Cannon, seventeen-feet long, designed to fire two-ton balls and so impractical that it, too, was never used.[62] Here and there, carpenters built tribunes. The Cathedral of the Assumption, where the crowning would take place, was closed in advance of the ceremony, but even a quick glance at the exterior left most tourists surprised at its modest size: Westerners, expecting *"great spaces and lofty arches, in which the voice returns in echo,"* wondered how so many important guests could be packed into so small a space.[63]

Other churches on Cathedral Square, though, were open, and the visitors poured through them in silent admiration. There was the Cathedral of the Annunciation, with nine golden onion domes shining above newly whitewashed walls. Passing through bronze doors inlaid with gold, the curious found a dim interior where icons, some by renowned Fourteenth Century painter Andrei Rublev, stared solemnly from frames of solid gold and silver, and faded frescoes encompassing *"all the good and evil spirits ever assembled"* jumbled together in a blaze of precious stones. Here, on a floor of jasper, agate, and cornelian, brought from a Sixteenth Century cathedral in Rostov, the Grand Princes of Moscow and the early Tsars had prayed before relics of Russian Orthodox saints. The windows of the Cathedral of the Archangel Michael were so high and so small that its jewels, the glitter of its gold, and its burnished shrines, were barely discernible against the dark walls.[64] Scattered throughout lay the tombs of the Rurik rulers, the Grand Princes of Moscow, and the first Romanov Tsars, including the unfortunate Dimitri, youngest son of Ivan the Terrible, whose mysterious death and innocent blood had symbolically washed away the sins of the Rurik Dynasty.

Everything spoke of the turbulent past. The Granovitaya Palata, the Palace of Facets, edged one side of Cathedral Square. Here, the unpredictable and despotic Ivan the Terrible held angry receptions; along its southern side, reached through elaborately carved open arches emblazoned with double-headed eagles, arose the fifty-eight steps of the ceremonial Red Staircase. In 1682, a young Peter the Great, clinging to his mother, watched in helpless terror as the Streltsy Guard – urged on by his half-sister, the Regent Sophia – revolted, seizing members of his family and throwing them from the top of the staircase onto their sharpened pikes below. It was a defining moment in the boy's life, cementing his hatred of Moscow and the Byzantine cabals of the Russian Court. Behind the staircase, sweeping in stepped tiers to a sea of golden onion domes and forest of crosses, stood the Terem Palace, where the Grand Princes and first Romanovs had lived in a succession of colorful, vaulted rooms. Against it all, rising atop ruins burnt during Napoleon's 1812 invasion of Moscow, was the immense, rust-colored Grand Kremlin Palace, built by architect Konstantin Ton for Nicholas I in a bombastic, neoclassical style infused with traditional Russian elements. *"Every silkworm in the world,"* gasped a visitor, *"must have been kept busy for months"* to provide the materials lining its *"extraordinarily sumptuous"* ceremonial halls. It was, he sniffed, *"not in the best of taste,"* but its cavernous rooms, malachite columns, gilded ceilings, and sparkling chandeliers *"exactly correspond with one's preconceived ideas of what an Emperor of Russia's palace ought to be like."*[65]

A view from inside the Cathedral of the Assumption. The dais at the bottom of the photo is the spot where the Tsar's coronation took place.

Climbing to the top of Ivan the Great's tall, whitewashed Bell Tower, John Logan was rewarded with a panorama of the city, its bright roofs and streamer-hung highways stretching in the distance. He remembered:

I never saw anything so bewitchingly beautiful as the views of Moscow. It was as if some rainbow had been broken up by the hand of some god and thrown down in splendid and yet symmetric confusion, the whole being sprinkled with gems of some genie of the east. At the very foot of the tower was the unrivaled collection of magnificent buildings within the walls of the Kremlin, huddled together with an opulent disregard of wealth, in a confusion of beauty. Beyond the city of Moscow – its squares, its brilliant thoroughfares, seen through the light of an early summer day – looked like a glittering stage spectacle viewed through gauze, with different colored lights thrown on the different objects, only that no stage spectacle was ever so overwhelming or quite so beautiful.[66]

A *"stage spectacle"* it may have seemed, an exotic, opulent setting for archaic pageantry endowed with symbolic myth. Moscow, *"charged with electricity,"* swelled with pride and anticipation, as the incessant rains of April gave way to May sunshine.[67] A good omen, people thought, as they stared *"with open-mouthed wonder"* at an extravagance of Autocratic power so at odds with a Twentieth Century world.[68]

Chapter IV

"*It must have looked,*" commented Aylmer Maude as he surveyed Moscow's crowded, newly decorated streets, "*as though Russia had gone mad with joy over the approaching festivities.*"[1] The weather improved as a million people poured into the city. Every day, Maude complained, "*newspapers were crowded with telegrams relating how Prince This and Count That*" had arrived to grace Moscow with their presence, a parade of the powerful and privileged exceeding anything previously witnessed in Russia – and all in honor of twenty-six-year-old Nicholas II.[2]

A million people brought a million headaches for members of the Coronation Committee: the influential had to be coddled, and the powerless shuffled to provide appropriately loyal decoration. Police could marshal the nameless throng behind barricades to cheer, knocking them out of the way with whips if they encroached on other areas, but official visitors required more diplomacy. Wars of money and influence waged over the coveted tickets allowing admittance to thousands of special tribunes built along the route of the State Entrance; over spots in stands overlooking the site of military reviews; and over places in pavilions surrounding the Cathedral of the Assumption. Ambassadors and extraordinary envoys advanced the causes of their visiting countrymen, insisting, bribing, and begging for the multitude of color-coded passes and special invitations issued by the Minister of the Imperial Court. These were high prizes, the recipients warned that they must keep the precious documents with them at all times.[3]

These headaches amplified when it came to the actual crowning itself. The Cathedral of the Assumption, which would serve as the *mis-en-scene* for the ceremony, may have been the most spiritually significant church in the Kremlin but it was also a building of relatively modest dimensions, capable of holding only a very tightly packed privileged thousand guests.[4] A hundred places went to the Romanovs and their Russian relatives, 246 to members of the diplomatic corps, and thirty-eight to "*foreigners of distinction.*"[5] Filling the remaining spaces was a logistical nightmare, as Richard Harding Davis noted. The Ministry of the Imperial Court had "*to decide between an aide-de-camp from Bulgaria and a Russian ambassador at home on leave, a Japanese Prince and an English general, a German Duchess and the correspondent of the Paris Figaro.*" It was, he said, "*a matter of so many square inches chiefly, and one man or woman who got in kept a dozen applicants for the space out; and the pressure that was brought to bear in order to gain a footing – and a footing was actually all one obtained – threatened the peace of Europe, and caused tears of disappointment and wounds that will rankle in the breasts of noble Russian families for years to come.*"[6]

Sacred rite though it was, the Coronation also resembled something of an illustrious family reunion. Fifty-two royal guests, many related by blood or marriage to either Nicholas or Alexandra or both, descended on Moscow, including eight future kings, two future queens consort, and a galaxy of reigning grand dukes and princes.[7] Plotting alliances and planning liaisons, rubbing up against one another's prejudices, gossiping, bickering and indulging themselves at every turn, they cavorted through these three weeks in Moscow as if the ceremonies were an extended Victorian house party of pleasant diversions and amorous delights.

"*You are going to be crowned under the admiring assistance of the world,*" Kaiser Wilhelm II wrote to Nicholas II.[8] Undoubtedly the egocentric Kaiser, who deemed himself "*Your most devoted friend and cousin*" in letters to the Emperor, would have treasured an invitation to the ceremonies, but tradition dictated otherwise. With the exception of the Emperor's mother, Imperial Court etiquette precluded any other crowned sovereigns from attending the ceremony. This was a practical as well as a symbolic exclusion, relieving Nicholas and Alexandra of

Chapter IV

Tsar Nicholas II of Russia and German Kaiser Wilhelm II.

Prince Henry and Princess Irene of Prussia.

ceding precedence to longer reigning monarchs while ensuring that they remained the sole focus of attention.[9]

Denied admission to the ceremonies, the Kaiser instead dispatched his younger brother Prince Henry of Prussia to Moscow. Henry was an obvious choice, for in 1888 he had married, much against the wishes of their shared grandmother Queen Victoria, his cousin Princess Irene of Hesse, the quietest and most unassuming of Empress Alexandra's siblings. Irene would have joined him, but a difficult pregnancy restricted her travel.[10] The Kaiser, for his part, worried and nagged that his brother be accorded proper precedence during the ceremonies. *"I should be very thankful,"* Wilhelm implored Nicholas II, *"if you would kindly see that the question of his rank is made out clearly."* Above all, he worried that Henry, as a mere Prince, would have to give way to reigning German Dukes, Grand Dukes, Princes, and their heirs, which the Kaiser considered *"out of the question. My House, as the Reigning One in Germany, is First, and the Princes belonging to it go before the sons of the reigning Princes in Germany."* Besides, he helpfully pointed out, *"He is your brother-in-law."*[11]

A gruff and dedicated sailor, by turns jovial and volatile depending on his audience, Henry came to Moscow expecting the worst and he found it. Officials got the time of his arrival wrong; when he stepped from his train, the Prince found not the usual guard-of-honor and regal welcome but a barren siding manned by several confused railway staff. Furious, he stormed off to his lodgings, letting everyone know that he was *"very annoyed"* at his reception. Finally, several Grand Dukes called on him and through obsequious apologies soothed his ruffled feathers.[12]

Prince Henry was only one of Queen Victoria's many descendants arriving in Moscow that May. Grand Duke Ernst Ludwig of Hesse and by Rhine and his wife Victoria Melita ("Ducky") came from Darmstadt, his sister's crowning a welcome diversion from their already troubled married life. Alexandra adored her artistically inclined, slightly foppish brother, but his engagement to the volatile Victoria Melita had helped push her toward finally accepting Nicholas's repeated proposals.[13] Both immature and ill-equipped for wedded life, Ernst and Victoria Melita flailed through two years of marriage until, she later claimed, she caught him in bed with another man.[14] Unhappy but determined to enjoy life, Victoria Melita willingly threw herself into the world of pleasure she soon discovered in Moscow.

A hint of scandal, too, hung over Alexandra's oldest brother-in-law Prince Louis of Battenberg, who came to Moscow with his wife Victoria, the Empress's eldest sister. A morganatic offshoot of the House of Hesse, the Battenbergs existed on the fringes of

The Grand Dukes of Hesse and by Rhine, Ernst Ludwig and Victoria Melita. Present at the Coronation, they were destined to drift apart.

the royal universe, never quite accepted despite Louis' marriage to Victoria and his brother Henry's marriage to Queen Victoria's youngest daughter Beatrice. Two years before marrying his Hessian Princess, Louis had carried on a highly publicized affair with *"professional beauty"* Lillie Langtry. When she gave birth to a daughter, Jeanne Marie, Louis accepted her as his child.[15] Blunt and intellectual Victoria, in some ways the antithesis of her emotional sister Alexandra, might have had a difficult time in Moscow had customs officials searched her luggage as thoroughly as they did that of the ordinary tourist; her favored reading included socialist philosophy, a subject that would have meant expulsion for any other foreign visitor.[16]

Then there were the Duke and Duchess of Saxe-Coburg and Gotha, Victoria Melita's parents and doubly related to the Imperial couple. Alexandra's uncle Alfred was Queen Victoria's second son, while his wife Marie Alexandrovna was Nicholas's aunt, only daughter of Alexander II. Fiery and difficult, Alfred was scarcely an ideal husband while Marie was an unwelcome, haughty presence at his mother's court, insisting that as the daughter of an Emperor she had precedence over all other royal ladies and draping herself in jewels so lavish that Queen Victoria stared at her *"like an angry parrot."*[17] Difficulties eased only in 1893, when Alfred abandoned his position as Duke of Edinburgh to rule his uncle's German Duchy where his wife, at least, could finally reign as undisputed first lady of the land.

Another of Alfred and Marie's daughters arrived in Moscow – the beautiful Crown Princess Marie of Romania, accompanied by her husband Crown Prince Ferdinand. Young Marie, known as Missy, was delighted to find herself the center of much attention. With her golden hair and fair complexion, recalled Kate Koon, she *"took the hearts of all the young men,"* and all the Grand Dukes seemed to flirt with her.[18] Coming from the somber Romanian Court, Marie was overwhelmed by *"the joy of it all, the glamour, the beauty,"* surrounding

The Duke of Edinburgh and Saxe-Coburg and Gotha. (1844-1900)

Grand Duchess Marie Alexandrovna.

Grand Duke Kirill, Tsar Nicholas II and Prince Ernst of Hohenlohe-Langenburg.

Crown Princess Marie of Romania and her sister Grand Duchess Victoria Melita of Hesse and by Rhine.

the coronation.[19] While her husband Ferdinand mumbled about feeling out of sorts among the Russians, Marie eagerly soaked in every enthralling experience. *"I lived them with all the ardor of my twenty years,"* she confessed later.[20] The two Coburg sisters, Victoria Melita of Hesse and by Rhine and Marie of Romania, made quite a pair in Moscow. Both were young, striking, and caught in unsatisfying marriages to men of doubtful fidelity. From balls to banquets, they indulged their love of pleasure, flirting openly with their cousins Grand Dukes Kirill and Boris, sons of Grand Duke Vladimir, and other handsome young men.

George, Duke of York (later King George V), first cousin to both Nicholas and Alexandra, had hoped his grandmother Queen Victoria would send him to the coronation. He and Nicholas had spent many happy summer days together on family holidays in Denmark, and enjoyed the occasional confusion generated by their remarkable resemblance to one another. But George was shocked when the Queen asked her third and favorite son Arthur, Duke of Connaught, and his wife Louise, to lead the British delegation. *"I was so certain that she would send us that I did not bother anyone about it,"* he confided to Nicholas, *"else I should certainly have written to you a long time ago and asked you to write to her to say that you would like us to come. And everybody in England expected that we were going, and when at last it was settled that the*

The Duke and Duchess of Connaught.

Prince Louis of Battenberg.

Connaughts were going I must say I was furious but there was nothing to be done."[21]

The Duke and Duchess of Connaught headed an impressive British delegation. Major-General Sir Francis Grenfell, Inspector-General of the British Army Auxiliary Forces, represented the military. As Sirdar (Head) of the Egyptian Army, he had met the future Nicholas II when he passed through Cairo during his Eastern tour; his position as Aide-de-Camp to Queen Victoria gave Grenfell a welcome ease with royalty. With him came attaché and future Member of Parliament Ian Malcolm, who would have a more personal connection to the Imperial couple. Alexandra later remembered him as *"a fair, curly-haired young man in a kilt."*[22] The kilt, in fact, caused difficulties in Moscow. Thinking he should appear in his national dress, Malcolm arrived at one reception only to be met by horrified looks. Eying his bare knees, Imperial footmen refused to admit him to the event, insisting that he was indecently dressed. Thereafter, he resorted to the more customary frock coat and trousers.[23] Six years after the ceremonies in Moscow, he married Jeanne-Marie Langtry, Prince Louis of Battenberg's presumed illegitimate daughter.

Comfortable indulgence and considerable pomp, so unlike the uncertain experiences of those who traveled as ordinary tourists, marked the British delegation's journey and arrival in Moscow. They traveled aboard a special train, enjoying sturgeon and herbed liqueurs for dinner and fresh caviar for breakfast as they rolled through the countryside.[24] Some 200 members of the Imperial Life Guards formed a guard-of-honor along a crimson-carpeted siding as their train pulled into Moscow, a regimental band launching into a noisy rendition of *God Save the Queen*. Grand Dukes Vladimir, Sergei, and Paul Alexandrovich greeted them, along with British Ambassador to Russia Sir Nicholas O'Conor and his staff, and waiting court carriages transported them through the city.[25] *"The Russian crowd lined the roads and looked on,"* Grenfell noted, *"very quiet and respectful, the men taking off their caps, and the women bowing to each carriage as it passed."*[26]

Similar ceremonial welcomes greeted the future Kings Ludwig III of Bavaria and Albert I of the Belgians, the diminutive Victor Emmanuel of Savoy, the fiercely proud Nicholas of Montenegro, and Prince Louis of Monaco. Crown Prince Frederick of Denmark (later King Frederick VIII) came on behalf of the *"Grandfather of Europe,"* King Christian IX, and to support his sister the Dowager Empress as she struggled through the emotional ceremonies. More distant relatives included the future King Gustav V and his wife Crown Princess Victoria of Sweden, along with a string of minor German princes and dukes. The iron rules of Imperial etiquette barring attendance by fellow sovereigns were broken so that Queen Olga of Greece could witness the crowning. Not only was she Nicholas II's aunt by marriage, but she was also a Romanov, granddaughter of Nicholas I and a first cousin to Alexander III. It was Marie Feodorovna who had forcefully pushed a marriage between her brother King George I and a very young Grand Duchess Olga; when the sixteen-year-old bride left Russia for Greece in tears, she carried a trunk filled with her favorite dolls.[27] Olga arrived in Moscow with three of her sons: the future King Constantine I, Prince Nicholas, and Prince George, who had been with the Tsesarevich when he was attacked in Japan and had deflected a second saber blow with his walking stick.[28]

Conspicuous in his arrival, and just as conspicuously ignored by this gathered *"royal mob,"* was Prince Ferdinand of Bulgaria, who swept into Moscow, said Richard Harding Davis, *"with hooked nose and jewels to his nails."*[29] German by ancestry, like so many Balkan monarchs, Ferdinand of Coburg took the Bulgarian throne in 1887 amid deep suspicions. Queen Victoria, to say nothing of the Romanovs, thoroughly disapproved of "Foxy Ferdinand," as he was derisively known. He was, Victoria insisted, *"totally unfit, delicate, eccentric and effeminate,"* a man who slept in a pink, lace-trimmed nightgown and proudly wore makeup.[30]

Ferdinand allayed Russian fears of his rule through a typically crafty move, baptizing his son and heir Boris into the Orthodox Church. The Romanovs were pleased, but not so the Roman Catholic Church. When Papal Nuncio Antonio Agliardi spotted Ferdinand at a reception in Moscow, he walked over and actually spat upon him. Not to be deterred, Ferdinand returned the favor as his fellow royals looked on in shocked delight.[31]

The hot-tempered Agliardi might have caused more scenes had he been in Moscow longer. As it was, religious sensibilities dictated that Pope Leo XIII's representative not arrive until after the actual coronation ceremony, to avoid the difficulties of attending an Orthodox service. People whispered that sending Agliardi, mere Archbishop of Caesarea, had been deliberately disrespectful. Agliardi himself despaired over the situation until a telegram arrived from Rome with word that he was immediately elevated to the rank of Cardinal. This at least permitted him to be received with royal dignitaries as a Prince of the Catholic Church. Thereafter, Agliardi was all smiles.[32]

Crown Princess Victoria of Sweden.

Similar difficulties surrounded the Church of England. No one of any importance, it seemed, wanted to go to Moscow: Edward White Benson, Archbishop of Canterbury, declined the invitation, as did Randall Davidson, Bishop of Winchester and Prelate of the British Order of the Garter. Mandell Creighton, Bishop of Peterborough, finally won the honor, perhaps more for his renowned love of High Anglican pageantry and ritual than for his own position, though the fact that his wife was of Baltic-German ancestry and her father was a former Russian subject, might have had some influence. Author of a history of the Papacy and a religious scholar of some repute, Creighton had never been to Russia himself, and arrived prepared to dazzle with a magnificently embroidered cope borrowed from the treasury at Westminster Abbey, a gold-sewn miter, and his own hooked crosier.[33] His welcome from British Ambassador Sir Nicholas O'Conor was something less than warm. O'Conor was Catholic, while Creighton, High Church but no Anglo-Catholic, believed that an Englishman who did not belong to the Anglican Church was disloyal to crown and country.[34] Clearly irritated, O'Conor ensured that Creighton's seat in the Cathedral of the Assumption was a badly situated affront to his office, and refused to present him to Nicholas II until the Emperor indignantly forced the issue.[35] Atoning for the slight, the Russians feted Creighton at every turn, with the notorious Pobedonostsev personally looking after his comfort and going out of his way to create a favorable impression.[36]

Christianity's complex divisions were just the start of diplomatic wrangling. Members of other faiths arrived in Moscow, trailing reminders of the Russian Empire's complicated history. Princes came from exotic lands, Rajas from India and khans from Central Asia, including the remarkable Emir of Bokhara. Son of a former Persian slave who had been one of his father's four legitimate wives,

Queen Olga of Greece and her brother Grand Duke Konstantin Konstantinovich.

Future King Ludwig III of Bavaria.

Sayed Abd al-Ahad Bakhadur-Khan was an imposing figure, fairly tall and hefty of girth, with a round, fleshy face, crimson-tinted beard, and dark eyes. Habitually wrapped in fur-trimmed, brocaded robes swishing with gold tassels, the Emir adorned himself with diamond-studded epaulets, ruby rings, and white or green turbans befitting a descendant of the Prophet Mohammad, complete with jeweled aigrettes or peacock feathers.[37] Despite his subordinate position in the Russian Empire, ruler of a former independent state reduced to the status of Protectorate, Abd al-Ahad enjoyed friendly relations with the Romanovs, and in Moscow he never failed, as one foreigner visitor recorded, to *"arrest everyone's attention"* with his elaborate dress and extravagant jewels.[38]

Prince Chira, grandson of the famous King Mongkut of Siam immortalized by English tutor Anna Leonowens, was a benevolent visitor well-disposed to Russia, but not so three other arrivals from the East, who landed in Moscow full of diplomatic maneuvers and political drama. Russian Far Eastern expansion worried Korea, Japan, and China, and each country saw the coronation as a chance to negotiate territorial concessions and secret treaties against the other. Korea, then breaking free of Chinese control, worried most: Japanese agents had murdered the Queen, and King Gojong – in sanctuary at the Russian Legation in Seoul – sent statesman Min Yông-hwan to Moscow to plead for Nicholas II's assistance. Japan, too, saw opportunity in Moscow. *"In view of the special circumstances in which Japan finds herself in regard to Russia,"* her Foreign Minister wrote to Nishi Tokijuro, the country's Minister in St. Petersburg, *"the Japanese Government must first consider profiting from the exceptional occasion of the Coronation."* Emperor Meiji dispatched General Prince Fushimi Sadanaru, recent commander in the First Sino-Japanese War, along with Extraordinary Ambassador Field Marshal Marquis Yamagata Aritomo, to press for Japanese interests in Moscow. They had a long, circuitous journey: by boat from Tokyo to San Francisco; a train to New York; a liner to Paris; and finally another train that carried them to Moscow.[40]

The most powerful member of this traveling triumvirate, though, was Grand Chancellor Count Li-Hung Chang, Extraordinary Ambassador from China. A former Viceroy and Minister of Beijing, Li-Hung Chang had served at the court of the powerful Dowager Empress Ci-Xi of China as both an Imperial tutor and a member of the Council of Empire. Popularly believed to be one of the world's wealthiest men, the diplomat was, recorded a coronation guest, *"a tall, dignified old gentleman in yellow silk, rather bent with age,*

Future King Albert I of the Belgians.

speaking in a low, clear, and rather sweet voice."[41] Li-Hung Chang had never before been outside of China, and neither he nor the Dowager Empress knew quite what to expect, the latter openly wondering how many eunuchs Empress Alexandra kept at court.[42]

Li-Hung Chang was nervous as he embarked on this journey to a country whose fearsome reputation preceded it in international imagination. *"In Russia,"* he noted, *"they kill their big officials whenever they can. I am told that a great secret band exists all over the Empire, and that the members thereof find their chief occupation and amusement in the killing of men of state and others in high positions."* He thought the journey an ordeal: though admitting that some of the country was "very beautiful," he was more often struck by the *"hundreds of miles"* of *"dreary waste"* where, he was convinced, voracious wolves attacked the unsuspecting.[43] Impressive and impressionable, Li-Hung Chang arrived quite aware that in his hands lay the collective fates of four proud and ambitious nations, though he denied all to inquisitive journalists.[44]

Victor Emanuel of Savoy, Prince of Naples.

Fascinated by the exotic Li-Hung Chang, many in Moscow sought out audiences with the aged diplomat. The attention soon went to emissary's head, and he barely avoided causing a few diplomatic incidents. Meeting the Duke of Saxe-Coburg and Gotha, Li-Hung Chang quizzed the Prince about his German duchy, all the while staring rather obviously at Alfred's enormous stomach. Through his interpreter and with a giggle, the Chinese diplomat said in mock astonishment: *"But it's such a small country! I should think you would find it difficult to live in it!"*[45] He directed a similar – though more offensive – bit of mischief at the Emir of Bokhara, whom he greeted haughtily. *"The Emir,"* reported Sergei Witte, *"was quite taken aback."* Not one to trifle with, the Emir – through a translator – informed the diplomat that *he* was a *royal* personage, and that he had called on the elderly gentlemen *"out of respect"* for the Chinese Emperor. Abd al-Ahad was full of solicitous questions about the Emperor and his mother, but gave no indication that his concern extended to Li-Hung Chang. The Chinese diplomat, in turn, launched into a seeming innocuous discussion of religion, asking the Emir about his Muslim faith and his ancestor the Prophet Mohammad, polite inquires that turned hostile when Abd al-Ahad rose to leave. Through his interpreter, the Chinese diplomat suddenly volunteered that he, too, knew of Mohammed, saying that the Prophet had been expelled from China as a convict before establishing his religion among the weakly naïve Bokharans. The Emir, too shocked to reply, departed and Li-Hung Chang, said Witte, returned to his room *"quite pleased with himself"* at having given offense.[46]

Giving offense was something more sensitive members of the Diplomatic Corps studiously avoided. Anxious to curry favor with the mighty Russian Empire and its new sovereigns, countries large and small worried over creating just the right impressions. That the ceremony demanded the presence of the entire diplomatic body in Moscow proved a logistical nightmare. The principal embassies and legations were all in St. Petersburg, Russia's capital; some countries kept a smaller establishment in Moscow, but most merely had a few rooms or consular offices. In advance of the coronation, officials scrambled to rent temporary residences appropriate to their dignity. The arrangements, as the German emissary Count Johann von Bernstorff admitted, were *"strenuous,"* and caused endless headaches.[47]

Most foreign governments spent lavishly, but Great Britain refused Sir Nicholas O'Conor more than the £6,000 (£600,000, or $810,000 in 2014) allocated for expenses at the previous coronation thirteen years earlier.[48] With this, O'Conor had to find suitable housing for his embassy and the British delegation. He eventually took the Morozov Mansion, residence of a wealthy Moscow merchant, that luckily occupied a prominent spot along Tverskaya Boulevard.[49] It was, remembered one guest, a *"palatial manor, standing in a spacious courtyard with grass plots and fountains facing the entrance."*[50] It was also expensive, renting at the hugely inflated rate of £1,200 (£120,000 or $162,000) for a mere three weeks.[51] This left O'Conor with a remaining £4,800 (£480,000 or $648,000) to pay for extra horses and carriages, temporary servants, decorations to the mansion's façade, and six formal dinners, including one in honor of Nicholas and Alexandra.[52]

O'Conor was fortunate to be able to worry about the aesthetic niceties of exterior decoration. American Minister Clifton R. Breckinridge constantly complained, and not without reason, that his own government refused to properly fund his embassy. In 1896, the United States allotted a mere $5,000 ($135,000, or £100,000 in 2014) to cover coronation expenses – then equivalent to a sixth of the sum O'Conor had. Breckinridge did what he could to stretch the money, but had to forgo the decorations that adorned every other embassy in the city.[53] *"Republican simplicity is all very well in its way,"* wrote John Logan, *"but I submit that self-respect is quite as important a factor in a nation's life. If we are going to send representatives to such functions at all it would be a wise policy to enable them to at least compete in appearance with other first class powers."*[54]

Prince Nicholas of Montenegro.

Breckinridge found the whole issue a headache. Son of former American Vice President John Breckinridge and himself a Democratic member of the House of Representatives from Arkansas, Breckinridge's long career had been blemished by accusations that he had plotted the murder of a political rival – something President Grover Cleveland willingly overlooked when he appointed him Minister to Russia in 1894. Like Nicholas II, Breckinridge felt himself inadequate to his new position. Diplomatic colleagues constantly complained that he spoke no foreign languages and failed to entertain in a style befitting his status; there were frequent insinuations that he and his wife Katherine were nothing but unsophisticated Arkansas hicks.[55] John Logan, with a subtle mixture of regional prejudice and contempt, deemed Breckinridge *"a delightful and thoroughly representative American,"* while Massachusetts-born Admiral Thomas Selfridge – another member of the official delegation – observed how Katherine Breckinridge was naïvely amazed that she had never seen Empress Alexandra in the same tiara twice.[56]

Breckinridge, for his part, loathed the ceremony of the Russian Court in general, and its sartorial requirements in particular. Having no military rank, he had no uniform – a nearly unforgivable state of affairs in a society so consumed with appearances. Russians, reported a visitor, *"cannot understand why Americans don't have uniforms. They can't conceive that the representative of a great power shouldn't be attired in velvet and gold."*[57] Etiquette demanded that Breckinridge had to appear in official court attire for ceremonial occasions: a black tailcoat with silver buttons, black knee breeches, black silk stockings, black patent leather shoes, and a black silk hat.⁵⁸ His fellow diplomats maliciously teased that people would mistake him for a waiter. Breckinridge, for his part, was convinced – correctly as it turned out – that the American press would lampoon him as a sell-out to monarchist foppery.⁵⁹ He did, though, have one important point in his favor. In the first year of Breckinridge's appointment to St. Petersburg, his wife Katherine became pregnant and befriended another stranger to Russia awaiting the birth of her first child: Empress Alexandra.⁶⁰ Aware that Imperial cordiality had been extended, Breckinridge's fellow diplomats eased off their criticism and treated Breckinridge with new respect. Influence allowed Breckinridge to include most of the visiting Americans on the List of Distinguished Strangers to the City, an anachronistic bit of public recognition that also won them entrée to many of the coronation events.⁶¹

O'Conor and Breckinridge struggled against financial limitations, but not so their French counterpart. No nation was quite as profligate as Republican France in celebrating the coronation of Russia's autocratic ruler. In 1892, Russia and France had signed a secret treaty, an unlikely union between despotic empire and bastion of Europe's revolutionary movements. Eager to impress its powerful new ally, the French Government armed its representatives with an inspiring 975,000 Francs (£4,000,000 or $5,500,000 in 2014) meant to dazzle Moscow.⁶²

Refined, witty, and elegant, Ambassador Louis Gustave, Count de Montebello, had swept into St. Petersburg a few years earlier with his beautiful and immensely wealthy wife Madeleine and they set about *"making for themselves an unparalleled position."* Lavish in their hospitality and popular in society, the couple relished their influence and looked with undisguised joy toward the ceremonies in Moscow.⁶³ The Count rented the Moscow Hunt Club for an extravagant 22,000 rubles a month ($297,000 or £220,000 in 2014) and transformed the building – the former Sheremetiev Palace – into an outpost of Gallic elegance; he paid some 178,000 rubles alone ($2,403,000, or £1,780,000 in 2014) merely to extend the terrace to more pleasing proportions.⁶⁴

Minister Clifton R. Breckinridge.

"The cost of these embassies alone," complained Aylmer Maude, *"would have been sufficient to lift thousands of families of Russian peasants from destitution to a state of comparative comfort."* As brass bands crashed noisily and flags fluttered, train after train delivered privileged potentates to a city unaccustomed to such displays of foreign power and prestige. The conspicuous excess was too much for this socialist son of an Ipswich minister, who looked on in horrified amazement at the *"labor needed to equip, to carry, and to feed all the thousands of idle rich."* It was nothing, he insisted, but a gigantic charade, appealing to the vanity of *"foolish children"* who cared only for *"flatteries and falsehoods."*⁶⁵ Maude, though, was a lone voice crying out in coronation-mad Moscow as the city edged ever closer toward its date with history.

Chapter V

Moscow's Nicholas Station was a hive of excited activity. Flags and bunting hung limply in the dull rain, shadowing a red carpet edged by soldiers stretching the length of the railway platform. A military band thundered into *God Save the Tsar* as a black locomotive, belching steam into the leaden sky, eased to a halt. Armed guards, eyes alert, clutched rifles as Grand Duke Sergei stepped toward the train amid an array of gold-braided courtiers and footmen clad in crimson liveries. And all of this impressive ceremony, so carefully choreographed and precisely enacted, greeted not some illustrious visitor but rather the Imperial Crown regalia on its arrival from St. Petersburg.[1]

This display hinted at things to come: even the transfer of jewelry meant for use in the coronation demanded a solemn, elaborate ritual. The indulgence was too much for Aylmer Maude. "To describe all the ceremonies attached to this important function," he growled, "would leave me but little space to tell of the rest of the coronation. The order in which crown and scepter and orb and other gew-gaws were counted, and put into boxes, and taken out again, and re-counted, was all elaborately arranged with far more care than was devoted to the feeding of starving men during the famine."[2]

Another whistling train delivered sixteen students from St. Petersburg's Imperial *Corps des Pages*, which educated young men in advance of military careers. Earlier that year, Count Feodor Keller, director of the institute, selected the best pupils to serve as Kammer Pages – Pages of the Chamber – to members of the Imperial Family during the coronation. They arrived in Moscow with their beds, desks, servants, and new uniforms: dark blue, hip-length tunics adorned with gold facings and gold embroidered collars and cuffs, white broadcloth breeches, knee-high black boots, and helmets with white plumes. They also arrived with unruly mops of hair: tradition demanded carefully curled waves. "Those of us who had a part in our hair," recalled a Page named Sergei Roop, "didn't look too bad after a while, but those who wore their hair in a short, brushed-up style looked rather terrible." By day there were lessons on Imperial etiquette and assisting ladies while avoiding stepping on or tearing the lengthy trains of their court gowns; at night the young men enjoyed four course dinners, served on china bedecked with Romanov double-headed eagles and washed down with wine handed round by liveried footmen.[3]

Duty assignments brought puffed up pride or groans of dread. All of the young men envied Sergei Cherkesov, the "handsome, elegant youth" appointed Kammer Page to the visiting Crown Princess Marie of Romania. "I am sure that you will fall in love with your Princess," *Corps des Page* director Count Keller warned Cherkesov. "She is ravishing."[4] Marie admitted the attention went to her head, and she was delighted by Sergei Cherkesov, so "*young and fair*," and thought it quite fitting that he was so obviously "*in love*" with her.[5] She showered her young page with extra attentions, frequently asking him to join her and her sister Victoria Melita of Hesse for intimate luncheons that cemented a bond of friendship between the lonely young woman and impressionable young man. Even after the coronation, the pair continued their friendship: though they never again met, they regularly exchanged letters until Cherkesov died shortly after the Russo-Japanese War, victim of "*an infection that he picked up during some carouses in Warsaw.*"[6]

Opposite page: Born Princess Marie of Edinburgh, in 1893 she married Crown Prince Ferdinand of Romania. Marie had the very unique distinction of being a first cousin to both Tsar Nicholas II and to his wife. Through her father, Prince Alfred, she was a granddaughter of Queen Victoria, while through her mother she was a granddaughter of Tsar Alexander II. Missing the Coronation festivities is not something she would countenance.

As the formal inauguration and spiritual cornerstone of Nicholas II's reign, his coronation demanded attendance by most of the Imperial Family. There were a few unavoidable exceptions. Tuberculosis kept his brother and heir Grand Duke

59

George confined to the Caucasus, and two cousins were also missing: Grand Duke Michael Mikhailovich, living in England after his morganatic marriage, and Grand Duke Nicholas Konstantinovich, declared insane after a notorious affair with an American adventuress and exiled to Tashkent. Grand Duchess Alexandra Iosifovna, Nicholas Konstantinovich's mother, also tried to excuse herself from the ceremonies. Icily regal and a stickler for etiquette, she had attended the coronations of Alexander II and Alexander III and argued that there was no magical pull for her in Moscow; only after Empress Alexandra begged her to come did the woman known as "Aunt Sanny" in the Imperial Family reluctantly agree.[7]

Attendance by the Romanovs was meant to emphasize a relatively modern idea of Imperial service to the nation. A hundred years earlier, beset by frequent palace revolutions and a high infant mortality, the Imperial Family had seemed under threat of extinction. Starting with Emperor Paul and continuing with his son Nicholas I, a string of lusty sons had not only ensured the Dynasty's survival but also provided a new national vision of a family consecrated to the Army, to Russia, and to the throne. Notions of sacrifice and duty predominated: at sixteen young Grand Dukes reaffirmed their allegiance in public oaths, destined to spend their lives serving in whichever capacity the Emperor thought fit.

Over time, though, the Dynasty faltered and turned on itself. A proliferation of Grand Dukes were left to go their own ways; Imperial appointments disappeared, leaving a slew of titled cousins determined to enjoy their wealth and shoulder few of the responsibilities. By 1896, once sacrosanct ideas of service were a thing of the past. Most of the Romanovs, commented a diplomat, were now entrenched in *"ideas that were centuries old."* They *"did not know how the rest of Russia lived, and did not want to learn. Fundamentally, they felt that Russia existed for the Romanovs, not the Romanovs for Russia."*[8] These Grand Dukes, insisted a relative, *"neither understand the aspirations of the democracy nor sympathize with them, for, reflecting the glory of Autocracy, they are more firmly convinced than any other Royal Persons in Europe that a gulf divides them from the rest of mankind. And this conviction is so deep that they appear to believe that the most ordinary actions are ennobled by the mere fact that they are performed by persons in whose veins flows the Imperial blood."*[9]

Grand Duchess Marie Pavlovna.

The closer to the throne the worse the attitudes seemed. Nicholas II actually feared his belligerent uncles Vladimir, Alexei, and Sergei Alexandrovich (the youngest, Paul, made a far less impressive opponent). The Emperor, said his brother-in-law Alexander Mikhailovich, *"dreaded to be left alone"* with them. Their *"bellowing"* and insistent attitudes, replete with shouts and fists loudly banging on desks, filled Nicholas *"with near awe."*[10] Arrogant and disagreeable though he was, Sergei was no match for his ambitious brother Vladimir. Vladimir had always considered his elder brother Alexander III too stupid to sit upon the Russian Throne; now he dismissed his nephew Nicholas II as an insipid non-entity, *"an immature schoolboy,"* equally unfit for the task.[11] There were constant clashes of will, with the Emperor complaining that his uncle was *"unfair to take advantage of my youth and position as your nephew."*[12]

Accompanying Vladimir to Moscow was his equally ambitious wife Marie Pavlovna. The Grand Duchess impressed nearly everyone with her social grace and flair for extravagant entertainments. During the days of Alexandra's indecision at Coburg in 1894, Marie Pavlovna helped convince her to accept Nicholas's proposal, promising that she would ease her adjustment to life in Russia.[13] Her efforts, though, met with resistance after Alexandra married and, offended, the Grand Duchess *"used her considerable influence in society to work against her new rival."*[14] Dislike of the pushy Marie Pavlovna was one of the few things on which the Dowager Empress and Alexandra agreed, but neither could dethrone the powerful Grand Duchess in her reign over smart society.[15] *"She's the woman we ought to have had as Empress!"* a government official commented, sentiments not lost on Alexandra.[16]

Other Romanovs arrived in Moscow with uncomfortable secrets. Poet and dedicated diarist Grand Duke Konstantin Konstantinovich seemed the model of probity, one of the most likeable and cultured of Grand Dukes, but his veneer of Orthodox virtue concealed a passion for anonymous homosexual encounters in public bathhouses.[17] Nicholas II's uncle Alexei, who had once served up a naked French actress garnished with rose petals as the centerpiece of a party, indulged in very public liaisons with one of his mother's maids-of-honor, with the wife of a cousin, and with a famous ballerina on whom he lavished extravagant gifts that made his private life the talk of St. Petersburg.[18] Then there was Alexei's shiftless brother Paul, a widower already involved in romantic misadventures with his future, morganatic wife. He marked his arrival in Moscow, according to stories that quickly passed through the city, by becoming so inebriated that friends had to carry his inert body out of a public restaurant, past a row of eagerly saluting officers.[19]

Hedonistic members of the ruling dynasty, lives and behaviors so at odds with the coronation's spiritual message, offered a scandalous prelude to the starring actors. Monday, May 6, the day on which Nicholas and Alexandra would arrive in the city, dawned over Moscow with unpromisingly thick clouds, cold winds, and flashes of intermittent rain. The day also marked the start of young Kate Koon's own heady adventures amidst *"the grandest spectacle and the greatest gathering of foreign representatives that we shall ever have the privilege of seeing,"* as she enthused.[20] Not until the last minute did her party learn that American Minister Clifton Breckinridge had arranged their presentation

Grand Duchess Alexandra Iosifovna.

that morning at Grand Duchess Elisabeth Feodorovna's reception for visiting foreign ladies. The news sent them into a panic. The Americans, perhaps more than any other group of western visitors to Moscow, constantly worried about sartorial issues, and officials met their original plan to wear simple black gauze dresses with matching hats with horror. Black, it was explained to the naïve young women, could only be worn if the Court was in mourning. Ransacking their steamer trunks, Kate and her sister Lou finally found suitable dresses, but a miserable ride in a leaky carriage across Moscow left them wet and bedraggled by the time they pulled up at the Governor-General's Palace on the Tverskaya.[21]

Spotting the two sisters desperately trying to shield themselves from the downpour with sheets of newspaper, a footman took pity and ushered them inside. A magnificent marble staircase led them to a ballroom crowded with excited ladies. Finally, they located the other Americans: Katherine Breckinridge, standing with Mrs. Logan, Mrs. Alexander, Mrs. Roebling, and the stately Mrs. Palmer, the latter *"beautifully dressed in pink silk"* and looking *"prettier than anyone else."* After a few uncertain moments, "gorgeously dressed" courtiers opened a set of doors and the Grand Duchess appeared, *"carrying herself like a queen,"* said Kate, *"and looking quite as beautiful and young as I had hoped she would. She began at the head of the line and shook hands with each one."* The graceful Elisabeth, in an *"exquisite old ivory silk gown trimmed with little gold embroidery,"* advanced slowly down the room; Kate watched not just the Grand Duchess but also the curtseys made by the gathered women, mentally practicing the unfamiliar move. When Elisabeth reached them, Kate recorded, *"we were introduced together as sisters, and that made it much easier and more informal. The Duchess spoke English most beautifully, and opened our conversation by asking when we had arrived."*[22]

Grand Duke Konstantin Konstantinovich.

By late afternoon, the reception was over, and the city's attention turned to Smolensk Station, where the train carrying Nicholas and Alexandra would arrive. A new pavilion modeled after the ornate wooden churches of medieval Russia stretched some 700-feet along the siding, its peaked roof outlined with thousands of electric lights and culminating in an immense, gilded double-headed eagle. Sofas and chairs, potted palms, and Oriental carpets adorned the Emperor's Waiting Room, a piece of luxurious extravagance that the Imperial couple used only for a few minutes on their arrival and then again on their departure.[23]

Nicholas and Alexandra had left St. Petersburg the previous night, joined on the train by their baby daughter Olga. Also aboard were Nicholas's sister Xenia and her husband Grand Duke Alexander Mikhailovich, known as "Sandro." Charming, quiet, and rather limited, Xenia was one of Alexandra's few early friends, though their relationship eventually soured. In 1896, though, Xenia and the tall, handsome Alexander relished their intimacy with the Imperial couple, especially the ambitious Grand Duke, who saw an opportunity to influence Nicholas for his own benefit. The pair, Nicholas once complained, embarrassed him with all of their *"kissing, embracing, and lying around on the furniture in the most improper manner,"* and the cramped situation on the overnight train did nothing to soothe nerves.[24] For the first time since his marriage, the amorous Nicholas complained to his diary, he had to sleep apart from Alexandra. It was also his twenty-eighth birthday, and the train halted several times to receive flowers and the traditional Russian welcome of bread and salt.[25]

It was just after five when the train finally pulled into Smolensk Station, *"in frightful weather-rainy, windy, and cold,"* Nicholas complained.[26] Members of the Imperial Family and many of the foreign princes lined the railway siding beneath the eaves to keep the rain off their bright uniforms and smart new gowns. A regiment of Her Majesty's Lancer Life Guards, clad in blue tunics, scarlet waistcoats, and plumed *shapkas*, was not as fortunate, standing in the deluge as their band played *God Save the Tsar*.[27] Nicholas stepped from the train first, wearing the uniform of the Ekaterinoslav Life Guards Regiment, followed by the Empress in a long, white dress and a hat bedecked with ostrich plumes.[28] As Governor-General, Sergei offered a formal welcome, informing Nicholas that *"Moscow lays down before you, Most Autocratic Monarch, its most loyal congratulations and its prayerful wishes that the coming year, in which an intensified blessing from the Holy Spirit will descend on your holy head, may be the entrance to a long range of tranquil and glorious years, to the gladness and happiness alike of your Imperial Family, and of the hundred million family of your loyal subjects."* "That," noted Aylmer Maude in disgust, *"is a fair, average specimen of the style in which people consider it reasonable to address a young man of twenty-eight."*[29]

Grand Duke Alexander Mikhailovich and Grand Duchess Xenia Alexandrovna.

The Imperial couple passed through the lavish new pavilion and climbed into a waiting carriage. Hoping to see the Emperor, John Logan had rushed to the station, but the surrounding crowd was *"so enormous that I only caught a most distant glimpse of him."*[30] The couple drove out into the rain, accompanied by the Lancer Life Guards Regiment, the Circassian Life Guards Regiment in long coats crossed with bandoliers and traditional *papakhii* hats of Astrakhan lamb, and men from the Hussar Life Guards Regiments, their sable-trimmed white dolmans draped over crimson jackets spotted by the downpour.[31]

Tradition kept Nicholas and Alexandra from entering the city center; instead, they drove to the Petrovsky Palace some five miles from the Kremlin. Built for Catherine the Great, it was, said Francis Grenfell, *"a curious, fanciful"* mélange of Gothic and neo-medieval Russian architecture that violated *"every principle of art,"* though he admitted that the effect was *"quaint and impressive."*[32] Here in the autumn of 1812, Napoleon had taken refuge with his

Moscow's Petrovsky Palace.

invading *Grande Armée*, awaiting a surrender that never came and watching in disbelief as Muscovites set their city on fire rather than capitulate.[33] Blessed with Holy Water as their carriage rolled through the palace gates and saluted by a guard-of-honor drawn from the Ekaterinslav Life Guards Regiment, Nicholas and Alexandra received another welcome of bread and salt from the citizens of Moscow before escaping to the private apartments.[34] *"The overcrowding of Moscow,"* Maude remarked dryly, *"does not appear to have reached the palace,"* where even the six-month-old Olga had an anteroom, a playroom, a bedroom, and a room for her nurse.[35]

"I wished in my heart of hearts that I was a true Russian!" enthused Therese Vianzone as she watched this procession. *"There is a true cult for the dear Imperial Family."* The Imperial carriage passed along the roadway, she said, amid *"frantic acclamations."*[36] Impressive on the surface, the demonstration – like so much of the coronation – was a carefully contrived bit of theatre, the streets lined only by the wealthy and well-connected who had been approved by the police.[37] Aylmer Maude cynically thought that the ovation seemed hollow, like that of *"the Paris mob"* that had *"cheered Louis XVI not long before the Revolution."*[38]

Sixteen-year-old Semen Ivanovich Kanatchikov was also on the Moscow streets that day. Recently arrived from the countryside, he took the only course open to the son of a peasant and became an apprentice at the Gustav List Factory. Here, he worked hazardous twelve-hour shifts in the metal foundry and lived in a grim, company-owned rooming house. More out of curiosity than loyalty, he decided to try to see the Emperor. Things *"ended very sadly,"* though, when a group of mounted Cossacks beat him and his comrades back with whips. They quickly retreated, bodies bruised, clothing torn and bloodied, *"with a feeling of shame and disgrace."*[39]

Thousands more had stood on Khodynka Meadow, watching as the distant carriage turned into Petrovsky Palace's gates. Though it lay just across the St. Petersburg Highway, an insurmountable gulf separated Petrovsky Palace from the people on the meadow, the ruling from the ruled. Ordinary Russians had come from across the Empire; many reached Moscow on foot, sometimes from neighboring villages, sometimes from hundreds of miles away.[40] Henry LaPauze learned that one group had spent a month traveling *"the hard way, feeding themselves across the Steppe with seeds of sunflower and hard black bread,"* walking from villages a thousand miles distant through the cold and uncomfortable spring months.[41]

Desperately poor and unfamiliar with the city, these peasants were excited, if not by a coronation they would never see then at least by the People's Feast. Day after day, ever more shuffled along the St. Petersburg Highway, past the Moscow Racecourse and Vagonovsky Cemetery to the desolate Khodynka.[43] Ordinarily a dusty, wind-swept expanse, it was now a muddy morass, a gigantic, open-air camp where people dared not venture too far across the field in search of higher ground.

Flyers plastered across Moscow promised *"every visitor to the field"* during the People's Feast pirozhki and pastries, beer and kvass, and special Imperial gifts. Some 400,000 souvenir bundles had been prepared. Each contained a half-pound of sausage, small bread rolls, gingerbread cookies, nuts, and sweets, tucked into white enamel mugs decorated with red and blue Imperial monograms, and wrapped in red and white cotton handkerchiefs woven with a view of the Kremlin on one side and portraits of Nicholas and Alexandra on the other – high and lasting prizes that would impress fellow villagers back home.[44]

Now these workers and peasants clustered around makeshift fires for warmth. Foreign visitors were fascinated. *"These people were never at rest,"* saw Richard Harding Davis. *"They apparently never slept or relaxed, but turned night into day and day into night, and formed a seething, bubbling cauldron of human beings, the like of which perhaps has never been brought together in one place."*[45] Kate Koon spotted a group of women whose *"short skirts and waists, and the kerchiefs over their heads were of the brightest cerise, red, yellow, and blue. There were women pilgrims, dressed in ragged, heavy short skirts, reaching only a little below their knees. Their feet and legs were bound in cloth, and upon their feet they wore sandals made of reeds. Over their shoulders they carried an extra pair of shoes and a bundle containing what they needed during their pilgrimage."*[46] Mary Hickley, too, found the kaleidoscope of colors bewitching – a woman in *"a yellow skirt, a magenta blouse, a scarlet shawl, and a spotted green kerchief on the head,"* standing next to another *"dressed in blue, orange, pink, and purple."*[47]

Grand Duke Sergei Alexandrovich and Grand Duchess Elisabeth Feodorovna.

Yet journalist Aubrey Stanhope, surveying this odd assortment of pilgrims, instinctively viewed them as subhuman, mere chattels in the Emperor's service. Peasants, he declared, embodied *"such childish naivety and absolute stupidity, full of superstition,"* in their *"reverence and adoration for the Great White Tsar."* They were, he insisted, stupid and slothful, *"not far removed from the animal,"* the *"wildest-looking creatures"* whose lives had *"no particular value."* Nicholas II might have agreed. To him, peasants and factory workers were abstract, nameless subjects, useful only for their labor; for background decoration; and for their cheers that bolstered the national myth of an unseen link between Throne and People. Amongst this immense crowd Stanhope sensed something else, something that official Russia had missed. If provoked, he thought, these *"humble, submissive, and obedient"* peasants might soon turn into wolves, *"dangerous and bloodthirsty*[48]

Rain poured upon the field all through the night; when Nicholas arose just across the highway the next morning, he saw the *"same foul weather"* that had greeted his arrival in Moscow.[49] An inspection of the temporary military camp at the edge of Khodynka Meadow and a ceremonial *Beating the Retreat* was scheduled for that morning. Then came word that Archduke Karl Ludwig, who had been expected in Moscow to represent his brother Emperor Franz Josef of Austria-Hungary, had died unexpectedly in Vienna. The niceties of Court mourning demanded that the public schedule be cancelled, at least for a day, out of respect for the late Archduke.⁵⁰ Nicholas was happy to forego ceremonial obligations in favor of familial indulgence: walks in the garden, lunches with Alexandra's siblings, and playful dinners with his boisterous Greek cousins.⁵¹

The family atmosphere carried over into private receptions. Francis Grenfell joined the Duke and Duchess of Connaught and members of the British delegation when they paid their respects to Nicholas and Alexandra that Tuesday. Entering Petrovsky Palace, he was startled by *"two enormous blacks"* standing stiffly before the doors leading to the private apartments.⁵² These were two of the Russian Court's famous "Abyssinian" Guards, imposing figures attired in a vague hodge-podge of Europe and Africa: jackets embroidered with Russia's double-headed eagles, red trousers, pointed Moroccan leather boots, and white turbans. Their only job was *"to open and close doors, and to signal by a sudden, noiseless entrance into a room that one of Their Imperial Majesties was about to appear."*⁵³ Grenfell was no stranger to the Imperial couple. Having first met Nicholas under the hot Cairo sun in 1890, he thought the Emperor now seemed curiously pale, though full of questions about Britain's expedition to conquer Khartoum, the rebellious Sudanese capital, which lay a little south of the scope of his 1890 trip to the sites of ancient Egypt. As for Alexandra, she was, said Grenfell, *"quite changed"* from the Hessian Princess he had encountered while serving as Aide-de-Camp to her grandmother Queen Victoria at Balmoral Castle in Scotland. He found the Empress *"stouter,"* but with more *"dignity and refinement."*⁵⁴

Archduke Karl Ludwig of Austria.

The Duke of Connaught, who appreciated feminine beauty in his own way, also thought that the little extra weight from her recent pregnancy suited his niece.⁵⁵ The Duke invested Nicholas with the Grand Cross of the Victorian Order, then turned to present the Queen's formal coronation gift, *"a very fine silver cup"* in a wooden case. The cup, though, was tightly wedged into its compartment, and the Duke could not pull it free. Straining, twisting, and turning the troublesome object, it took several men to finally free the cup as Nicholas and Alexandra tried unsuccessfully to suppress their laughs.⁵⁶

The weather finally improved the following day, the sun appearing in bursts that, said Nicholas, *"instantly made it more cheerful."*⁵⁷ Behind closed doors, the Imperial couple worried over their coronation. Princess Marie Golitsyn, Alexandra's Mistress of the Robes and Chief Lady-in-Waiting, twisted her ankle and a very nervous Princess Elisabeth Naryshkina-Kurakina stepped in at the last minute. *"I was somewhat terrified at this summons,"* recalled the Princess, *"for I knew practically nothing about the details of the coronation ceremony. But a refusal was impossible."* She rehearsed fastening the Empress's coronation mantle with an *"extremely heavy"* and difficult diamond studded clasp and fretted over the actual moment of crowning.⁵⁸

During Alexander II's coronation, Empress Marie Alexandrovna's crown slipped from her head and nearly crashed to the floor; in 1883 a careless lady-in-waiting stabbed Marie Feodorovna's scalp inserting a hairpin to hold her crown in place.⁵⁹ Hoping to avoid such misfortunes, Alexandra wanted to practice. The Princess found her mistress in a dressing room, the Emperor standing nervous and smoking *"one cigarette after another"* as he opened a wooden case and withdrew the small, diamond-encrusted consort's crown to place it atop his wife's head. A hairdresser was showing the Princess how to insert a diamond-studded hairpin when Alexandra let out a piercing scream. Exactly as feared, the pin had gone too far and drawn blood.[60]

That Wednesday, an overnight train delivered Dowager Empress Marie Feodorovna and her two youngest children Michael and Olga to Moscow from the South of France. Their holiday, Nicholas noted, had left them all terribly sunburned.[61] Nearly eighteen, handsome, and already taller than his brother, Michael was a naïve young man who *"believed without hesitancy anything and everything anyone told him,"* while his fourteen-year-old sister Olga, plain and unassuming, was excited at her first taste of Imperial ceremony.[62] The Dowager Empress, though, was overwhelmed with emotion. As she explained to her mother Queen Louise of Denmark, attending her son's Coronation in Moscow was a *"great sacrifice."* Unable to forget her husband's crowning, she looked at the ceremonies as *"awful beyond description,"* a *"duty"* to be endured. Twenty-eight-year-old Nicholas, she thought, was *"so young"* to be burdened with the Throne; she could only hope that he would *"walk in his angelic father's footsteps"* throughout his reign.[63]

Intermittent sunshine finally burst over Moscow in a blazing orange sunset as Mary Hickley saw what she thought must be *"half the grandees of Europe,"* rushing through the city in carriages pulled by *"fiery black horses, all silver chains, flying tassels, and tinkling bells,"* toward Petrovsky Palace.[64] Members of the Moscow Imperial Opera, the Russian Choral Society, the Moscow Concert Society, and the Moscow Philharmonic Orchestra – some 1,200 people in all – crowded the courtyard to serenade the Imperial couple with selections from Dargomyzhsky's opera *Rusalka*; Gounod's *La Nuit*; Ladow's *Au Bord de la Riviere*; Tchaikovsky's *Sleeping Beauty*; and Mendelssohn's *Nur Hat Dich, du Shöner Wald*.[65] Nicholas and Alexandra stepped out onto the balcony at nine. Below, hundreds of singers held lanterns, turning the courtyard into *"a sea of flickering lights."*[66] Mary Hickley was moved by *"the very sweetest and wildest of music – grand old choruses and plaintive folksongs, wailing always in a minor key – the Russian landscape put into music."*[67] *"Let's applaud,"* Nicholas urged his guests after the first song.[68] Like many other foreign visitors, Mary naïvely saw such insignificant moments as clear evidence of the Emperor's presumed liberal intentions.[69]

The Dowager Empress Marie Feodorovna with their younger children: Olga, Michael and George, who was afflicted with very poor health.

"The night," wrote Grand Duke Konstantin Konstantinovich, *"was quiet and luminously soft, bathed by a new moon in the sky above,"* as people reluctantly abandoned the magical scene.[70] Nicholas II would make his State Entrance into Moscow the following morning. The *"garlanded streets"* were already *"thronged with people,"* who had camped out along the route.[71] They watched through the night as workers tore up tramlines, replacing them with cushioning layers of sand to protect carriage wheels and newly shod horses.[72] Few slept: buoyed by excitement, they talked, drank, and sang through the night as Moscow, *"dressed up like a bride on her wedding day,"* awaited the splendid pageant of the following day.[73]

Chapter VI

A "radiant" sunrise broke over Moscow, fanning out across its *"gilded domes, its bulbous bell-towers, its roofs in tender green or reds."*[1] It had rained in the night – *"just enough,"* said John Logan, *"to lay the dust"* on the roadways. A soft, warm breeze swept across the city, perfuming the air with the scent of spring flowers.[2] It was, Nicholas's cousin Grand Duke Kirill Vladimirovich thought, as if nature itself wished to celebrate the Emperor's State Entrance into Moscow.[3]

Nearly a million people had gathered along the five flag and flower bedecked miles that Nicholas II would travel from Petrovsky Palace to the Kremlin.[4] Pavilions, tribunes, and stands held some 100,000 *"specially privileged"* onlookers; others crowded windows, balconies, and doorways: *"ladies in exquisite toilettes, men in all kinds of uniforms, sisters of mercy, nuns, priests,"* all *"very carefully dressed"* and awaiting the procession.[5] The Emperor's humble subjects, though, were carefully kept back. Two solid rows of soldiers in a rainbow of colored uniforms lined the streets. There were members of the exclusive Preobrazhensky Life Guard, their restrained dark blue broadcloth uniforms brightening into the Lancers' more vivid blue; His Majesty's Own Cossack *Konvoi* Regiment, with scarlet *kosakhins* and long Circassian coats that set off the gorgeous crimson and gold worn by the Hussars; and Chevalier Life Guards, in white tunics and silver cuirasses.[6] Behind them, mounted Cossacks, uncomfortable in heavy coats of crimson wool and black Astrakhan *kolpakhi* hats, eased their restless horses, while another 92,000 men – police and special agents – stood between roadway and members of the public, ensuring that the people saw nothing.[7]

Intense security reminded foreigners of Russia's dangerous history. *"This country,"* shuddered Mary Hickley, *"is a hotbed of anarchists and Nihilists."*[8] Buildings along the route had been searched, basements and attics sealed, permits checked, and even fire escapes boarded over, lest some revolutionary miscreant clamber onto a roof and toss a bomb.[9] Police made the visiting Americans flash their passes several times before allowing them to sit in the windows of their rented rooms at the Hotel Dresden.[10] They were enjoying the spectacle of diplomats and princes crowding onto the balcony of the Governor-General's Palace across the avenue, when a mass of black smoke suddenly billowed from the building.[11] An inexplicable fire in the chapel sent Grand Duke Sergei rushing from his guests and salvaging clothing from the rooms occupied by his sister-in-law Princess Victoria and her husband Prince Louis of Battenberg before the flames spread.[12] After a few nail-biting minutes, wagons equipped with water tanks arrived and firemen extinguished the mysterious blaze.[13]

Moscow swelled with expectation, but the man at the center of the spectacle was filled with dread. Despairing lack of confidence had marked Nicholas II's accession to the Throne; now, he faced his *"first difficult day"* in Moscow, riding through the city as his father had done thirteen years earlier, a reluctant sovereign clinging to the Autocracy yet seared by personal doubts.[14] Nor was Alexandra filled with enthusiasm at this most public of ceremonial obligations. It was her first real introduction to the Russian people, an opportunity to create favorable impressions, but symbolic implications meant less to her than private feeling. The ride, she complained, would be *"dull,"* and she would have to travel *"all alone"* on her journey.[15] Unimpressed by the pageantry, Nicholas and Alexandra viewed the State Entrance as an ordeal, less an occasion for public rejoicing than a tiresome, private tribulation.

Nearly 200 guests joined the Imperial couple for luncheon at Petrovsky Palace, while a few rooms away, cadets from the *Corps des Pages* shared their feast of caviar, lobster, wild fowl, and assorted wines.[16] Finishing his meal early, Francis Grenfell wandered into the courtyard to match a numbered ticket to his assigned mount. He found

A coronation poster depicting the arrival at the Cathedral of the Assumption of Tsar Nicholas II with Empress Alexandra Feodorovna and the Dowager Empress Marie Feodorovna. Behind them, in the middle of the drawing, is Grand Duke Sergei Alexandrovich, who was partly responsible for the Khodynka Field tragedy.

Emperor Nicholas II's ceremonial entry into Moscow.

"*a big bay horse, looking very sleepy, having probably been exercised since 4 AM.*"[17] Others soon filled the courtyard, "*a motley crew,*" said a page, in a cacophony of uniforms and speaking "*a perfect babble of languages.*"[18] All members of the Imperial Family, along with foreign royal guests and delegations, would ride in procession with the Emperor. There was one exception: his wife Katherine might be on good terms with the Empress, but American Minister Clifton Breckinridge was excluded from the procession, presumably because he was a commoner with no military rank.[19]

At half-past two, a twenty-one-gun salute shook the Moscow sky, announcing the start of the procession.[20] The charges were so powerful that a startled Semen Kanatchikov heard "*the sounds of glass breaking in the nearby houses.*"[21] A single shot signaled the moment when Nicholas appeared in the Petrovsky Palace courtyard; a second when he mounted his horse; and a third when he rode out of the gates.[22] Bells peeled, people along the street crossed themselves, and men doffed their hats in respect as the procession began.[23] For ninety minutes, "*a panorama of majesty and wealth and beauty,*" as Richard Harding Davis put it, unfurled along Moscow's streets.[24] "*Never before had we seen such an amount of gold,*" enthused Henry LaPauze. "*Perhaps we had imagined it in Versailles or the Trianon, but had not expected to see such a sight in the present hour.*"[25]

A contingent of twelve mounted members of the Moscow Police, led by their Chief Vlassovsky, opened the pageant, followed by a Master of Ceremonies in gold-braided uniform, riding a sleek black horse flanked by fourteen mounted officers with shining helmets.[26] "*The crowd's admiration burst forth into hurrahs and shouts of pleasure,*" declared *The New York Times* as four squadrons of His Majesty's Own Cossack *Konvoi* Regiment galloped out, leading the Astrakhan Kuban Cossack Regiment, the Cossack Life Guards Regiment, and mounted horsemen of the Cossack Guard, their Atamans, or Chiefs, all attired in long scarlet or blue coats and clutching fierce-looking lances.[27] As the very exemplification of the Emperor's grip over his nation, the legendary Cossacks always made a dramatic impression on foreigners, and John Logan thrilled at their "*swarthy faces, black hair, and piercing eyes.*"[28] "*Dark, impassive men,*" representing "*the subjugated Asian tribes,*" followed, including the Emir of Bokhara and the Khan of Khiva. Mary Hickley thought them "*very magnificent in gold and silver embroideries, velvets and silks of exquisite dyes, sables, and priceless jewels,*" while John Logan, ever the military man, saw visible representations of colonial power, of "*the extent of the victories won by the arms of Russia through all the mighty wastes of Central Asia.*"[29]

Prince Peter Trubetskoy, Marshal of Moscow's Nobility, rode at the head of sixty aristocrats, followed by Major-General Baron Stackelberg leading his Court Orchestra as it played rousing and patriotic tunes. Major-General Prince Golitsyn, Grand Master of the Imperial Hunt, surrounded by State Trumpeters and his Huntsmen in green

An image of Tsar Nicholas II during the ceremonial entry into the Moscow Kremlin.

and red caftans, came behind them, followed by four members of the Abyssinian Guard in scarlet coats and white turbans, and sixty Imperial Footmen in red velvet knee breeches, white silk stockings, powdered wigs, and Tricorn hats.[30] As the minutes ticked steadily by, the drama of horses and men gave way to stately gilded carriages holding Chief Grand Master of Ceremonies Prince Alexander Dolgoruky, lesser Masters of Ceremony, and elderly members of the State Council and the Imperial Senate, lulled by the hot sun and gently rocking vehicles and *"sleeping like babies."*[31]

Twenty-four Gentlemen-of-the-Bedchamber and twelve Chamberlains *"in uniforms covered with gold"* and *"Tricorn hats with white feathers"* rode in front of yet more carriages.[32] The Grand Marshal of the Imperial Court sat in a state phaeton pulled by horses caparisoned with waving ostrich plumes, escorted by squadrons of Chevalier Guards in white tunics with gold lace, silver cuirasses, and silver helmets topped with double-headed eagles; and *Gardes à Cheval* in white tunics, polished gold cuirasses and gold helmets topped with double-headed eagles.[33] Horse by horse, carriage by carriage, the procession continued leaving the crowd stunned. *"There is so much gold that the eye is dazzled,"* gaped one newspaper. *"It is no longer possible to distinguish mere valets from important governors."*[34] Only the Americans, watching from the Hotel Dresden, thought the cavalcade was overblown. They mocked the circus atmosphere and laughed at how seriously Russians seemed to take their pomp.[35]

"And now," said John Logan, *"the supreme moment in the procession had arrived. A hush fell over all."*[36] Following the tradition established by Emperor Paul at his 1797 coronation, Nicholas II appeared on horseback, riding Norma, a thirteen-year-old, dapple gray English mare fitted with silver shoes held in place with silver nails.[37] He wore the dark green uniform of a Commander in the Semenovsky Life Guards Regiment, the light blue moiré sash of the Order of St. Andrei across his chest and his gold epaulettes and aiguillettes shining in the sun.[38] At least one onlooker was

Tsar Nicolas II leading the procession on its way to the Moscow Kremlin.

immediately disappointed. He seemed *"a small, slight figure, contrasting vividly with his father thirteen years before."*[39] From the windows of her hotel, ballerina Mathilde Kschessinska watched as her former lover rode in triumph down the wide boulevard. *"I tried to suppress my grief,"* she recalled, *"to appear carefree; but I was living a terrible torment! It was agonizing to watch the Tsar pass."*[40] Nicholas, everyone agreed, was *"pale,"* with *"a mystical expression on his face"* as his right hand remained frozen at the brim of a round Astrakhan cap in salute.[41] Finally, though, the enthusiasm broke through his anxiety and reserve, and the young Emperor rewarded the crowd with *"an almost wistful smile."*[42]

"The house-tops rocked," wrote Richard Harding Davis, *"and the sidewalks seemed to surge and sway with waving caps and upraised hands."* The cheering, he said, was unworldly, a *"curious moaning"* that issued from the crowd – *"a strange, hoarse"* roar *"full of feeling,"* to Mary Hickley.[43] To the most impressionable foreign onlookers, it seemed the mightiest and most heartfelt of receptions. The cheers, reported *Le Figaro*, were more like *"a terrible roar...curious and indescribable,"* that *"rose like a wave."*[44] Kate Koon, who could not understand a word of Russian, insisted that people shouted, *"We would die for our Tsar!"*[45] Most enthusiastic of all was Therese Vianzone, as she gazed on his *"peaceful and good looking face"* filled with *"redoubtable majesty."* No one seeing him, she declared, could doubt his *"great intellectual vigor and chivalry"* as he rode along the Tverskaya to an *"unbelievable"* ovation. *"How one heard the conviction, the love in the cheers! How they loved the Emperor, the Russian people! There was nothing contrived, nothing prepared. What their hearts felt, their voices acclaimed. It is unique, it is unforgettable: and nothing would be an understatement of what happened."*[46]

Reality, though, was somewhat different. Princess Catherine Radziwill recalled *"no spontaneity in the greeting of the crowd, no enthusiasm,"* and that most of the cheers came from the troops lining the roadway.[47] She was prejudiced against Nicholas and Alexandra, but others confirmed Radziwill's impressions. Ian Malcolm thought that the crowd was restrained in its acclamations as the Emperor passed, while Francis Grenfell recorded that the cheering, *"though continuous, was subdued, and appeared to be controlled,"* with *"no wild enthusiasm."*[48] Even the official coronation account insisted that emotion and reverence accounted for the notably subdued greeting.[49]

Romanov Grand Dukes, adjutants, foreign princes, and members of the extraordinary embassies rode behind the pale and anxious Nicholas; it was an escort, said Logan, which *"would have graced the retinue of a world conqueror in the zenith of his glory."*[50] Galloping with this contingent and taking in *"the grandest thing I had ever seen,"* Francis Grenfell sought distraction in the *"enormous crowd"* along the roadway. It was all very interesting, he thought, though he failed to spot even *"one pretty woman"* among the spectators.[51]

Enthusiasm reached a crescendo when Dowager Empress Marie Feodorovna appeared. She rode alone, in Catherine the Great's crimson and gold Imperial State Coach awash with carved and gilded cherubs and topped by a replica of the Imperial Crown. White-wigged grooms in scarlet and gold liveries led eight white horses whose bobbing heads were bedecked with waving ostrich plumes. Two coachmen in Tricorn hats guided the vehicle; at the rear, two Kammer Pages,

The Dowager Empress Marie Feodorovna riding in the gold Imperial Stage Coach.

"*upright and motionless,*" held gold tasseled cords gathered at the sides of the carriage. Ober-Stallmeister Count Orlov-Davidov and his assistant galloped on either side of the coach, flanked by six mounted Kammer Pages, four members of the Cossack *Konvoi* Regiment, and two squadrons of Chevalier Guards, surrounding the vehicle like survivors of a shipwreck clutching at a piece of jetsam.[52] The entire extravaganza, sniped Aylmer Maude, would have made "*any respectable woman from a circus*" blush.[53]

In her Russian Court gown of silver tissue embroidered in gold thread, Marie Feodorovna was a vision of stately magnificence. Throat hidden by the 470-carat Imperial *Riviere*, the single largest diamond necklace in the world, and dark hair crowned with a "*fantastically gorgeous*" diamond tiara, her jewels flashed miniature fires as sunlight poured into the carriage.[54] Everyone agreed that the "*almost deafening*" cheers that greeted the Dowager Empress were "*extraordinarily sincere*" and the loudest acclamations that day.[55] Ian Malcolm thought that the crowd "*was quite quiet*" until Marie Feodorovna appeared.[56] The Dowager Empress, noted Kate Koon, "*provoked more cheering from the people than did her son.*"[57] And Francis Grenfell was struck by the fact that "*the Dowager Empress met with the greatest reception.*"[58] "*The Russian people's reverence for the Tsar's mother was apparent,*" reported *Le Matin*, noting that she was the object of "*special sympathy and respect.*"[59] Marie Feodorovna smiled but seemed sad, and "*the bows with which she acknowledged the enthusiasm of the people were indeed far from being happy ones.*"[60]

Empress Alexandra followed in a second, smaller carriage made for Catherine the Great, a "*sumptuous jewel box*" adorned with crimson and gold carving shimmering between the Kammer Pages and galloping ranks of the Cossack *Konvoi* Regiment.[61] Black, white, and gold ostrich plumes bobbed from the heads of eight white horses led by grooms in scarlet and gold. No expense had been spared: postilions sat in saddles of red Moroccan leather engraved in gold and stitched in silver, atop saddlecloths of gold lace woven with the Imperial Coat-of-Arms at Maison Roduwart Brothers in Paris at a cost of a million dollars.[62] "*Each horse,*" mused Richard Harding Davis dryly, "*would have preferred a mouthful of oats*" to the enormous gold bits, "*as big around as a man's thumb,*" that now encumbered them.[63] Alexandra, Kate Koon thought, "*looked beautiful*" in her gown of silver brocade adorned with sparkling diamonds and bowed "*most graciously*" to the crowd.[64] Others, though, remarked that she "*blushed*

A view of the Imperial procession. In it we can see the carriages of the Dowager Empress and of her daughter-in-law Empress Alexandra Feodorovna.

furiously," perhaps overcome by the emotion of the moment, and seemed *"immovable, like an Indian goddess."*[65] She sat, said the correspondent for *Le Figaro*, *"like an idol, glorying in her youth."* [66]

The crowd, *"already hoarse,"* claimed John Logan, *"seemed anxious to expend its last fragment of lung power"* as Alexandra appeared.[67] Nicholas was impressed, calling it a *"hearty and triumphant success, as perhaps it can only be in Moscow."*[68] Yet there was something odd: the deafening cheers that had greeted Marie Feodorovna ebbed rather for Alexandra. Although it was not the *"dead silence"* Radziwill later claimed, the lesser enthusiasm was notable.[69] The Dowager Empress was familiar to the country, loved and respected in society and a figure of sympathy; in contrast, Alexandra was young and unknown, a foreigner who had come to Russia in gloomy circumstances she had yet to outgrow.

More carriages followed, each drawn by six white horses, *"giving one the impression that their occupants were not quite so heavy as the two Empresses,"* said Maude.[70] Within rode foreign princesses and ladies of the Imperial Family, including Nicholas II's excited and miserable fourteen-year-old sister Grand Duchess Olga.[71] It was her first time wearing a formal, floor-length Russian Court gown – *"the armor,"* as Imperial ladies termed it – and it was an ordeal. For all of their elaborate cherubs and fittings of velvet and lace, the carriages were also terribly uncomfortable. Lacking modern springs, they bounced and bumped along, jostling passengers at every rough spot in the road. Worse, most of the windows could not be lowered: in the warm May afternoon, they became miniature infernos.[72] Draped in cumbersome gowns and trapped in glass prisons dictated by their biology, the unfortunate ladies must have felt like the sequestered princesses of medieval Muscovy, passing their days in the isolated Terem and trotted out only on festive occasions.[73]

Away from all of this pageantry, anxious Kammer Pages had embarked on a wild race across Moscow. After assisting the two Empresses into carriages at Petrovsky Palace, they were to rejoin them just outside the Kremlin. Boris Engelhardt, Marie Feodorovna's page,

Opposite page: A view of Red Square and St. Basil's Cathedral. The square was festively decorated with garlands and banners commemorating the Coronation of Tsar Nicholas II.

had no difficulties, but the landau carrying his comrades Alexander Mandryk and Alexei Ignatiev broke down. Clad in their full dress uniforms, they tore through the crowded streets on foot, finally flagging down a passing coach that delivered them to Red Square with just minutes to spare.[74]

From their positions, the pages heard the roar as the Emperor's horse approached. Nicholas passed through the Triumphal Arch commemorating Napoleon's defeat and into the city, where his uncle Grand Duke Sergei, as Governor-General, welcomed him on behalf of Moscow with the traditional bread and salt.[75] The Mayor, members of the City Duma, merchants, and artisans all offered congratulations along the route before Nicholas dismounted at the edge of Red Square.[76] Hot and bothered, the young pages rushed forward and helped the two Empresses from their carriages, maneuvering the fifteen-foot-long trains of their court gowns along a length of red carpet as Nicholas led his wife and his mother to the Iversky Chapel. *"Overcome by grief"* as she approached the Chapel, the Dowager Empress *"let her tears freely flow."*[77] Having kissed a cross and being blessed with holy water, the trio crowded into the small chapel and venerated the icon of the Iberian Mother of God in symbolic obeisance to Russia's history and Church. Prayers and blessings, thought Aylmer Maude, formed *"an important part"* of the Imperial couple's theocratic *"work"* needed before they could enter Red Square.[78]

Chimes in the Kremlin's Spassky Tower rang out the hour of four just as Nicholas appeared in Red Square on his white horse.[79] Some 200,000 spectators jammed the vast expanse, specially invited dignitaries and representatives from across the Empire who waved and cheered from immense tribunes ringing the square and rising against the Kremlin walls.[80] *"All Moscow felt the inexpressible breath that unites the Tsar with his people,"* the official account insisted. Eyes were *"filled with tears of joy, and the immense force constituting the love of the people for their Tsar penetrated into the depths of everyone's soul."*[81]

"The terrifying enthusiasm of the onlookers was without end," reported *Le Petit Parisien*. *"The crowd cheered with a frenzy."*[82] Soldiers from the Semenovsky and Preobrazhensky Life Guards Regiments, stationed along the Kremlin battlements between vast pennants in the Romanov House colors of white, gold, and black, saluted; bands struck up *God Save the Tsar*; church bells rang out; and guns thundered artillery salutes.[83] Nicholas, said one onlooker, seemed *"excited, with a pale, pinched face."*[84] But just as he reached the Kremlin's Spassky Gate, the rigidly orchestrated ceremonial temporarily went awry. A stray dog loped into the scene, sat on its haunches a few feet in front of the Emperor's horse Norma and scratched away at unseen fleas, blithely unconcerned at its act of *lèse-majesté*. Finally, someone managed to shoo it off and the faithful Norma carried Nicholas into the Kremlin.[85]

The cacophony of bells and bands, cannon and cheers, followed Nicholas through the Gate, where representatives from the provinces in their Sunday best, bureaucrats in tailcoats, nuns in dark habits, and schoolchildren in starched uniforms continued the ovations. Lamas from Tibet, in *"yellow satin robes and brass headdress,"* and tradesmen looking uncomfortable in new suits, looked on from tribunes as the Emperor dismounted in Cathedral Square.[86] Pale and seemingly preoccupied, he failed to return several regimental salutes.[87] The two Empresses followed on foot, Alexandra flushed and excited and Marie Feodorovna again close to tears, as courtiers led them to the Cathedral of the Assumption.[88] Metropolitan Sergei of Moscow, robed *"in vestments of cloth-of-gold,"* waited at the southern door with members of the Holy Synod and high-ranking clergy, blessing the trio and ushering them inside the church as its bell rang out and artillery on the Kremlin towers fired an eighty-five gun salute.[89]

Swaying ranks of priests, carrying icons, gonfalons, and swinging censers of fragrant incense, led Nicholas, Alexandra, and Marie Feodorovna through the church to the strains of the hymn, *This Day Hath the Grace of the Holy Spirit Assembled Us* before a solemn *Te Deum* began.[90] At its end, the Metropolitan was to conduct them across the square, to pray before icons and venerate relics in the Cathedral of the Archangel Michael and the Cathedral of the Annunciation. The elderly Sergei of Moscow, though, marched off in the wrong direction as Nicholas looked on in confusion. Grand Duke Vladimir, a few steps behind, halted the procession, correcting the mistake by shouting at the top of his lungs, *"Emperor at the back! Emperor at the back!"*[91]

Tsar Nicholas II, with the Dowager Empress Marie Feodorovna and Empress Alexandra Feodorovna, arriving at the Cathedral of the Assumption. Standing immediately behind them is Grand Duke Sergei Alexandrovich. This is the scene that served as inspiration for the poster used on page 69.

Honor done to icons, relics, and the tombs of those somewhat questionably described as their ancestors, Nicholas and two Empresses crossed Cathedral Square. At the bottom of the Red Staircase Count Konstantin van der Pahlen, Chief Grand Marshal of the Imperial Court, formally welcomed Nicholas II to the Kremlin with more bread and salt.[92] *"The sun was getting low,"* Francis Grenfell recalled, *"and the gilded domes of various churches in the Kremlin caught the rays and were a blaze of light."*[93] At the top of the stairs, Nicholas and Alexandra turned to the crowd below and bowed three times before disappearing inside. As they passed from view, guns thundered out a final 101 shots in salute and the Imperial Standard rose above the Grand Kremlin Palace.[94] Nicholas II, declared Henry LaPauze, had *"taken possession of the capital."*[95]

The first great event in the coronation festivities had ended. Worries over security had proved groundless; even the weather, so dismal and uncertain that first week of May, had cooperated in the triumphant spectacle. *"What there was to triumph about,"* Aylmer Maude complained, *"is not obvious."*[96] The pageantry left him cold. *"If the Government existed to compete with the circuses in giving shows to the people at the people's expense,"* he mused, *"it would all be easier to understand."*[97] Others, though, proved more susceptible to the extravaganza. "Western Europe," commented *The Times of London*, "has nothing to show at all comparable to the sustained splendor and long-drawn magnificence of the coronation of the Tsar. Splendid and lavish ceremonial has a significance and a value in Russia which Western nations understand only with an effort."[98] It had, thought Richard Harding Davis, been *"a picture of fairyland,"* an opulent *"dream"* marking *"the entry of the first gentleman in Europe."*[99]

The *"first gentleman,"* though, was unimpressed. Even at this supreme moment, he could not summon any enthusiasm. Nicholas confessed that he was *"secretly bored"* by the ceremonies and felt *"rather lonely in the midst of all the grandeur."*[100]

Chapter VII

At the end of a day filled with public processions and pageantry, Nicholas and Alexandra escaped to the privacy of the suburban Neskuchnoye Palace.[1] Set on a bend of the Moskva River and ringed by a large garden, the neoclassical palace offered the isolation they so treasured.[2] Here, between afternoon walks, cozy teas, and light-hearted family evenings, they fasted and prayed with an almost medieval devotion in advance of the coronation.[3]

Ceremonial obligations interrupted pious prayers as the mood shifted from symbolism to diplomacy. The day after the State Entrance, Nicholas and Alexandra returned to the Kremlin to receive members of the Extraordinary Embassies in another meticulously choreographed pageant of pomp and power. Flattering attentions surrounded Russia's only ally, France. Led by General Raoul Le Mouton de Boisdeffre, Chief of the General Staff of the French Army and the man who had negotiated the 1892 mutual defense treaty between Republican France and Imperial Russia, the mission from Paris had arrived in Moscow to a regal welcome. A detachment from the Pavlovsky Life Guards Regiment lined the railway siding, and the regimental orchestra played the two national anthems as arms were presented and salutes delivered. Such honors, usually reserved for visiting royalty, underlined the ties between the two countries.[4]

This Friday, Henry LaPauze stood outside of the former Sheremetiev Palace as gold-braided courtiers and gilded carriages arrived at the temporary French legation to collect his nation's representatives. Smartly attired in full dress uniforms, Count de Montebello, General de Boisdeffre, and other members of the French delegation set off for the Kremlin in style. They rode in court carriages manned by grooms specially dressed in liveries mirroring the French flag, with blue breeches, white waistcoats, and red and gold jackets.[5]

Arriving at the Grand Kremlin Palace, the French delegation ascended the wide, gray marble Parade Staircase between ranks of Chevalier Life Guards to the State Vestibule. Sunlight from a leaded glass dome poured over a monumental painting by Ilya Repin of Alexander III receiving peasant delegations during his coronation in 1883. The picture may have seemed an unfortunate comment on the republican nation, but their route was deliberate, a circuitous path designed to impress and inspire awe. They passed down the 200-foot length of the Hall of the Order of St. George, where a guard-of-honor from the Preobrazhensky Life Guards Regiment saluted beneath a vaulted ceiling hung with six immense gilt and ormolu chandeliers newly electrified for the coronation. A turn took them beneath the lofty pink, cream, and gold dome of the Hall of the Order of St. Alexander Nevsky, past a staggering array of gold plate shining in the sunlight; and into the palace's sanctum sanctorum, the blue and gold Hall of the Order of St. Andrei, its thrones sheltered beneath an elaborate canopy of cloth-of-gold and ermine set below a gilded sunburst ornamented with the Romanov Coat-of-Arms.[6]

Two silent members of the Abyssinian Guard opened doors to the adjoining Hall of the Order of St. Catherine as Grand Marshal of the Imperial Court Prince Alexander Dolgoruky tapped his ebony staff of office on the mahogany and rosewood floor to announce the delegation. Etiquette demanded that the diplomats make three deep bows or, for the republican French, incline their heads in respect: first at the threshold, then again at the center of the Hall, and finally when facing the dais, where Nicholas and Alexandra stood framed between columns of malachite and gold.[7] Formal congratulations were delivered, gifts presented, and diplomatic niceties exchanged to ensure friendly relations. Armed with the 1892 mutual defense treaty between their two countries

Opposite page: A newspaper drawing depicting Tsar Nicholas II, Empress Alexandra Feodorovna with their daughter Grand Duchess Olga Nikolaievna, and the Dowager Empress Marie Feodorovna.

The French Delegation to the Coronation.

and a promised state visit to Paris that autumn, the French delegates emerged triumphant, unknowingly having cemented the ties that would lead to an all-out European war in 1914.[8]

Those weeks in Moscow also cemented another unsuspected debacle looming on the horizon, the disastrous Russo-Japanese War. France might be Russia's only European ally, but these were ties to a republican country, a defensive agreement offering no opportunity for expansion. That chance, Nicholas was sure, lay in the Far East. By 1896, China, Korea, and Japan all seethed with intrigue and uncertainty. The first two were vulnerable and decrepit, but the Japanese Empire's sun was very much in the ascendant as her military and political system modernized. Nicholas used Japan's 1894 invasion of China to extend Russian influence. Alexander III had left his son a grand economic project: construction of the Trans-Siberian Railway from Moscow to Vladivostok. Russia now offered China protection in exchange for permission to continue the railway into Manchuria.[9]

"One of the dangerous features of the sovereign," said Nicholas II's Minister of War, *"is his love of mysterious countries."* No one was more responsible for this tendency than Prince Esper Ukhtomskii, who had accompanied the then Tsesarevich Nicholas on his Far Eastern tour.[10] Ukhtomskii, a scholar of Asian culture, insisted that Russia had a spiritual mission to fulfill in the Far East. *"In Asia, for us,"* Ukhtomskii wrote, *"there are in reality no borders, and there cannot be any other than those uncontrollable ones of the spirit of the Russian people....All the peoples of the Orient know the power of the White Tsar, at whose feet lies all of Asia."*[11] Nicholas actually believed Ukhtomskii's propaganda that Asia desired Russian subjugation. *"The Orient,"* the Prince declared, *"believes in us as far as we cherish the best of what was bequeathed to us by the past: Autocracy. Without this, Asia is not able sincerely to*

Neskuchnoye Palace.

love Russia and identify with it painlessly."¹²

Officials decried Ukhtomskii's influence over the impetuous and susceptible Nicholas II. The Minister of War blamed the Prince for inspiring *"fantasies of the greatness of the Russian Tsar as master of Asia,"* potent ideas that Nicholas accepted without question.¹³ During his Far Eastern tour Nicholas conflated imperialism with religious dogma, envisioning himself as theocratic leader for Asian peoples who loved God and revered an autocratic monarchy. It was a cocktail of lethal ambition and religiosity that now bubbled to the surface in negotiations over Russia's future role in Asia.

The Chinese Delegation to the Coronation.

"I wonder why Russia asked the Throne to send me?" mused Chinese diplomat Li Hung-Chang on his arrival in Moscow.¹⁴ Li Hung-Chang was being disingenuous: he knew that Russia needed a high-ranking Chinese emissary to enter into secret talks. The Russian Government went out of its way to win him over, filling his temporary lodgings with exquisite works of art, porcelain, antique furniture, and exotic flowers: some £4,000 (£400,000 or $540,000 in 2014 terms) alone was spent on the decoration of a single room.¹⁵

Meetings with Nicholas II left the elderly Chinese diplomat unimpressed; he thought the Emperor *"a small man to rule a great Empire."* Deeming him *"pale and listless,"* Li Hung-Chang concluded that Nicholas rarely set foot outside his palaces for fear of assassination, while he was sure that Alexandra was *"a good woman as well as a good Empress"* merely by looking at her face.¹⁶ He bowed to Nicholas, but neglected to kiss Alexandra's outstretched hand. The Imperial couple's looks of embarrassment turned to pleasure, though, when he placed a large jade ring – a gift from the Dowager Empress of China – into Alexandra's hand instead. Sliding it onto her finger, she reached out to show the diplomat, and an excited Li Hung-Chang fell to his knees and grasped both of her hands in his own.¹⁷

Deriding *"all this western flattery,"* Li-Hung Chang was nevertheless impressionable enough to negotiate away important concessions. Russia would be allowed to build railroads across Manchuria; Tsarist

Chinese diplomat Li-Hung Chang.

The Japanese Delegation to the Coronation.

soldiers would later use the lines to mass along the Korean Peninsula. In exchange for this Russian incursion, he walked away with a substantial personal bribe and forced loans for China.[18]

Fearing such developments, Japan used the festivities in Moscow to exert their own claims in the Far East. General Prince Fushimi Sadanaru and Extraordinary Ambassador Field Marshal Marquis Yamagata Aritomo offered congratulations from Emperor Meiji, whom Nicholas had briefly met during his visit to Japan in 1891, but spent most of their time locked in secret meetings with Russian Foreign Minister Prince Andrei Lobanov-Rostovsky. For them, the fate of Korea was at stake. Finding the Russians amenable to destabilization of the country, Japan signed a secret agreement with Lobanov-Rostovsky essentially carving the Korean Peninsula into spheres of respective influence. These concessions convinced Nicholas II he could pursue his expansionist policies in the Far East without fear of Japanese retaliation.[19]

Korea, the third of the Far Eastern players in Moscow, knew nothing of these negotiations but suspected everything. Ambassador Extraordinary Min Yông-hwan arrived in the city seeking protection for his country against Japanese incursions, but soon heard talk of Korean partition. Despite friendly assurances from Lobanov-Rostovsky, Min was certain the Russians were lying. Nicholas II did his best to avoid Min altogether, trying to limit their contact to a formal reception on May 10, but the Korean statesman uncomfortably pressed the issue. *"No, no!"* Nicholas insisted when asked about Korean partition; but the Emperor was also lying, aware that his government was doing precisely as the ambassador feared.[20]

The Russians seemed to go out of their ways to belittle Min and his country. Min spoke no Russian, and relied on translator Kim To-il to offer his congratulations. Kim caused offense when he referred to Marie Feodorovna as *"the Emperor's mum."* Nervous and agitated, Min stumbled through his congratulatory speech before presenting Korea's gifts to the Imperial couple: a two-tiered, purple shell box, two embroidered screens, two brass braziers, four bamboo blinds, four floral mats, and four hand-painted hanging scrolls. *"These might pass for a present from a private Korean to a*

The Korean Delegation to the Coronation.

private Russian," an official complained. *"But as a gift of a King to an Emperor they are shamefully poor."*[21] Then there was the matter of the actual Coronation ceremony. Knowing that Min desperately wanted to attend, Russian officials callously toyed with him. He could witness the crowning, they said, but only if he removed his formal headdress, an act of submission in Korean culture. Representatives from China, Persia, and the Ottoman Empire, Min was told, agreed to comply with this rule. When he reluctantly conceded, the Russians withdrew the invitation altogether, explaining that tradition dictated that only Christians be allowed inside the Cathedral of the Assumption. They had lied merely to humiliate, and Min never forgot the affront. The following year, attending Queen Victoria's Diamond Jubilee, he ordered a formal morning suit and had his hair cut to ensure a place at the ceremony.[22]

Diplomats preoccupied with secret negotiations gave way to renewed public spectacle as the week unfolded. Religious rite though it was, the coronation and its attendant ceremonies also allowed official Russia to wallow in intricate ceremonial. Even an event as mundane as distribution of Coronation proclamations, a tradition that dated back to the 1724 crowning of Peter the Great's second wife Catherine as Empress, was wrapped in carefully orchestrated splendor.[23]

Armed with the parchments, Masters of Ceremonies rode across the city in gilded carriages, each accompanied by four Assistant Masters of Ceremonies, two Secretaries of State, and grooms in scarlet and gold liveries. An Adjutant-General, two Adjutants, and two Lieutenant-General-Adjutants galloped on horses sporting ostrich plumes and gold saddlecloths embroidered with double-headed eagles; two squadrons from the Chevalier Guards and two from the *Gardes á Cheval*, in white uniforms and silver cuirasses, provided a military guard.[24]

The Russian Court deemed this martial display a necessary adjunct to the Imperial Heralds, who offered an unintended comic burst amid outward sobriety. Sitting atop snow-white horses, the Heralds looked as if they had stepped from the pages of Charles Perault's *Puss in Boots*. Nearly every inch of their golden brocade dalmatics, gold moiré *beshmets* or tunics, and loose trousers in the Romanov House colors of gold, black, and white silk, bristled with colored fringes, tassels, embroidered heraldic emblems, and double-headed eagles sewn in silk thread, embellishments in keeping with their manufacture in the St. Petersburg workshops of the Imperial Theatre. Gold, black, and white ostrich feathers waved from their flamboyant, wide-brimmed red suede and felt hats. Even their red and gold Moroccan leather and suede boots, embroidered in gold thread, sported gilded spurs engraved with double-eagles.[25]

The same sense of theatricality extended to the ceremony itself as these picturesque corteges spread across Moscow. At each stop, State Trumpeters and

Heralds reading the Imperial proclamation announcing the Coronation of Tsar Nicholas II.

Kettle-Drummers, necks draped in gold, black, and white silk scarves, blared salutes as Heralds took illuminated parchments from gold-fringed crimson velvet bags adorned with ormolu double-headed eagles and read the proclamations:[26]

A beautiful poster heralding the upcoming Coronation of Tsar Nicholas II.

Our Most August, Most High, and Most Autocratic Sovereign, The Great Emperor Nicholas Alexandrovich, having acceded to the Hereditary Throne of the Empire of Russia, and of the Kingdom of Poland, and the Grand Duchy of Finland, which are inseparable there from, has deigned to Order, after the example of the Most Pious Sovereigns His Glorious Ancestors, that the Holy Ceremony of the Coronation and Anointment of His Imperial Majesty should, with the Help of the Almighty, take place on the 14th day of May; furthermore, His Majesty has commanded that His August Spouse, The Empress Alexandra Feodorovna, should participate in this Holy Function. By the present proclamation this solemnity is announced to all the Faithful Subjects of His Majesty, in order that on this ardently desired day, they may raise their most fervent prayers to the King of Kings, so that of His Unfailing Grace He may deign to Bless His Majesty's Reign, and preserve the public peace and tranquility to the Greater Glory of His Holy Name and the unalterable Prosperity of the Empire.[27]

Thus Moscow learned, as if there had been any doubt, that the coronation would soon take place.

"*The display was very imposing and interesting,*" observed John Logan, who witnessed the proclamation in Red Square, "*and highly successful in all respects save the reading, which was scarcely a first class elocutionary effort.*"[28] The quality of reading was not, however, the only thing that was wrong. The parchments, with illuminated borders by Ivan Petrov-Ropet and lithographed text in gold, were "*objects of much desire.*"[29] Deprived of any opportunity to share in the festivities, people wanted some tangible reminder of the event and its profligate expense and the parchments became prized souvenirs. Logan saw no copies distributed at all in Red Square, and paid some enterprising Muscovite 2 rubles for the one he eventually secured.[30] He was lucky, for there were "*epic battles*" over these sheets of paper.[31] People climbed onto carriages and surrounded horses, ripping parchments from the hands of startled officials and terrified Heralds. One angry crowd overturned a coach, pulled out its velvet upholstery, and pried off its carved and gilded cherubs; at another stop, they attacked the gold-braided courtiers, tearing epaulettes and medals from uniforms.[32] Francis Grenfell viewed these scenes as "*people fought for the copies*" as amusing entertainment, but the riots were not so lighthearted for the eighteen people crushed to death that day in the struggles.[33] The Government suppressed word of what had happened; the deaths of these unfortunate, nameless victims, it decided in an ominous taste of events to come, must not be allowed to cast a shadow over the celebrations.[34]

Aristocratic Moscow unknowingly celebrated while families of the eighteen victims collected their battered and bloody dead. With unfortunate, ironic timing, the city's fashionable society organized a charity bazaar to raise funds for the poor. *"Delicately scented, dressed in silks and satins, with beautiful jewels and ornaments, white kid gloves and expensive headdress,"* Aylmer Maude reported in disgust, these ladies spent a minor fortune adorning their hall with fresh flowers and elaborate garlands to welcome their wealthy friends. A few sold glasses of champagne at outrageous prices; others stood over booths offering vases, paintings, bits of lace, and other *"more or less useless knick-knacks."* The several thousand rubles eventually raised for the poor merely paid for the cost of staging this benefit. It was, said Maude, a complete waste of time, another example of the hypocritically selfish attitudes justified through the coronation festivities.[35]

The Hall of the Order of St. Andrei in the Grand Kremlin Palace.

The afternoon of Saturday, May 11, offered another piece of theatre with the blessing of the Imperial State Banner. Much time and money had been lavished on this symbolic representation of Nicholas II's dominion over his Empire. Nuns at Moscow's Novodievechy Convent spent months embroidering the banner's gold brocade field with coats-of-arms and double-headed eagles in colored silk threads, while famed jeweler Peter Karl Fabergé created its staff of chased gold topped with a gilded double-headed eagle.[36]

The Imperial Family, foreign royal guests, and members of the Imperial Suite crowded into the Hall of the Order of St. Andrei in the Grand Kremlin Palace for the ceremonial blessing, watching as officers and ranks of priests solemnly escorted the Banner to the canopied dais at the west end of the St Andrei Hall. Father Ioann Yanishev, Personal Confessor to the Imperial couple, sprinkled the standard with holy water and led the assembly in prayers as a choir sang *God is With Us*, a martial, militaristic hymn in keeping with the Banner's symbolic role.[37] Yanishev's prayer was a call to obedience:

Most Pious Sovereign! Divine Providence has entrusted You, by virtue of the law of succession to the Throne, Autocratic Leader of the Peoples of the Russian Empire, with this Holy Standard, symbol of the unity and of the power of the Nation. We pray to the Heavenly Father that this Standard will unite all peoples in boundless loyalty to the Throne and the Motherland, and in the devoted fulfillment of patriotic duty. Redoubtable to the enemies of Russia, may this Standard be for You a Sign of God's Protection, which will help You against all obstacles, bravely to lead Your People in His Name and in the Orthodox Faith, in well-being and justice, to prosperity, greatness, and glory. Let the People know that God is with You![38]

He ended with an appeal to the Emperor: *"May the Lord God Help Us, under this newly Consecrated Banner, to follow the Path of Truth firmly and steadfastly in all things, for the benefit of the State and the Good of the People. And may we all be delivered from the snares of vanity and return to simplicity and sincerity in aims and tasks. Great*

The Duke of Edinburgh and Saxe-Coburg and Gotha

Prince Arthur, Duke of Connaught.

things are achieved by simple means and it is not vanity that leads to glory."[39]

Queen Victoria turned seventy-seven that Sunday. The Bishop of Peterborough presided over a special Anglican service, using his sermon to draw unlikely parallels between British reverence for the elderly Victoria and what he believed to be Russia's unbounded love for its own young sovereign. Creighton's adoration for his monarch flowed unchecked, rising to such heights that Victoria's son Arthur, Duke of Connaught, was moved to tears.[40] Nicholas and Alexandra presided over a celebratory luncheon for the Queen's visiting relatives, and that night British Ambassador Sir Nicholas O'Conor gave a dinner marking the occasion.[41] Nicholas and Alexandra, in retreat, did not attend, but seventy-seven others – many of the Queen's descendants, including her two sons Alfred and Arthur and a dozen of her grandchildren – sat down at tables in the Morozov Mansion's white and gold ballroom. Between toasts to her grandmother the Queen and to her brother-in-law the Emperor, Princess Victoria of Battenberg dominated the room with her *"amazingly clever and well-informed"* conversation.[42]

The following afternoon, another piece of ritualized pomp unfolded as courtiers transferred the Imperial Regalia

Prince Louis and Princess Victoria of Battenberg.

from the Armory to the Grand Kremlin Palace. All the outward symbols of sovereignty were marshaled to envelope the Emperor in an aura of majestic power. Most important was that supreme symbol of sovereignty, the crown. Nicholas toyed with using the fabled Cap of Monomakh at his coronation. Its history was heroic, its alleged associations with Byzantium and with medieval Russia were evocative and, at a mere two pounds, the little sable-fringed hat would rest easy on his head.[43] Grand Duke Konstantin found the idea absurdly sacrilegious. *"How,"* he quizzed his sister Queen Olga of Greece, *"could Nicky be installed with the Cap of Monomakh? After all, we've been an Empire for almost two-hundred years....One cannot repudiate history."*[44]

The Grand Duke need not have worried: tradition forced Nicholas to use the Imperial State Crown. Created by Swiss-born Court Jeweler Jérémie Posier for the coronation of Catherine the Great in 1762, it was modeled on crowns used by Holy Roman Emperors and shimmered with more than 5,000 diamonds. Two hemispheres, entirely covered in diamonds, were set within a silver framework of palms, oak leaves, acorns, and garlands. Bands of perfectly matched pearls circled the base and arched over these hemispheres between twenty-eight large diamonds, rising to a diamond cross set with an uncut ruby of 415 carats, bought in 1676 by the Russian Ambassador in Peking as a gift for Tsar Alexei. It was a work of blinding brilliance, its 5,000 diamonds totaling some 3,000 carats.[45] It was also, at nine pounds, exceptionally heavy. The crown would rest atop the sensitive scar Nicholas bore from the sword attack against him in Japan; to cushion the weight, a padded red velvet lining was added.[46]

The Imperial State Crown glowed with magnificent,

The Imperial Regalia.

privileged power, but a coronation ceremony also invested the sovereign with another half-dozen representations of symbolic authority. The Emperor would wield two additional pieces of regalia once he was crowned and enthroned. Made for the coronation of Catherine the Great, the Imperial Scepter represented judicial rule over the Empire in the form of a long rod of chased and burnished gold. Divided into three sections by bands of double diamonds, it was topped by the fabled 193-carat Orlov Diamond and a golden, double-headed eagle. Catherine had also commissioned the Imperial Orb. A highly polished ball of red gold, circled by double rows of diamonds and surmounted by a diamond cross holding a 47-carat oval sapphire from Ceylon, the Orb symbolized the Emperor's dominion as a Christian sovereign over the world. One adjutant would hold the diamond-encrusted Sword of State, added by Alexander II for his coronation in 1856, and another, the gold and diamond State Seal. Around his shoulders, Nicholas would wear one final piece of regalia, the Diamond Chain of the Russian Order of St. Andrei. Named for the Russian heraldic award, the chain alternated jeweled double-headed eagles with diamond emblems of the order, and would replace one of simpler design Nicholas would wear when he entered the Cathedral.[47]

Use of an Imperial Mantle to clothe the Emperor *"in glory and righteousness"* remained consistent from reign to reign, though each coronation demanded new robes.[48] Three identical mantles for Nicholas II, Empress Alexandra, and Marie Feodorovna were created in 1896, designed by A. Trombitsky of St. Petersburg and assembled in the Imperial capital by the famed couturier Madame Olga Bulbenkova, who held a warrant as dressmaker to the Russian Court. Of

A portrait of Empress Alexandra Feodorovna wearing Coronation robe and regalia.

heavy gold brocade woven with black double-headed eagles in the Sapoznikhov Factory, each of the twenty-one-foot-long mantles was lined with white silk and edged with ermine supplied by furrier Paul Sorokumovsky & Sons of St. Petersburg; in all 897 ermine pelts adorned these robes. During processions, pages used seven small silk straps beneath the ermine borders, three along each side and one at the rear, to maneuver the robes – a necessity as each weighed twenty-eight pounds.[49]

Unlike her husband, Alexandra would be invested only with an Imperial Mantle, a smaller Diamond Chain of the Order of St. Andrei, and a new Consort's Crown.[50] Created as a smaller version of the Imperial State Crown, the Consort's Crown was first worn by Empress Marie Feodorovna at the 1797 coronation of her husband Emperor Paul, and by all subsequent empresses thereafter. Two Empresses, though, would be present for the coronation in 1896: etiquette demanded that the Dowager Empress appear throughout the service in the original Consort's Crown bestowed on her by Alexander III in 1883, just as Alexandra would receive her crown from her husband. To solve this dilemma, the Imperial Court commissioned a new Consort's Crown for Alexandra from Court jeweler Kurt Hahn. Identical to the 1797 original, this small crown, encrusted with some 2,000 perfectly matched diamonds from South Africa, cost 76,200 rubles ($1,029,000, or £762,000 in 2013), making it the single most expensive item created for the Coronation.[51]

Tradition demanded that the Regalia be moved with as much ceremony as had greeted its arrival in the city. Bells rang out announcing the "solemn" event to all of Moscow as members of the Golden Grenadiers Regiment, sporting tall gilded helmets copied from those worn by Frederick the Great's soldiers, escorted the regalia along a crimson carpet from treasury to palace. Masters of Ceremonies and military generals carried the precious pieces on specially woven cushions of gold, black, and white velvet, in ascending order of importance, from the lowest diamond-encrusted military award to the massive Imperial State Crown. Courtiers carefully arranged this staggering array of bejeweled splendor in the Hall of the Order of St. Andrei on a table draped with golden cloth edged in ermine; ropes of silver chain, clutched in the beaks of silver eagles atop silver posts, guarded the display.⁵² To this the Imperial Court added its own absurd touch. Every now and then, an elderly man clambered across the floor on his hands and knees like a dog, up one row of the soldiers guarding the table then down the other to silently polish their boots.⁵³

Dowager Empress Marie Feodorovna wearing Coronation robe and regalia.

Similarly comic scenes took place as Count Keller put his pupils from the *Corps des Pages* through their paces in the Kremlin's Palace of Facets. Prince Alexander Dolgoruky, Master of Ceremonies, instructed them on maneuvering and arranging the heavy Imperial mantles. Alexander Mandryk played Nicholas II, Alexei Ignatiev stood in for Alexandra, and Boris Engelhardt took the role of his mistress the Dowager Empress. Draped in *"robes of thick canvas, several yards long,"* to simulate the mantles, they walked through rooms and up and down staircases as their comrades practiced carrying the cumbersome cloths around doorways and across floors. The Imperial couple's personal pages then told them of the expected maneuvers; Alexei Ignatiev had to deliver his report in French as Alexandra was still not proficient in Russian.⁵⁵ Alexander Mandryk, attached to Nicholas, found him *"a dear, well-intentioned, and fascinating human being, who treated me with great attentiveness and kindness."* Alexandra, in contrast, *"always seemed cold, even in those moments when she was making a conscious effort to be kind and hospitable."*⁵⁶

Twilight fell over Moscow. Workers scurried over Cathedral Square, hanging last minute decorations, sweeping cobbles, and laying down crimson carpets as officials moved through tribunes, placing names and numbered cards on seats reserved for dignitaries. Anticipating the following day's coronation, a crowd swarmed around the Kremlin; when Nicholas and Alexandra arrived to spend the night, their landau could barely pass through the streets.⁵⁷ The Imperial couple prayed in the Kremlin's Church of the Savior Behind the Golden Gate and dined with the Dowager Empress before Father Ioann Yanishev heard their confessions. *"May the Merciful Lord God come to our aid,"* Nicholas wrote in his diary, *"may He give us strength tomorrow and bless our life and peaceful work."*⁵⁸

Chapter VIII

After months of anticipation and weeks of worry, coronation day finally arrived. Tuesday, May 14 broke over Moscow in a brilliant sunrise. *"There was not a single cloud,"* recalled Grand Duke Konstantin Konstantinovich. *"The shrill cry of swallows could be heard, soaring high up in a blue sky."*[1] Moscow awoke *"merry and animated,"* said Henry LaPauze, anxious and excited.[2] By six the streets and squares around the Kremlin were already crowded as *"a blazing sun poured torrents of light and heat"* across the city. Twenty-one shots boomed out from the Kremlin, joined by church bells in *"a lovely medley of sound"* summoning the city to greet the momentous day.[3] That morning, a poet wrote in commemoration, two distinct beings – man and God – would be inextricably fused together when Nicholas II was crowned.[4]

Moscow stirred from its unsettled slumber. Lacking great wealth or court connections, Kate Koon had assumed she would have to make do with hearing second-hand accounts of the ceremonies. The night before, though, Clifton Breckinridge had descended on the American visitors armed with heavy vellum invitations embossed with double-headed eagles in gold:

By Order of His Majesty the Emperor the Chief Grand Master of Ceremonies has the honor to inform Mademoiselle Koon that Tuesday, the 14th of May, is the day of the Solemnity of the Coronation and of the Consecration of Their Imperial Majesties. Mademoiselle Koon is invited to the tribune on the Cathedral Square at the Kremlin. Arrive at 8:15 in the morning by the steps of the Winter Garden of the Palace of the Kremlin.[5]

A courtier followed, handing over little cards with *"explicit instructions"* for appropriate dress.[6] This, as the ladies discovered, demanded gowns with décolleté necklines, long white gloves, and aigrettes in the hair. The words *"Court Train"* sent Kate into a panic. She quickly unpacked her most elaborate dress and its twelve-foot, shoulder hung train, smoothing out the blue satin adorned with pink poppies and flounces of tulle, and hoping that the wrinkles would disappear by morning.[7]

Invitations meant early mornings: *"Breakfast at six o'clock, and maids and valets in attendance at four,"* as one lady recalled. Some guests simply sat up all night, holding impromptu dances or playing endless games of cards to ensure that they were on time.[8] The Americans slept little. Tossing and turning in her room at the Hotel Dresden, an excited Emily Roebling duly rose a little after four that morning.[9] Across town, Kate Koon crept to her bedroom window and saw *"the promise of a glorious, warm day."* After another anxious, restless hour, she finally woke her sister Lou.[10]

Preparation was frenzied. Maids served an early breakfast and the Americans ate voraciously, warned that their next meal would not come until late afternoon. *"Everyone was to display everything in the way of full dress which he or she possessed,"* John Logan recalled, and the only full-length mirror in the house was *"much in demand."* Finally, just before seven, they heard carriages arriving in the dusty courtyard, and Logan helped the ladies into the waiting vehicles, pushing and tucking their trains – *"corpulent bundles of silk and satin"* – into the crowded compartment before finally setting off.[11]

Opposite page: A very detailed drawing of Tsar Nicholas II and Empress Alexandra Feodorovna during the Coronation. One can recognized to Nicholas' right his brother Grand Duke Michael Alexandrovich. To the Tsar's left is his uncle Grand Duke Vladimir Alexandrovich, Surrounding empress Alexandra Feodorovna are Grand Dukes Paul and Sergei Alexandrovich. Looking in the distance, standing under the dais is the Dowager Empress Marie Feodorovna.

Badges like this one were given to those invited to attend the ceremony.

All foreign guests first stopped at the Turkish Embassy, to follow Ambassador Zia Husny Pasha – senior member of the diplomatic corps – in procession to the Kremlin.[12] Standing outside the Legation a few minutes before seven, Ian Malcolm watched the *"brilliant sight"* as *"the state coaches of the different countries and the smart equipages of the foreign diplomats circulated up and down the street."*[13] Louis Gustave de Montebello and his wife arrived in a gilded coach trailing Gallic splendor, their grooms adorned in a new variation on the *Tricoleur* consisting of red velvet breeches, blue velvet jackets, and white Tricorn hats with gold and white plumes. The Countess was *"ravishing"* in a gown of cream-colored satin embroidered in pearl-studded palm fronds.[14] A little before eight, the diplomats finally set off, through a city whose very air, said Logan, *"was charged with electricity."*[15]

Double lines of soldiers struggled to clear the roadways for passing carriages.[16] The processions gave Muscovites brief glimpses of the pageantry reserved for privileged eyes. There were cheers but also jealous shouts as the vehicles drove to the Kremlin. *"We shall have to wait till all the guests who have come from a distance are provided for before there is any room for us!"* some yelled. An interpreter assured the Bishop of Peterborough that the public simply wanted the foreigners to enjoy the day.[17] The words, though, exemplified the alienation many of the Emperor's common subjects clearly felt at being ignored and deprived of any part in the festivities.

"The high banks of the Kremlin," reported Richard Harding Davis, *"the streets around it, the bridges and open squares, and the shores of the river that cuts Moscow in two, were black with the people who had spent the night in the open air."*[18] Henry LaPauze was entranced by *"the emerald of its bell towers, the sparkle of its gilded domes"* against the blue Moscow sky as they rolled through the complex, past walls draped with fluttering Imperial Standards and ranks of uniformed soldiers.[19] A distracted coachman delivered Kate and Lou Koon to the wrong gate. Their invitations allowed them inside the citadel, but they had no idea where to go, and no one spoke English. With bundled trains over their arms, they pushed through crowds of plainly dressed women, feeling *"rather odd being so overdressed"* themselves, before an official came to their rescue.[20] Finally, Masters of Ceremony in white and gold costumes with plumed, cocked hats pointed with ebony wands to the coveted stands.[21]

Ian Malcolm thought the transformed Cathedral Square seemed like some gigantic set from *Lohengrin*.[22] State Trumpeters stood along the Grand Kremlin Palace's terrace, instruments *"shining in the sun like burnished gold,"*[23] ready to blare out salutes. A scarlet-robed court orchestra filled one corner, *"playing soft and sensuous strains,"* including V. I. Glavatch's official *Coronation March*, an unequivocal paean to the autocracy:

> *Glory to the dawn of Joy!*
> *Glory to the Orthodox Holiday!*
> *Glory to the Autocratic Throne of the Tsar of All Russia!*
> *Glory, glory, glory to the Reigning Couple!*[24]

A view of the Moscow Kremlin at the time of the Coronation. To the left of the Ivan the Great Bell Tower is the Cathedral of the Assumption. This structure is followed by the Cathedral of the Archangel, the Cathedral of the Annunciation and the corner of the Grand Kremlin Palace. The open space between Ivan the Great's Bell Tower and the various cathedrals is known as Cathedral Square.

An elevated walkway covered in crimson velvet and railed by a white balustrade stretched from the bottom of the Red Staircase to the Cathedral of the Assumption's southern door.[25] More red carpet flowed to the Cathedrals of the Archangel Michael and the Annunciation, sectioning off the square; along its length stood Chevalier Guards in white uniforms, crimson cuirasses with the Cross of St. Andrei, eagle-topped helmets, and broadswords held in rigid salute.[26] Behind and between them crowded soldiers, nobles, merchants, bureaucrats, and peasant delegates; when they removed their hats, said journalist Arthur Sykes, *"the forest of brown heads of hair resembled nothing so much as a gigantic swarm of bees."*[27]

By eight the tribunes were nearly full. Rising in tiers and draped in white, black and gold velvet, their ornately carved columns supported roofs bedecked with double-headed eagles flanked by waving ostrich plumes. They transformed Cathedral Square into a vast arena. Ian Malcolm found his seat in the same tribune where the Golitsyns had secured a place for Mary Hickley, on the eastern side of the square directly opposite the Red Staircase.[28] Kate Koon thought that the seats given to the Americans, in an open stand to the side of the Red Staircase, were *"the best place in the entire Kremlin."* Staring across the battlements, she could barely make out *"the hazy green"* of the surrounding countryside.[29] Emily Roebling disagreed about the seating, for more prosaic reasons: wearing a heavy evening gown, and with only a tiara and feathers to shield her face, she wondered how she would endure several hours beneath the hot sun.[30] The only relief would come at eleven, when liveried footmen handed around sandwiches, pastries, champagne, and refreshing ice cream.[31]

Looking around the tribunes, John Logan saw *"a blaze of glory. Jewels without number and without price bedecking women as fair as a poet's dream could paint them,"* mingled with *"brilliant uniforms, flashing with decorations and putting the rainbow to shame for variety and splendor of color."* Diaphanous veils cascaded from the traditional *kokoshniks* of aristocratic Russian ladies, clad in court gowns of crimson or emerald green embroidered in gold. Young Maids-of-Honor, gowned in virginal white with red velvet trains, clustered in another stand next to uniformed

The Emir of Bokhara (at center) surrounded by members of his delegation.

officers. Sunshine poured down upon the *"solid masses of gold"* bedecking courtiers, and bounced back off diamond aigrettes, crescents, tiaras, and stars, in dazzling, blinding shards of brilliance.[33]

It was, everyone agreed, *"the most interesting crowd imaginable."*[34] Mary Hickley admired the *"barbaric splendor"* of chiefs from Central Asia, their robes a *"shimmering, shining mass of rainbow colors and jewels."*[35] One stand seemed full of exotically costumed men: *"There were Persians,"* Kate wrote, *"each wearing a black fez; Turks with their red ones; Bokharans with white or colored turbans;"* and members of the Korean delegation, *"with the queerest black headdresses."*[36] The Emir of Bokhara cut a spectacular figure in a purple silk caftan and turban studded with jewels. Nearby sat Li-Hung Chang, *"conspicuous in a yellow jacket"* and little hat adorned with a waving peacock feather.[37] After several hours, the elderly diplomat found the hot Moscow sun too much of a strain and disappeared into the palace, but Kate struck up a friendly conversation with several men in his suite. *"They seemed very nice,"* she said, *"and spoke English beautifully."*[38]

Nicholas II and Alexandra Feodorovna entering the Assumption Cathedral.

Charles Moisson, Lumiere's chief cine engineer, stood on a plinth with his young assistant François Doublier, armed with sixty-foot long rolls of celluloid and a Kinematophone camera to film the processions to and from the Cathedral.[39] The twenty reporters selected to witness the ceremony in the Cathedral of the Assumption had arrived early that morning. Richard Harding Davis, who thanks to his own wheeler-dealing was one of two American reporters granted a place in the church, spent the better part of an hour passing through checkpoints, showing one ticket to get past the lines of police and soldiers; another to enter the Kremlin; a third to reach Cathedral Square; and a forth before he was finally admitted to the Cathedral.[40] The remaining journalists reported from a tribune built along the side of the Cathedral of the Archangel Michael overlooking the square, notebooks and pens ready to record details of the great day.[41] An enthusiastic Therese Vianzone – the rare female journalist among the group – was happy when her French comrade Henry LaPauze shared his impressions of events in the church.[42]

The journalists, artists and designers who worked at the Coronation.

Just 200 yards separated the Grand Kremlin Palace from the Cathedral of the Assumption yet the Imperial Court deemed it necessary that anyone entitled to an ounce of gold braid on his uniform be on display. A thunder of artillery at half-past eight announced the first of more than fifty processions.[43] Accompanied by a fanfare of trumpets and the roll of kettledrums, a group of pages marched down the Red Staircase, between ranks of Chevalier Guards and followed by footmen in crimson liveries, military officials, and two-dozen Masters of Ceremony in an opening salvo of splendor.[44] Representatives and delegations from across the Empire followed. *"We wondered,"* said Kate Koon, *"how the small church was going to hold all of them, together with the royal guests who had not yet gone in. The question was soon solved, for by watching another side door we could see the two processions file out."*[45]

The Cathedral's confining walls, crowded by the invited congregation, necessitated this bit of stagecraft.[46] Built in 1479 by Italian architects for Ivan III, the whitewashed church nestled beneath five newly gilded onion domes. Red velvet –sewn with crowns, double-headed eagles, and laurel wreaths in gold thread – cloaked the lower walls; above, frescoed saints daubed *"in dark blues and reds and greens"* rose against shimmering gold to a vaulted ceiling hung with solid silver chandeliers weighing 800 pounds.[47] Pearls, rubies, emeralds, and diamonds glistened in an iconostasis, sheathed in five tons of gold leaf, shielding the sanctuary.[48] *"Here,"* enthused a visitor, *"is the real Russia…ancient Muscovy."*[49] Aylmer Maude, though, had a starkly different view. The small, dark Cathedral, he

The Red Staircase.

thought, perfectly reflected a religiously medieval Autocratic system that *"shut out the light of Heaven."*[50]

Rising in tiers and covered in crimson velvet sewn with the Imperial couple's monograms and double-headed eagles in gold, wooden stands ringed three sides of the Cathedral.[51] Here, in keeping with Orthodox tradition that it was disrespectful to sit in the presence of God, the thousand guests would stand for five hours. This had always been an ordeal. In 1883, when a diplomat's wife complained to the newly crowned Marie Feodorovna, the Empress was *"quite indifferent"* to the discomfort. *"Evidently she didn't think it was of the slightest consequence whether we were tired or not."*[52] Nor had Marie Feodorovna been any more sympathetic to Grand Duchess Marie Pavlovna, wife of Grand Duke Vladimir Alexandrovich. Recovering from a serious illness at the time of Alexander III's Coronation, Marie Pavlovna had asked if she might have a folding chair available nearby in case she felt faint. The Empress, already at daggers-drawn with her sister-in-law, refused, selfishly declaring that she herself *"had to stand all the time, too."*[53]

An artist's rendering of Emperor Nicholas II and Empress Alexandra Feodorovna walking up the Red Staircase.

Four huge columns, wrapped in red velvet, edged a central, crimson-covered dais facing the iconostasis. Above hung a canopy of crimson velvet embellished with gold thread, fringe, tassels, and plumes of gold, black, and white ostrich feathers.[54] Reached by twelve broad steps and ringed by a gilded balustrade, the dais – *"no bigger than the stage of a New York theatre"* as Richard Harding Davis aptly described it – would become the very epicenter of the Russian Empire that day.[55]

The congregation would stand, but the monarchs would sit on this dais in three thrones, visible expression of semi-divine status. Nicholas II would use the Ivory Throne of Ivan the Terrible, a high-backed open armchair entirely covered with carved ivory panels showing Biblical scenes. According to legend, Zoe Paleologue had brought it from Constantinople on her marriage to Ivan III – ties to Byzantine rule that appealed to Nicholas's theocratic conception of his rule. Alexandra would sit upon the Throne of Michael Feodorovich, created for the first Romanov Tsar and faced with panels of chased gold set with rubies, sapphires, and pearls. The Dowager Empress would watch from the Diamond Throne of Tsar Alexei Mikhailovich, its surface covered with gold and silver panels adorned with some 870 diamonds. For comfort, all three thrones had been cushioned in crimson brocade woven at the Sapoznikhov Factory in Moscow and sewn with the Imperial monograms in gold silk thread.[56]

From his spot in the Cathedral's northeastern corner, Francis Grenfell had *"a perfect view of the thrones."*[57] Vividly attired in his golden cope and glittering miter, the Bishop of Peterborough found a prominent place to the right of the dais that the Catholic British Ambassador Sir Nicholas O'Conor had sought to deny him.[58] Journalists were quick to note his *"weird manner of dress, which attracted much attention and added a discordant note in the Cathedral."*[59]

The twenty correspondents selected to witness the crowning jostled for position near the eastern wall, some delighted, some perturbed, by views both panoramic and, for those behind the columns, restricted.⁶⁰ Anxious to create favorable impressions, they sported an odd array of military uniforms, frock coats, and evening dress, *"which at that hour of the morning,"* said Richard Harding Davis, *"made them look as though they had been up all night."*⁶¹ French artist Henri Gerveux and Danish Court painter Laurits Regner Tuxen stood in a corner, sketching the scene for monumental canvases they would later paint.⁶² The congregation watched through the clouds of incense as priests conducted a *Te Deum*.⁶³ All members of the clergy wore new robes, miters, collars, and stoles of gold and silk brocade adorned with gems, copied from Seventeenth Century models displayed in the Kremlin Armory.⁶⁴

An artist's rendering of Emperor Nicholas II and Empress Alexandra Feodorovna kissing during the Coronation ceremony.

Anticipation filled the Cathedral; across the square, anxiety reigned in the palace. The young men serving as Kammer Pages had been up since four. Fearing hunger, they wolfed down cold meat, ham, bread, coffee, and tea in a gluttonous frenzy before donning their stiff uniforms. Then it was on to a barber, to have their hair arranged in the embarrassing, delicate waves demanded by tradition, before rushing to the start of their ceremonial duties.⁶⁵

Fourteen-year-old Grand Duchess Olga Alexandrovna was having her own bad hair day. A hairdresser interrupted her breakfast to curl her bangs into an unbecoming fringe to support her white *kokoshnik*. Then she hurried off to don her light blue Russian Court gown adorned with satin roses. Hungry and hot, she found the dress *"heavy and wearisome."*⁶⁶ Her brother Michael, *"hurrying me all the time,"* dragged her along to join the rest of the Imperial Family waiting in the State Drawing Room.⁶⁷

The Dowager Empress was, as usual, too preoccupied to worry over her younger children. The day of her son's coronation was an emotional ordeal. Her participation in ceremonies felt like a *"great sacrifice." "I would always have reproached myself,"* she confided to her mother Queen Louise of Denmark, *"if I had not been there,"* but she made little effort to disguise her feelings as the day progressed.⁶⁸

When Kammer Pages Deruzhinsky and Boris Engelhardt entered her rooms at half-past eight, they found Marie Feodorovna a statue of splendor.⁶⁹ She wore a Russian Court gown of silver brocade ornamented with designs in silver thread and sewn with pearls; hairdressers had already pinned the Consort's Crown, with its mass of glittering diamonds, atop her head.⁷⁰ Her *"pride of ruling and the determination not to lay it down"* was on full display in the abundance of jewels Marie Feodorovna had so jealously kept for herself and now wore.⁷¹ Around her neck flashed the famous Imperial *Riviere*, with its five rows of enormous diamonds; above these, she wore a single strand of large, perfectly matched pearls, while diamonds sparkled from her earrings and the brooches adorning her bodice. It was an embarrassment of jewelry that, Princess Anatole Bariatinsky could see, *"attracted everyone's attention."*⁷²

Grand Duchess Xenia Alexandrovna.

Grand Duke Michael Alexandrovich.

Grand Duchess Olga Alexandrovna.

Deruzhinsky and Engelhardt bundled the fifteen-foot-long train of Marie Feodorovna's gown into a small elevator, racing up the stairs to meet her on the floor above and guide her to the ceremonial State Bedchamber. Here, they draped a twenty-one-foot-long Imperial Mantle of gold brocade around her shoulders, while maids sewed its ermine collar to the back of the gown to ensure that the weighty garment remained in place.[73]

It was a quarter-to-nine when Marie Feodorovna, escorted by her brother Crown Prince Frederick of Denmark and her brother-in-law Grand Duke Alexei Alexandrovich, joined members of the Imperial Family in the State Drawing Room.[74] *"Our hearts bled at the sight of her,"* wrote Grand Duke Konstantin. Her face *"was full of suffering,"* and she looked like *"a sacrificial victim."*[75] Though smiling, she seemed *"almost overcome with emotion."*[76] Even the unsentimental Princess Victoria of Battenberg, Empress Alexandra's sister, saw past the forced smile: *"I have never seen sadder eyes than hers,"* she wrote to Queen Victoria.[77]

Kammer Pages gathered in the frescoed Tsaritsa's Golden Chamber with a detachment of Golden Grenadiers, awaiting the start of the Dowager Empress's procession. Just as she approached, one of the young men, crammed full of breakfast, vomited all over a luckless baron. *"We could do nothing but stand at attention without moving,"* remembered Kammer Page Sergei Roop as he watched the mess drip down the poor courtier. Someone pushed the offending page through a door before Marie Feodorovna could witness the scene; the courtier was not as fortunate and had to set off with the procession drenched in vomit.[78]

A *"roar of cheers"* greeted Marie Feodorovna's appearance at the top of the Red Staircase.[79] Trumpets blared, kettledrums rolled, cannon thundered, church bells pealed, and massed regimental orchestras launched into the National Anthem at different times and in different keys, *"a noisy, unintelligible mess"* that left ears ringing.[80] The crown atop her head glowed with *"a thousand flames of dazzling radiance"* as the Dowager Empress slowly descended the stairs.[81] Crisply uniformed Chevalier Guards marched in rigid ranks, their numbers giving way to fancifully dressed Heralds with their ostrich-plumed hats and chamberlains so covered in elaborate galloon that their coats

Crown Prince Frederick of Denmark.

Grand Duke Alexei Alexandrovich.

Grand Duke Konstantin Konstantinovich.

seemed *"almost of solid gold."*[82] Six adjutants carried her Imperial Mantle and the train of her gown. Behind them walked a moving rainbow: her white-gowned Mistress of the Robes and the *Dames á Portrait*, wearing jeweled miniatures of their mistress on bows pinned to the left side of their bodices; ladies-in-waiting in green and gold; and maids-of-honor in crimson velvet trailing veils of white tulle from their *kokoshniks*.[83] Two rows of Kammer Pages followed a group of military officials, and members of the Dowager Empress's household, all trying to avoid the *"strong stench"* of vomit emanating from the unfortunate Baron's coat that grew ever more noticeable in the unforgiving sun.[84] At the bottom of the Red Staircase, Marie Feodorovna stepped beneath a canopy of cloth-of-gold and velvet held aloft by more than a dozen Major-Generals. Embroidered with double-headed eagles, crowns, and Imperial monograms in colored silk threads and fringed in heavy gold bullion, its twelve black, white, and gold ostrich plumes waved in the breeze as she followed the ribbon of red carpet through the cheering square.[85]

Metropolitans Ioannikius of Kiev, Palladius of St. Petersburg, and Sergei of Moscow waited at the Cathedral of the Assumption's southern door. Their new gold vestments glowed *"like pillars of fire"* in the sunshine.[86] Anointing Marie Feodorovna with Holy Oil, they escorted her into the church.[87] *"Pale and anxious,"* she moved through the congregation and ascended the dais between rows of Chevalier Guards, their unsheathed broadswords held rigidly upright in salute.[88] *"It took some time,"* reported Francis Grenfell, for the officers to arrange her train and Coronation Mantle as she sat on the Diamond Throne.[89]

Kate Koon watched as Romanovs and royal guests passed down the Red Staircase and into the Cathedral. *"All the women had on diamond diadems and wore magnificent jewels,"* she wrote. *"One woman had sapphires which were in her headdress, around her neck, and embroidered down the front of her dress. The gowns were perfect wonders."*[90] Inch by inch, they filled the floor of the church, ladies to the right of the dais facing the iconostasis, gentlemen to the left.[91] Young Olga Alexandrovna thought herself lucky to be jammed against one of the central columns – it gave her something to lean against for the next three hours.[92] The near-sighted Queen Olga of Greece examined the crowd, lorgnette held to her right eye.[93] Her mother, the equally formidable Grand Duchess Alexandra Iosifovna,

The Tsar crowning the Empress. When the Tsar had duly received his crown, the scepter and the orb, he summoned the Empress to him. Her Majesty approached and knelt on a cushion before the throne. The Tsar took off his crown and, after touching her head with it, resumed it himself. He then placed upon her head a smaller crown, which was adjusted by four ladies-in-waiting. The Empress was thereupon invested with the Collar of St Andrei and the imperial robe, and the Tsar embraced her and raised her to her throne upon the dais.

stood imposingly rigid, snow-white hair crowned with a diamond and sapphire tiara.[94] Nor did younger beauties of the family disappoint. Elisabeth Feodorovna was coolly elegant in a gown of cream-colored velvet sewn with fuchsias in gold thread. Dark-haired and aloof, Victoria Melita of Hesse looked every inch a Romanov descendant in white satin and cloth-of-gold; nearby, her sister Marie of Romania sparkled in cream brocade embroidered with pearl-studded roses.[95]

Flickering flames of a thousand votive candles and shafts of sunlight streaming through windows bathed the crowd in suffused light. *"The very atmosphere seemed golden,"* said Marie of Romania, the diamonds, rubies, sapphires, and emeralds flashing *"like stars in God's Heaven."* A choir robed in blue and silver sang *"chants so solemnly beautiful that they were almost unearthly. They rose and swelled, filling the Church with such might waves of harmony that one's heart felt like bursting, but when the strain became next to unbearable, the volume of sound would gradually decrease, almost dying away into a whisper; and a great peace, which was a strange blending of joy and pain, would flood the soul and one was as though released."*[96]

The cheers, bells, trumpets, and cannon had permeated the palace as Nicholas and Alexandra dressed. It would be, Nicholas confided in his diary, *"a great and splendid, solemn day, though for Alix, Mama, and me, a hard one, in a moral sense."*[97] For this most important day in his life, Nicholas followed the tradition established by Emperor Paul and donned the full dress uniform of a Colonel in the Preobrazhensky Life Guards, the most senior of Russia's Imperial Regiments.[98] Red broadcloth collar and cuffs, embroidered with oak leaves in gold thread, adorned a thigh-length, double-breasted dark blue broadcloth tunic made in the St. Petersburg workshops of the fashionable military tailor Nordenstrem. White trousers disappeared into black, knee-high boots lined in white doeskin, to match the white doeskin gloves from the St. Petersburg firm of Morrison that Nicholas wore. The light blue moiré sash of the Order of St. Andrei stretched across his chest, held in place by the order's eight-pointed diamond star; three rows of gleaming medals, the Diamond Star of the Order of St. Vladimir, and gold-tipped aiguillettes, also bedecked the tunic's front. Diamond-studded epaulets trimmed in gold bullion,

IMPERIAL DIAMOND CROWN.

SCEPTRE OF EMPRESS.   ORB OF EMPRESS.   DIAMOND CROWN OF EMPRESS.

CROWN OF KAZAN.

CROWN OF POLAND.

GRAND IMPERIAL ORB OF THE RUSSIAN EMPIRE, BYZANTINE, TENTH CENTURY.   CROWN OF SIBERIA.   CROWN OF PETER THE GREAT.

denoting his rank as Adjutant-General to his late father, draped Nicholas's shoulder; atop them hung the gold Lesser Chain of the Order of St. Andrei. No detail was too small to demand attention and extraordinary expense: even the tunic's buttons, specially crafted by the St. Petersburg firm of Skosyrev, were gilded and engraved with double-headed eagles.[99]

Lady's maids dressed Alexandra in her coronation gown. Tradition dictated the style but not the manufacture. In 1883, Marie Feodorovna wore a gown commissioned from renowned Parisian couturier Charles Frederick Worth that, along with her extensive coronation toilette, cost an unbelievable 120,000 rubles (approximately $1,620,000 or £1,200,000 in 2013).[100] Alexandra proved more frugal and patriotic, wearing an elaborate gown of silk, silver tissue, and silver brocade woven at the Sapoznikhov Factory in Moscow and created by St. Petersburg couturier Madame Olga Bulbenkova. A fitted, boned bodice with low, boat-shaped décolletage rested above a bell-shaped underskirt of white silk; beneath this, Alexandra wore stockings of white, semi-transparent silk, and shoes of silver brocade adorned with seed pearls, made by St. Petersburg designer Ivan Egorov. Over the bodice, a floor-length jacket and overskirt trimmed with gauze and silk split down the middle and flowed back to form a fifteen-foot train. Nuns at Moscow's Ivanovsky Convent had embroidered the bodice, jacket with its

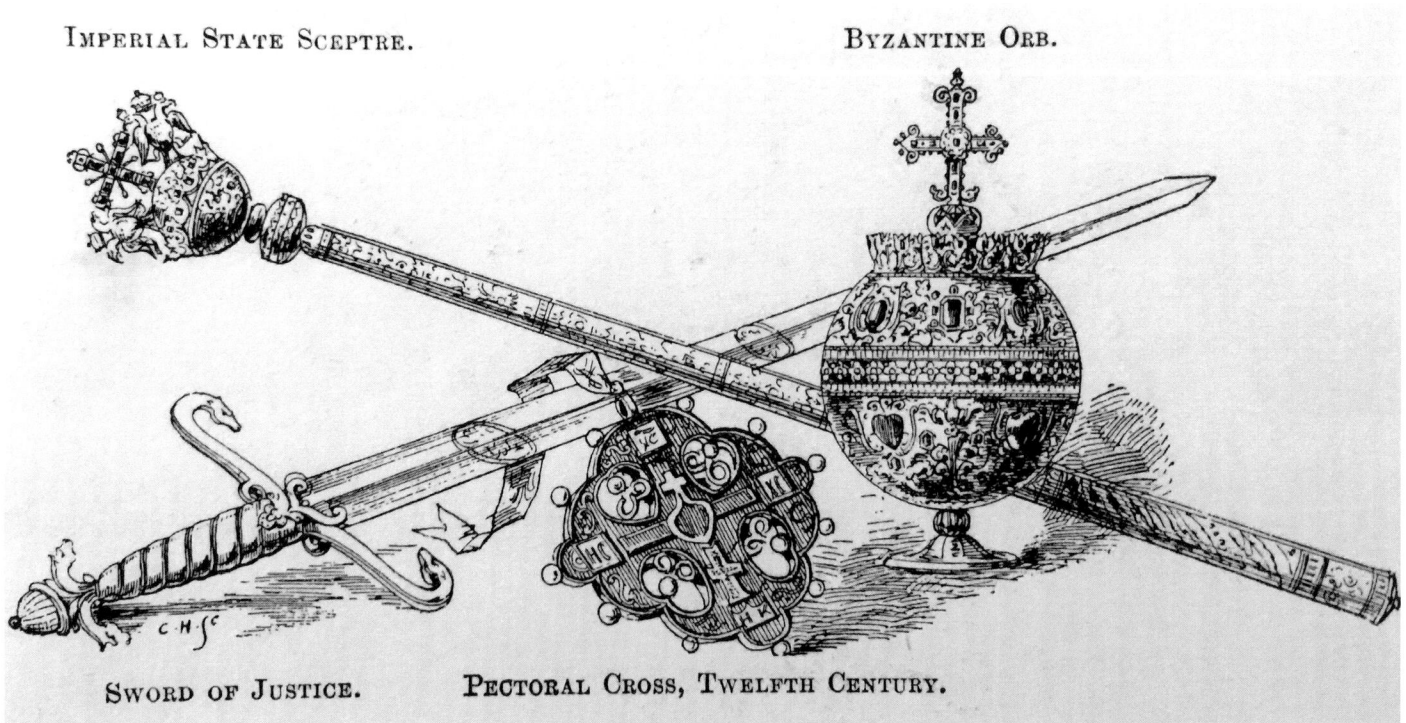

IMPERIAL STATE SCEPTRE.   BYZANTINE ORB.

SWORD OF JUSTICE.   PECTORAL CROSS, TWELFTH CENTURY.

open, hanging sleeves, and skirt with shimmering *rocailles* and flowers in silver and gold thread ornamented with 10,000 seed pearls. The end result cost 4,920 rubles (approximately $66,400 or £49,200 in 2013). Jewels and silver brocade weighed the dress down; adding the Imperial Mantle brought the ensemble to a staggering 46 pounds and left Alexandra nearly immobile.[101]

Like Nicholas, the young Empress went to the coronation without a crown, her hair twisted into long, twin side-curls demanded by tradition. She compensated with jewelry. A diamond-studded star held the crimson sash of the Order of St. Catherine, the oldest of the Imperial Heraldic Orders for distinguished ladies, in place across her bodice. To honor the late Emperor, she wore the *sautoir* created by Fabergé as an engagement gift from Alexander III and Marie Feodorovna, its long cascade of pearls coiled five times around her neck and ending in a large pearl drop. To this she added a single strand of pink pearls and matching pink pearl-drop earrings, engagement gifts from her husband.[102] These sentimental choices reflected Alexandra's belief that the coronation was a religious extension of her own wedding vows, a consecration to her new country.

Intense and overblown though it had been, the ceremonial of the early processions paled next to Nicholas and Alexandra's appearance in Cathedral Square. A few minutes after ten, a fanfare of trumpets announced the start of Their Majesties' Procession.[103] Hundreds of people preceded Nicholas and Alexandra. A detachment of Chevalier Guards, leading twenty-four Imperial Pages in dark tunics and white-plumed hats came first, followed by a contingent of Kammer Pages in their white breeches and tunics embellished with gold embroidery, and Masters of Ceremony in gold-braided uniform. Then came a surprising break in the parade of glittering uniforms, as hundreds of the Emperor's ordinary subjects, all specially selected and investigated by the police, marched down the Red Staircase. Rural representatives and peasant delegations had come from across the Empire, along with members of the provincial assemblies Nicholas had so publicly chastised the previous year. The drab, Sunday-best clothing of university presidents, educational officials, merchants, artisans, industrial barons, bankers, civil authorities, financiers, and mayors finally gave way to Cossacks in scarlet coats; the President and members of the Moscow Stock Exchange; a delegation from Russian-controlled Finland; and members of Russia's nobility, clad in somber black uniforms awash with glittering decorations.[104]

Konstantin Pobedonostsev, surely proud that his former pupil was about to be crowned unquestioned Autocrat, marched down the staircase with his Holy Synod, followed by Secretaries of State, and members of the Imperial

Members of the Russian Nobility attending the Coronation of Tsar Nicolas II.

Senate, the Council of Ministers, and the State Council.[105] Two elaborately costumed Heralds led three Grand Marshals armed with golden maces, while Adjutant-Generals, and Major-Generals à la Suite accompanied the Imperial Regalia, each item greeted with its own fanfare of trumpets. Aristocratic courtiers carried the items on red velvet cushions embroidered with double-eagles in silver thread and edged with gold bullion in ascending order of importance, from the Lesser Diamond Chain of the Order of St. Andrei for Empress Alexandra to the Imperial State Crown. Standing at the Cathedral's southern door, Metropolitans Sergei and Ioannikius blessed the items with Holy Water and incense before courtiers placed the Regalia on a gold brocade-draped table atop the dais.[106]

A dozen more processions followed down the Red Staircase. Chevalier Guards; Adjutants, Adjutants-General, and Major-Generals à la Suite represented the Emperor's Military Entourage. The Minister of War continued the martial aspect, walking with Generals and Admirals of the Imperial services, the Commander of the Chevalier Life Guards Regiment, the Adjutant-General of the Day, and the Major-General à la Suite on Duty. The gold-braid reached a crescendo when the highest-ranking courtiers appeared: Masters of Ceremony, followed by the Grand Master of Ceremonies, the Grand Marshal of the Imperial Court, the Head of the Imperial Chancellery, the Commandant of the Imperial Residences and, finally, Count Hilarion Vorontsov-Dashkov, Minister of the Imperial Court.[107] Above, watching from the terrace, a nurse held six-month-old Grand Duchess Olga Nikolaievna. She was too young to ever remember the scene, but her parents nevertheless wanted their daughter to witness this most important day in their lives.[108]

All the plans and parades, processions and pageantry, finally culminated at half-past ten. Tchaikovsky's *Fanfare* sounded from the Court Orchestra, State Trumpeters saluted, drums thundered, bells rang, and artillery fired into the blue sky as Nicholas and Alexandra appeared.[109] Cathedral Square erupted. *"Hats were thrown into the air, handkerchiefs waved, and men and women cheered, and cheered again until they were hoarse,"* said John Logan.[110] Nicholas and Alexandra walked arm-in-arm, flanked by the Emperor's uncles Vladimir, Sergei, and Paul, and by his eighteen-year-old brother Michael; four ladies-in-waiting, four maids-of-honor, Kammer Pages, military officials, and six officers in the Chevalier Life Guards Regiment with drawn swords, followed.[111] Nicholas seemed to shrink beside his tall uncles; even his young brother Michael noticeably towered over him as they descended the staircase.[112] At her husband's side, Alexandra was "*extraordinarily beautiful*," though "*everyone noticed how shy and nervous she seemed.*"[113] Her face, "*charged with profound emotion,*" reminded one onlooker of "*a martyr, walking with measured steps to her funeral pyre.*"[114]

At the bottom of the Red Staircase, the couple stepped beneath a second, more elaborate canopy adorned with sixteen ostrich plumes. No less than sixteen Major-Generals à la Suite held it aloft on ebony poles inlaid with mother-of-pearl, while sixteen Adjutants-General clutched at its trailing gold cords and tassels.[115] Aylmer Maude waspishly wondered if these proud military men, sheltering the couple beneath this extravagant prop, were "*ashamed of wasting their time, holding an unnecessary covering in such fine weather over the heads of two young people who were taking a short walk.*"[116] Symbolism above Nicholas and Alexandra's heads was echoed beneath their feet: priests had sprinkled the entire length of crimson carpet with Holy Water and strewn it with palm fronds, deliberately invoking an image of the Emperor following in the footsteps of Christ toward his own religious sacrifice for mankind.[117]

The Metropolitans of Moscow, of St. Petersburg, and of Kiev waited beneath the Cathedral of the Assumption's copper-hooded southern door. Nicholas and Alexandra were incensed and anointed with Holy Oil, then bowed their heads to hear the first of the day's many prayers reinforcing the idea of a divine Autocracy. Metropolitan Sergei intoned:

Most Pious Sovereign! Your solemn progress amidst outstanding splendor has an exceptionally great end. You come into this ancient sanctuary to assume the Crown and be anointed with Holy Oil. Your Hereditary Crown belongs to You alone, Autocratic Emperor. Yet all Orthodox Christians are worthy of the unction that is given but once. And should You be blessed through this sacrament to perceive a new life, the reason is this: that as there is no power higher, so there is no power on earth more arduous than the power of the Emperor, no burden so wearisome as his duty. Through this visible anointment may the invisible might of Heaven descend upon You to augment Your abilities as Emperor and light the way for Your Autocratic pursuit of the welfare and happiness of Your devoted subjects.[118]

Grand Duke Paul Alexandrovich.

A final "*tumultuous and triumphant*" cheer burst over the square.[119] The couple kissed a golden cross and turned toward the open doorway.[120] With slow, measured steps, Nicholas and Alexandra crossed the threshold, passing from bright sunshine into the subdued, golden interior to keep their appointment with destiny.

Chapter IX

A thunderous cheer signaled Nicholas and Alexandra's entrance into the Cathedral of the Assumption, so loud that it seemed to shake the very walls and startle the congregation.[1] A thousand heads turned to the Imperial couple, small figures momentarily silhouetted against the blinding sunshine streaming through the open, fifteen-foot-high doors. Enveloped in a swirl of fragrant incense, they moved slowly through the church as the choir intoned the 101st Psalm.[2] With three bows to the iconostasis, they ascended the central dais between rows of officers from the Chevalier Life Guards Regiment, Nicholas taking his place on the Ivory Throne at the center, with Alexandra on the Throne of Tsar Michael Feodorovich to his left.[3] Turning to his right, he caught his mother's eye and they exchanged *"a deep and tender glance"* as the choir's deep melodies echoed through the church.[4]

Nicholas looked *"grave and serious"* as his pale face surveyed the scene.[5] His mystically inclined cousin Grand Duke Konstantin thought the Emperor had *"an expression of piety and supplication"* that seemed *"to radiate majesty."*[6] Alexandra, *"violently blushing,"* appeared *"more sad-looking than ever,"* to Richard Harding Davis.[7] She kept her eyes lowered throughout the ceremony and at times trembled as if overcome with emotion, though as the service continued, said her sister Victoria, she *"grew quite calm."*[8]

The 101st Psalm gave way to the plaintive strains of *Misericordiam et Judicum Cantabo Tibi Domine*.[9] As its ghostly echoes faded, Metropolitan Palladius approached the throne and addressed Nicholas: *"Our Most Pious and Great Lord, Emperor and Autocrat of All Russia! Whereas by the Mercy of God and by the Act of the Holy and All Hallowing Spirit and by Your Desire, in this Temple is to take place the Coronation and the Anointing with Holy Oil of Your Imperial Majesty, may it please Your Imperial Majesty to follow the custom of Ancient Christian Monarchs and of Your Ancestors Crowned by God, by confessing the Orthodox Faith."*[10] Nicholas stood. In *"a clear, loud voice,"* the Emperor read the Nicene Creed from a large, illuminated book before a Deacon intoned an intercessory chant in a *"rich bass voice."*[11] A martial call followed these peaceful words, as Palladius prayed: *"Let the Lord of Hosts strengthen His weapons; subdue under His Feet every enemy and opponent, and may His Coronation and that of His Spouse, the Most Pious Sovereign Empress, be blessed by the King of Kings and Lord of Lords."*[12]

Readings from the Books of Isaiah, Matthew, and Romans followed, each announced and blessed by celebratory bursts from the choir.[13] As a minister's son, Aylmer Maude found the context offensive. The exclusive focus, he concluded, was not the spiritual welfare of the Russian people but rather religious justification of unlimited power, with God co-opted as assistant in the name of the Autocracy.[14] Everything said in the church that day, Maude insisted, might be condensed to a single phrase, *"Render unto Caesar the things that are Caesar's, but unto God the things that are God's,"* with *"as much accentuation of the first clause and as little of the second as possible."*[15]

Nicholas stood as courtiers presented the Imperial Regalia. Grand Dukes Vladimir, Sergei, Paul and Michael removed the Lesser Chain of the Order of St. Andrei from his neck then draped the gold-brocaded Imperial Mantle around his shoulders, fastening the diamond and emerald clasp of Empress Elisabeth across his chest.[16] Then came an unfortunate accident. As Grand Duke Vladimir arranged the Diamond Chain of the Order of St. Andrei atop the mantle's ermine collar he missed a catch; the decoration clattered to the carpet with a thud. He quickly replaced it around his nephew's shoulders, but not before those nearby had witnessed what, to the superstitious, seemed an ominous omen of disaster.[17] *"After the ceremony,"* recalled Court Chamberlain Alexander Izwolsky, *"all of those who saw it were ordered not to speak of it."*[18]

Opposite page: A artist's rendering of Tsar Nicholas II crowning his wife.

Nothing was said and the service continued as Palladius prayed:

To Thee alone, King of Mankind, has He to Whom Thou has entrusted this Earthly Kingdom bowed His head with us. And we pray Thee, Lord of All, to keep Him under Thine Own Shadow; strengthen His Kingdom; grant that He may do continually those things Pleasing to Thee; make to arise in His days Righteousness and Abundance of Peace, that in His tranquility we may lead a tranquil and quiet life in all Sober Godliness. For Thou art the King of Peace and the Savior of Our Souls and Bodies, and to Thee we ascribe Glory.[19]

Nicholas bowed his head as Palladius crossed his hands atop his forehead and prayed:

O Lord our God, King of Kings and Lord of Lords, Who through Samuel the Prophet did choose Thy servant David and did anoint him to be King over Thy People Israel: Hear now the supplication of us, though unworthy, and look forth from Thy Holy Dwelling Place and vouchsafe to anoint with the Oil of Gladness Thy Faithful Servant Nicholas Alexandrovich, whom Thou has been pleased to establish as Sovereign over Thy Holy People whom Thou has made Thine Own by the Precious Blood of Thine Only-Begotten Son. Clothe him with power from on High; set on his head a Crown of precious jewels; bestow on him length of days, set in his right hand a scepter of Salvation; establish him upon the Throne of Righteousness; defend him with the panoply of Thy Holy Spirit; strengthen his arm; subject to him all barbarous nations; sow in his heart fear of Thee and feeling for his subjects; preserve him in the Blameless Faith; make him manifest as the Sure Guardian of the Doctrines of Thy Holy Orthodox Church; that he may Judge Thy People in Righteousness and Thy Poor in Judgment, and save the Sons of those in Want and become Heir to Thy Heavenly Kingdom.[20]

The Metropolitan anointing Tsar Nicholas II with the holy chrism. After the ceremony of Coronation, the first part of the Communion Service was celebrated. The Tsar was then summoned by two Archpriests to his anointing, and advanced to the steps of the High Altar. There the Metropolitan anointed his Majesty with the Holy oil on the forehand, eyes, nostrils, mouth, ears, breast, and hands, saying, "The Seal of the Gift of the Holy Spirit." The completion of the rite was proclaimed by a peal of bells and a salute of 101 guns. The Empress then advanced and was anointed in like manner, but on the forehead only.

Laurits Tuxen's rendering of the Coronation. In this majestic painting, rays of sunlight exalt the figure of the Dowager Empress Marie Feodorovna.

A second prayer asked for divine guidance but also emphasized that Nicholas *"alone"* had been entrusted with protecting God's *"Earthly Kingdom."*[21]

Crossing himself three times, Nicholas called for the Imperial State Crown. Dimitri Nabokov, an elderly Councilor of State and future grandfather to novelist Vladimir Nabokov, shuffled across the dais clutching a cushion bearing the crown. Then at this most solemn of moments came disaster. Suffering from the stomach flu, Nabokov was suddenly *"stricken with diarrhea."* He could do nothing but offer the crown as he stood in silent embarrassment, dark stains spreading over his white trousers and pooling around his boots as the awful aroma mingled with the smell of vomit soaking his nearby companion in misfortune.[22]

As with the clattering Diamond Chain of the Order of St. Andrei, everyone on the dais tried to ignore this unfortunate scene as Palladius took the crown from Nabokov. *"Most Pious Autocrat and Great Emperor of all the Russias,"* he declared, *"this visible ornament upon thy head represents the invisible act of Christ, King of Glory, who consecrates You Head of the Russian Nation and with His Blessing confirms Your Unlimited Power over Your People."*[23]

Opposite page: An artist's rendering of Tsar Nicholas II kissing his mother the Dowager Empress Marie Feodorovna after the Coronation.

"With the greatest calm and modesty," said the Dowager Empress, Nicholas placed the crown atop

Chapter IX

his head.²⁴ *"It looked a simple enough gesture,"* remembered his sister Olga, *"but from that very moment Nicky's responsibility was to God only."* Echoing her brother's own conception of his role, she termed it *"a most solemn and binding contract between God and the Sovereign, His servant."*²⁵

Other items of regalia followed: Nicholas clutched the Scepter in his right hand, and the Imperial Orb in his left, *"visible representations of the Autocratic power which the Almighty gives You to Rule over Your People,"* Palladius declared. The Emperor returned to his throne for a few moments before handing the Orb and Scepter to adjutants and, *"in exquisitely sweet and tender tones,"* summoned his wife.²⁶ With head bowed, Alexandra approached. *"So young, so fair,"* Aubrey Stanhope scribbled in his notes as she knelt on a crimson cushion at her husband's feet, *"with all the shyness of a girl brought up after the English fashion."*²⁷

It was the moment, wrote Richard Harding Davis, when *"the peasant girl became a queen."* The peasant girl, in this case, was a former Princess now made Empress, clad in her $66,000 silver brocade gown adorned with jewels, but Davis insisted that she looked as simple as *"a child going to her first communion."* *"Of all the women there,"* he wrote, *"she was by far the most beautiful."* He saw that *"the color in her cheeks was high, and her eyes were filled with that shyness or melancholy that her pictures have made familiar; and in contrast with the tiaras and plumes and necklaces of the ladies of the court surrounding her, she looked more like Iphigenia going to the sacrifice than the queen of the most powerful Empire in the world waiting to be crowned."*²⁸

When the Coronation ceremony was ended, Tsar Nicholas II and the Empress passed in State procession under a great baldachin to the Cathedral of the Archangel Michael, where they paid their devotion at the tombs of the Tsar's ancestors. Their Imperial Majesties then visited the Cathedral of the Annunciation, where they kissed the Cross and were sprinkled with Holy Water. After a brief service they left the Cathedral and passed to the Red Staircase. here the procession held whilew the Metropolitan of St Petersburg withdrew, after making the sign of the Cross, and the Tsar and Empress then entered the Palace.

Implicitly invoking the connection between marriage vows and coronation ceremony, the official account portrayed Alexandra as *"the ideal image of submission incarnated in feminine beauty and grace"* as she knelt down before her husband on a crimson cushion edged in gold lace.[29] Four ladies-in-waiting draped an Imperial Mantle around her shoulders and hung the Lesser Diamond Chain of the Order of St. Andrei around her neck.[30] Briefly removing his crown, Nicholas touched it to her head, signifying that her power and status came solely through his grace, before setting the new Consort's Crown on his wife, *"in a gesture of eerie force,"* reported the correspondent from *Le Figaro*.[31] Whispering, *"Careful!"* he watched as Princess Naryshkina-Kurakina inserted a diamond-studded hairpin in place to hold the crown, then drew his wife forward and kissed her *"in a gesture full of tenderness,"* said a witness. *"The scene was both immensely solemn and as graceful as can be imagined."*[32] The tenderness touched even the practical Princess Victoria of Battenberg, who worried about the symbolic weight of a crown resting atop her youngest sister's head. Nicholas, though, she assured Queen Victoria, used *"so much gentle care that it was pretty to see."*[33]

Aylmer Maude offered a more cynical interpretation. Nicholas, he concluded, was so quick to get the crown back onto his own head because he feared that his wife *"might keep it."* His thought was prescient. Alone among chroniclers, he foresaw a day when the strong-minded young Empress would become the power behind the throne. He also detected jealousy. The apparently mild and gentle Nicholas, he perceived, would carefully guard his power – not from his wife, as Maude assumed, but from his own people.[34]

In a stroke of serendipitous stagecraft beyond even the Russian Court's tight control, a *"glorious ray of rainbow color"* pierced through a high window and shone *"directly upon the heads of the new Emperor and Empress of all the Russias"* – or so Aubrey Stanhope remembered.[35] There was, said Marie of Romania, *"the light of the mystic"* in the Emperor's eyes, but his heavy vestments seemed to overwhelm him. Even *"the prodigious crown of his ancestors"* looked too heavy for his head. It was her cousin Alexandra who seemed most impressive, *"beautiful and dignified."* Alexandra towered over her husband, crown in place, mantle cascading around her. *"Her face was flushed,"* Marie wrote, *"her lips compressed; even at this supreme hour, no joy seemed to uplift her, not even pride; aloof, enigmatic, she was all dignity, but she shed about her no warmth."*[36]

This was the voice of one who knew them, accustomed to the moods and melancholies of Nicholas and Alexandra. Many onlookers, though, saw exactly what they wished. It was the Imperial couple's youth, Davis reported, that made the whole event most impressive. Nicholas had *"the dauntlessness"* of a boy, and Alexandra a *"sweet girlishness of manner."* To the American, they were not rulers, not political figures, but rather a young couple in love whose apparent dedication lent them

…an inexpressible hold on your interest and sympathy. It was not as though they had been looking forward to this hour for many years, until it had lost its first meaning and was now the payment for a long period of apprenticeship, until it had been lived so often in anticipation that when it came it was only a form. It was not as though he had grown cynical and stout, and she gray-haired and hardened to it all; but, instead, she looked like a bride upon her wedding day, and you could see in his face, white and drawn with hours of prayer and fasting, and in the tears that wet his cheeks, how strongly he was moved.[37]

Official Russia had no desire to humanize the couple. Seated on their thrones, they listened as a Proto-Deacon, in tones *"throbbing with exultant joy,"* loudly declaimed the Emperor's portentous string of titles.[38] *"The Lord's Enlightened and Merciful Mediator, the Orthodox and Pious and Christ-Loving, the Absolute Autocrat and Great Lord by the Grace of God, Nicholas Alexandrovich,"* had now become not merely *"Emperor and Autocrat of all the Russias,"* but also Emperor, Autocrat, Tsar, Sovereign, Grand Duke, Prince, Heir, or Lord of a territories and provinces large and small, encompassing one-sixth of the globe.[39]

Opposite page: An artist's rendering of Tsar Nicholas II and Empress Alexandra Feodorovna receiving congratulations.

"God save the Emperor!" Metropolitan Palladius cried out at the end of this recitation, "God save the Empress!" The congregation bowed three times toward the dais and the choir burst into the congratulatory chorus *Many Years!*[40] Beyond the church's thick walls, 101 guns and pealing bells announced the moment to all of Moscow; the sound was so loud, wrote one correspondent, that *"the walls of the church seemed to vibrate."*[41] *"Massed bands brayed the National Anthem as loud as they could,"* said Mary Hickley, *"in the vain hope of being heard in the tremendous din."*[42] A guest on Cathedral Square saw the throng of people filling the tribunes rise *"as if by one simultaneous movement"* and fall upon its knees, *"an extraordinary spectacle of devotion which alone would have made the morning memorable."*[43] At the same time, the softer yet equally insistent click of telegraph machines sparked word of the moment across the earth, *"to Odessa,"* said Davis, *"to Constantinople, to Berlin, to Paris, to the rocky coast of Penzance, where it slipped into the sea and hurried on under the ocean to the illuminated glass face in the Cable Company's tall building on Broadway, until the world had been circled, and the answering congratulations came pouring into Moscow while the young Emperor still stood under the dome of the little chapel."*[44]

Nicholas and Alexandra sat upon their thrones as relatives paid homage. The Dowager Empress came first and seeing her in tears, Nicholas embraced her repeatedly. *"It could not have been a more charming scene,"* recorded Henry LaPauze.[45] Francis Grenfell thought that she *"nearly broke down"* as the tears streamed down her face.[46] *"I swept a deep curtsey,"* the Emperor's sister Olga recalled, *"raised my head, and saw Nicky's blue eyes looking at me with such affection that my heart glowed. I still remember how passionately I vowed to dedicate myself to my country and her sovereign."*[47] The foreign relatives, though, seemed *"quite as embarrassed as any young debutante."* Some rushed through the act. Davis decided that the myopic Queen Olga of Greece *"scowled at the young couple like Lady Macbeth."* Only the Duke of Connaught kissed Alexandra, while the Prince of Naples was so flustered that he offered the couple his own hand and *"backed away as though he were afraid they would kiss him."* Most of the royals *"looked as though they were saying 'Good night' to their hostess, assuring her that they had had a very pleasant evening."*[48]

Awkward obeisance over, Nicholas stood, crossed himself, and read out the words of his coronation prayer:

O Lord, God of Our Fathers and King of Kings, Who Has Created all things by Thy Word, and in Thy Wisdom has made Man, that he may Govern the World in Holy Righteousness: Thou Has Chosen me as Sovereign and Judge over Thy People. I confess Thy inscrutable Providence in selecting me, and bow in gratitude before Thy Majesty. I beg You, My Lord, to aid me in the task You have given me and guide me in this Great Mission. May the Wisdom which descends always from Your Throne always be with me. May it descend to me from On High, that I may understand what is pleasing in Thy Holy Heavens and in Thy Eyes, and may Govern according to Thy Commandments. May my Heart be in Your Hand, that I may Order all I do for the advantage of the People Thou has entrusted unto My Care and to Thy Glory. Guide Me, O Lord, that at the Day of Judgment I may render, without condemnation, My Account to Thee.

The Dowager Empress Marie Feodorovna.

Grant to Me Thy Mercy and Bounty, through Thine Only Begotten Son, with Whom, and with Thy Holy and Life-Giving Spirit, Thou has Blessed the World unto All Ages.

These words, reported the official account, were *"eagerly repeated by the Emperor's subjects, who prayed to the Lord to strengthen the Sovereign in his great, heroic feat in service of his Homeland."*[49]

The prayer had been cut down substantially from the traditional text *"to spare the Emperor spending more time on his knees."*[50] No one agreed about the result. Princess Victoria of Battenberg optimistically thought her brother-in-law delivered it *"in a clear and moving voice."*[51] Russians who understood the words, though, perceived indecision. Grand Duke Konstantin scarcely heard the Emperor, and Alexei Suvorin thought that Nicholas recited the prayer *"hesitatingly and without confidence."*[52]

Though trimmed for comfort, this prayer became the most significant and ultimately fatal moment of the service. The coronation ceremony had no oath, but Nicholas and especially Alexandra mistakenly took these words as a solemn pledge between Emperor and God to preserve the Autocracy intact. Uncertain knowledge of the Russian language and the religious ecstasy of the moment left Alexandra convinced that any concessions would violate a pledge that Nicholas never made. In later years there would be constant references to this phantom oath as justification for rejecting reform. A constitution, Alexandra once warned her husband, would be *"against what you swore at your coronation."*[53]

Many in the closely packed congregation caught only brief glimpses of the unfolding pageant. Courtiers and officers, Grand Duke Konstantin complained, *"blocked my view, so that I saw almost nothing."*[54] *"Except in the case of a very tall man or a particularly lofty tiara,"* remembered Richard Harding Davis, *"you saw only those who stood in the front rows."* Crowded into every available inch of space, people could not kneel during prayers. Several men saved themselves from the embarrassment of tumbling onto the floor only by flinging their arms around the shoulders of those clustered in front of them.[55]

Nicholas stood and the congregation knelt while Palladius prayed that God *"endow with wisdom the Most Pious Emperor."*[56] When it was done, the choir burst into the hymn, *We Praise Thee, O Lord*. Yet another *"staggering ray of sunshine,"* insisted an onlooker, filtered down from the dome, *"lighting up for a moment the great mass of diamonds"* in the crown atop Nicholas's head like the halo over one of the frescoed saints looking on from the walls.[57]

Empress Alexandra Feodorovna.

The chorus faded and the Liturgy began. *"May Your Majesty deign to approach the Great Door of the Sanctuary in this Holy Cathedral,"* Palladius invited.[58] Nicholas handed his regalia to an adjutant and, together with Alexandra, followed the Metropolitan on a special covering of scarlet edged in gold lace, unrolled as they walked by Grand Duke Sergei Alexandrovich, to the center of the iconostasis.[59] Standing upon a square of gold brocade, they bowed as Palladius approached with the jasper ampulla of Ivan the Terrible, filled with white wine, spices, and oil that had been brewed together in a special Holy Chrism during Lent.[60] Using a golden rod, Palladius anointed Nicholas on the forehead, eyes, nose, lips, ears, breast, and both of his hands, pronouncing, *"The Seal of the Gift of the Holy Spirit,"* as a salute of 101 guns and the ringing of bells marked the monument. Alexandra was anointed only on the forehead.[61] Both Nicholas and Alexandra viewed those anointing them merely as earthly expressers of divine will. *"God,"* the Empress later insisted to her husband, *"anointed you at your coronation, He placed you where you stand,"* sentiments the mystical Nicholas shared.[62]

For the only time in his life, Nicholas entered the Sanctuary to celebrate the Eucharist. Extended only during a coronation, this privilege, as Richard Wortman noted, revealed the Emperor *"as the most favored of the lay population rather than as a member of the clergy."* Tradition dictated that the Emperor take Eucharist with the Royal Doors of the iconostasis open and in full view of the congregation; according to Canon law, only ordained priests took communion out of sight. For a hundred years sovereigns had followed this custom. Not so Nicholas II: once he entered the sanctuary, the Royal Doors closed behind him.[63] It was an extraordinary piece of symbolism, an expression of autocratic power enforcing the idea that Nicholas was a man apart, his reign a mixture of temporal and spiritual rule.

Within the Sanctuary Bishops removed the Emperor's Imperial Mantle and replaced it with a clerical dalmatic of golden brocade.[64] Even his communion was exceptional: Nicholas took the wafer and wine separately, a privilege reserved for actual members of the clergy.[65] *"What contrast,"* Aylmer Maude wondered, *"could be greater than that between the Last Supper and this gorgeous ceremony?"* It was, he insisted, a *"pompous performance"* by *"a man who renders no manual service to others but claims much for himself and has many possessions,"* perverting the inclusive nature of communion to deliberately elevate his own status.[66]

Grand Duke Kirill Vladimirovich.

Attention wandered with Nicholas out of sight. Standing below the dais, his cousin Grand Duke Kirill Vladimirovich listened to the choir. *"The waves of harmony rose and fell, rolled and broke like the sea in tones which were scarcely of this world, vibrating throughout the length and breadth of the cathedral, filling it to its smallest recesses. From sudden thunder, it would dwindle to a still whisper. It implored, it triumphed, and it sorrowed, it conveyed an idea of the infinite and while it lasted brought heaven down to earth."*[67] Through *"dense clouds of incense,"* Prince Nicholas of Greece looked out at *"icons and gold ornaments, glittering and sparkling in the light of the candles, the gorgeous uniforms and court dresses of the ladies with their incomparable jewels."*[68]

After hours of standing, the congregation was restless and tired. Pressed together in the stifling cathedral and weighed down in their heavy gowns, several of the women fainted.[69] Some people ignored the solemn prayers and hymns, chattering away *"as though at an afternoon tea,"* said Richard Harding Davis.[70] Surprised journalists saw the Bishop of Peterborough hand snuff to his Orthodox colleagues.[71] Scanning the crowd for distraction, Francis Grenfell spotted *"a man of very dark complexion"* burst into the church and make straight for the dais. Officials dragged him away before he disrupted the service, but most of the foreign visitors were sure that they had actually seen a member of that legendary Russian species, the Nihilist, bent on some terrible, dastardly deed.[72]

Nicholas finally emerged from the sanctuary, wrapped in his mantle, the Imperial State Crown atop his head, and *"tears streaming down his cheeks."*[73] The Dowager Empress, as she admitted, *"was about to burst from emotion and compassion"* as Nicholas kissed her *"with such great love and tenderness."*[74] As Alexandra followed him, Marie Feodorovna reached out to her daughter-in-law *"and tenderly kissed the young Empress in a poignant scene."*[75] Palladius offered a final prayer before the chorus again intoned *Many Years!* Nicholas and Alexandra stood, bowed to the congregation three times, and descended the dais, moving through the church and pausing as blinding sunlight spilled over them through a southern door now standing open to the square beyond.[76]

It was five minutes to one. Bells rang, artillery thundered, and the crowd again erupted in cheers as Nicholas and Alexandra appeared. Wearing his crown, holding the Orb and the Scepter, and trailing his golden mantle, Nicholas walked at the front of the raised canopy, Alexandra following behind him. Their diamond crowns flashed like *"veritable suns"* as they crossed the square.[77] *"Very human emotions,"* saw Mary Hickley, were visible on their faces as the Imperial couple passed: Nicholas *"was white as a sheet,"* while Alexandra seemed *"agitated,"* both *"profoundly awestruck and impressed with the heavy responsibility and burden"* of their positions.[78]

Tradition called for the newly crowned sovereigns to pray before tombs and relics in the Cathedrals of the Archangel Michael and of the Annunciation.[79] Kammer Page Alexander Mandryk saw that Nicholas was *"absolutely dripping sweat"* as he approached the cathedral doors. Hands encumbered with the Orb and the Scepter, the Emperor paused as his uncle Vladimir continually wiped his brow with a handkerchief.[80] As he crossed the square, though, Nicholas faltered and seemed, to one onlooker, about to faint; Vladimir and his other uncles quickly leaned over and supported him.[81] Nearly crushed by the heavy mantle, exhausted by the ceremony, crown askew and eyes blinded with sweat, he nearly stumbled again on reaching the Cathedral of the Archangel Michael; some in the crowd even thought that he had fainted or dropped the scepter.[82] According to the somewhat questionable Princess Catherine Radziwill, a murmur went through the square at this *"sign of weakness, not only of a physical but also of a moral character."*[83]

At the Cathedral of the Archangel Michael, the Bishop of Kostroma blessed them as they entered and made a circuit of praying before sacred icons and the tombs of previous rulers.[84] The Archbishop of Kherson led them through a similar ritual at the Cathedral of the Annunciation before Nicholas and Alexandra reached the bottom of

Prince Nicholas of Greece.

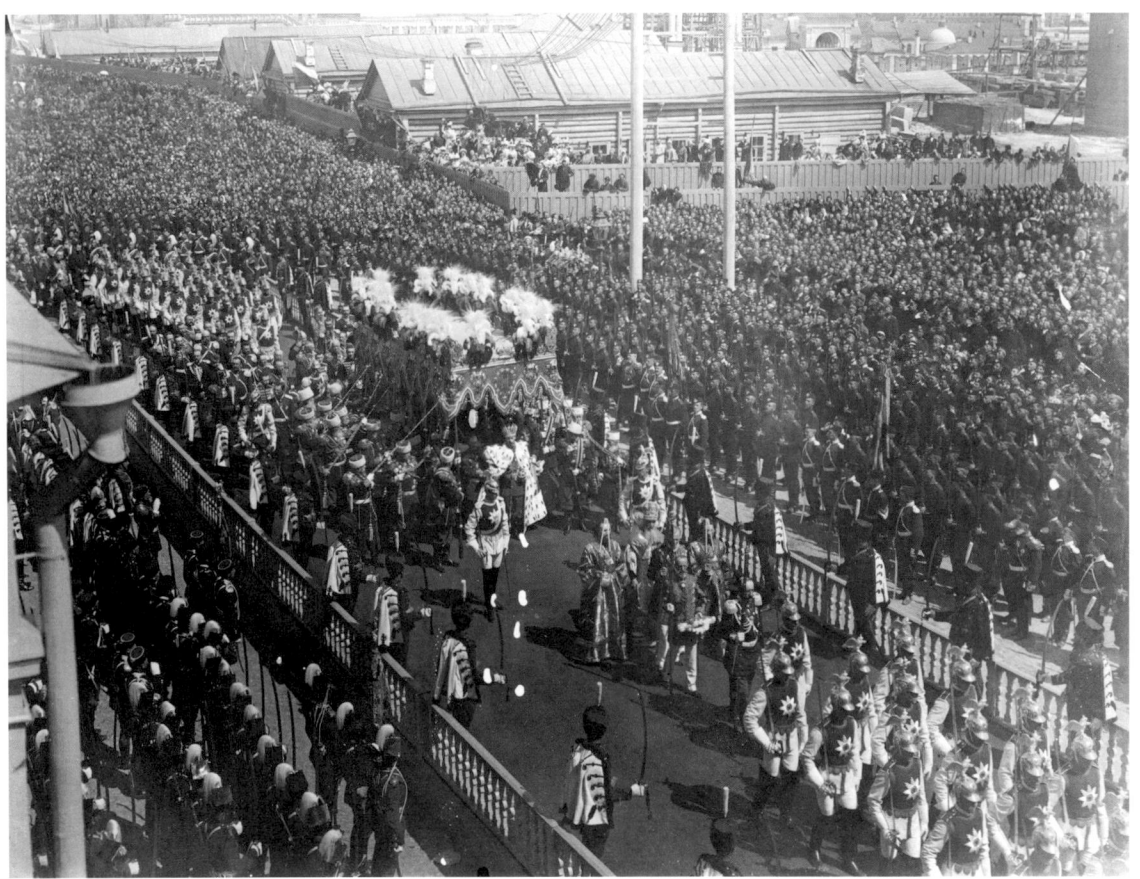
The Tsar and the Empress after the Coronation (she was walking under the canopy).

the Red Staircase.[85] Palladius again blessed them before they abandoned their canopy and ascended the carpeted steps.[86] Much closer now, the Americans watched them pass. Nicholas, said John Logan, *"looked tired;"* his crown was *"tilted slightly"* and seemed *"a bit large for his head."*[87]

Nicholas and Alexandra ascended the Red Staircase. At the top, they turned and followed Nicholas I's precedent of bowing three times to acknowledge the *"deafening"* cheers of the crowd below.[88] *"The Regalia sparkled,"* wrote Bavarian Ambassador Baron Carl Moy, *"the uniforms shone, the warm sun poured down on this whole picture, a light breeze ruffled veils and fans, all the bells rang, the cannons thundered, fanfares sounded, and it all mixed together to drown out the hurrahs of the crowd."* Moy saw what the Government wished, *"an unforgettable glimpse of the deepest reverence for Monarchy, Russia, and Orthodoxy."*[89] These acclamations seemed sincere, but they were as carefully cultivated as the ceremony just concluded. As far as the eye could see, noted Kammer Page Alexei Ignatiev, Cathedral Square brimmed with *"the military, functionaries, and ladies in hats,"* a crowd of privileged beings specially selected to provide a moving tableaux of Holy Russia worshipping its Emperor. The *"people,"* thought Ignatiev, *"were just what was missing."*[90]

Interest dissipated as soon as the Imperial couple disappeared into the Grand Kremlin Palace. Valet Alexei Volkov found the Emperor *"very pale and tired"* when he entered the bedroom. Pointing at his uniform, Nicholas exclaimed, *"Look what they have done to me!"* There were small threadbare patches on the knees of his breeches, the result, Nicholas complained, of having knelt so much during the ceremonies.[91] The Emperor also had a headache. Despite the new cushioning, the nine-pound Imperial State Crown rested heavily on the sensitive scar from his attack in Japan; he was happy to be rid of it when he and Alexandra fled to their private apartments.[92] Crown and scar exemplified the Emperor's life. The first, symbolizing his destiny and privileged position, was an unwanted burden that now, even in his moment of greatest glory, oppressed him with literal pain. And the second, mark of an assassin's saber, was visible expression of his belief that an unfortunate fate awaited him. Together they became Nicholas's personal trappings of office, inescapable and inexorably woven together in his mystical mind.

With the Imperial couple gone, Cathedral Square, said Kate Koon, became *"a moving mass of gorgeousness"* as people scurried from tribunes.[93] Having stood for six hours or more, the diplomats and dignitaries, Romanovs and royal guests, and courtiers and Kammer Pages who now gathered in the palace collapsed in exhausted heaps. Young men from the *Corps des Pages* lay sprawled unceremoniously across the dais in the Hall of the Order of St. Catherine, flirting with equally fatigued maids-of-honor when Grand Duchess Marie Pavlovna burst into the room. Brushing aside their efforts to bow and curtsey, she waved them back into place and ordered wine and pastries sent up from the palace kitchen to replenish their flagging energies.[94] The pages appreciated this unusually thoughtful gesture from a woman whose husband they did their best to avoid. When not barking out orders, Grand Duke Vladimir amused himself by chasing the young men, grabbing hold of their carefully waved hair, and tugging at the curls until they screamed out in pain.[95]

The Tsar and the Empress at the top of the Red Staircase.

Clad in his own voluminous robes, Mandell Creighton, Bishop of Peterborough, shared Nicholas II's discomfort at the unrelenting heat. He found a quiet corner of the palace and asked a footman to bring him some tea. The tea appeared promptly, and so did Konstantin Pobedonostsev, eager as ever to ingratiate himself and promote his country's image with the British cleric.[96] Most of the foreign guests were left to their own devices. The Americans wandered through the palace, admiring furniture and fittings, thankful to be out of the hot sun. Feeling like an inadequate, rather common tourist, the proud Emily Roebling consoled herself by assuring her companions that back home in Trenton, New Jersey, *she* was the object of curiosity, and people walked around *her* rooms peering at her possessions when she held a reception.[97]

After an hour's rest, Nicholas and Alexandra reluctantly donned their mantles and crowns and, at three, stepped out onto a terrace high above the Moskva River.[98] Alexandra's brother Ernst Ludwig cast etiquette to the wind and clambered out on his hands and knees alongside them, hiding behind their robes and peering over the railing to gaze at the crowd along the river banks. "*It seemed as though a million people stood below them, and the endless cheers reached them like waves breaking in a giant storm, soaring up the two sun-bathed, glittering people.*" It was, he said, "*one of the greatest moments of my life.*"[99]

These were the people excluded from Cathedral Square, a *"dense mass"* determined to see some small moment of the day otherwise denied them. They had been gathering for days, crowding the streets, cramming the quays, even waving from a flotilla of boats bobbing on the placid river. For the factory workers and shopkeepers, pilgrims and peasants, this was their only chance to see the Tsar of national myth: wrapped in golden robes, glittering crown on his head, benevolent father of the Russian people. With each of the Imperial couple's three bows, the ovations increased, a roar so deep, so prolonged, and so enthusiastic, said Francis Grenfell, that *"it actually drowned out"* the accompanying artillery salutes and ringing church bells.[100]

A fanfare from the State Trumpeters signaled the start of the Coronation Banquet[101]. Eighteen hundred guests, served by 4,500 footmen in crimson and gold liveries, partook of the meal, though only 200 dined with Nicholas and the two Empresses.[102] Diplomats, foreign royals, and distinguished guests feasted in the palace's enormous ceremonial halls and in large tents erected on terraces and in the quadrangle.[103]

Processing through the palace, Nicholas and Alexandra reached the Holy Vestibule. As Nicholas neared the doorway to the Palace of Facets, recalled Page Boris Engelhardt, Marie Feodorovna *"quickly went into the line behind him. Empress Alexandra stopped and allowed her mother-in-law's suite to go before her own."*[104] Ignoring the possible slight implicit in this strict exercise of precedence, Alexandra followed as the opening polonaise from Glinka's *A Life for the Tsar* marked Nicholas's entry to the hall.[105]

A single, seventy-seven-foot square hall whose vaulted ceiling rested on a massive central pier, the Palace of Facets had served Muscovite tsars as a throne room. It dazzled in the afternoon sun, whose light glanced off golden frescoes, four immense bronze chandeliers, magnificent engraved salvers, and Imperial regalia resting atop a brocade-draped table during the meal.[106] A dais – carpeted in crimson and draped in a canopy of cloth-of-gold sewn with double-headed eagles, edged with ermine, and bedecked with colored ostrich plumes – stood in the southeastern corner. Nicholas, Alexandra, and Marie Feodorovna ascended steps lined by two Heralds in their fanciful medieval uniforms, Kammer Pages, and four officers of the Chevalier Guard, and took their places on the three thrones that had been used in the cathedral. Nicholas sat in the middle, flanked by Alexandra to his left and Marie Feodorovna to his right. Behind them stood chamberlains, marshals and military officials.[107] It was a disconcerting spectacle for Nicholas and Alexandra, who sat *"with very serious expressions on their faces;"* a Kammer Page even thought that the Emperor was depressed.[108] Here, the Imperial trio would dine in ceremonial splendor, like the unfortunate stars, as the Dowager Empress complained, of some Wagnerian opera.[109]

The Tsar and the Empress during the procession in Cathedral Square.

Five toasts preceded the meal, each heralded by a fanfare of trumpets as the ostentatiously titled Grand Cup Bearer announced, *"His Majesty deigns to drink!"*[110] Each toast called for a different goblet of solid gold and accompanying artillery salute fired from the Kremlin walls. Sixty-one shots boomed out in honor of the

Emperor, fifty-one for his wife and his mother, thirty-one for the Romanov Family, and twenty-one – firmly establishing their place in their hierarchy of Imperial Russia – for the Orthodox Church and Nicholas II's subjects. Tradition excluded foreigners from the banquet hall. Diplomats were admitted to toast the Emperor's health before shuffling from the room, clumsily walking backward before the doors were closed.[111]

Another blast of trumpets heralded the food. The precise, ordered etiquette of the Russian Court dictated that a contingent of privileged officials carry the Imperial plates. It took the Grand Marshal of the Imperial Court, the Chief Grand Master of Ceremonies, the Grand Esquire Trenchant, and two officers from the Chevalier Life Guards to convey each course through the hall. At the steps of the dais, they handed the plates to Kammer Pages, who in turn handed them to elderly members of Moscow's nobility, who then presented them to the Imperial trio.[112] Standing on the steps of the dais, Gustav Mannerheim, an officer in the Chevalier Life Guards Regiment and future President of Finland, watched with trepidation as, *"with trembling hands,"* the old gentlemen shakily ascended the dais.[113] Grand Duke Vladimir stood close by, guiding uncertain hands and sopping up spilled soup with a napkin when one man sloshed it all over the table.[114] This scene was increasingly at odds with the glorious harmonies filling the hall as a stringed orchestra accompanied a choir performing the new *Coronation Cantata* by Alexander Glazunov, a paean to the glories of Autocracy.[115]

Although tradition kept foreigners from the Palace of Facets, Konstantin Pobedonostsev asked Mandell Creighton, Bishop of Peterborough, to join male members of the Imperial Family, courtiers, and senior Orthodox clergy in the hall. Creighton thought this surprising gesture was a courtesy *"to the English Church."* In fact, Pobedonostsev – always conscious of the power of propaganda – likely imagined that feting the impressionable Bishop would create favorable impressions of Russia.[116] Creighton found himself sitting with the legendary and popular Father John of Kronstadt. They had no language in common but, as Creighton said, *"chummed"* and smiled happily at one another before the *"rather hungry"* Bishop made his way through the meal.[117]

Foreign royal guests and extended members of the Imperial Family looked on from a crowded gallery above the Palace of Facets. This was a relic of Muscovite rule, when women confined to the Terem and excluded from public functions had watched the pageantry through high interior windows. The crush to see the Imperial diners was immense as Grand Dukes and Duchesses, Princes and Princesses, stumbled over voluminous trains and pressed against the little openings in the oppressively hot gallery. *"Sweat poured down many*

Princess Victoria of Battenberg (on the floor) with her sister Grand Duchess Elisabeth Feodorovna and their Aunt Beatrice of Battenberg (née Great Britain).

The Palace of Facets.

august foreheads," said a courtier, *"and some looked quite apoplectic."* The portly Prince Ludwig of Bavaria, clad in a heavy wool uniform, nearly fainted in this hothouse.[118] Abandoning this scene, Alexandra's sister Victoria stumbled on a *"strange mixture of people"* crowding a nearby hall: *"men in uniform, some in plain clothes, and even one or two in peasants' dress."*[119] The picturesque if somewhat odd sight gave way a chilling explanation: all descended from those who had, at one time or another through the centuries, saved the life of a Russian sovereign.[120] It was an unsettling reminder of the precarious nature of the Imperial throne.

Those excluded from the Palace of Facets found diversion in the lavish banquet. Kate Koon thought herself lucky to be seated in the Hall of the Order of St. Vladimir, serenaded by a company from the Bolshoi and Mariinsky Operas, and not in one of the hot, airless tents beneath the Moscow sun. Caring less about food than about her thirst, she finally convinced a scarlet-coated footman to bring her *"one small glass"* of iced water.[121] An array of English silver, Irish crystal, and colorful plates, saucers, cups, and bowls crowded the tables: pieces from the cobalt-bordered Coronation Service of Nicholas I; green, red, gold, and blue medieval Muscovite-style designs atop the Kremlin Banquet Service; and black double-headed eagles crowning the simple white of the New-Style Coat-of-Arms Service commissioned for the Coronation of Alexander III.[122] Silk tasseled cords bound parchment rolls at each place. Untying them revealed a menu elaborately illuminated by artist Viktor Vasnetsov, with a scene from the Coronation of Michael, the first Romanov Tsar framed with crowns, peacocks, and colorful foliate ornaments, medieval allusions appealing to Nicholas II's own Muscovite leanings.[123] Lettering in Old Church Slavonic read:

The Holy Coronation of the Sovereign Emperor Nicholas II and the Sovereign Empress Alexandra Feodorovna: Glory to God in the Heavens, Praise to Our Sovereigns on This Earth! Glory to All the Russian People! Glory to His Faithful Servants! Glory to His Distinguished Guests! Glory! May Truth be in Russia a Shining Glory more Fair than the Sun! This Song We Sing to Bread! We Sing to Bread! We Render Honor to Bread! Glory to the Old People for Consolation! To Good People, for Listening to Glory! Glory Forever and Ever! Glory![124]

Below this, guests found the menu: *Rassolnik*, a soup with meat and pickled cucumber; borscht; pirozhki stuffed with meat; steamed sturgeon; roasted spring lamb; pheasant in aspic; roast capon in cream sauce; salad; asparagus; sweet fruit in wine; and ice cream.[125]

Francis Grenfell, always the gourmet, thought it *"an excellent lunch"* and devoured everything, but others were

During the long Imperial procession, following the Coronation at the Church of the Assumption, Tsar Nicholas II and Empress Alexandra Feodorovna walked under a richly-decorated baldaquin (canopy). Portions of the Imperial procession were filmed and can be easily watched online even today.

less certain.[126] Though special dishes had been prepared for him, Chinese diplomat Li-Hung Chang complained that they *"do not taste like the foods at home, or those of our own cooks which we have with us."* His only comfort was his own tea, brought from China and specially brewed for him in the Imperial kitchen.[127] Hot and tired, Emily Roebling admitted that the food looked *"magnificent"* though the dishes *"were not always very good"* when tasted. More interested in the champagne, she toasted her absent husband, proudly celebrating his fifty-ninth birthday in far-off Trenton, with one of the Emperor's crystal glasses, only to receive a nasty shock. The champagne, she found, was *"strong enough to knock your head off."*[128]

A mere hour passed from the first blare of trumpets to the final salute marking the banquet's end. Thoroughly relieved, Nicholas, Alexandra, and Marie Feodorovna walked one last time through the palace, crowned and trailing golden robes as the crowd looked on.[129] Last glimpses cemented the day's impressions. Nicholas, said Kate Koon, was pale, *"quite worn out,"* and nearly *"enveloped"* in his mantle.[130] Alexandra looked beautiful but shy, while Marie Feodorovna seemed *"distressed,"* her face marked by profound sorrow.[131]

Evening fell over Moscow, and with the arrival of dusk, celebrations switched from the theatrically medieval to the dazzlingly modern. *"It was a hot summer night,"* recalled Mary Hickley, *"with the throb of a great national excitement in the air."*[132] The streets were thick with carriages and crowds of people making their way toward the Kremlin. Anticipating this night, electricians had strung hundreds of thousands of tiny electric lights along roofs, over windows, down walls, above doorways, and across domes. They flowed atop triumphal arches, outlined churches, shone upon fountains and statuary, and sparkled in the delicate spring foliage of trees – so many lights that authorities had to build Moscow's first electrical station to absorb the load.[133]

Preparations for the illumination had been intense and, in some cases, filled with danger. A few weeks earlier, one British correspondent had reported the scene at the Kremlin:

I watched a cool headed sailor climbing about the Russian eagle which surmounts, at a height of 170 feet, the handsome tower of St. Savior's Gate. Every now and then the electric current would be turned on and a few lamps fail to light up. The sailor then had to climb, wholly unaided and carrying tools with him, round and about the huge eagle, it measures about twenty feet across the wings, stepping on and holding by the outspread wing feathers for the most part, until he succeeded in reaching and putting to rights the defaulting lamps. The risk, in the cold, raw weather, at such a height, was immense and it was a relief when, after nearly an hour's labor, he reached comparative safety a few yards below the peak on which the eagle stands. The moment his hands were at liberty the man devoutly crossed himself three times, turning towards the sacred places within the fortress, an action which indicated pretty surely his own opinion of the feat just accomplished and sent a thrill through the spectators below.[134]

Now, a half-million people hovered around the Kremlin, full of *"suppressed excitement and enthusiasm."*[135] At nine Nicholas and Alexandra stepped onto the terrace above the Moskva River, below a moon that shone *"like a great lantern suspended in the firmament."*[136] Immense projectors lined with mirrors shot streaks of brilliant white light into the night, catching the couple in their glare as the crowd burst into *God Save the Tsar*. An official presented Empress Alexandra with a silver tray topped by a bouquet of white roses. Removing the flowers tripped a hidden switch to the power station concealed inside the Kremlin: in an instant some 200,000 lights flickered on in the medieval citadel.[137]

"The picture that the Kremlin presented," enthused the Coronation's official account, *"was truly fairy-like, amazing, unimaginable!"*[138] Richard Harding Davis saw *"colored glass bowls in the form of gigantic stars and crowns and crosses,"* along with Imperial ciphers burning *"against the darkness like pieces of stationary fireworks."*[139] This *"embroidery of diamonds,"* thought John Logan, was like a *"mirage"* of *"pearls, rubies, diamonds and sapphires"* that blazed with *"fantastic and scintillating light."*[140] Green lights shone upon the Spassky Tower, outlining its steep roof and its golden, double-headed eagle that *"seemed to be made of diamonds;"* crimson, gold, white, and blue lights bathed the tops of the other towers, a necklace of jewel tones sparkling against the night.[141] Everyone in the British party, said Francis Grenfell, *"agreed that we had never seen anything more beautiful."*[142] Mary Hickley was enchanted by this *"dream of beauty,"* struggling to take in the *"mass of golden domes, huge palaces, the encircling crenellated wall with its fantastic towers and turrets,"* and *"bridges spanning the river below"* that *"scintillated in myriads of fairy lights – ruby, sapphire, emerald, amethyst!"*[143] Even the cynical Aylmer Maude was stunned. *"I was for a moment,"* he wrote, *"half inclined to forget what injury to human life and limb and what tremendous cost and labor had been needed to prepare it all."*[144]

Magical splendor could not overcome human nature. Pressing along with the curious, jovial spectators, several of the foreign correspondents were victimized by pickpockets.[145] Still, they were lucky: Aylmer Maude barely escaped disaster when a mounted Cossack tried a little too enthusiastically to control the masses and backed his horse into the crowd. This customary rough treatment sat uneasily with the celebratory atmosphere so carefully cultivated. Later that same night, after several similar incidents, crowds pulled four members of the Cossack Guard from their horses and beat them severely.[146]

Sitting in the Grand Kremlin Palace that night, the newly crowned Emperor turned to the pages of his diary:

A great and splendid, solemn day, though for Alix, Mama, and me, a hard one, in a moral sense. From eight in the

A photo taken of the Moscow Kremlin after Tsar Nicholas II lit 200,000 flickering lights.

morning we were on our feet, though our procession did not start until half-past ten. Fortunately the weather was excellent; from the Red Staircase we had a radiant sight. Everything that took place in the Cathedral of the Assumption, although it really seemed like a dream, I shall never forget my entire life. We got back at half-past two. At three there was a similar procession to the Palace of Facets for the meal. At four it was happily at an end. Had dinner with Mama, who has borne up wonderfully under this long ordeal. At nine we went to the upstairs balcony and there Alix lit up the electric illuminations on the tower of Ivan Velikii and then, one by one, the towers and walls of the Kremlin were illuminated as well as the embankment opposite and along the Moscow River. Went to bed early.[147]

Thus the introverted Nicholas described the day of his crowning. The contrast between majestic pageantry and private feelings reveal a monarch reluctant to embrace the ceremonial demands of office while desperately clinging to a divine Autocracy. Throughout, he had seemed pale, insignificant, lost beneath the trappings of Imperial power. Subsumed by the public grandeur of the occasion, he retreated to comfortable banality, to complaints about having stood for so long, and to the domestic concerns dominating his life.

Others, though, conveyed something of the exalted conception that had escaped the Emperor's customarily terse diary. The coronation, wrote Donald Mackenzie Wallace, was mute evidence of *"the almost sacred character of the Tsar."*[148] Mandell Creighton saw the ceremony as an expression of popular will, *"an attempt to set forth in a becoming way the sentiments of the people, who wished their ruler to feel how entirely their hopes were set upon him, and who commended themselves and him alike to God's guidance and direction."* The atmosphere, he thought, was *"charged with a simple, childlike earnestness, and intensity of faith and hope."*[149] The day, Henry LaPauze aptly summed up, had *"started in triumph, and finished in apotheosis."*[150]

Chapter X

Moscow awoke the next morning like a drunk reeling from a festive hangover. Tired, still dazed by the coronation and its spectral illuminations, people dizzily struggled out of bed. Even the overcast, rainy weather reflected the subdued mood.[1] Ten days of balls, a theatrical gala, and the People's Feast, still stretched enticingly ahead as a salve to the sense of anticlimax.

Newspapers that Wednesday morning carried the Emperor's Coronation Manifesto. It was a chance for Nicholas II to cultivate loyalty and appeal to public sympathy but, aside from 300,000 rubles for new university housing in Moscow and in St. Petersburg, the manifesto focused almost exclusively on the Empire's criminals. Outstanding taxes were forgiven or reduced; minor criminal offenses symbolically pardoned; and certain political prisoners granted review and reductions of their sentences provided they showed *"sincere repentance."* Some political exiles received right of return to Russia, with permission to conduct business, but there were few attempts to favorably influence them toward the new reign. In most cases, civil rights were not restored and freedom, even when granted, came with severe residency restrictions, lest these troublesome elements spread philosophies pernicious to the Autocracy.[2]

By contrast, 876,758 rubles ($11,850,000 or £8,767,580 in 2014), three times the benefit allotted to university housing, was lavished on decorations and orders for the privileged receiving Imperial honors. There were jeweled badges, brooches, snuffboxes, and commemorative medals, including copper coins for common soldiers, and 5,000 gold, silver, and bronze medallions and jetons for more illustrious coronation guests. Monogrammed watches and signed photographs went to Kammer Pages, while the Metropolitans of Kiev, St. Petersburg, and Moscow received diamond crosses to wear atop their miters.[3]

The Coronation Honors List poured out awards and orders in an Imperial bounty: dignified bureaucrats became Senators, and worthy members of the State Council, the Imperial Court, the Imperial Suite, and the military all received promotions. Fourteen *"Foreign Visitors of Distinction"* received the Russian Order of the White Eagle, including Baron Alphonse de Rothschild, a French banker and one of the very few Jews so honored by the anti-Semitic State.[4] The list left contradictory impressions. *"Many people were happy,"* recorded Alexei Suvorin, *"but plenty were unhappy."* Many who had heavily – and obviously – campaigned to be included in the list were, as Suvorin noted, *"in despair,"* particularly those who had used fortunes to advance their cause. *"Money isn't everything!"* sighed Hilarion Vorontsov-Dashkov, clearly exasperated at the more insistently ambitious.[5] Among those singled out for special mention was Nicholas's former tutor Konstantin Pobedonostsev, Ober-Procurator of the Holy Synod, who was raised to the rank of a Knight in the Order of St. Vladimir. Citing his *"enlightened service"* and *"strengthening the truth of the Orthodox Faith,"* the honor actually awarded Pobedonostsev's odious nationalistic policies, a mantle of religious credibility supporting the autocracy.[6]

Social inequities came into sharp focus that morning. Festive bunting and cheerful flags hung in limp discontent across the soggy streets; the air was still, unmoving, uncomfortable.[7] Nicholas and Alexandra received congratulations at the Grand Kremlin Palace. Restless delegations from Government institutions, the Holy Synod, the Nobility, the Diplomatic Corps, and provincial and rural assemblies shuffled along the 300-foot length of the Hall of the Order of St. Andrei, across its floor inlaid with twenty varieties of rare woods, toward a dais where the Imperial couple, he in the uniform of the Egersky Life Guards Regiment and she in a salmon-colored gown embroidered in silver thread, stood impassively for two-and-a-half hours.[8] Russians came armed with elaborately engraved gold and silver plates

Royal guests, from the left: Crown Princess Marie and Crown Prince Ferdinand of Romania, Grand Duke Ernst Ludwig of Hesse and by Rhine, Grand Duchess Marie Alexandrovna, Duke Alfred of Saxe-Coburg and Gotha, Grand Duchess Victoria Melita of Hesse and By Rhine, and Hereditary Prince Alfred of Saxe-Coburg and Gotha.

holding traditional gifts of bread and salt; Aylmer Maude thought that Nicholas II *"will probably never even have the time to examine"* the plates.[9] Providing these salvers bankrupted many small towns. Moscow spent only 5,000 rubles ($67,000 or £50,000 in 2014) on its plate, but the Polish delegation paid an astronomical 24,000 rubles ($324,000 or £240,000) for its single silver tray.[10] The money, complained Grand Duke Konstantin, *"could have been put to so much good elsewhere."* [11]After receiving nearly 300 of these trays, even the Emperor agreed.[12] Rural representatives, small towns, factories, and ordinary people, he declared, should not bother with such *"useless"* and *"expensive"* presents. Thoughtful as the sentiments were, they offended loyalist sensibilities and provincial pride.[13]

Religious themes dominated the remainder of the day. Antonio Agliardi, the Papal Nuncio, had – by careful design – arrived in Moscow the previous day, setting foot in the city only after the coronation service was over. Clad in his new cardinal's robes and all smiles, he offered Leo XIII's congratulations to the Imperial couple.[14] Even the dinner that night, a banquet for 286 guests, demonstrated unity between State and Church. Aristocrats belonging to the first two tiers in Peter the Great's famous Table of Ranks joined members of the Holy Synod and high-ranking clergy in the Palace of Facets.[15] Nicholas, Alexandra, and their secular guests sat on one side of the table in uniforms and dainty toilettes; on the other, churchmen lined up in contrasting rows of rich purple robes and dark headdresses.[16] There was food, wine, and music, but little in the way of enjoyment, at least for the Imperial couple. *"The heat was appalling!"* Nicholas complained in his diary. He was happy to escape early, to spend the evening with the Dowager Empress and his Greek cousins.[17]

Formalities continued at half-past eleven the next morning as Nicholas and Alexandra received congratulations from the Emperor's non-Christian subjects in the Hall of the Order of Andrei. It was a brilliant day: bright sunshine streamed through the tall windows overlooking the Moskva River, washing over the room's gilded piers and profusion of ornaments. Nicholas, wearing the uniform of the Ismailovsky Life Guards Regiment, led an Alexandra in silver brocade and diamonds to the dais.[18] Crown Princess Marie of Romania thought the scene straight out of *A Thousand and One Nights*. The Emir of Bokhara led an exotic parade of *"quaintly-garbed envoys from the North, South, East, and West of their mighty Realm,"* *"mysterious-looking Chinese"* and other *"picturesque personalities"* all offering declarations of loyalty to their Imperial master.[19] Nicholas and Alexandra looked tired from the start, and boredom quickly set in.[20] Some of the foreign royal guests and even members of the Imperial Family chatted and laughed; a few even ignored protocol and climbed onto the dais behind the crowned couple for better views. *"Ella!"* whispered an infuriated Grand Duke Michael Nikolaievich, *"Tell them that it's not permissible to stand by the Throne!"*[21]

People scattered at the ceremony's end. Nicholas and Alexandra ran off to Neskuchnoye, as they would do at every opportunity, to escape their formal duties, to walk in the garden, and to spend time with each other.[22] The immensely wealthy aristocratic Yusupov family treated the British delegation to a lavish dinner and Gypsy concert in the forbidding halls of their medieval house that had once served as hunting lodge for Ivan the Terrible.[23] For seven thousand people scattered across Moscow, though, the hours of leisurely freedom ended at eight, when flickering lights and pealing bells summoned them to the Grand Kremlin Palace, and the Coronation Ball.

The crush in the palace was enormous: by nine o'clock, people could scarcely move through the cavernous halls. *"Through the open windows of the palace,"* wrote one correspondent, *"we could hear the noise of the crowd in the distance as they cheered."*[24] Chevalier Guards, in breeches of white elk skin, so tight that it took several men to pull them on, struggled to clear paths through the rooms.[25] The Americans, in particular, were stunned by a *"scintillating magnificence difficult to exaggerate."*[26] John Logan saw *"uniforms glittering with orders, varied in color and design as widely as the imagination can possibly conceive, mingling with the costumes of the great ladies of the Court, some of whom seemed oppressed by their weight of diamonds; and to accentuate the splendor of the scene appeared here and there the bizarre costume of some Oriental potentate, a Chinese dignity, or a Siamese Prince."*[27] *"Jewels elsewhere are as nothing,"* Kate Koon marveled. *"On all sides women were wearing necklaces, pins, and*

Grand Duke Michael Nikolaievich.

The Siamese Delegation to the Coronation.

tiaras that almost covered their heads and necks. Some of the jewels were as large as robin's eggs." The resulting "blaze," she wrote, "makes ones eyes fatigued."²⁸

At last, the Grand Master of Ceremonies appeared in gold-embroidered splendor. Striking the floor three times with an ebony staff topped by a silver double-headed eagle, he cried out, "Their Imperial Majesties!" and the crowd fell silent.²⁹ With a white, sable-trimmed dolman draped over the shoulder of his crimson and gold Hussar Life Guards uniform, Nicholas led his wife toward the crowd. Alexandra wore a light pink-colored Russian Court gown of silver tissue, embroidered in silver with pale tulle roses embellished with diamonds, matching the diamond tiara atop her head and a wide diamond stomacher draped across the bodice.³⁰

The orchestra launched into the polonaise from *A Life for the Tsar*, but dancing was scarcely the point.³¹ The ball was pure theatre, with Nicholas and Alexandra on majestic display as they circled the palace halls. Only members of the Imperial Family, foreign royal guests, and diplomats joined them in a polonaise of bobbing heads and gliding steps, musical accompaniment almost incidental to the exercise. Winding through the crowded rooms, the Emperor and Empress changed partners seven times to honor relatives and diplomats in turn. For the second circuit, Nicholas led his aunt Queen Olga of Greece, while Alexandra walked on the arm of the Turkish Ambassador, the highest-ranking member of the Diplomatic Corps.³² Zia Husny Pasha, the Turkish Ambassador, was in an unfortunate position. *"Being tone deaf and having no sense of rhythm,"* said one acquaintance, his efforts at dancing *"made quite a comic scene."*³³ Walking on the arm of her cousin Nicholas II, Crown Princess Marie of Romania seemed to be *"the most exquisite creature"* at the ball, a woman who *"took the hearts of all the young men present."*³⁴ Prejudice colored impressions: the Duke

The Turkish Delegation to the Coronation.

of Connaught, thought Kate Koon, *"walked along in his pompous manner, like a true Briton,"* at the side of his niece Alexandra.³⁵ The Empress seemed regal, a *"noble, girlish beauty,"* in John Logan's romantic words, but Kate thought the Emperor short and slight, *"not at all kingly."*³⁶

The Americans hoped to be back in the palace the next morning, when the Imperial couple received distinguished ladies and the wives of the Diplomatic Corps. A little after eleven, Nicholas and Alexandra entered the Hall of the Order of St. Andrei, he uniformed as a colonel in the 44th Nizhegorodsky Life Guards and she draped in a dark blue gown sewn with golden flowers.³⁷ Alexandra's friend Katherine Breckinridge, wife of the American Minister to Russia, was there in the court finery her husband so disliked, but not so her countrymen. *"We never understood why,"* Kate lamented. In fact, a court chamberlain had delivered the coveted invitations to the American Legation, but an overworked Breckinridge absentmindedly failed to pass them along.³⁸

Queen Olga of Greece (née Grand Duchess Olga Konstantinovna).

Those who did arrive followed the careful sartorial instructions printed on the bottom of their invitations calling for the same elaborate court gowns, long trains, tiaras, and feathers they had worn on the day of the Coronation ceremony. Chamberlains and Kammer Pages guided them to the palm-bedecked Winter Garden, where a court photographer captured their resplendence for posterity before they crowded into the halls. Nerves were unsteady: worried that ignorance or excitement would bring disaster, Grand Duchess Elisabeth Feodorovna took it upon herself to roam through the palace, offering impromptu lessons in Imperial etiquette and managing the bows, curtsies, and kissing of hands while reminding ladies how to walk backward in the cumbersome gowns and not trip over the long trains. Her efforts were wasted: there were too many ladies, too many foreign languages, and too much confusion, for the Grand Duchess to communicate successfully. Finally, an exasperated Grand Duke Alexei Alexandrovich took the matter into his own hands. Announcing that he would play the Empress, the portly Grand Duke walked to the center of the room and extended his hand as the graceful Grand Duchess curtsied and kissed it for the benefit of the amused ladies looking on.³⁹

Outside the palace, hundreds of thousands of Nicholas II's common subjects headed for Khodynka Meadow, site of the following day's People's Feast. Some 25,000 alone arrived by train that afternoon from surrounding villages.⁴⁰ They poured onto the dusty Khodynka throughout that Friday. By dusk, a sea of heads circled the ornate, medieval-style pavilion where Nicholas and Alexandra would appear. Thousands pressed against covered tribunes for 400 dignitaries and surrounding open stands for the 12,000 who had purchased tickets from the Ministry of the Imperial Court to gaze upon the fete.⁴¹

Games and prizes filled carnival booths scattered across the field; new pairs of boots, hats, scarves, and even shining samovars hung from gaily decorated posts, rewards for the lucky few.⁴² Taking the stage, actors would amuse with comedic scenes from *The Humpbacked Horse* and the popular *Ermak Timofeyevich*, singers would delight with extracts from *Ruslan and Ludmila*, and musicians would offer rousing and patriotic tunes as the crowd awaited the Imperial couple. Strolling minstrels and magicians would entertain, and the thousands of children could laugh at performances by Durov's Trained Animals and the Brothers Nikitin Circus.[43]

Covetous eyes gazed on a line of wooden stands slung across one end of the field, where flimsy shelves held 400,000 souvenir bundles for their distribution at ten the following morning.[44] Vassili Krasnov, a worker camped out on the field, thought it was *"plain stupid"* to wait until morning for his gift. Strangers from outside Moscow, he worried, would craftily make off with all the spoils before ten o'clock came. *"Am I going to live to see another coronation?"* he wondered. *"To be left without a reminder of such a celebration seemed to me – as a Muscovite through and through – a disgrace: was I to be like some corner of a field they'd forgot to sow? They said the mugs were very pretty and would last forever....Back then, enamel cups and things were a real marvel."*[45]

Grand Duchess Elisabeth Feodorovna.

Employees at Moscow's Gustav List Factory also fretted about the supply of gifts. Hoping to avoid a long wait, the foreman told his workers that he would take them to the field at eight the following morning; there were, he assured them, plenty of souvenir bundles to be had. Semen Kanatchikov heard *"contradictory, ominous rumors"* throughout the evening: the crowd, already huge, was growing by the hour, and the gifts might be gone by morning. A few of his worried friends set off for the field, but seventeen-year-old Kanatchikov remained behind in his humble lodgings, impatiently waiting for morning to come.[46]

An immense throng pushed ceaselessly toward Khodynka as Friday's sunset gave way to a warm, moonless night.[47] No one knew how many came: estimates ranged from between 500,000 to a million – the latter more than twice the number expected by officials.[48] Journalist Vassili Nemirovich-Danchenko saw peasants who had walked from Siberia in their *bast* shoes; they clustered around bonfires, drinking vodka or kvass, strumming balalaikas, and singing folk songs. Thousands more pushed against perilously flimsy wooden railings separating them from booths stacked with Imperial gifts.[49] The ground itself eventually disappeared beneath this tightly packed, unrelenting human wave. Each new arrival forced the crowd further from the Imperial Pavilion and across the field, where the dusty plain gave way to pits and ravines hastily covered with rotted planks. Relief was impossible: two distant vats of water, at the edges of the field, remained out of reach, and authorities provided no medical personnel or aid stations.[50] A line of twelve mounted Cossacks, forty-six soldiers from the Moscow Garrison under command of Captain Lvovich, and two police constables – sixty-one anxious men in all – stood between the crowd and Imperial gifts.[51]

Five miles away, fashionable Moscow made its way to the Bolshoi Theatre. That night there would be a gala performance, entertainment on an imposing scale meant to reinforce loyally nationalistic feeling. Nicholas I introduced such secular diversions at his coronation and, as with his triple bow from the top of the Red Staircase, monarchs after him repeated the tradition.[52] For Alexander II and his guests, there had been a performance of Donizetti's romantic opera *L'Elisir d'Amore*, light, European, and cosmopolitan like the Emperor himself, a slice of sugary confection dropped into the middle of sacred Russian Orthodox ritual. The tone, like everything else in Russia, changed under Alexander III. Marius Petipa choreographed a new folk ballet appealing to Slavic tastes, and a chorus performed the first and last acts of Michael Glinka's opera *A Life for the Tsar*, whose tale of heroic self-sacrifice by peasants to ensure their sovereign's survival became a leitmotif echoing the coronation's larger themes.[53]

Grand Duke Vladimir Alexandrovich.

In 1896, there would be a new ballet, a celebration of this most renowned of Russian arts that came with its own high sexual drama. Petipa choreographed *La Perle*, a frothy paean to romantic love set to the music of Riccardo Drigo, Orchestral Director of St. Petersburg's Mariinsky Ballet Company.[54] Ivan Vsevolozsky, Director of the Imperial Theatres, drew up a program that, not unnaturally, featured Mathilde Kschessinska, the Mariinsky Ballet's principal dancer, in the starring role. Kschessinska might be a star, but she had also been Nicholas II's mistress before his marriage. Appeasing her own wounded ago, she clung to a fantasy that her former lover had been forced into his marriage with Alix of Hesse as *"an unavoidable necessity,"* although he had *"only a vague feeling"* for the Princess[55]. She now lived openly with his cousin, weaving her personal life, said one furious critic, into the *"stinking, cynical wreath of human offal and vice"* that she called art.[56]

Somehow the Dowager Empress obtained an advance copy of the ballet schedule. Reviewing the program, she was shocked to find her son's former lover listed as the evening's star, and quickly drew a line through it. If Kschessinska appeared, she said, there would be *"a scandal."* Vsevolozsky was forced to give visiting Italian dancer Pierrina Legnani the coveted starring role as the White Pearl, an odd choice for such a nationalistic event, but one dictated by the uncomfortable circumstances.[57]

Armed with a sense of entitlement matched only by an unbounded ego, Kschessinska was insulted that she would not dance the lead role as an excruciating doppelganger in front of the Emperor's newly crowned wife. Furious at the perceived slight, she ran to Grand Duke Vladimir, a man with a weakness for young ballerinas. The Grand Duke, she wrote, *"had always shown me friendship and kindness,"* and he alone *"could intercede for me and would understand the shocking injustice with which I had been treated."* Vladimir proved sympathetic indeed, and went straight to Nicholas II, insisting that the program be changed. Faced with his forceful uncle, Nicholas gave in. Vsevolozsky was forced to completely redo the planned gala, with new music, and choreography by Petipa, added just for Kschessinska who, having disrupted the schedule, could only be worked into the gala by being given a special solo appearance. Undoubtedly this appealed to her vanity, making her the centerpiece of the festivities, but it caused much resentment among members of

the Mariinsky Corps.⁵⁸ Concession relieved Nicholas of an unpleasant confrontation with his uncle, but at the cost of placing his former mistress on stage in front of a tittering aristocratic audience aware of their shared sexual past.

It was a warm Friday night, the sunset glowing red over Moscow's onion domes and smilax-bedecked buildings. Twilight transformed the Bolshoi Theatre's elegant neoclassicism into a bastion of blazing decorations.⁵⁹ John Logan gazed in awe at the *"mammoth spectacle"* of *"fantastic and scintillating light"* that greeted the

The Bolshoi Theater at the time of the Coronation.

guests. Crimson and gold velvet draperies, sewn with golden double-headed eagles and heraldic shields, wrapped the Ionic columns supporting the pediment; an enormous canopy, dripping gold fringe, crowned the main entrance; flags embroidered with monograms and laurel wreaths fluttered, and gigantic decorative crowns crowded the massive rooftop statue of Apollo in the Chariot of the Sun from view. Every inch of the theatre had been picked out in strings of tiny electric bulbs, cascading down walls, outlining statuary, and silhouetting cornices in twinkling fires culminating in real flames that burned in rooftop Rostral columns against the encroaching dark.⁶⁰

The Government devoted some 12,000 rubles ($162,000, or £120,000 in 2014) to adorning the Bolshoi exterior; another 50,000 rubles (approximately $675,000, or £500,000) was spent enlarging the Imperial box to accommodate sixty-three guests; repainting the auditorium; wiring the chandeliers for electricity; gilding stucco ornaments; and re-cushioning seats in crimson velvet.⁶¹ The 3,000 guests were rigidly segregated by seniority and rank. Minor diplomats and lesser gentlemen of the aristocracy occupied the first thirteen rows of the Orchestra; behind them were provincial nobility and minor courtiers, and finally members of the Imperial Court, Suite, Entourage, and Household. Ladies of the Imperial Family, the Diplomatic Corps, and Extraordinary Embassies filled the first tier stretching out from the central Imperial Box; above them, in lessening importance as they neared the ceiling, came more diplomats, courtiers, and government officials.⁶²

Everyone of importance wanted a seat in the Bolshoi that evening. Antonio Agliardi, the Papal Nuncio, was a notable exception, absenting himself from what he apparently considered a secular spectacle. By contrast, Mandell Creighton, Bishop of Peterborough, was delighted to receive a last minute telephone call offering him a coveted invitation.⁶³ The crowd, said John Logan, was *"a gorgeous display of wealth and beauty, of variety in design, of wild revelry in color, of jewels of untold value."*⁶⁴ An equally enthusiastic Henry LaPauze spotted *"some famous heroes, wearing the Grand Cross of St. Andrei or the Grand Cross of St. Alexander Nevsky,"* their uniforms *"streaming with gold and diamonds."*⁶⁵ Epaulettes and aiguillettes, medals and orders, tiaras and necklaces, all glistened in the light, turning the auditorium into *"a cascade of gold, diamonds, and shimmering crystals."*⁶⁶ If they tired of this display, guests could study the program, a colorful, bold design of brazenly bare-breasted nymphs frolicking beneath art nouveau-styled waves.⁶⁷

Nicholas and Alexandra arrived at eight and walked to the edge of an immense Imperial Box framed by caryatids to acknowledge the cheering crowd. The orchestra played *God*

Opposite page: From the left: Grand Duke Paul Alexandrovich, Prince Adolph of Schaumburg-Lippe, Empress Alexandra Feodorovna, Grand Duke Sergei Mikhailovich, Tsar Nicholas II, the Duke of Leuchtenberg, Grand Duchess Marie Pavlovna, Duchess Evgenia Maximilianovna of Oldenburg, the Duchess of Leuchtenberg, Grand Duke Sergei Alexandrovich and Grand Duke Vladimir Alexandrovich.

Save the Tsar as they stood in the light, he in the dark blue dress uniform of the Preobrazhensky Life Guards Regiment, she in a gown of silver brocade with innumerable strings of pearls around her neck and a magnificent diamond tiara on her head.⁶⁸ "*Perhaps the Theatre, with its resounding walls, echoing and re-echoing the great shouts,*" wrote Logan, "*served to augment the enthusiasm and make it seem even greater than it was. But be that as it may, the welcome which the Imperial couple received was as warm as one could wish and they seemed to be deeply moved.*"⁶⁹

Imperial and Royal ladies attending the Coronation. From the left, standing: Duchess Olga of Württemberg, Grand Duchess Vera Konstantinovna, Grand Duchess Anastasia Mikhailovna, Grand Duchess Marie Pavlovna, Grand Duchess Elena Vladimirovna, Grand Duchess Elisabeth Mavrikievna, Princess Helena of Saxe-Altenburg. At front: Duchess Elsa of Württemberg, Grand Duchess Alexandra Iosifovna and the Duchess Connaught.

Bathed in "*yellow and scarlet, green and blue, gold and purple, white and maroon and pink*" calcium lights, singers took the stage as the orchestra thundered into Glinka's opera.⁷⁰ For the next ninety minutes, the story of Ivan Susanin and his sacrifice to save the life of the first of the Romanov Tsar unfolded in patriotic splendor. With its famed *Glory Chorus* and triumphant scenes of Michael Romanov's crowning, nothing could have been more suited to the occasion. It was, Francis Grenfell admitted, an enjoyable spectacle, though the performance did not quite measure up to its gilded surroundings: the lead tenor, he grumbled, sang his part badly.⁷¹

As guests smoked, sipped champagne, and ate caviar during the interval, reality briefly intruded on fantasy. With amazement, then concern, and finally fear, the sixty-one men standing guard on Khodynka Meadow had watched as the crowd continued to swell that evening. After a few hours, a desperate Captain Lvovich contacted headquarters and dispatched his deputy to the Bolshoi, where both Count Vorontsov-Dashkov and Chief of Police Colonel A. A. Vlassovsky sat watching the spectacle. Despite his earlier concerns and "*usually only too prompt and vigorous*" in enforcing security, Vlassovsky dismissed pleas that he visit the field.⁷² The deputy had better luck with Vorontsov-Dashkov, who scribbled an urgent note asking for additional troops. After ten increasingly frantic messages from Lvovich, Vlassovsky finally ordered 100 mounted Cossacks onto the field before returning to the auditorium to enjoy the ballet.⁷³ Almost as soon as the men had arrived at Khodynka, though, they were inexplicably ordered back to their barracks, leaving the crowd in chaos.⁷⁴

Unaware of the growing tensions at Khodynka, the privileged audience filling the Bolshoi now turned their eyes to the spectacle of *La Perle*. "*Knights clad in gleaming armor of coral and richly colored shells,*" remembered John Logan, "*fought for mermaids whose fairy forms were resplendent with the soft light of opals and shimmering pearls.*" Music swelled and dancers – including Kschessinska – swirled across the stage as "*mammoth green sea monsters with flaming eyes of scarlet crept about, in and out of gigantic shells.*" It was a phantasmagoria of surreal images and shifting hues that entertained and delighted.⁷⁵ "*The Emperor,*" thought a foreign visitor unaware of the irony, "*must have been greatly pleased in the certainty that his guests had enjoyed themselves immensely.*"⁷⁶ In his diary, Nicholas made no mention of his former mistress dancing in front of his own White Pearl; it had been, he recorded, "*a glorious spectacle,*" with a "*charming*" ballet.⁷⁷

It was still warm when Nicholas and Alexandra left the Bolshoi and drove back to the Kremlin. Moscow slumbered beneath its festoons of light, quiet and peaceful. *A Life for the Tsar* had greatly impressed the foreign guests at the theatre. The romantically heroic drama on the Bolshoi stage, though, proved no match for the tragic drama unfolding across town. On Khodynka Meadow, the opera's theme of peasant sacrifice played out in real life and to catastrophic effect, destined to haunt the Coronation forever.

Chapter XI

The darkness of night gave way to an opalescent dawn as sunrise crept over the crowd gathered on Khodynka Meadow that Saturday, May 18. The field, recorded one correspondent, looked *"like an anthill: the only thing visible was a swarm of human heads."*[1] *"The morning was calm,"* said one man on the field, *"without any wind. There wasn't a breath of fresh air, and in the crush it was harder and harder to breathe."*[2] A cloud of steam, *"like the mist over a swamp,"* hovered across the field. Here and there, people had fainted; the crowd was pressed so tightly together, *"as if in a vise,"* that the unconscious stood upright, jostled back and forth in this sea of humanity. Journalist Vladimir Giliarovsky spotted a *"handsome old man"* who had *"had long since stopped breathing: he suffocated in silence, died without a sound, and his corpse had grown cold."* People vomited but could not lower their heads.[3]

With the first rays of sun, a few men handed out Imperial souvenirs to friends or sold them to those armed with rubles, four hours before the booths were to open.[4] Word went through the crowd, recalled one man, that *"factory workers would receive their gifts first, and then us peasants."*[5] Worried that supplies would run short, those pressed against the rails screamed, *"Distribute! Distribute!"*[6] Faced with this angry mob, men in first one booth and then another hurled packages into the air.[7] The crowd surged forward, breaking through wooden rails and stampeding toward the coveted gifts, fighting with each other as they tried to catch the bundles and *"tearing the booths to pieces."*[8]

A wave of human dominoes, *"unable to resist,"* said one man, moved forward as panic swept the field. *"Everything happened so fast."*[9] Stumbling on the uneven ground, people tumbled into ravines and plunged through rotted planks to the depths of abandoned wells.[10] Fists, elbows, and arms pressed men, women, and children to the dusty ground, from their feet to their knees, and from their knees to their stomachs as those behind pushed on relentlessly. *"There were desperate cries and calls,"* said one man, *"as we all fell on top of each other. I was among the last to reach the trenches, and I had to walk on others. I was pushed down and crawled over hands and feet, as under me they shouted, wept, and groaned for help. I did not dare look back until I was out of danger."*[11]

"It was impossible to stop," a man agonized.[12] *"Women and children,"* reported one French correspondent, *"carried away by the tremendous pressure, were pushed into a trench. Everyone that fell was doomed to death."*[13] Bodies were trampled, arms broken, and faces smashed into bloody pulps as screams rose above the meadow, *"horrible, heart-rending groans and howls,"* Giliarovsky said.[14] Aubrey Stanhope saw *"a big, fat peasant woman"* stumble and fall in front of him; *"two people in their flight fell over her, twenty over them in the same manner, and in a few minutes, there lay a heap of struggling, cursing, biting, scratching humanity, tearing each other's scalps off, fighting in an awful death struggle with the frenzy of despair."*[15] Entire families were crushed within seconds in this *"terrible whirlpool of unconscious force,"* later found desperately clinging to one another in death.[16] *"People were shoving me toward them,"* sobbed one man. *"I curled up and rolled into a ditch. I shouted and raised my hand – someone took it. I heaved myself up, pulled myself by the arms, and fell into another hole. People fell on my legs and chest. That's what it was like, trench after trench."*[17] The crowd tore at each other in terror: groups of peasants and workers huddled together in bloodied nakedness, their clothing shredded as they tried to escape.[18]

Hoping to film the Imperial couple's arrival later, French cinematographers Charles Moisson and François Doublier had arrived at Khodynka early that morning. Perched on top of a booth, Moisson scanned the field as seventeen-year-old Doublier pushed through the crowd. *"I heard shrieks behind*

Opposite page: A painting depicting the massive crowd that gathered at Khodynka Field.

me," said Doublier, *"and panic spread through the people. I climbed onto a neighbor's shoulders and struggled across the top of the frightened mass."* Ignoring people tugging and even biting at his legs, Doublier clambered to Moisson's side, both watching in horror as the stampede continued.[19] Cossacks rode into this melee, galloping over bodies, trampling on the injured, and beating back the crowd with whips as they tried to escape.[20] Brutality bred brutality: the crowd pulled Cossacks from their mounts, beating both men and horses to death. Francis Grenfell felt nauseated at the sight of horses and riders *"stamped into a jelly and torn limb from limb."*[21] Storming the stalls, the wounded, thirsty, dangerous crowd found the barrels of beer fitted with rubber plugs that prevented more than a trickle. In a rage, they smashed the barrels apart, filling cupped hands, hats, upturned shirts – even boots – as the liquid gushed across the parched ground.[22]

"No such holocaust of human victims has ever before been caused by a crowd in the open air," Donald Mackenzie Wallace reported in The Times of London, *"and probably no such ghastly disfigurement of the dead has ever been seen on any modern battlefield."*[23] Terrible, mournful wails soon replaced the frenzied push: there were screams for help, hundreds of desperately shouted names in a search for the missing, and sobs from mourning relatives. The dead and dying lay everywhere, their black, purple, and blue faces *"crushed beyond recognition."*[24] Blood oozed from ears and noses; broken bones protruded from twisted arms and legs; engorged tongues filled mouths frozen in silent screams; eyes hung from gouged sockets; and brain tissue seeped through shattered skulls.[25] Pregnant women, caught in the stampede, had gone into premature labor, their newborns dragged across the dusty ground by umbilical cords when the crowd pressed forward.[26] One woman clutched a baby in her arms, both dead from the crush; three young brothers lay with cold arms curled around each other; a dead father held the hands of his two dead sons.[27] A few people, though, had risked their lives to save others, passing children and babies over heads to safety before they were consumed in the panicked waves.[28]

Alexander Izwolsky.

Shock settled over the field. *"Never shall I forget that awful odor of stale beer, leather, and corpses all mixed up together under the heat of a burning sun,"* wrote Aubrey Stanhope. *"And those unfortunate bodies, having been squashed well-nigh to a pulp, began to decompose with visible rapidity. Those poor faces swelled to twice their natural size."* He saw *"dozens of scalps"* piled in a bloody heap; nearby a woman, clutching her child, sobbed over her husband's body; a man sat beside the crushed and lifeless form of his wife, eyes vacant, *"staggered and speechless."*[29] Alexei Ostrukhov, a doctor living near Khodynka, rushed to the scene to help the victims. Wandering through the mounds of corpses, he spotted movement – unconscious, barely-breathing victims who had quickly been hurled into piles with the dead.[30]

Crossing this meadow of misery, Aylmer Maude fulminated in silent rage at the *"reckless neglect of necessary precautions for the lives of thousands of human beings, while thousands upon thousands of trained men were engaged in securing the safety of one young man, whose business is supposedly to serve the people."*[31] He saw that some of the corpses had a few copper kopecks thrown atop them, left by mourning relatives to pay for their burial; once the Moscow Police turned up, though, the money vanished.[32]

Opposite page: The Imperial Stand on Kohdinka Field designed by Fyodor Schechtel.

Peasants celebrating at Khodynka Field before the tragedy.

After the shock of the initial disaster passed, French cinematographers Moisson and Doublier started filming the scene, turning their camera on *"the shrieking, milling, dying masses around the Imperial Pavilion."* The film ran out, but neither man dared abandon the safety of their perch until the police arrived. Rather than provide them with an escort, police arrested the pair of Frenchmen and hauled them off to the Moscow City Jail.[33]

A little before eight, when Semen Kanatchikov and his comrades from the Gustav List Factory arrived at the field, they were confused by groups of hysterical peasants scrambling away from the scene. *"Oh my God!"* someone cried out, *"oh my God! How many people have been crushed! They're taking away the corpses by cartloads!"* Stunned, they listened as the terrified survivors passed: *"You can't imagine how many people fell into the wells!"* one sobbed. *"There's this deep, deep well – people kept falling into it even when it was already packed!"* Another likened what had happened to *"waves on the sea,"* the crowd moving without restraint toward a seemingly inexorable doom. The young men from the List Factory had heard enough. *"We never received our gifts,"* remembered Kanatchikov, *"and we were certainly in no mood for them."* They turned and began the long walk back to their lodgings, *"happy and thankful that we hadn't left for the field in the evening."* Carts piled with corpses rumbled along the road – *"arms, legs, and heads could be seen dangling out,"* he said.[34]

Amid the sobs, Kanatchikov heard something else, an ominous hint of things to come: *"They say the wells were left open on purpose!"* one man declared.[35] This idea spread as the crowd dispersed, many flinging their precious Imperial souvenirs into roadside ditches in silent protest.[36] *"It's a conspiracy!"* someone shouted. The crowds marching off Khodynka, Alexei Suvorin saw, were *"grim and angry."* He, too, heard the protests: *"The organizers!"* a survivor yelled. *"They should be sent to Sakhalin! Or to a desert,*

An artist's rendering of the stampede that caused the Khodynka tragedy.

or worse! Vampires! They drank our blood." Seeing the carnage, the piles of bodies, the ravines and deep wells hastily covered with rotted wood, Suvorin understood the suspicions. *"It's not without reason,"* he wrote in his diary, *"that people think this was planned."*[37]

An urgent telephone call woke Chief of Police Colonel A. A. Vlassovsky that morning and summoned him to the field. Arriving at Khodynka shortly after eight, he stumbled in shock through rows of corpses and screaming victims before someone in the crowd,

A ghastly scene at Khodynka Field, where thousands found an untimely and horrific death.

recognizing him, shouted out, *"Tear Vlassovsky to pieces!"* Police barely managed to save him from the mob.[38] Thoroughly unnerved, Vlassovsky rode straight to the Governor-General's Palace to deliver the tragic news. Grand Duke Sergei, recalled a courtier, was *"very depressed by what had happened,"* and asked for hourly reports.[39]

The Grand Duke and the city's Chief of Police faced a crisis. Both needed to downplay any responsibility for the tragedy, not only to avoid personal repercussions but also because they though any guilt attached to Sergei or his protégé would be an affront to the Imperial Family's dignity. An urgent telephone call had also alerted Minister of Justice Nicholas Muraviev of the disaster; after viewing the scene at Khodynka, he rushed off to the Governor-General's Palace early that morning.[40] He, too, was Sergei's protégé, and owed his position to the Grand Duke.[41] An investigation into the disaster was certain, and it is likely that the three men decided on a unified front to save Sergei's reputation. *"Accidents often happen in crowds,"* Vlassovsky asserted, a line Sergei soon echoed.[42]

A photograph of one of the thousands of victims at Khodynka.

Another early telephone call sent Count Paul Shuvalov racing to the Governor-General's Palace that morning. Hearing of the disaster from his father-in-law Count Vorontsov-Dashkov, Shuvalov thought that Sergei, whom he served as adjutant, would immediately visit Khodynka and wanted to accompany him. Instead, he found the Grand Duke stubbornly resolute. There was no need, Sergei said, to go to Khodynka: Vlassovsky had given him a full report on events at the field, and *"nothing serious had happened."* Shuvalov protested but Sergei was unmoved. The Grand Duke did, though, find the time to pose for souvenir photographs with a group of bewildered officers from the Preobrazhensky Life Guards Regiment in the palace courtyard.[43]

Festive commemoration over, Sergei reluctantly set off with Shuvalov for the Kremlin to break the news to Nicholas II. The Emperor *"became pale as a sheet"* and there were tears in his eyes as he listened to the report.[44] It was, said Nicholas, *"ghastly,"* an event that *"left me with the most appalling impression!"*[45] Alexander Izwolsky, who later served as his Minister of Foreign Affairs, heard that Nicholas's first thought was to cancel the remaining coronation festivities and retire to a monastery in prayer.[46]

The question of how to respond to the catastrophe occupied the rest of the morning. Khodynka, most people agreed, changed everything. The grand and glorious festivities surrounding the Coronation, they thought, must cease out of respect for the dead; the Imperial Court, it was assumed, would be plunged into mourning.[47] This at least was the view held by Nicholas and Alexandra, though they faced an immediate clash between personal desire and public obligation. The People's Feast – whatever remained of it and no matter the depth of the disaster – could not simply be cancelled in a few hours. Too many people – hundreds of thousands from across the Empire – remained at Khodynka. To avoid disappointment, Nicholas and Alexandra would attend the fete as scheduled. What had happened, Nicholas said, was *"a tragedy,"* but he agreed with Sergei that it should *"not be permitted to cast a shadow over the joyous occasion of the coronation."*[48]

A commemorative cup given at Khodynka Field and a bust of Tsar Nicholas II.

Seven days and nights of ceremonies still remained. Though casualty figures remained uncertain, Vorontsov-Dashkov believed that the disaster demanded an overt expression of Imperial compassion, and his advice echoed the Imperial couple's private inclinations. He suggested that Nicholas declare a state of mourning and cancel that evening's ball. A memorial service for the victims at Moscow's immense Cathedral of Christ the Savior, the Minister advised, would demonstrate the Emperor's sorrow and sympathy with his people. As a final gesture, he recommended that Nicholas and Alexandra visit the city's hospitals to console the many hundreds of wounded.[49]

That evening's ball, however, was not mere entertainment. It was to be given in the Imperial couple's honor by Ambassador Count Louis Gustave de Montebello on behalf of the allied French nation. Just as no other nation was quite as profligate in funding its extraordinary embassy to the coronation, so, too, was Republican France intent on extravagantly commemorating the event. *"Russia is celebrating,"* Le Petit Parisien told its readers on coronation day, *"and the whole of France is keen to share her joy."*[50] The French government had declared a public holiday to mark the occasion and ordered elaborate and costly decorations across the city that made, as Le Matin declared, *"the Tsar's coronation a real Parisian national holiday."*[51] Government buildings were hung with *"wonderful flowers, banners, and flags;"* theatres *"wore their finery like trophies;"* and avenues were draped with the Russian flag and the French Tricolor in matching bursts of white, blue, and red. Public monuments were illuminated and bedecked with Russian Coats-of-Arms; even the French Army joined in the festivities, having been granted an official holiday so that they, too, could celebrate, a gesture by his country's only European ally that Nicholas II deemed *"deeply moving."*⁵²

To provide a suitably regal backdrop for the ball Montebello would give in the Imperial couple's honor, rooms in the rented Sheremetiev Palace were refurbished and tapestries, bronzes, marbles, porcelain, gold plate, and Marie Antoinette's furniture from Versailles and Fontainebleau arrived on special trains from Paris, along with 100,000 roses – at a cost of 50,000 Francs ($280,000, or £205,000 in 2013) – from the South of France.⁵³ It was, recalled an aristocrat, the most anticipated ball of the entire coronation schedule.⁵⁴ *"For several months,"* reported *Le Figaro*, *"the possession of one of these little invitations became a serious concern for thousands of people. It was expected to be a marvel of taste, a costly and historic evening."*⁵⁵

Grand Duke Sergei and his brother Grand Duke Paul during the Coronation.

"The number of people who requested invitations," Le *Petit Parisien* informed its readers, *"is enormous. It was difficult to withstand the pleas, but the number of officials invited made it impossible to satisfy all requests."*⁵⁶ Early that Saturday morning, as the tragic scene was unfolding at Khodynka, florists and carpenters were building arbors in the Sheremetiev Palace and arranging the hundreds of thousands of flowers, which had just arrived from the South of France by train.⁵⁷

Word of the Khodynka tragedy shocked Paris. The news, noted *Le Petit Parisien*, *"has caused in France as painful an impression as in Russia. As we share Russia's rejoicing, so we also share its deep and sincere grief."*⁵⁸ French President Felix Faure immediately telegraphed his government's condolences to Nicholas II, assuring him of *"the deep feelings of sympathy and affection"* between the two countries, and adding, *"no one, a few days ago, could imagine that our friendship and sympathy with the Russian people would so soon have an opportunity to be demonstrated under such sad circumstances."*⁵⁹ Now, the Count de Montebello sat by his telephone, fully expecting that at any moment word would come from the Imperial Court that Nicholas and Alexandra would have to cancel their appearance that evening and the ball be abandoned.⁶⁰

Neither Nicholas nor Alexandra, his sister Olga remembered, wanted to attend.⁶¹ The tragedy at Khodynka, said a courtier, *"upset"* the Empress's *"sensitive nature,"* and the idea of the ball was *"a nightmare"* to her.⁶² *"She did all in her power to try and have it put off,"* recalled her cousin Marie of Romania, and *"begged to be allowed to abstain from any festivity that night."*⁶³

Ultimately, the decision lay with Nicholas II, who now found himself beset with insistent opinions. Konstantin Pobedonostsev, his notorious Minister of Religion, declared that canceling the remaining festivities served no purpose; it would, he insisted, *"upset the minds of the people,"* and *"produce a bad impression"* among the foreign visitors to Moscow.⁶⁴ Prince Andrei Lobanov-Rostovsky, the Minister of Foreign Affairs, pointed out reasons for the couple to attend that evening's ball. If they failed to appear, he suggested, Russia might alienate its only European ally and provoke a diplomatic incident.⁶⁵

Nicholas listened to these arguments; his sister Olga later blamed these men entirely for what followed, asserting that it was solely the ministers who had *"insisted that he must go as a gesture of friendship to France."* Olga, though, was wrong. She insisted that Grand Duke Sergei was *"in such despair"* over Khodynka that he *"offered to resign at once."*[66] In fact, it was Sergei, along with his brothers, who provided the decisive pressure.

Nicholas II's four uncles Grand Dukes Vladimir, Alexei, Paul and especially Sergei turned on him, badgering their nephew into submission. Theirs was a unified, belligerent front. Accidents, they insisted, *"were always likely to happen when a crowd gathered."* The deaths of those loyal subjects on Khodynka, they said, *"should not be exaggerated."* The Emperor should ignore the tragedy; he should attend the ball that night as planned; he should keep to the remaining schedule of festive events without interruption. What he should not do – could not do – they declared, was acknowledge the catastrophe by holding a public memorial service for the victims or call for a period of mourning.[67] These were not suggestions: they were threats. If Nicholas followed the advice of his Minister of the Imperial Court, the four Grand Dukes threatened to immediately resign their official offices and positions: Vladimir from his post as Infantry General of the Russian Army and Commander of the Imperial Guard, Alexei from his post as General-Admiral of the Russian Navy and Commander of the Imperial Fleet, Sergei from his post as Governor-General of Moscow, and Paul from his position as Commander of the Imperial Guards Cavalry Division.[68]

Soon enough, competing voices added to the chorus of advice. Grand Duchess Elisabeth took her husband's side, arguing with her sister Alexandra that the ball was of such *"political importance"* that the Imperial couple simply had to attend.[69] The Dowager Empress, all emotion, was horrified by the tragedy. *"One just does not understand how it could have happened,"* she wrote to her mother, *"since it is not a new thing, and in 1883 it went so splendidly without costing any human life,"* apparently forgetting the thirty-two lives lost on Khodynka during her husband's coronation.[70] Siding with Vorontsov-Dashkov, she insisted that it was impossible to go on as if nothing had happened.[71]

The four Imperial uncles. Clockwise from top right: Grand Duke Vladimir Alexandrovich, Grand Duke Alexei Alexandrovich, Grand Duke Serge Alexandrovich and Grand Duke Paul Alexandrovich.

In this, Marie Feodorovna found unexpected support from her son-in-law Grand Duke Alexander Mikhailovich and his brothers Nicholas, George, and Sergei. Grandsons of Nicholas I, the four Mikhailovich Grand Dukes – cousins once removed to Nicholas II – were populists, often derided as *"dangerous radicals"* by more reactionary members of the Imperial Family.[72] A distinguished historian and noted Francophile, Nicholas Mikhailovich had been christened *"Philippe Egalité"* by his fellow Guards officers for his liberal beliefs, and he now indignantly argued against Nicholas II's four uncles.[73] Nicholas, he began, should abandon all future festivities starting with the ball that evening; but he was interrupted by an angry Alexei Alexandrovich. The Mikhailovich brothers, Alexei declared, were playing politics, unfairly trying to magnify the tragedy to harm Sergei and seize the Governor-Generalship of Moscow. Things ended badly, Nicholas Mikhailovich shouting his own dire warning: *"Remember Nicky, the blood of those five thousand men, women, and children will forever remain a blot on your reign! You cannot revive the dead, but you must show sympathy for their families. Do not let the enemies of the regime say that the young Tsar danced while his murdered subjects were taken to the Potter's Field."*[74]

Eventually Marie Feodorovna offered a compromise. For the sake of diplomacy, Nicholas and Alexandra could appear at the French ball for thirty minutes but leave before the dancing began. Sensing an opening, the uncles argued that the Imperial couple must dance at least one dance to honor Russia's ally, but agreed that they could then leave. Caught in the middle of an uncomfortable family argument, Nicholas quickly agreed to this proposal.[75]

The dilemma posed by the remaining ceremonies was not so easily resolved. Nicholas was torn between the autocratic and imperious path suggested by Alexander III's brothers and the more humane and publicly aware response supported by

The Mikhailovich brothers. Clockwise from the top right: Grand Duke Nicholas Mikhailovich, Grand Duke George Mikhailovich, Grand Duke Alexander Mikhailovich and Grand Duke Sergei Mikhailovich.

his mother and the four Mikhailovich Grand Dukes. Should he follow the advice of his uncles, plunging forward with the remaining ceremonies as if the tragedy had not occurred? Or should he take the advice of his mother, his Mikhailovich cousins, and his Minister of the Imperial Court and risk public scandal if his uncles made good on their threats and resigned their posts? Though inclined to cancel the festivities, he could not summon the personal courage needed to stand against his uncles' threats. Placing more importance on avoiding a family quarrel than on demonstrating sympathy for the dead, Nicholas made a fateful decision. The ceremonies would continue; there would be no mourning; he would not call for a public memorial for the victims. Visits to the wounded in Moscow's hospital would be his only concession.

"We won!" This was the verdict Sergei delivered to his adjutant Count Paul Shuvalov after a morning spent with the Emperor. Shuvalov understood: Nicholas II had given in and agreed to ignore the tragedy. It was scarcely a victory for the younger Count, who had sided with his father-in-law Vorontsov-Dashkov, and he took the Grand Duke's cavalier attitude badly. It was not merely in poor taste, but also dismissed the deaths on Khodynka as beneath the Emperor's concern. In disgust, Shuvalov – in contravention of Imperial etiquette – refused to accompany the Grand Duke to that evening's ball.[76]

The imperiously triumphant Grand Duke was not yet done. Returning to his palace, he ordered that word of the Khodynka disaster be suppressed.[77] French cinematographers Charles Moisson and Francois Doublier, arrested earlier that morning, spent most of the day in jail, alongside dozens of other journalists rounded up on Sergei's directive lest they spread news of the tragedy. When the two Frenchmen finally walked out of jail, they did so without their precious rolls of film, seized by police and presumably destroyed.[78] A British journalist, filing his report by telegram that afternoon, found that officials – on the Governor-General's orders – refused to forward it. Someone complained to Vorontsov-Dashkov, who went straight to the Emperor. True to his habit of agreeing with whoever stood in front of him, Nicholas granted the Count's request and had Sergei's orders rescinded. Soon, there was an official Government communication on the tragedy. Reports flashed around the world to the furious click of telegraph machines, appearing on front pages of newspapers from Moscow to San Francisco.[79] Even so, press freedom came with conditions: the Correspondents Bureau requested that journalists *"refrain from all rhetoric when writing of the sad accident"* on Khodynka. A censor warned one reporter to either avoid mention of the "deplorable incident" altogether or to merely quote the terse official account without comment.[80] *"The publicity courted by the regime,"* writes one historian, *"now spread the news of its incompetence and inhumanity to the world."*[81]

Just how incompetent the regime had actually been no one could yet know, nor could anyone accurately determine just how many had perished. Sergei clung to his assertion that *"nothing serious had happened."* Shuvalov spent the rest of the day telephoning police precincts and hospitals; the actual casualty figure, he found, was *"almost a hundred times that reported"* by Sergei. Vorontsov-Dashkov took these numbers to the Dowager Empress, who gave them to her son. Nicholas, though, dismissed them, insisting that he believed only the lower figure reported by his uncle.[82]

Marie Feodorovna was furious, especially with her brother-in-law Sergei, writing that his *"behavior is incomprehensible to me."*[83] Shocked by the tragedy, she tried to show conventional sympathy for the victims by sending each of the injured a bottle of Madeira and visiting the wounded that afternoon – the only Romanov to do so.[84] *"It was truly horrifying to hear the survivors' descriptions, so that I really can think and talk only about it!"* she wrote to her mother Queen Louise of Denmark. *"I am completely disconsolate."* Some, she reported, *"had lain under the dead for long periods, completely blue in the face, so greatly had they been pressed down, while others continued to walk over them. They looked terrible, and almost all of them had several broken ribs, and collarbones and breastbones pressed in, so that they could hardly breathe."* Although aghast at what she saw, the Dowager Empress shared what would become the official view: that the tragedy was as much one suffered by the Emperor as by the victims. She found it *"touching"* that so many of the victims *"said it was their own fault, and that they especially regretted having caused Nicky that sorrow."*[85]

As the Dowager Empress made her rounds through hospital wards, a very different scene took place on Khodynka. Invited guests poured onto the hot and windy field throughout the morning,

Opposite page: An artist's rendering of Emperor Nicholas II and Empress Alexandra Feodorovna at the Montebello Ball.

An artist's rendering of the Imperial celebrations at Khodynka Field.

past ranks of soldiers covered with dust to take prized seats in flower-bedecked stands and tribunes flanking the ornate Imperial Pavilion. To Kate Koon's surprise, the road leading to Khodynka *"was lined with peasants coming back to town, each with a bundle done up in a handkerchief."* Their faces, she thought, *"did not look as happy as they should on such a bright and festive day."* She spotted a wagon, *"a dozen or more boots sticking out"* from beneath a tarp but, unaware of the tragedy, dismissed the ominous image.[86] As journalist Pierre d'Alheim of *Le Temps* rode out to the field, he met *"crowds of people,"* walking back toward the city with *"gloomy, downcast looks."* Police frantically waved vehicles aside as carts rumbled into view, the *"hands, legs and blue, swollen heads"* of dead bodies jostling beneath the rough tarps.[87] Mary Hickley heard *"rumors of an accident,"* but said *"little was made of it."* Nearing the field through *"a stifling hot fog and red dust,"* she, too, saw *"a continuous stream of peasants, all pouring away from, instead of towards, the fete."* The downcast eyes and somber faces seemed strange: *"How sadly these people take their pleasures!"* she thought. A few soldiers, *"exhausted and battered, as if after a fight,"* walked alongside carts *"heaped high with a quivering load of the dead – poor, crushed peasants, still in their gaudy, festive clothes."* It was, she said, *"a most horrifying sight,"* one *"stamped on the memory forever."*[88]

Mary Hickley.

"As far as the horizon," saw Francis Grenfell on arriving at Khodynka, *"on every side, the ground was black with people."* He thought at once of Derby Day, but this crowd was three times the size.[89] Soon, word of the disaster spread among the distinguished guests, whispered and repeated from seat to seat, row to row, tribune to tribune. Some 2,000, Mary Hickley heard, had perished, *"yet in this somewhat barbarous country,"* she recorded, *"where human life seems of little account, the Fete was still going on, nearly as gaily as if nothing had happened."* She saw groups of people in the distance, clustered around theatre stages, booths, gypsy dancers, and circus animals performing tricks, a *"foreground of jollity concealing from us the scene of horror and carnage behind."*[90] Arriving in his silken finery, Li-Hung Chang asked Sergei Witte if the rumors were

true. When Witte confirmed the tragedy, the Chinese diplomat seemed stunned, not at the loss of life, but by the fact that Nicholas had been told of the disaster. *"If I were an important personage serving your Emperor,"* he advised Witte, *"I would of course have kept all this from him. Why should I give pain to the poor man?"*[91]

Authorities did indeed do their best to shield Nicholas and Alexandra from the brutal realities of that morning when their open landau rolled onto Khodynka shortly before two. A regiment of Chevalier Life Guards lined the entire route; behind them double rows of soldiers blocked the view. The Imperial couple saw nothing but others did. From atop his horse, Chevalier Life Guard Gustav Mannerheim spotted *"a column of open vehicles,"* heaped with corpses, rumbling along behind the troops.[92] Aubrey Stanhope saw *"hundreds upon hundreds of rough country wagons"* headed away from the field. *"They were filled with dead bodies,"* he wrote, *"just thrown in and piled carelessly one atop the other, the legs, arms, heads to be seen waggling loosely"* as the vehicles jostled over the uneven ground.[93] Young Grand Duchess Olga Alexandrovna, riding behind her brother, also glimpsed a vehicle loaded with protruding arms and legs. *"At first,"* she recalled, *"I thought that people were waving to us. Then my blood froze. I felt sick. Those carts carried the dead-mangled out of all recognition."*[94]

There were cheers as the Imperial couple passed, but also anger. *"Go and see what has happened down there!"* groups of peasants and workers shouted in unheard protest.[95] Entering the Imperial Pavilion at five minutes past two, Nicholas and Alexandra stepped to the edge of a carved balcony and greeted the crowd, he in uniform and she *"in white, sparkling with diamonds."*[96] Artillery batteries saluted, bells rang out, and V. A Safonov, Director of the Moscow Conservatory, led three orchestras and a choir of 1,800 in *God Save the Tsar*.[97] *"On this mighty plain, and stretching as far as the eye could reach,"* remembered John Logan, *"there was a great mass of human beings, face to face now with the Tsar they had come so far to see."*[98] *"We in England,"* wrote the Bishop of Peterborough, *"would have shrunk from further demonstrations of loyalty, and would have dispersed sadly to our homes in mourning. It was not so in Moscow.... There was no cessation of the shouts."*[99] Mary Hickley was overwhelmed at this *"grand display of loyalty and affection"* and *"deep roar of melancholy Russian cheers,"* as hats were tossed into the air, hands waved handkerchiefs, and people crossed themselves and bowed to the ground in supplication.[100]

Grand Duchess Olga Alexandrovna.

Nicholas stood before the crowd, in an Imperial Pavilion whose very floorboards concealed dozens of dead bodies hastily rammed beneath the building.[101] It was, thought Alexei Suvorin, the *"one day"* when the cheer, *"Cesar, the dead salute you!"* would have been appropriate.[102] The cheering crowd, in fact, was a bit of official artifice: worried about unpleasant demonstrations, authorities had quickly filled the entire area surrounding the pavilion with handpicked spectators to ensure the appropriate responses. *"Great enthusiasm,"* noted Sergei with approval when he saw the results.[103] Security forces had been notable earlier that morning only by their absence, with less than a hundred men to control a crowd of over a half-million; in contrast, more than 3,000 police and soldiers now stood between the Emperor and his subjects to ensure his safety.[104] Despite these precautions, some who witnessed the tragedy reached the pavilion, hurling caps filled with human excrement and shouting, *"Presents for you!"* at the Emperor; the *"people,"* a few crude notes declared, were *"returning"* the Imperial gifts.[105]

It was a surreal scene: the selected, cheering mass gathered in front of the Imperial Pavilion and, cut off from view by lines of soldiers, a crowd of wounded, mangled bodies, and sobbing relatives. Dead bodies bloated in the sun, next to a gaily-singing Gypsy choir; corpses crammed into the remaining stalls and kiosks rapidly expanded in the heat, threatening to burst through flimsy walls.[106] *"The atmosphere,"* said Vladimir Nemirovich-Danchenko, *"was hardly cheerful."* The scene *"felt like a nightmare."*[107] Even Nicholas's sister Xenia saw the horror: *"While we were there, they were still carrying the bodies away."*[108] Solicited cheers against this devastating background offended sensibilities. *"From this,"* declared a disgusted General Alexei Kuropatkin, *"the view follows that the People's Feast is organized not for the people, that the people should present only a majestic living decoration, and that this decoration at the appropriate moment must cry, 'Hurrah' and throw their hats into the air."*[109]

Tsar Nicholas II and Empress Alexandra Feodorovna receiving rural district elders on May 18, 1896 in the yard of Petrovsky Palace. Artist: Ilya Repin.

"The people," declared the official account of the Coronation festivities, *"understood the suffering and emotion of their Emperor, and showed sympathy for his sorrows,"* greeting his appearance at Khodynka with *"a touching display of the communal feeling"* they shared with Nicholas II.[110] With this deft turn of phrase, the Imperial Court positioned Nicholas II as victim, the object of sympathetic pity. Refusing to call for national mourning or a special service for the victims, Nicholas confined his public expression of sentiment to an official statement released later that day by the Ministry of the Imperial Court. The Emperor, read the text, was *"deeply distressed at the occurrence,"* and ordered that *"each bereaved family"* would receive 1,000 rubles ($135,000, or £100,000 in 2014).[111] He spoke no words, though, as he stood at the edge of the balcony, receiving prompted ovations from a hand picked crowd as the tragedy continued across the field. *"Rather than a prayer for the peace of the thousands perishing at the People's Feast as a result of the inefficiency and inaction of the Tsar's servants,"* one man commented, *"the Orthodox Tsar marked the catastrophe"* with what he termed the ongoing *"idiocy"* of carnival barkers, songs, dances, and performing animals.[112] There was no mention of the dead, no moment of silence – *"it was like nothing had happened,"* Nicholas wrote baldly in his diary.[113]

No words, no prayers, no moment of silence – and not more than twenty-five minutes passed on Khodynka Meadow before Nicholas and Alexandra climbed back into their landau and left the field *"accompanied by a lot of noise,"* said Alexei Suvorin, who saw that the crowd nearest to them *"showed no animosity."*[114] With them went all interest in remaining at the terrible scene. Covered with dust, hot and tired, Kate Koon and her fellow Americans found a crowded café just down the St. Petersburg Highway. *"We had a hard time getting anything to eat,"* she complained, until they spotted a minor Russian courtier John Logan had befriended. Using his linguistic skills, they refreshed themselves with *"salads, ices, and champagne"* and now heard for the first time of the disaster.[115] Mary Hickley, too, was initially disgruntled by *"a horrible drive back in suffocating heat,"* though the *"crowds of weeping peasants"* shocked her out of self-pity as carts with their *"ghastly*

loads-sickening sights to English eyes, unaccustomed to such scenes in the streets of a great city," crowded the roadway back to the center of Moscow.[116]

The twenty-five minute Imperial appearance at Khodynka gave way to festivities at Petrovsky Palace, as hundreds of representatives congratulated Nicholas and Alexandra. Clergy from the Cathedral of Christ the Savior and from the Cathedral of the Assumption prayed; impoverished workers from seven wool factories offered a box of vermeil, gold, and bronze; delegations from Moscow's sectarian community of Old Believers presented a diamond-studded silver tray; management of the Imperial Theatres; officers and enlisted men from the Georgievsky Life Guards Cavalry Regiment bowed; carpenters, electricians, florists, and contractors who had decorated the city congratulated; and deputations from the Moscow Association of Coachmen, the city's German Colony, the Hunting Society, and the Moscow Racing Club enjoyed their moment of Imperial favor. There were even bakers, men who had prepared the little commemorative loaves of bread in the souvenir bundles distributed at Khodynka Field.[117]

Congratulations duly offered, the guests sat down to lunch, the tents for provincial officials on one side of the palace courtyard facing those for peasant elders on the other, a visible reminder of the enormous gulf separating the ruling from the ruled.[118] It was only the second time that peasant representatives had been included, following a tradition established by Alexander III.[119] The symbolic message of a mythical, unbreakable link between Throne and People, coming within hours of Khodynka, could not have been more unfortunately timed. Two orchestras played military tunes as guests washed down borscht, veal, and roast spring chicken with champagne, wine, and soft drinks for the Emperor's Muslim subjects.[120] Nicholas, said Sergei Witte, watched with a face that *"showed grief; in fact, he looked sick."*[121] He soon recovered. *"The Empress and I heartily thank you,"* Nicholas told his guests, *"for your expressions of love and dedication. We do not doubt that these feelings are shared by your fellow villagers."* He ended with words that, under the circumstances, were pregnant with irony: *"Care for your welfare is as close to my heart as it is to that of our Father and Blessed Savior."*[122]

With this duty over, Nicholas and Alexandra disappeared from public view for the rest of the day. Contrary to the memoirs of his sister Olga, who insisted, *"I know that both Nicky and Alicky spent the whole of that day in visiting one hospital after another,"* the Imperial couple passed the afternoon and evening taking tea and spending their time cloistered behind palace walls.[123] There were no visits to any hospital, a decision that played into an atmosphere already charged with tragedy and ugly insinuations that turned grisly as twilight descended over Moscow. Reports now shared one thing in a common: an undeniable escalation in the number of the dead. Minimal figures offered by Sergei could no longer be trusted as Shuvalov and Vorontsov-Dashkov delivered the news: first it was some 200 killed; then *"up to 300"* were said to have perished; then 360 were known dead.[124] By nightfall, everyone knew that at least a thousand had perished, and possibly as many as 2,000.[125] When Nicholas went to dinner with his mother, he left *"in tears, deeply upset."*[126]

"Is it worth the hassle of canceling a ball for such a little thing?" a commander in the Chevalier Life Guards Regiment callously asked earlier in the day on hearing of Khodynka.[127] Such attitudes were devastating and fed a growing perception that the Imperial Court and its Emperor disregarded the lives of ordinary Russians. If Nicholas II's humble subjects needed further proof of their miserable place in the autocratic system and in Imperial sympathies, they found it in the glowing accounts of that evening's ball, *"a kaleidoscope of guests, of beauty, of youth,"* enthused Alexei Suvorin's newspaper *Novoe Vremya*.[128]

Nicholas and Alexandra – he in the uniform of a Colonel in the Uhlan Life Guards Regiment with the cordon of the French *Legion d'Honneur* across his chest, she in a white gown of silver brocade embroidered in gold, and diamond necklace and tiara – arrived at half-past ten, greeted by a choir intoning *God Save the Tsar*.[129] General Boisdeffre and Count de Montebello and his wife Madeleine, the men wearing the cordon of the Russian Order of St. Alexander Nevsky and she in *"an exquisite golden brocade gown"* of pink satin covered with

General Raoul de Boisdeffre.

An artist's rendering of the ill-fated ball.

gold-sequined tulle and a diamond tiara, welcomed their Imperial guests in the palm-bedecked foyer.[130] In what some took as a deliberate nod to republicanism, Montebello failed to kiss Alexandra's hand; over a thousand lay dead, but it was this unfortunate breech of etiquette that seemed to most infuriate the Imperial couple as the evening began.[131]

Nerves, it soon became obvious, were on edge all around. Though trained from birth to control his emotions in public, Nicholas, said Sergei Witte, was *"obviously distressed."*[132] His courteous smile was forced; rather than join in the festive mood, he *"looked pale and sad,"* as if *"oppressed by the calamity."*[133] Alexandra, never able to disguise her feelings in public, seemed *"in great distress, her eyes reddened by tears."* [134] *"It nearly broke my heart,"* she later declared, to *"go on with all the celebrations."*[135]

The ball, said Alexander Izwolsky, was *"dismal,"* and *"the effort it caused"* them the Imperial couple to attend *"could clearly be seen in their faces."*[136] Other guests looked sad or embarrassed. *"Everything seemed beautiful,"* said Kammer Page Boris Engelhardt, *"but a severe oppression was felt by all."*[137] Though Count de Montebello asked that the tragedy not be mentioned, Khodynka seemed to be the only topic of conversation.[138] It was, said Marie of Romania, *"dismal,"* the atmosphere strained; French journalist Pierre d'Alheim *"felt sick,"* while his Russian counterpart Vladimir Nemirovich-Danchenko summed up the opinion of many that night, calling it *"the saddest ball ever given."*[139]

Only one person seemed unmoved. Grand Duke Sergei remained proudly defiant, *"a broad smile"* on his face as he watched the proceedings of an event he thought was *"superbly arranged."*[140] The public show of indifference was appalling, leading *"foreigners to believe that the Romanovs had lost their minds,"* as Grand Duke Alexander Mikhailovich recalled. Together with his brothers, Alexander had come only to protest. When Nicholas and Alexandra entered the ballroom, the four Mikhailovich Grand Dukes turned and made a pointed, theatrical exit. Watching them leave, Grand Duke Alexei spat out, equally melodramatically, *"There go the four Imperial followers of Robespierre!"* [141]

The orchestra of the Preobrazhensky Life Guards Regiment struck up the national anthem, and a choir robed in blue and silver medieval-style costumes sang *God Save the Tsar* as Nicholas and Alexandra entered a ballroom hung with Gobelin tapestries and garlands of roses.[142] Lively music announced the opening quadrille: Nicholas danced with the Countess, while the Count led Alexandra; General Boisdeffre led the Empress in the second quadrille, while Nicholas chatted with members of the French mission.[143] Tea was served at midnight. Nicholas and Alexandra retreated to the reception room, which had been hung with tapestries depicting the tale of Don Quixote; in the middle of the room, the Countess had installed a fountain illuminated by colored lights. The Imperial couple sat in two antique chairs covered in Beauvais tapestry, specially brought from Paris.[144]

During tea, hundreds of other guests roamed through the halls admiring the tapestries and furniture, or took to the gardens, illuminated with colored lanterns, as the choir entertained with Russian folk songs.[145] When Nicholas and Alexandra again entered the ballroom, they joined in a mazurka and then watched a cotillion arranged by Countess de Montebello. At the end of the dancing, French munificence was on display as all of the ladies received lavish bouquets and fans in the national colors shared by the two countries – white, blue, and red.[146] Alexandra thought that the fan presented to her, painted by Leloir, was particularly beautiful, and thanked the Countess for the exquisite work.[147]

On the surface, all seemed to be going well, but soon *"a very strained conversation"* erupted between Nicholas II and his uncle Sergei in a corner of the ballroom.[148] Keeping to his earlier agreement, Nicholas wanted to leave, but now his uncles protested.[149] This evening, this ball, the four argued, was *"the exact place to show boundless Imperial power."*[150] If Nicholas and Alexandra left, Grand Dukes Vladimir, Alexei, Sergei, and Paul declared, it would not be understood and would be a sign that they had given in to *"sentimentality"* for the dead.[151]

"Sentimentality" for the dead – this was the argument advanced as just a few miles away mounds of bloated corpses lay unburied and Moscow's hospitals were full of the wounded. Just as unbelievably, Nicholas gave in. The Emperor and Empress remained; they danced, drank champagne, and at one in the morning they sat down to a lavish supper as if nothing extraordinary had taken place earlier that day. Four round tables had been arranged for them in the reception room: Nicholas and Countess de Montebello presided over one, Alexandra, General Boisdeffre, and the Count a second, while members of the French delegation, foreign royal guests, and members of the Imperial Family took their places at the remaining two.[152] Cascades of flowers shipped from the South of France adorned the tables, along with stiff cards showing a scene painted by Gerveux and listing the elaborate menu: *Consommé froid, Truite à la Souveraine, Filets mignons Parisienne, Poularde du Mans La Vallière, Salade de laitue à la crème, Asperges d'Argenteuil sauce mousseline, Biscuit glacé Princesse, and Gaufrettes*, all washed down with endless bottles of Champagne de Montebello.[153] Throughout, Nicholas later said, he and Alexandra held napkins to their faces to conceal their true feelings during the meal.[154] *"I could only think of the unfortunate dead,"* a devastated Alexandra explained to a friend.[155] After three-and-a-half lavish hours, the Imperial couple finally departed at two in the morning.[156] It had been, they assured the Count and Countess, an evening of *"sumptuous and beautiful French hospitality."*[157]

That night before going to bed, Nicholas sat down and, keeping to his inalterable habit, made a laconic, 224-word entry in his diary. What happened on Khodynka, he recorded, was *"a very grave sin,"* in which *"about 1,300 people were trampled."* Word of the disaster, he wrote, *"left me with the most appalling impression."* He noted that it had been a *"melancholy people's holiday"* only in passing, before describing the festivities, the luncheon at the Petrovsky Palace, *"dinner at Mama's,"* and the *"very beautifully done"* French ball, where *"the heat was unbearable."*[158] Thus he recorded one of the most momentous days of his reign, his words chilling evidence that he did not comprehend public opinion surrounding the disaster. He went to bed that night oblivious to the fact that with his fatal decisions he had taken the first steps on a road toward revolution.

An artist's rendering of Tsar Nicholas II and Empress Alexandra Feodorova at the Coronation Ball. Following them is Queen Olga of Greece.

Chapter XII

A baking sun rose over Khodynka Meadow on Sunday, May 19. Police and peasants crowded the dusty stretch of ground, searching through pits and ravines in the desperate hope that someone might still be alive. Thirty-six bodies pulled from an abandoned well joined the grim cortege making its way down the St. Petersburg Highway, past lines of the same soldiers conspicuously absent the previous morning, to Vaganovsky Cemetery for burial.[1]

"Don't go, it's too awful!" a soldier warned Aubrey Stanhope as he entered the cemetery. Guards stood about, lower faces obscured by makeshift mufflers soaked in disinfectant to block out the smell of decay. Corpses lay in rows, *"reduced to pulps"* in the stampede, covered with flies, bloated and rotting in the sun. Friends and relatives crowded around water cans, washing blood and dirt from bodies in a feeble effort to restore some semblance of dignity to the dead while clerks, arrayed along trestle tables, recorded names of the victims. Carpenters knocked together flimsy coffins for those who could afford the expense; for unclaimed victims or those whose injuries made identification impossible, peasants dug deep trenches for mass burial. A few priests prayed for the dead – provided that they were paid; those unable to afford their fees held their own quiet services.[2] Coffin after coffin, shrouded body after shrouded body, disappeared into endless graves eventually marked by a tall obelisk engraved with the simple inscription, *"18 May 1896."*

"An oppressive feeling of gloom," said a courtier, descended over Moscow.[3] Henry LaPauze thought that, *"the celebrations are virtually over."*[4] The *"severe shock"* left Mary Hickley depressed.[5] It enveloped everyone, this *"black veil over all the splendor and glory,"* as the Dowager Empress wrote.[6] It was *"an evil omen,"* and people already compared Nicholas and Alexandra to the ill-fated King Louis XVI and Marie Antoinette. Khodynka, they said, just like the tragedy during the Dauphin's wedding, when a Parisian crowd panicked during a fireworks display and some 800 were killed.[7] *"The coronation of Nicholas II, so marked by celebrations and unforgettable splendor,"* declared one Paris newspaper, *"is now a disaster, whose tragic reports echo the deaths surrounding the marriage of Louis XVI and Marie Antoinette."*[8]

Most foreign visitors, insulated from reality and impressed by the pageantry of the Russian Court, had little sympathy for the victims of Khodynka. To them, it was the Emperor's tragedy. Emily Roebling recalled a tragic crush on her own Brooklyn Bridge soon after it opened, and her sympathies went out to Nicholas for the way in which a *"terrible accident"* had spoiled *his* celebrations.[9] *"The poor Emperor!"* Henry LaPauze echoed. *"This is the first blood spilled for him."*[10] Such ideas, later repeated in the official coronation account, depicted a Nicholas suffering on Russia's behalf. *"This national disaster and common grief,"* thought Mary Hickley, *"may draw Sovereign and People closer: it has revealed how deep is the love between them."*[11] Ian Malcolm spoke of *"the sympathy, sincere and immediate, which on this shocking occasion was poured upon the people by the Tsar,"* which would be forever cemented *"as one of the most striking and touching features of his reign."*[12] And John Logan thought Khodynka proved to *"the entire Russian people that their new ruler has a kind, a brave, a manly heart."* It *"laid the foundations of sympathy between the great under-class of the Russian people and the Throne,"* and showed the people *"how much they were loved by the Tsar."*[13]

Opposite page: Grand Duchess Maria Pavlovna, Tsar Nicholas II's ambitious aunt, in Imperial splendor.

Surrounding Nicholas with sympathy and absolving of him guilt, these foreign visitors had little doubt as to who bore real responsibility for the disaster. Those gathered on Khodynka had brought about the disaster themselves, went their reasoning. Uneducated factory workers and peasants were unruly at the best of times; gathered together, and influenced by alcohol, they were a dangerous force. It had been a typically Russian crowd, argued Kate Koon, illiterate, drunk, and belligerent.[14] Only the correspondent for *Le Figaro* noted that, *"the organizers of the festival must share in the blame with the people for this disaster."*[15]

Workers and peasants heard the talk blaming them. *"Now they'll say that it was the peoples' fault!"* one man complained.[16] Twenty-four hours after the tragedy, the Government admitted to 1,438 victims: 979 dead and 459 seriously injured.[17] Semen Kanatchikov thought that the lists in newspapers *"clearly underestimated the number of victims."* Many others agreed: there was, Kanatchikov remembered, *"enormous outrage"* over tales that the Government was deliberately suppressing the scope of the disaster.[18] French correspondents reported varied numbers of the dead. That Sunday, reporters *Le Figaro* and from *Le Petit Parisien* told their readers that 1,138 had perished, 159 more victims than the official government figures that day.[19] The correspondent from Le Matin reported that, *"2,281 were actually killed and taken to Vagonovsky."*[20] On Monday, the government estimated that some 3,000 people had died, but this number – picked up and reported by foreign correspondents – was quickly withdrawn.[21] A mass grave for 150 at Vaganovsky Cemetery, Aylmer Maude reported, actually contained 350 corpses.[22]

Khodynka, Kanatchikov said, *"was the only thing discussed at our factory."* There was *"enormous outrage"* over the disaster.[23] The *"old, blind faith in the Tsar,"* he remembered, dissipated in the wake of the tragedy.

People were indignant at the *"irresponsibility, the impunity of the authorities who had destroyed thousands of lives,"* and stubbornly went on with the ceremonies.[24] This anger spilled across Moscow. Workers, students, and members of the middle class hurled accusations against the authorities in general, Grand Duke Sergei in particular, and the Emperor as the ultimate, uncaring head of a heartless autocratic system.[25] A reporter for the *New York Times* heard it that Sunday, not once but again and again, harsh exclamations against the authorities and the Imperial Throne.[26] That evening, Moscow Police arrested a young woman named Maria Shishkova for reading a piece of anti-Imperial propaganda to passers-by on the street. Meant as an indictment of the Government, it contrasted the corpses from Khodynka, *"thrown like herrings in a barrel"* into mass graves, with the *"smiling celebrities in a festive mood"* as the Imperial couple enjoyed the lavish Montebello ball.[27]

Grand Duke Sergei Alexandrovich his wife Grand Duchess Elisabeth Feodorovna. While Sergei Alexandrovich did his utmost to cover up his responsibility, his wife became his main apologist.

Anger not directed at Nicholas fell on Moscow's Governor-General. People blamed the unpopular Grand Duke Sergei for the catastrophe, and even those who held him innocent of personal responsibility were stunned by his attitude. His failure to visit Khodynka, threats of resignation, and attempts to shift the blame onto others, left even his relatives shocked.[28] Within hours of the disaster, Sergei loudly insisted, to anyone and everyone he encountered, upon two points: that he bore no responsibility for the catastrophe, and that Vorontsov-Dashkov was at fault for the loss of life.[29] *"I have never heard of such an injustice before,"* complained Dowager Empress Marie Feodorovna, *"and Sergei's behavior in the matter is incomprehensible to me."*[30] Grand Duke Konstantin, who genuinely liked his cousin Sergei, found it impossible to defend him. *"It seems obvious,"* he wrote that Sunday, *"that the main responsibility must lie with the Governor-General, who should be stricken with grief, and neither hide nor diminish what has happened, but rather should reveal it all in its full horror. Yet it's not like this at all."*[31] Konstantin was torn. He wanted to speak to his cousin: *"I love him dearly, we have been friends since childhood, and now I have to listen to condemnation of him from all sides, yet I cannot offer a single word in his defense."*[32]

Konstantin was one of the few who remained sympathetic to Sergei. Nicholas II's sister Xenia bluntly complained that their uncle *"washed his hands of everything."* Sergei, she noted, insisted that the disaster had *"nothing to do with him,"* but that Vorontsov-Dashkov was *"responsible for everything."* Like her mother, she found her uncle's behavior *"beneath contempt."*[33] Grand Duchess Elisabeth simply parroted her husband's excuses and blamed the Minister of the Imperial Court. With all of the Romanov Family talking about Sergei, said Marie of Romania, Elisabeth's *"despair was pitiful to see."*[34] Xenia found her aunt stubbornly insistent. *"I kept trying to tell Ella my opinions about everything that had happened,"* she recorded. But Elisabeth would only repeat, *"Thank God Sergei has nothing to do with all this!"*[35]

Having unsuccessfully attempted to pit Paul Shuvalov against his father-in-law Vorontsov-Dashkov, Sergei again tried to make trouble, this time complaining to his adjutant that the Minister of the Imperial Court was allowing the press too much freedom to discuss the tragedy. Vorontsov-Dashkov, insisted the Grand Duke, was conducting propaganda against him, undermining his position as Governor-General and implicating him unfairly in the eyes of the public. Shuvalov was furious. Though he had served as the Grand Duke's adjutant for five years, and his wife Alexandra was friendly with Elisabeth Feodorovna, Shuvalov could take no more. Bluntly, he told Sergei that he would tender his resignation as adjutant as soon as the ceremonies ended.[36]

Sergei was not the only Grand Duke behaving badly. The city reeled in shock after the tragedy as a somber mood settled over Moscow. Yet the brash Grand Duke Vladimir chose that particular Sunday afternoon to host a shoot for his family and foreign royal guests. They took to an estate adjoining Vaganovsky Cemetery, the sound of their guns echoing over the burials underway. Conservative newspaper editor Alexei Suvorin was appalled. The public, he rightly predicted, would take the shooting for the Romanov Dynasty's indifference over the disaster.[37]

A dual narrative unfolded in the wake of the Khodynka disaster and the Montebello ball. Moscow's papers were filled with accounts of both events, offering readers an intentional contrast between suffering victims and celebrating Emperor and Empress.[38] Many were stunned by the lack of public sympathy. *"In the evening, theatres gave their performances as usual,"* recorded one incredulous French correspondent, *"and no public orders have come to close such institutions."*[39] On June 1, Count de Montebello, displaying more public concern than Nicholas II for the victims of Khodynka, went to Vaganovsky Cemetery to pay his respects and lay a wreath on behalf of his country.[40] The city government of Paris voted to send 50,000 Francs ($273,000, or £205,000 in 2014 figures) to the Russian Government to assist the families who had lost loved ones.[41]

German diplomat Count Johann von Bernstorff took

Grand Duchess Xenia Alexandrovna.

official indifference as evidence of *"the Court's callousness toward the suffering of the people."*⁴² Even the Empress's grandmother Queen Victoria was horrified at this decision: *"It is simply ghastly!"* she wrote of Khodynka to Alexandra's sister Victoria of Battenberg. *"Would it not have been better to have stopped the balls, etc., for it looks so unfeeling to go on just the same?"*⁴³

Attendance at the French Ball, though, set the tone for the remainder of Nicholas and Alexandra's time in Moscow: there would be no deviation from the official schedule of festivities. Over the coming week they would attend two special church services celebrating members of the Imperial Family; a military review; two lavish dinners given by foreign ambassadors; a pleasant musical concert; three splendid balls; a sumptuous state dinner; and make visits to the Moscow City Assembly and the Troitsky-Sergievskaya Monastery. And with each luxurious dinner, each elegant ball, each unapologetic step, Moscow shuddered at the grim contrast.

Giving in to threats from his uncles, Nicholas rejected the idea of a memorial service for the victims at the Cathedral of Christ the Savior. Aware that the response to Khodynka had damaged the prestige of the Imperial Throne, Grand Duke Konstantin wrote Nicholas a letter, imploring him to hold a public service for the victims before leaving Moscow. *"What a calming impression it would make on everyone!"* he ended. Nicholas, as the Grand Duke noted sadly, did not even bother to acknowledge his suggestion.⁴⁴

Instead, Nicholas and Alexandra, along with most of the Imperial Family, confined sympathies and prayers to a private, regularly scheduled service that Sunday morning in the Kremlin's Church of the Nativity of the Virgin. A priest briefly invoked Khodynka, referring to

Princess Victoria of Battenberg.

the *"devoted servants of the Tsar who unwittingly gave their lives"* the previous day. Any lingering reflections dissipated as the Imperial Family sat down to a lavish luncheon of turtle soup, salted fish, fillet of beef with vegetables, cold grouse with *paté de foie* gras, roast turkey, cauliflower, baked pineapple, and ice cream.⁴⁵

The Emperor and Empress at least followed Vorontsov-Dashkov's suggestion to visit those wounded at Khodynka, making a single call on patients that Sunday afternoon at Moscow's St. Catherine's Hospital. Sergei and Elisabeth accompanied them. There were so many injured, Nicholas recorded in his diary, that the wards were full and many of the *"poor, unfortunate victims"* were consigned to tents on the hospital grounds. Sergei counted or was told of 160 wounded patients, but was mainly concerned was that the event had *"almost"* cast a shadow over the *"happy time."* On the other hand, he was pleased to see that his nephew was being *"surprisingly calm and sensible"* about everything.⁴⁶ They spent just over an hour at St. Catherine's Hospital, returning to Neskuchnoye as soon as possible so that the Imperial couple could have *"a good walk,"* take tea, and rest for five uninterrupted hours.⁴⁷ Night found them back at the Kremlin – irritated at having to abandon their private leisure – to preside over a glittering State Dinner in the Hall of the Order of St. Alexander Nevsky for 432 guests.⁴⁸ Thankfully, Nicholas recorded, it *"did not go on too long."* They found the time to visit Sergei and Elisabeth and examine decorations in the Governor-General's palace, and to spend the evening over an enjoyable family tea with Alexandra's sister Victoria and her husband Louis and Nicholas's uncle Grand Duke Paul.⁴⁹

Moscow's mood was somber as it struggled to make sense of Khodynka, even as Nicholas and Alexandra carried on with seven days of pageantry. This seeming reckless indifference to the suffering of Nicholas II's subjects displaced memories of splendid ceremonies. The Imperial couple's last week in Moscow began with yet another misstep. They could not find time to hold a public memorial service for the dead, but on the morning of Monday, May 20, the entire Imperial Family attended a special *Te Deum* in the Kremlin's Chudov Monastery to honor Grand Duke Kirill Vladimirovich, Vladimir's eldest son. Nicholas appointed Kirill a personal adjutant as his cousin swore allegiance and guns in the Kremlin fired a salute of 101 shots. In theory, it marked the Grand Duke's transition to a life of service to his imperial cousin and their nation; in practice, it and the accompanying celebratory luncheon of grouse soup, pirozhki, sturgeon, roast fowl, game, salad, and ice cream burnished with raspberry sauce only seemed to cruelly underline the Imperial Family's distance and self-absorption in the face of national tragedy.[50]

From the left: Grand Dukes Boris and Kirill Vladimirovich, Grand Duchess Marie Pavlovna, Grand Duke Vladimir Alexandrovich, Grand Duke Andrei Vladimirovich and Grand Duchess Elena Vladimirovna.

The Imperial couple followed this poorly timed, insensitive piece of theater with an hour-long visit to the Khodynka wounded at the Marie Hospital. It was a heart-rending sight as they toured wards filled with the maimed. Sergei counted sixty victims this time, but he had no further observations. There were, Nicholas noted, *"three or four cases that were very bad."*[51] It was his last mention of the tragedy. From this day forward, as if erasing the event from memory, Nicholas made no reference to Khodynka in his diary.

Good intentions aside, the brevity of these visits suggested an Imperial couple unable or unwilling to meaningfully demonstrate sympathy with their people. Their responses were almost mechanical, leaving a widespread impression that neither Nicholas nor Alexandra cared about their subjects. It was unseemly but not altogether unexpected that the entitled and imperious Grand Duke Vladimir would offend public sensibilities by holding a shoot next to the cemetery as Khodynka victims were buried; it was quite another thing, though, for Nicholas and Alexandra to act as they did. The *Te Deum* and luncheon for Kirill Vladimirovich consumed more of their time than did their two hospital visits, a dangerous error at a time when Moscow was still reeling with shock.

Yet Nicholas and Alexandra made no further efforts to appease opinion. They could have visited more hospitals; they could have remained longer with the patients. But they chose personal desire over public obligation, a fact underlined by their schedule that Monday afternoon. Six free hours stretched before them: they had no events planned, and spent their time alone at Neskuchnoye, walking, reading, resting, before taking tea with the Duke and Duchess of Connaught and dining privately with the Dowager Empress.[52] Over the coming week, they found time to dance, to dine, to take leisurely walks – eighteen hours alone of leisurely walks – but refused to extend themselves beyond brief two hospital visits, totaling three hours, to the wounded.[53] This inability to adjust to circumstances, to reconcile private inclination with the obligations imposed upon them as monarchs, revealed a Nicholas and Alexandra alarmingly unprepared for the demands of a changing Empire.

Grand Duke Konstantin Konstantinovich was critical of his cousin Grand Duke Sergei Alexandrovich's handling of the Khodynka tragedy. He did not mince words, in fact, even going as far as repproaching Tsar Nicholas II for mishandling the tragedy. He, not surprisingly, was ignored. From the left: Grand Duchess Elisabeth Mavrikievna, Grand Duke Konstantin Konstantinovich, the Dowager Empress Marie Feodorovna and Empress Alexandra Feodorovna.

Nothing changed, nothing altered, and on the heels of the hospital visit that Monday came yet another disastrous decision: Nicholas and Alexandra attended a magnificent ball given by Sergei Alexandrovich. *"One would have thought that Sergei would cancel the ball,"* Grand Duke Konstantin wrote amidst murmurs of Imperial indifference toward the Khodynka victims.[54] The symbolism could scarcely have been worse. If attending the Montebello ball was defended as a diplomatic necessity, no one could find any such justification for Nicholas and Alexandra throwing themselves into festivities hosted by a man many openly blamed for the tragedy. People excused their presence at the French ball; public opinion was not as forgiving when Nicholas and Alexandra continued with the celebrations as if nothing had happened.

For all the vocal complaints by the four Mikhailovich brothers, or private worries by Grand Duke Konstantin, only the Dowager Empress seemed distressed by Khodynka and adjusted her behavior accordingly. Having visited the wounded within hours of the tragedy, she felt it impossible to carry on with celebrations she already found onerous. This her Kammer Pages learned on arriving at the Governor-General's Palace that Monday night, when an unusually charming Grand Duke Sergei told them that the Dowager Empress would not attend the ball.[55] She was, Sergei explained, *"sorry that because of her absence you have been deprived of seeing many triumphant ceremonies,"* and wanted the young men to remain and witness the Ball. *"I am happy to fulfill the wishes of the Empress,"* the Grand Duke told them, *"and I would like for you to feel that while you are here, you are not Kammer Pages of Her Majesty, but my guests,"* adding that they should mingle freely and enjoy the champagne.⁵⁶

Fashionable Moscow took its cue from the Imperial couple, and carriages and landaus filled the square in front of the palace as society rushed to the ball. *"The windows were all lit up,"* reported Alexei Suvorin. *"Brilliants silhouettes of ladies and gentlemen came and went in the salons."*⁵⁷ Dancing in the ballroom began as soon as Nicholas and Alexandra arrived at half-past ten: a polonaise, a waltz, and lively polkas played by the orchestra of the Preobrazhensky Life Guards, the partners paired up by a Grand Duke Sergei anxious to create just the right impression.⁵⁸ One pairing had unsuspected consequences when the diminutive Prince of Naples partnered the striking Princess Jelena, daughter of Nicholas I of Montenegro – the start of a romance that led to their marriage and eventually made her Queen of Italy.⁵⁹

Princess Elena Nikolaievna of Montenegro.

Few of the guests gave any thought to Khodynka. Francis Grenfell was delighted to find that, despite 1,500 guests, the crowd at the Governor-General's Palace *"was much more select"* than that at the French Ball. There was *"room to move about, and see the house,"* though it was *"very hot, and the Emir of Bokhara, in a hairy hat, made us feel hotter."*⁶⁰ Liveried footmen embowered in a flowery pavilion offered cooling fruit, ices, and champagne. A lavish supper at one and a final round of festive dancing preceded Nicholas and Alexandra's departure at half-past two that morning.⁶¹

The late night had no adverse effect on the Imperial couple. They abandoned the idea of any further hospital visits: *"we got up late,"* Nicholas noted, *"to a marvelous morning"* spent together.⁶² At noon, though, they were back at Khodynka Meadow attending a military review on the same dusty ground where, just eighty hours earlier, over a thousand had died. Joined by ladies of the Imperial Family and foreign princesses, Alexandra watched from the pavilion balcony as Nicholas rode forth like a triumphant hero on his white horse. He sat in stony silence, hand frozen at the brim of his cap in salute as General Von der Launitz led thousands of troops across the dusty field.⁶³ There was no mention of the tragedy, though Nicholas and Alexandra took the time to chat with Count de Montebello and ask him to

The Prince of Naples.

Initially, the Austrian Delegation was to be headed by Archduke Karl Ludwig, Emperor Franz Josef's brother. However, the Archduke died weeks before heading to Russia. In his stead, the Austrian government sent Archduke Eugen to support the Austro-Hungarian Ambassador Prince Franz of Liechtenstein. Archduke Eugen (in light uniform) and Prince Franz (in dark uniform) are at the center of this photograph featuring other delegation members.

telegraph President Faure their *"satisfaction at having been at the French Embassy Ball and admiration for their hosts."*[64] In his diary, Nicholas meticulously recorded the names of various regiments reviewed but not the ironic significance of the location. By the time it ended he wanted only to escape, fleeing with Alexandra to Neskuchnoye so that they could stroll through the gardens and enjoy their treasured privacy.[65]

Duty intruded at seven, when Nicholas and Alexandra attended a dinner given by the Austrian Ambassador Prince Franz of Liechtenstein. Though in no way Russia's ally, Austria planned to honor the Imperial couple with a magnificent ball that, not coincidentally, would put the riches of the Habsburgs on proud display. Prince Franz had a new parquet floor laid in his rented palace, and a train from Vienna brought paintings, tapestries, furniture, and gold plate to regally adorn the rooms.[66] The sudden death of Archduke Karl Ludwig, though, plunged the Viennese Court into mourning and the niceties of Imperial etiquette demanded that the ball be cancelled.[67] The irony was not lost on the more astute gathered in Moscow: the passing of an Austrian Archduke made festivities unseemly, but the deaths at Khodynka were not deemed of sufficient importance to alter the remaining celebrations. *"To be able to make head or tail of the Coronation proceedings,"* wrote Aylmer Maude, *"one has to grasp the idea that human beings are not brothers, sons of one Father as Jesus taught, but that they are made of various qualities of dirt, and therefore an Austrian Archduke may well, in the sympathies of the Court of Russia, outweigh thousands"* of ordinary Russians.[68]

And so, lest Imperial sensitivities be offended, a dinner replaced a ball, a dinner that ended early so that fashionable Moscow could rush off to yet another ball. Over 4,000 guests descended on the old neoclassical Dolgoruky Palace, where members of the Nobility Club followed the pleasant strains of a distant orchestra up a crimson-carpeted staircase. They crowded into the immense and lofty Hall, ringed by twenty-eight white Corinthian columns and hung, said Kate Koon, with *"the prettiest"* crystal and gold chandeliers she had ever seen.[69] It was, Kate complained, *"frightfully warm,"* while Ian Malcolm thought it was *"too crowded to be absolutely enjoyable."*[70] Potted palms, strings of floral garlands along the balconies, and artful cascades of roses and lilies relieved the stark white of the walls – *"you cannot imagine how well the bright colors looked,"* Kate enthused in a letter.[71] There were, she said, *"men in the most stunning uniforms,"* all *"resplendent with their decorations,"* while the ladies shimmered in their jewels.[72]

When not watching the dances, guests pushed toward the buffets, quenching their thirst with punch ladled from bowls carved of solid ice.[73]

The inevitable polonaise from Glinka's *A Life for the Tsar* heralded the Imperial couple's arrival at a quarter-to-eleven, Nicholas leading Princess Trubetskoy, wife of the Marshal of Moscow's Nobility, down the middle of the parquet floor while Prince Peter marched along with Alexandra.[74] The polonaise gave way to a quadrille, which Alexandra danced with Sergei, who on his own admission was feeling very cheerful that night, followed by a waltz, a mazurka, and a polka before the Imperial couple retreated to a dais at one end of the hall; above them, peering over the galleries, Moscow's noble children looked on with eager eyes.[75] *"It was terribly hot,"* was Nicholas's only comment, though he once again sought out Count de Montebello, thanking him for Saturday's ball and explaining *"in the warmest terms"* that he *"would have wonderful memories"* of the evening.[76] In a blue gown and *"ablaze with jewels"* – diamond tiara, diamond necklace, and a wide diamond stomacher that seemingly encircled her waist – Alexandra, thought Kate, *"looked as sweet as ever, and quite as sad."*[77]

The gown represented a personal triumph. Marie Feodorovna had selected a series of dresses for her daughter-in-law to wear at receptions, hoping to mould the gauche young Empress into her own image. Not to be outmaneuvered, Alexandra caused equal offense by insisting that the gowns were not to her taste and refusing to wear them. Though aggrieved by Khodynka, the Dowager Empress still found time to complain to her sister the Princess of Wales about the insult:

Imagine, she did not put on a single one of my wonderful, beautiful dresses. I regret that I was so stupid, throwing away good money that I can ill afford....It is such a demonstration of cheek, rudeness, heartlessness and unceremonious behavior, the like of which I cannot recall. I would never have dared to act like that with my mother-in-law....Perhaps she did not do mean to do anything wrong, perhaps this is simply the absence of a keen sense of tact – something you cannot acquire later, if you have not been born with it.[78]

Marie Feodorovna snapped out of her self-pity and isolation on Wednesday, May 22, joining her son, daughter-in-law, most of the Imperial Family, and an assortment of foreign guests, in a ceremony to which no one could possibly object: a visit to the Troitsky-Sergievskaya Monastery some fifty miles northwest of Moscow.[79] A train ride took them from Yaroslavl Station deep into the forested countryside. After two hours, the monastery appeared in the distance, its *"lofty battlemented walls rising grandly in the air"* against a carpet of green. Whitewashed palaces and churches clustered over a hilltop, alongside towers of pink brick and cathedrals dotted with blue and gold onion domes in what Francis Grenfell called a *"most striking"* array of surprising color.[80] The train slowed as it approached, passing fields thick with reverential groups

Empress Alexandra Feodorovna.

of peasants who repeatedly crossed themselves knowing that within rode their Emperor, on his way to Russian Orthodoxy's holiest shrine, the home of the monks whose prayers and advice were credited with driving back the Tatar occupation.[81] The Bishop of Peterborough, primed by Pobedonostsev, understood the visit's significance. It was, he thought, intended to transport Nicholas *"back to the lives of simple men, instinct with faith, who supplied the motive power and maintained the principles...round which the Russian nation had been formed."*[82] No one, least of all Grand Duke Sergei, who thought the whole ceremony *"very touching,"* noted the irony of elevating these long-dead *"simple men"* to the autocratic roster of honor while so many present-day workers and peasants lay unvisited in Moscow's hospitals.[83]

Marie Alexandrovna, Duchess of Saxe-Coburg and Gotha.

Standing in the Cathedral of the Holy Trinity, beneath frescoed walls painted by the great Andrei Rublev, the Imperial party listened to the chanting choir, prayed before icons, and venerated the relics of the monastery's founder St. Sergei of Radonezh before presenting a magnificently embroidered pall to adorn the shrine.[84] *"It was very lovely and solemn,"* wrote the Dowager Empress, *"but it was horribly hot."*[85] After visiting the Cathedral of the Assumption, final resting place of Boris Godunov, they moved on to the Sacristy.[86] *"How Napoleon's mouth would have watered!"* Grenfell gasped. There were "silver and gold cups, jeweled miters, curious and beautiful enamels," and *"Gospels and Litanies in gold and silver bindings thick with jewels."* He was particularly taken with a Gospel given to the Monastery by Michael, the first Romanov Tsar, its cover *"exquisitely ornamented with enameled flowers and arabesque patterns in enamel, with a large ruby cross emblazoned on it, surrounded by emeralds of great size and beauty."*[87] The sun was sweltering, and Nicholas and Alexandra declined the offered tea in favor of beer. By four, they were back on the train, armed with crafts, souvenir crosses and boxes of cypress. Alexandra, at least, made a gesture to the Khodynka victims, purchasing some 500 icons to be distributed – by officials – to the wounded while she and Nicholas retreated to the comfort of Neskuchnoye.[88]

The following day, May 23, was again free of obligations until early afternoon, yet Nicholas and Alexandra followed their predictable pattern of choosing privacy over hospital visits. It was swelteringly hot when, at two, they visited the Moscow City Assembly Hall – the first time a sovereign deigned to so publicly acknowledge the existence of a representative body. A choir of schoolchildren sang out their welcome, but a nervous little girl burst into tears presenting Alexandra with a bouquet. With a sudden disdain for Imperial etiquette, the Empress swooped down and kissed her – a spontaneous gesture before a distressed child contrasting sadly with the couple's subdued and suppressed response to Khodynka. After the usual congratulatory addresses and presentation of bread and salt, the Assembly offered its gifts: two golden goblets set with the Emperor's initials in rubies and those of the Empress in sapphires. It was all over in thirty brief minutes.[89] *"We came home at 2:30,"* Nicholas recorded, *"racing"* to Neskuchnoye *"as fast as possible"* to spend the afternoon and early evening idly taking tea and chatting among themselves.[90]

Seven o'clock found the Imperial couple at the temporary British Embassy, Nicholas clad in the uniform of the Scots Greys Regiment, of which he was Colonel-in-Chief, as he and Alexandra attended a dinner given in their honor by Sir Nicholas O'Conor.[91] Like the Austrian dinner, it ended early so that guests could attend the State Ball at the Grand Kremlin Palace. Marie Feodorovna again sat out the festivities, listening as the crowd slowly filled the immense halls above her rooms. The Khodynka disaster merely added to the veil of searing grief through which she viewed the ceremonies, painful reminders of days at her husband's side in Moscow thirteen years earlier. "I hear music playing over my head," she wrote to her mother. "It all seems so strange, as you can understand, as if one were dancing on my open grave."[92]

Prince Henry of Prussia.

For others, though, there was no hesitation as Nicholas and Alexandra began the familiar Glinka polonaise through the palace a few minutes after ten that evening. It was hot and crowded: some 2,229 invitations had gone out to Imperial and royal guests, diplomats, clergy, aristocrats, and government officials.[93] Princess Anatole Bariatinsky, overwhelmed by the oppressive heat, had collapsed into a corner chair, trying to appear as inconspicuous as possible when the formidable Duchess of Saxe-Coburg and Gotha spotted her. *"You are young,"* Marie Alexandrovna chastised, *"and if everybody thought the same, no one would dance! You must do so, especially on such an occasion as this. In my time, we should not have dared to sit out before my father Emperor Alexander II!"*[94] Energetic mazurkas and polkas, interrupted only by hot tea at eleven, did nothing to cool an exhausted crowd, who faced a lavish midnight supper of *consommé, pirozhki,* cold grouse, roasted fowl, salad, asparagus, and ice cream. Alexandra, on show at the center of a long raised table in the Hall of the Order of St. Alexander Nevsky, could do nothing but sit silently in this sweltering environment. Only Nicholas found relief, wandering from table to table throughout the banquet, offering each guest the chance to say that they had once dined with the Emperor before the Imperial couple left at half-past one in the morning.[95]

No official obligations intruded on the following morning of May 24. Nicholas and Alexandra spent their time leisurely before taking lunch with Prince Henry of Prussia. Only at half-past two did they face more unwelcome ceremonial, when the Papal Nuncio said his farewells. The Imperial couple also met privately with a few of the foreign royal representatives, including Prince Fushimi Sadanaru, who presented them *"with some remarkably beautiful gifts,"* as Nicholas noted, from the Emperor of Japan. They found time to return to Neskuchnoye: Nicholas had a *"delightful walk in the rain. I gathered a large bunch of lilies of the valley for Alix."*[96]

Five hours later, at nine, it was Imperial Germany's turn to honor the couple, in an evening fraught in nearly every way with disappointment and disaster. Prince Hugo von Radolin, the German Ambassador, waited too long to make arrangements in Moscow, and found that every mansion and palace suitable to the dignity of his country had already been leased.[97] Necessity eventually forced him to rent the Von Dervitz mansion at Krasnoye Vorota.

At 7,000 rubles, it was a bargain in coronation-crazed Moscow, and with good reason: it was some distance from the city center, and was far too small to host a ball or even a decent reception.[98] Kaiser Wilhelm II sent his own gold plate from Berlin, hoping to create a favorable impression, but lack of space forced the Ambassador to issue a mere 400 invitations to a simple musicale in honor the Imperial couple.[99] Alexandra asked for Schiller's *Wallenstein*, while the Kaiser insisted that the overture and chorus from Wagner's *Die Meistersinger von Nurnburg* also be included in this unlikely evening of song. At least the music was of the highest quality: a trainload of the best singers, along with a choir and the entire Berlin Philharmonic Orchestra, descended on Moscow for a mere two days for their starring roles, at a cost of some 24,000 Marks ($162,000 or £120,000 in 2014).[100]

Diplomacy and Imperial *politesse* demanded that Nicholas appear in German uniform, which his mother had raised him to hate. He came dressed as a general in the Prussian Hussar Life Guards, complete with light blue tunic, black trousers, and plumed white hat.[101] Bizarrely, during the intimate dinner, recalled Count Bernstorff, *"only English was spoken-an unmistakable sign of the influence exercised by Queen Victoria."* It was hot and nerves were on edge: Prince Henry kept referring to his brother-in-law as *"Nicky."* Perturbed, the Emperor finally let out, *"in a friendly but determined tone,"* with a loud whisper: *"Don't call me Nicky in public!"* During a toast, a Prussian official referred to the *"suite of German Princes"* surrounding Prince Henry. *"We're not vassals!"* shouted back an angry Prince Ludwig of Bavaria.[102] Nicholas was annoyed that their Kammer Pages had not been fed – *"Pages of the Chamber always eat at the same table as the other guests!"* he scolded Radolin.[103] The evening's end at half-past one that morning brought one last annoyance: Nicholas grabbed his plumed hat only to find that someone had left it on a plate covered in some sticky sauce.[104]

The following morning, Saturday May 25th, Alexandra awoke to a serenade by the Court Orchestra, playing beneath her open bedroom window: a surprise arranged by her husband. *"The second birthday my dear, darling Alix has celebrated in Russia,"* Nicholas wrote in his diary. *"God grant that there will be many more such days in our life."*[105] The couple, along with members of the Imperial Family and the foreign royal guests, attended a special *Te Deum* in the Kremlin's Church of the Nativity of the Virgin to mark the event, followed by a celebratory luncheon in the Kremlin that lasted into the afternoon.[106] There were a few private meetings with foreign representatives before Nicholas and Alexandra escaped to Neskuchnoye at four for a quiet afternoon of taking tea and walking *"alone together,"* as the Emperor recorded in his diary.[107]

Grand Duchess Victoria Melita of Hesse.

Duty again intruded that evening, in the form of a state dinner for 700 at the Kremlin.[108] The usual assortment of dignitaries and diplomats gathered in the Hall of the Order of St. George dined on steamed Don Sturgeon in champagne sauce, truffles, and *soufflé froid de foie gras* as a chorus from the Bolshoi serenaded them with selections from Wagner's *Die Meistersinger*, and from *Ruslan and Ludmilla*.[109] The days of impeccable pageantry, the tremendous heat, and the unrelenting evenings filled with rich and heavy food in crowded halls – it was all becoming too much for many, and few troubled to hide it. Kate Koon noticed that the royal ladies *"looked as though they must be very bored."*[110]

Conflicting impressions emerged side by side – glory and censure, triumph and tragedy – as three weeks of ceremonies came to an end. It was Sunday, May 26, the *"last day, thank God,"* Nicholas wrote in his diary, of the Coronation festivities.[111] A beautiful, cloudless day, though again terribly hot: Mary Hickley likened Moscow to *"sitting on the Equator."* With tragic irony, the final public event was a massive military review held on Khodynka Meadow. *"The brown plain of baked mud lay sweltering under a brazen sky,"* Mary wrote, *"and the stifling air was heavy with thick red dust that, like a fog, greatly interfered with the grand military spectacle before us."*[112] At eleven, Nicholas, wearing the uniform of the Ekaterinoslav Life Guards Regiment, mounted his horse and rode from Petrovsky Palace to Khodynka; behind him, Empress Alexandra rode in an open phaeton pulled by four white horses, accompanied by her sister-in-law Grand Duchess Victoria Melita of Hesse and by Rhine and her cousin Crown Princess Marie of Romania.[113] A mounted contingent of Grand Dukes, foreign princes, foreign military attachés, and members of Extraordinary Embassies waited near the Imperial Pavilion. *"We were tightly packed,"* recalled Francis Grenfell, who complained about the *"broiling sun."*[114]

Elegantly dressed ladies, colorful parasols raised against the sunshine, packed the tribunes. Nicholas took the salute as the troops marched past: 38,565 enlisted soldiers, 1,960 officers, sixty-seven generals – just over 40,000 men in all.[115] It was a *"magnificent sight,"* said Mary Hickley, a brilliant, *"unending procession,"* the Meadow ringing with continuous cheers as troops filed past the Emperor. She saw Chevalier Guards, *"grand men in white and gold"* who from a distance *"looked like a line of sparks"* as the sun gleamed on their cuirasses; *"fierce"* Cossacks *"of furiously martial bearing;"* Cavalry regiments, *"picturesque"* in their blue and green uniforms trimmed with fur; smart Artillery squadrons; and even ordinary soldiers, *"plainly-clad and businesslike in appearance."*[116] Nicholas was impressed, as he rarely failed to be by well-orchestrated military display. *"It was,"* he noted, *"a brilliant parade in every respect, and I was delighted that all the troops showed such spirit in front of the foreigners."*[117]

After two hours under the relentless sun, the review ended with an artillery salute and thousands of voices filling the air with *God Save the Tsar*. The Imperial couple returned to Petrovsky Palace for lunch as guests filtered out of the Meadow, carriages jostling along the highway side-by-side with troops all *"smothered in dust."* To Mary Hickley, it seemed quite inspiring, at least until her carriage rumbled past Vaganovsky Cemetery. Even from the road, she could see *"rows and rows of new graves, like the furrows of a ploughed field,"* and mourners wandering *"sadly among them."*[118]

Crown Princess Marie of Romania.

There were farewells at Petrovsky Palace, including a worn out Li-Hung Chang. He was desperately tired, and only managed this final meeting after a Russian doctor shot him up with some unknown drug and made him drink a large bottle of wine. By the time he met the Imperial couple, the elderly man recorded, *"I was feeling like a boy."* Tongue loosened and inhibitions lowered, Li-Hung Chang stumbled into Nicholas and Alexandra's presence, declaring that he was glad the ceremonies were over as he found them much too long and the heavy smoke of incense had nearly made him sick. Nicholas erupted into laughter.[119] Before he left, Nicholas and Alexandra gave the diplomat a sable robe, luxuriously lined with purple satin; duly impressed, he promised that he would wear it *"only when the most auspicious occasions fall upon the coldest days."*[120]

A State Dinner for the remaining royal guests, diplomats, and officials in the Kremlin's Hall of St. Alexander Nevsky ended the official coronation program. The

consommé, Rassolnik soup, pirozhki, steamed Gatchina trout, roast lamb, chicken breasts stuffed with truffles, cold lobster, roast duck, artichokes in mushroom sauce, salad, and ice cream came in waves like nausea.[121] A little before nine, joined by Sergei and Elisabeth, Nicholas and Alexandra left the Kremlin, driving through the twilit Moscow streets as crowds, said the official account, cheered their last view of their Emperor and Empress.[122]

A military guard-of-honor snapped to attention as Nicholas and Alexandra arrived at Moscow's Brest Railway Station.[123] A new railway carriage, lavishly upholstered in velvet and filled with ornate, gilded carvings at a cost of £3,500 (£350,000, or $472,500 in 2014), waited to carry them eighteen miles to Sergei and Elisabeth's estate at Ilinskoye, to spend three quiet weeks with their closest relatives, relaxing in the countryside. Any crowds who came to watch them go were as silent now as if they had been at a funeral. *"Not a single cheer,"* wrote an aristocratic observer.[124] If Nicholas noticed, he said nothing about in his diary, where his one preoccupation was relief that the strain and exertion of public appearances were over. *"The chief consolation,"* he wrote, *"is to know that all these festivities and ceremonies are at an end!"*[125]

The Imperial trains steamed off into the night. Three weeks of superbly regal parades and processions, banquets and balls – all the pageantry the Russian Court could muster – had fallen victim to an unforeseen clash with brutal reality. In 1825, Nicholas I had come to the Imperial Throne amid the Decembrist Rebellion. Danger, he believed, demanded decisive action, and he reluctantly spilled the blood of his subjects as his reign began. Yet he turned this bloodshed to his own advantage, portraying himself as a stern, paternalistic, and competent bastion of order, guarding Russia against chaos. Three-quarters of a century later, faced with bloodshed at the symbolic beginning of his reign, his great-grandson Nicholas II let a disastrous situation spiral out of control. A sensitive and generally well-meaning man who saw himself as embodying Russia's sorrows, Nicholas II faced a tragedy that offered a similar chance for Imperial clarity, an opportunity to display a sorrowful unity with his people and give body and meaning to his own vision at the most public moment of his reign. Instead, consumed with appeasing his uncles, ignoring his own instincts, and unable to weigh the effect of indulging his personal craving for peaceful solitude with his wife against the public desires of his injured subjects, he fed the embittered perception that he was a foolish, callous youth, hopelessly inept and lacking in basic human sympathy. He left his coronation in Moscow having unknowingly taken the first steps along a tortured road that would lead many of his subjects – and history – to condemn him as *"Nicholas the Bloody."*

Opposite page: A painting of Tsar Nicholals II during the Coronation.

Epilogue

With the end of the Coronation, Nicholas and Alexandra escaped to Ilinskoye, Sergei and Elisabeth's Moscow country estate. It was, Nicholas confided to his diary, *"wonderful"* to put the ceremonies behind them, to know *"that one can now live for oneself."*[1] He spent his days walking, swimming, playing tennis, taking tea, picking flowers, and enjoying long naps in the bucolic grounds.[2] For the first time since she had given birth, he and Alexandra went out on horseback together.[3] Forty miles of railway track separated Nicholas II from Moscow, but he apparently never considered infringing upon his holiday to visit the wounded still dying in the city's hospitals. The two short hospital visits he and Alexandra had made in the first forty-eight hours following the Khodynka tragedy were deemed sufficient evidence of Imperial concern.

To Nicholas, the idea of indulging popular feeling was an alien concept. *"What have I got to do with public opinion?"* he angrily demanded of Sergei Witte.[4] Having concluded the ceremonies, he was in no mood to discuss Khodynka. *"I don't want to talk about Moscow,"* he grumbled to his brother George, *"it makes me sick to remember. It's not particularly comforting to think about the sad side of the Coronation."* In one of his more unfortunate comments, Nicholas wrote not of the dead or wounded, but rather complained that it had been *"a year of hard labor, with Alix and me as the martyrs."*[5] While this echoed the stance adopted in official literature – that Khodynka had been a personal tragedy suffered not by the victims but rather by the Emperor – it was also keenly selfish. The Imperial couple compounded their tragic judgment by retreating to Ilinskoye. As Helen Baker has noted, this stay with the controversial Grand Duke Sergei – increasingly blamed for Khodynka – *"suggested to the Russian populace that the Tsar would not contemplate punishing a member of his own family, no matter how deserving."*[6] It also aligned Nicholas firmly in the eyes of public opinion with the bitterly unpopular Grand Duke.

Was Sergei deserving of punishment? It was a question that found no official public answer. That something had gone horribly wrong at Khodynka was abundantly clear. *"Who could have foreseen such a tragedy?"* pondered Alexei

Epilogue

A family gathering at Ilinskoye. Standing in the back, from the left: Crown Prince Ferdinand of Romania, Tsar Nicholas II, Grand Duke Sergei Alexandrovich, Grand Duchess Victoria Melita and Grand Duke Ernst Ludwig of Hesse and by Rhine. Seated, same order: Grand Duke Dimitri Pavlovich, Crown Princess Marie of Romania, Empress Alexandra Feodorovna with her daughter Grand Duchess Olga Nikolaievna, the Duchess of Saxe-Coburg and Gotha with her granddaughter Princess Elisabeth of Hesse and by Rhine, and Grand Duchess Elisabeth Feodorovna. On the floor, same order: Princess Beatrice of Saxe-Coburg and Gotha, Grand Duchess Marie Pavlovna the Younger, Grand Duke Paul Alexandrovich and Princess Victoria of Battenberg.

Suvorin.⁷ Yet signs pointing toward likely disaster had been ignored. In 1826, the crowd attending Nicholas I's popular feast overwhelmed expectation, exhausting free alcohol, fighting for scraps of food, and smashing booths and tables. Similar scenes took place in 1856 for Alexander II's feast, and in 1883 the size of the crowd exceeded estimates and the push for souvenirs left thirty-two dead. Eighteen people died the week before Nicholas II's fete, fighting for coveted Coronation proclamations.⁸ In 1896, the warnings from history were ignored.

Details chronicling the disaster emerged in two competing investigations, both commissioned nearly simultaneously by an Emperor unwilling to make difficult decisions and enforce the consequences. The day after the tragedy, he asked his Minister of Justice Nicholas Muraviev to conduct an inquiry into Khodynka. Muraviev was to determine how the disaster had occurred and who bore responsibility. Aware that Muraviev owed his appointment to Grand Duke Sergei, many speculated that his inquiry would inevitably absolve the Governor-General of any guilt and instead blame Vorontsov-Dashkov.⁹ Yet as Grand Duke Konstantin heard, Muraviev actually promised that he would conduct his investigation in such a way as to clear both Sergei and Vorontsov-Dashkov, regardless of the facts.¹⁰ This piece of official cynicism, in which an inquiry meant to establish facts and assess guilt was conceived with a predetermined outcome meant to protect those closest to the Emperor, suggests that no one – from Nicholas II down – was interested in discovering the truth.

Grand Duke George Alexandrovich.

The Minister of Justice devoted a mere two weeks to his inquiry. With rumors that both Sergei and Vorontsov-Dashkov would be cleared, attention turned to Chief of Police Vlassovsky. Although he had merely followed the Grand Duke's directives in refusing to cooperate with security arrangements, everyone knew that he would be made to pay for the Governor-General's decisions. Aware of what was coming, Vlassovsky was said to have unsuccessfully tried to kill himself at the end of the coronation festivities.¹¹

Copies of Muraviev's report, never released publicly, circulated within the Imperial Government. Sergei Witte read it and thought that Muraviev *"was quite objective in his description of the details of the tragedy, but he was far less objective and was often evasive in dealing with the question of responsibility."*¹² He blamed Moscow bureaucrats for the disaster, singling out Vlassovsky and members of the Khodynka committee.¹³ As promised, he attached no responsibility to either Grand Duke Sergei or Count Vorontsov-Dashkov.¹⁴ Alexei Suvorin read the report in utter disbelief: *"Thank God,"* he said sarcastically, *"the guilty have been found! Any time a train is derailed, it's always the signalman who is to blame!"*¹⁵

Muraviev's report provided the Government with its official verdict on the question of responsibility. The press reported rumors that Vlassovsky would be arraigned with other Moscow bureaucrats before the Imperial Senate and put on trial.¹⁶ The possibility of a public trial, though, was unwelcome on all counts. Not only would it ensure continued discussion of the tragedy – something no one in official circles wanted – but, more to the point, the Government would lose control of its carefully structured narrative and its defendants. Faced with the possibility of censure, imprisonment, or worse, Vlassovsky might well talk, exposing Sergei's negligence. A talkative and desperate Vlassovsky would have undermined Muraviev's charge to clear the Governor-General of responsibility. Nicholas dismissed Vlassovsky from his post in July but ensured his compliance through a series of Machiavellian moves. All further public inquiries into Khodynka were cancelled. In a Ukase signed on July 15, 1896, the Emperor, while admitting that *"the cause of the misfortune ought to be sought in the Moscow authorities,"* declared that he alone would assess and administer any punishments.[17] Vlassovsky was denied the right to appeal his dismissal. But the same government, under Sergei's orders, that deemed him responsible for Khodynka bought his silence with an annual pension of 3,000 rubles ($40,500, or £30,000 in 2014).[18] This, notes Helen Baker, *"infuriated many Russians,"* who knew that Khodynka victims received much less; critics took it as proof that the Imperial Government cared more about protecting its officials than it did about the lives of peasants and workers.[19]

Although Vlassovsky was out of the way, Sergei continued to worry about the activities of the *"Vorontsov clique"* who had access to the Emperor at court.[20] A few days after Khodynka, Vorontsov-Dashkov asked the Emperor for a second inquiry, one independent of that conducted by the Grand Duke's protégé Muraviev. Once the coronation ceremonies ended, the Count said he would withdraw to his country estate and await the results: if evidence showed that he had been at fault, Vorontsov-Dashkov would resign.[21] Nicholas agreed, and appointed Count Konstantin von der Pahlen to head a Senatorial Extraordinary Investigation.[22]

Grand Duke Sergei Alexandrovich.

The Emperor's acquiescence only underscored a larger problem. Nicholas, ever reluctant to make potentially controversial decisions and face conflict directly, instead submitted to whatever pressures were brought to bear on him. The decision to appoint a new, independent investigation before Muraviev had concluded his own inquiry certainly undermined the Minister of Justice's efforts, whatever the nature of his mandate. Yet Nicholas, eager to appease everyone, saw no dilemma in ordering two rival, simultaneous investigations into the Khodynka tragedy.

Pahlen, a former Minister of Justice under Alexander III, was a respected figure, a *"very honorable man,"* said Sergei Witte.[23] He was also a former Minister of the Imperial Court and had worked closely alongside Vorontsov-Dashkov in an official capacity. Grand Duke Sergei had not objected when *his* political protégé Muraviev was asked to examine his responsibility for Khodynka; when the tables were turned, though, Sergei was outraged and accused Pahlen of bias.[24] Learning of this second investigation, the Grand Duke and his brothers again threatened Nicholas. If the Emperor authorized Pahlen's Senatorial inquiry, they would all immediately resign from official posts in protest.[25]

Minister of Religion Konstantin Pobedonostsev threw himself into the battle: accusations against Sergei, he insisted, would be taken as indictments against the Imperial Family as a whole and undermine the "*monarchical principle*" of autocracy.[26] There was, Nicholas laconically recorded in his diary, "*a lot of excitement in the family*" over the Pahlen investigation.[27] True to form, he gave in to the threats. "*In three days,*" Grand Duke Konstantin complained, "*the Emperor has changed his mind as many times. How outrageous can you get – to allow yourself, in an autocratic nation, to give an ultimatum to the Emperor, to threaten and frighten!*"[28] He summed up what must have been on many minds when he wrote: "*Oh, if only the Emperor was more decisive!*"[29]

Though Nicholas agreed Pahlen would not be allowed to conduct a proper inquiry, he lacked the courage of his convictions, even convictions forced upon him. He permitted the Count to continue his investigation privately. Only Nicholas would see the results. Shrouded in Imperial secrecy, hopes for a responsible inquiry evaporated in the Moscow spring.

Although Pahlen's report was secret, copies circulated within Government and Imperial circles.[30] Future Russian Foreign Minister Alexander Izwolsky was in a unique position to learn its contents: not only was he Muraviev's cousin but his wife was also Pahlen's niece. Through these connections, Izwolsky followed the investigation and knew its conclusions, as did several others. Pahlen's report exonerated Vorontsov-Dashkov of the most serious charges, while placing the majority of the blame for Khodynka on Grand Duke Sergei.[31] Pahlen recommended that the Grand Duke receive a "*severe disciplinary penalty.*"[32] "*Whenever a Grand Duke was given a responsible post,*" Pahlen candidly remarked, "*there was sure to be trouble.*"[33]

Grand Duchess Alexandra Iosifovna.

Nicholas, commented Sergei Witte, read Pahlen's report "*favorably*" and accepted its conclusions against the Grand Duke as correct. Sergei and his brothers protested, but to no avail.[34] "*Nicky,*" wrote the Emperor's sister Xenia, "*now understands about the Uncles, and says that he won't try to keep them on if they take it into their heads to resign.*"[35] He even dared demonstrate his continued faith in Vorontsov-Dashkov, asking the Count to accompany the Imperial couple as they set off on a tour of Russia later that summer.[36] Furious, Grand Duke Sergei retaliated with a public snub that August, abruptly leaving Moscow with his wife the day before Nicholas and Alexandra arrived in the city.[37] The insolent Sergei, insisted Grand Duchess Alexandra Iosifovna, would have been exiled to Siberia "*in his lawn tennis outfit*" had her father-in-law Nicholas I still been on the Russian Throne.[38]

The tide soon turned, as Sergei and his brothers worked to exact revenge. At the beginning of August, Grand Duke Alexei essentially forced Grand Duke Alexander Mikhailovich from his position in the Imperial Navy, punishment in part for his vocal opposition to continuing the coronation festivities in the wake of Khodynka.[39] "*In general,*" wrote Nicholas II's brother George, "*our dear uncles have behaved in a thoroughly improper manner recently. I am amazed at their effrontery.*"[40]

Yet the Emperor's apparent resolve quickly crumbled in the face of familial tensions. "*To avoid quarrels and strain in the family,*" Nicholas candidly wrote that autumn, "*I constantly concede, and end up looking like an idiot, without will or character.*"[41] Alexandra, it was said, had thrown herself into a "*complex political question*" resulting from Khodynka, siding with Sergei against Vorontsov-Dashkov and Pahlen's inquiry.[42] The Dowager Empress supported Vorontsov-Dashkov and Pahlen's report, excoriating her daughter-in-law Alexandra and the *"unreasonable"* Grand Duchess Elisabeth for their bad influence on Nicholas. Her own friends assured her that the young Imperial couple were *"nothing"* without her and could regain their popularity only with her help. A *"muted antagonism,"* said Grand Duke Konstantin, erupted between the two Empresses over responsibility for Khodynka. *"It's all so unfortunate and embarrassing,"* he commented sadly.⁴³

Whether it was pressure from Alexandra, desire to present a united imperial family to the world, or threats by Sergei and his brothers, something changed Nicholas's mind. That autumn, he abandoned Pahlen's verdict. He and Alexandra made a great show of traveling with Sergei and Elisabeth, who complained to Queen Victoria of *"abominable lies"* about her husband. Sergei, she insisted, was the victim of *"jealous intriguers,"* whose actions were *"simply disgusting."*⁴⁴ Proof that Sergei had won the battle came in December, when Nicholas appointed his uncle chairman of a committee designing a memorial for Alexander III, a public sign that the Grand Duke would never be held accountable for his role in the tragedy.⁴⁵ Even the victorious Grand Duke Sergei seemed stunned by this whirlwind of reversals, complaining of Nicholas II's *"lack of character"* as he watched him vacillate and cast aside one decision after another.⁴⁶

Nicholas II's embrace of Sergei spelled disaster for many who had battled against him. Though he had tendered his resignation, Count Paul Shuvalov remained the Grand Duke's adjutant for several months, hoping that they could part on friendly terms. *"We had,"* remembered Shuvalov's wife Alexandra, *"established a very close relationship with the Grand Duke and Grand Duchess. I had permission to ring up and ask whether I could lunch with her on this or that day, and they used to visit us informally."* Time, though, brought no thaw in relations: Elisabeth refused to take her friend's telephone calls, refused to receive her husband's adjutant, and even pointedly snubbed the couple's relatives at public functions. Reconciled to his status as an outcast, Shuvalov left the Grand Duke's employ that autumn.⁴⁷ Later ironically appointed to the post of Chief of the Moscow Police, Shuvalov was assassinated by terrorists in 1905.

Grand Duchess Elisabeth Feodorovna.

Count Konstantin von der Pahlen's punishment was subtler. *"From this time on,"* recalled Witte, he *"was never to receive a substantial appointment."* Though Nicholas II was polite, it was clear, said Witte, that Pahlen was out of favor.⁴⁸ The Count left his post as Chief Grand Master of Ceremonies shortly after the Coronation, confiding that he could no longer serve the Emperor after Nicholas II refused to hold Sergei accountable for the Khodynka disaster.⁴⁹

In requesting the Pahlen inquiry, Vorontsov-Dashkov had sought and received vindication of his own role in the Khodynka tragedy. Had the results been otherwise, the Count promised that he would resign his post as Minister of the Imperial Court.⁵⁰ When Nicholas assured Vorontsov-Dashkov that he accepted the inquiry's conclusions and invited the Count to accompany him on his tour of Russia, the issue seemed settled – at least until others intervened. It took six months, but the Minister's fall was inevitable: on May 6, 1897, Vorontsov-Dashkov was relieved of his post through a typical piece of Imperial subterfuge. The Count, it was announced, had tendered his resignation; in fact, as both Witte and Alexander Mossolov, who headed Nicholas II's Court Chancellery, recalled, he was dismissed, informed *"when nothing could have been farther"* from his mind that his *"resignation"* was accepted.⁵¹ Conflict with Sergei over Khodynka, said

Witte, and the Grand Duke's *"considerable influence"* on the Emperor, brought the Count's demise; Mossolov ascribed it more directly to pressure exerted by Alexandra, though not necessarily over Khodynka.[52] Privately, Vorontsov-Dashkov supposedly complained that he was *"not used to working with people who could not keep their word."*[53] Although Nicholas appointed him to the State Council and listened to his views behind the scenes, the former Minister's career as an influential courtier in St. Petersburg was over. In 1905, Nicholas made him Viceroy of the troubled Caucasus, a post the Count held until 1915, the year before his death.

Tsar Nicholas II.

Public opinion took these developments poorly. They suggested an Emperor more concerned with protecting his uncle than with punishing those responsible for the Khodynka disaster and tending to the welfare of his humble subjects. These impressions were unfortunately borne out by the cynical way in which the government dealt with victims of the tragic affair.

Precisely how many perished at Khodynka would be a matter of confusion and angry assertions for years to come. *"The number of persons killed, crushed, trampled, smothered,"* recorded British journalist E. J. Dillon, *"never accurately ascertained, was variously estimated at three, five, or seven thousand,"* though he noted that authorities in Moscow told him that *"a little over 4,000"* people had died.[54] This latter figure was widely circulated and believed.[55] On May 18, Alexei Suvorin recorded in his diary that *"up to 2,000 people were crushed,"* although it is not known if he included in this figure both the wounded and the dead.[56] On Sunday, May 19, correspondents from *Le Figaro* and *Le Petit Parisien* reported that 1,138 had been killed.[57] That same day, the official number of dead increased: now, Suvorin, as well as correspondents from *Le Figaro, La Croix, Le Matin*, and *Le Petit Parisien*, reported 1,282 casualties.[58] The correspondent from *Le Matin*, though, noted that 2,281 had actually died as of May 20, a figure taken from the actual number of corpses recorded at Vagonovsky Cemetery.[59] On May 22, the Russian Government announced that some 3,600 had been killed, but quickly retracted the figure.[60] In their own contemporaneous accounts, Francis Grenfell said that there was *"little doubt the numbers exceed 2,000"* dead, Henry LaPauze reported *"several thousand deaths,"* Kate Koon wrote of 1,800 victims, and Mary Hickley noted that *"two thousand people had been crushed to death."*[61]

Casualty figures swelled as the days passed. *The Illustrated London News* reported that *"more than 3,000 persons had perished, and many hundreds besides had been fatally or seriously injured,"* while *The New York Times* conservatively placed the number of dead at *"no less than 4,000."*[62] Sergei Witte spoke of "several thousand" dead, while future Foreign Minister Alexander Izwolsky, with extremely close ties to both the Muraviev and Pahlen investigations, said that 3,000 had perished.[63] Aylmer Maude suggested that at least 3,000 had been killed, while Grand Duke Nicholas Mikhailovich, arguing against attendance at the Montebello Ball, asserted that 5,000 people had been killed.[64] John Logan confidently wrote of 2,836 victims, a precise number repeated by Mary Hickley.[65]

The Russian Government offered official numbers that were certainly at odds with these reports. On May 19, the count stood at 1,438: 979 dead and 459 seriously injured. This increased to 2,004 by May 26: 1,360 dead and 644 seriously wounded. By the end of May, there were 2,690 victims, of whom 1,389 had died. The final Government count declared that 1,429 had died, among them 118 children.[66]

The official figure of 1,429 dead apparently agrees with Moscow police and hospital records, at least to the end of May 1896, but the number of eventual fatalities grew with the passing weeks as the wounded succumbed to their injuries. A later study revealed that several thousand died in the months and years following from fatal fractures, consumption, and internal damage suffered on the field.[67] Ultimately, no one would ever know precisely how many people died from the tragedy.

The casualty numbers were critical when it came time for the Government to honor Nicholas II's public promise to give 1,000 rubles to each victim's relatives. The pledge, most agreed, was a sympathetic gesture, though journalist Aubrey Stanhope presciently speculated that it would not be kept. He blamed not Nicholas, whom he called *"little more than a prisoner in his own country,"* but rather the *"wall of officialdom"* separating Government and People.[68]

Few aspects of the Khodynka disaster were as grim as the Government's treatment of the bereaved. The same officials who shielded those responsible for the loss of life further aggrieved sensibilities by fighting with the bereaved families over fulfilling Nicholas II's public promise that relatives of each victim would receive 1,000 rubles. Alexander Bulygin, Grand Duke Sergei, and the Minister of the Interior headed a special commission assessing a total of 1,768 claims.[69] Less than half of the surviving families – 634 of the 1,429 killed – were compensated.[70] Only 277 received the full 1,000 rubles Nicholas had promised to each family; relatives of other victims were given 750 rubles, 500 rubles, 350 rubles, and similarly decreasing amounts depending on what the Government thought each individual life had been worth.[71] Under this cold bureaucratic calculation, the committee rarely gave any money for the deaths of children or of the elderly.[72]

Alexander Bulygin.

Many received nothing, while others had only minimal compensation. A woman whose daughter had supported her was granted a mere 250 rubles for the loss of her child: the bereaved mother, the Government declared, could subsist on charity.[73] One widowed peasant was so badly injured that she could never work again: the committee agreed to give her 1,000 rubles, but only if she put her child in an orphanage.[74] To save itself money, the Government gave most payments as annual pensions of between 20-60 rubles rather than outright grants.[75] As a final insult, authorities made quite clear that they were to be considered free of blame for the tragedy. Payments were not an admission of guilt or recognition that the Government owed the victims anything. They were officially described as *"financial aid,"* as if a benevolent Government was tending to the welfare of those who had actually fallen victim to its own incompetence.[76]

After months of wrangling, the commission eventually paid out 390,000 rubles, less than a third of the sum pledged.[77] This money, it has frequently been said, came from the Emperor's own pocket. *"Nicky spent thousands and thousands of rubles to provide pensions for those disabled at Khodynka and for the widows and orphans,"* his sister Olga declared. *"He did not want to embarrass the Treasury."*[78]

In fact, Nicholas II paid nothing: the grants came not from his personal funds but rather from the State Treasury.[79] In abdicating responsibility to ensure that his pledge was fulfilled, the Emperor only added to the growing resentment against his Government.

This incompetence fed a tide of discontent that had been raging among peasants, workers, students, and the intelligentsia since the catastrophe. A few days after the Coronation festivities ended, Moscow Police arrested distributors of a radical broadsheet called *"Butchery on Khodynka,"* in which the anonymous author railed against Grand Duke Sergei, Vlassovsky and, more damagingly, Nicholas II. Such a disaster, it argued, was possible only in a country like Russia, where an autocrat was more concerned with spending *"200 million rubles on the Coronation, Tsarist feasts, and balls"* than with the safety and happiness of his subjects.[80] Similar publications repeated and amplified the charges. Khodynka, an émigré pamphlet published in Geneva, pointed out that Nicholas II had used his power not to punish the guilty but to protect them.[81] The Emperor, the pamphlet declared, proved himself *"incapable of observing even the outward signs of decency"* in the tragedy's wake.[82]

Grand Duke Vladimir Alexandrovich.

Protests marked the six-month anniversary of the Khodynka disaster. In Moscow, police ordered into the streets by Grand Duke Sergei clashed with demonstrators across the city.[83] Hundreds of students descended on Vaganovsky Cemetery, where most of the Khodynka victims were buried, to hold a memorial service. Denied entrance, they prayed outside the gates before troops arrived and beat them back with whips. More than 700 were arrested and expelled from Moscow University on Serge's orders.[84] These heavy-handed measures, said Semen Kanatchikov, *"caused great agitation"* among his fellow workers. *"For the first time,"* his comrades *"looked upon the students not as pointless malcontents but as seekers after justice."*[85]

Few Russians could separate joyous ceremonies from catastrophe. The single most important event in Nicholas II's reign became inexorably linked with tragedy. Yet the Emperor never understood just how deeply Khodynka pervaded the Russian conscience. Initial reactions of horror over the event swelled into popular outrage as the ceremonies continued.[86] Layers of officialdom and bureaucracy separated Nicholas II from personal responsibility for Khodynka, but in autocratic Russia, where the Emperor symbolized and gloried in the nation's triumphs, he could not escape its tragedies, particularly one so intimately aligned with the most significant occasion of his reign.

The twenty-four-hours following the disaster revealed a monarch incapable of adjusting to unexpected circumstance, of adapting his actions to suit momentous changes, and of following his own instincts in the face of familial pressures. It was not that Nicholas II was unmoved by what had taken place: as historian Robert Warth noted, *"Weakness and poor judgment should not have been taken for lack of compassion."*[87] He failed, though, to sufficiently demonstrate his own sympathy and grief, and quickly consigned the tragedy to memory. Giving in to pressure from his uncles, Nicholas refused to cancel the remaining festivities or call for national mourning; he appeared as scheduled at Khodynka, making no mention of the tragedy, and compounded the damage by celebrating at the Montebello ball that night as his subjects lay dying. Prayers for the dead came not at a public memorial, as Vorontsov-Dashkov had suggested, but rather during a private church service in the Kremlin. He announced an investigation into the disaster, but the inquiry was at best superficial and at worst predetermined in its outcome. Visits to the wounded seemed shallow, leaving the impression that they stemmed from dutiful obligation rather than actual concern. Nicholas and Alexandra spent a total of three hours visiting the wounded in two hospitals, yet found eighteen hours to enjoy private walks together at Neskuchnoye. Neither understood that the burdens of the crown, especially in the wake of a tragedy like Khodynka, called for some personal concession to public distress.[88]

What happened in the wake of Khodynka, wrote Richard Wortman, revealed an Emperor *"who could not make proper amends."*[89] Along with a sense of careless ineptitude went a feeling that "any display of sympathy or feeling" would be interpreted as personal weakness, that compassion would reveal Nicholas II as subject to the whims and ways of ordinary mortals.[90] This was the argument advanced by Grand Dukes Vladimir, Alexei, Sergei and Paul Alexandrovich against Vorontsov-Dashkov's proposals: *"Sentiment,"* they had declared, had no place in the autocracy. For many of his subjects, Nicholas II emerged from Moscow as an uncaring, self-absorbed, and heartless autocrat, unconcerned with their fate and unwilling to atone for the fatal mistakes committed in his name.

Grand Duke Alexei Alexandrovich.

Khodynka and its tragic tendrils quickly subsumed the coronation's legacy. In many ways, the callous response proved more damaging than the loss of life. People viewed Nicholas II as heartless, or incompetent, or both. Perhaps the clash was inevitable. As industrialization took hold, disparity widened, and dissatisfaction grew, fewer people could be impressed into loyalty by magnificent parades and costly court spectacles. Insight and action, though, might have saved the situation even after Khodynka. In dismissing the tragedy and its victims with a shocking haste, Nicholas finally shattered the Imperial vision of a benevolent Tsar and adoring, unquestioning subjects.

***

Those gathered in Moscow to witness the ceremonies scattered to the ends of the earth when the pageantry ceased. Grand Duke Sergei, restored to Imperial favor, remained a highly unpopular Governor-General.

Muscovites, sure that he was to blame for the tragedy, christened him with the name *"Prince Khodynka." "Prince Khodynka has come back to keep an eye on the Vaganovsky Cemetery"* read placards greeting his return to Moscow in the autumn of 1896.⁹¹ Foreign newspapers reported that Sergei had received a letter disguised as an Imperial rescript. When opened, a disturbingly accurate forgery announced that Nicholas was appointing him *Prince Khodynka* in recognition of his role in the deaths of so many people. News of this hoax leaked out at once, and later in the evening Serge was cheered at the theatre with cries of *"Bravo, Prince Khodynka!"*⁹² He met his fate in February 1905, victim of a terrorist bomb that literally blew him to pieces as he was leaving the Kremlin. His widow Elisabeth Feodorovna, who helped convince her sister Alexandra to attend the Montebello ball and who so strenuously defended her husband, turned to religion, founding a convent whose veil she was wearing when, in 1918, Bolsheviks cast her and other members of dethroned Romanov Dynasty down an abandoned Siberian mineshaft to die.

Journalists and writers covering the Coronation recorded its extravagant ceremonies, and revealed its devastating climax. Alexei Suvorin remained editor of the influential *Novoe Vremya*, a conservative voice respected by Nicholas II for his reactionary views until his death in 1912. Together with his wife Louise, Aylmer Maude returned to England, where they devoted the rest of their lives to progressive causes and translating the works of Leo Tolstoy. A leading member of the Fabian Society, Maude died in 1938. And Richard Harding Davis became one of the most eminent reporters of his day, befriending future President Theodore Roosevelt during his coverage of the Spanish-American War and continuing as a journalist in the First World War. He died suddenly in 1916, at the early age of fifty-two.

Of the diplomats who had witnessed the ceremonies in Moscow, Sir Nicholas O'Conor went on to be Britain's Ambassador to Constantinople and died in 1908; Major-General Sir Francis Grenfell, who wrote his memoirs of the Coronation, served in senior positions in the Egyptian and Irish armies before his death in 1925. The famous Li-Hung Chang played a major role as a Chinese negotiator in the Boxer Rebellion before his death in 1901, a controversial figure suspected of working against Chinese interests in his talks with Russia. American Minister Clifton Breckinridge returned to Arkansas in 1897. He remained active in politics until his seventies, and died in 1932. And Louis Gustave, Count de Montebello, whose splendid ball proved so fatal to Nicholas's public image, remained France's Ambassador to Russia until 1902, presiding over a triumphant visit by President Faure. In 1901, Nicholas II stood godfather to Montebello's grandson, an event commemorated by Proust in *Remembrance of Things Past*.

Among less prominent but no less vocal figures, Semen Kanatchikov never forgot the coronation or the tragedy of Khodynka. The day off that he and his colleagues had enjoyed when the Emperor was crowned, and the unexpected eight-hour days – with

Grand Duke Paul Alexandrovich.

lunch breaks – became aspirations. Khodynka seared him to the core. Searching for a better life, he joined the future Communist Party in 1898, and later became a Bolshevik official, recruiting delegates in Ekaterinburg and across the country. By 1918, when the Romanovs were imprisoned in Siberia, Kanatchikov had become a leading Party official in Tomsk and then with the Perm Soviet. He died in 1940. John Logan returned to America, wrote an awestruck account of his time in Moscow, and resumed his army career. In 1899, while leading troops at San Jacinto during the brief Philippine-American War, he was shot and killed at the age of thirty-four; his mother Mary outlived him by twenty-four years. British attaché Ian Malcolm married Jeanne-Marie, daughter of Lily Langtry and, it was presumed, Prince Louis of Battenberg. Malcolm became a Member of Parliament, maintaining links with Russia and meeting the Empress several times. Mary Hickley left Moscow after the coronation for a trip to the Caucasus, one of those ostensibly quiet and prim unmarried ladies who showed a great spirit of adventure. Though she returned to England, her connection with Russia was far from over: in 1906, her family offered the Golitsyns refuge from the turbulence of the previous year's failed revolution, opening their Somerset home to the aristocratic family employing their sister. An amateur poet and memoirist, Mary died in 1932. Emily Warren Roebling, pioneering female manager and engineer, died in New Jersey in 1903, and the great Chicago society hostess Bertha Palmer died in 1918. The two Koon sisters returned to Minneapolis. In 1898, Kate married manufacturing industrialist Charles C. Bovey. The author of a set of privately published memoirs about the Coronation, she died on July 17, 1964 – ironically the forty-sixth anniversary of Nicholas and Alexandra's execution.

***

Grand Duke Sergei Alexandrovich.

"The Coronation," declared one St. Petersburg periodical in 1896, *"sealed the unbreakable union of the Russian Autocrat with the Orthodox Church. In the person of the Crowned Sovereign, the people, hundreds of millions strong, joined in this grace, for the Russian people are inseparable from their Tsar."*[93] For Nicholas II, it was a moment of religious intensity, when he pledged himself to his country's service with genuine, heartfelt conviction. Alexandra viewed it as *"a kind of mystic marriage,"* in which she *"became one with Russia, sealed forever a Russian in heart and soul."*[94] Absorbing this aura of divine sanction and mystical power, the couple clung to Byzantine conceits of a religious autocracy starkly at odds with the dawn of the Twentieth Century.

Encouraged by a wife uncomfortable in her ceremonial role, Nicholas retreated into insignificance, to a private world where domestic concerns crowded out the reality of a Russian Empire crumbling around him. Unrest, strikes, and political assassinations followed the Coronation in rapid succession. Officials across the Empire fell victim to terrorist bombs and guns, students and factory workers went on strike, pogroms erupted with the blessing of authorities, and discontent swelled into revolution during Russia's disastrous war with Japan. In January 1905, troops in St. Petersburg shot down unarmed groups of workers attempting to march on the Winter Palace to present Nicholas II with a petition calling for industrial and governmental reform. *"Bloody Sunday,"* as the massacre came to be called, left ninety-two dead, at least according to the Government, though few believed the official tally. It was Khodynka all over again.

Russia's defeat at the hands of Japan and a summer of unpredictable violence forced Nicholas II to do the unthinkable that October of 1905. Under enormous pressure, he reluctantly granted a parliament, the Duma, transforming the Empire from autocracy to the germ of a constitutional monarchy. The Duma was an inconvenient, troublesome reminder of a moment of weakness. Ignoring the pressures that had forced him to act, Nicholas clung to the fantasy that he had granted these concessions as a gesture of munificence, and continued to regard himself as an autocrat with unlimited power.[95] Over the next decade he unsuccessfully attempted to revoke the Duma and curtail the civil liberties granted in 1905 no less than five separate times.[96] Alexandra viewed

Tsar Nicholas II and Empress Alexandra Feodorovna.

the situation through her husband's eyes: despite the October Manifesto, she continued to insist that the Emperor remained autocrat, solely responsible for the Russian Nation.

Tsesarevich Alexei Nikolaievich.

After four daughters, Alexandra finally gave birth to a long-desired son and heir, Tsesarevich Alexei, in 1904, only to learn that he had inherited hemophilia. Nothing could be done, and the Imperial couple, fearing the public's reaction, kept his condition a secret for years. Passive acceptance dominated Nicholas, while Alexandra gave in to unbalanced religiosity, seeking comfort in a succession of holy fools and peasant healers that culminated in the infamous Gregory Rasputin. Nicholas grew tired and disillusioned, Alexandra's health declined, and the brilliance of the Russian Court became a relic of the past as they disappeared behind palace walls and alienated public sympathies. Thereafter, Nicholas lived in a shadow world of fantasy. An unprecedented authorized biography in 1913, whose pages Nicholas personally corrected, presented him as the living embodiment of all virtues, talents, and intellect, a man unlike any other on earth, whose role as *"the Lord's Anointed"* could not *"be compared to any obligation of our own."*[97]

The First World War merely accelerated looming disaster as Nicholas, often isolated at Army Headquarters, increasingly and deliberately relied upon his autocratically minded wife. Church matters, bureaucratic issues, and ministerial appointments – the

Tsar Nicholas II relaxing in his study, an island of isolation where the empire's troubles were minimized to fit his vision of a Russia that no longer existed.

concerns filled page after page of Alexandra's incessant letters to her absent husband. As the end neared, she urged him to "*Show to* all *that you are the* Master & Your *will* shall *be obeyed-the time of great intelligence and gentleness is over-now comes your reign of will and power and they shall be* made *to* bow *down before you…Be Peter the Great, Ivan the Terrible, Emperor Paul – crush them all under you.*"[98]

Devastating losses and military setbacks, disorders and food shortages, innumerable ministers dismissed as the government devolved into chaos, and an Empress apparently in thrall to the disreputable Rasputin all came to a head in 1917, when discontent swelled into Revolution. On a cold March day, isolated at the Pskov train station, Nicholas signed away the throne in a document all the more remarkable for its curious interpretation of the circumstances. The Revolution, Nicholas declared, was *"a harsh new ordeal,"* sent down by *"the Lord God"* upon Russia. Even in his last act as Emperor, he viewed abdication as God's vengeful judgment upon a nation disobedient to Imperial authority, not as the consequence of his own failings upon the Throne.[99]

Khodynka christened Nicholas II's new reign in blood, enveloping the coronation in sorrow and unease. Like a perverse mirror image of the tale of Ivan Susanin in *A Life for the Tsar*, the sacrificial blood shed on Khodynka only amplified the tragedies of the Romanov Dynasty, and disillusion, not expiation, followed the disaster. Failing to understand the precarious situation, the Emperor displayed insufficient public sympathy for the victims, allowed the guilty to escape punishment, and evinced no interest in fulfilling his promises to the bereaved. Members of the execution squad who shot Nicholas and his family in the summer of 1918 viewed the blood they spilled in a dingy Siberian cellar as retribution for the Dynasty's crimes. Then and today, others viewed Nicholas II's death as penitential sacrifice, the passing of a Tsar-Martyr innocent of guilt who died for Russia's sins.

A Life for the Tsar: Triumph and Tragedy at the Coronation of Nicholas II

The Imperial House of Russia

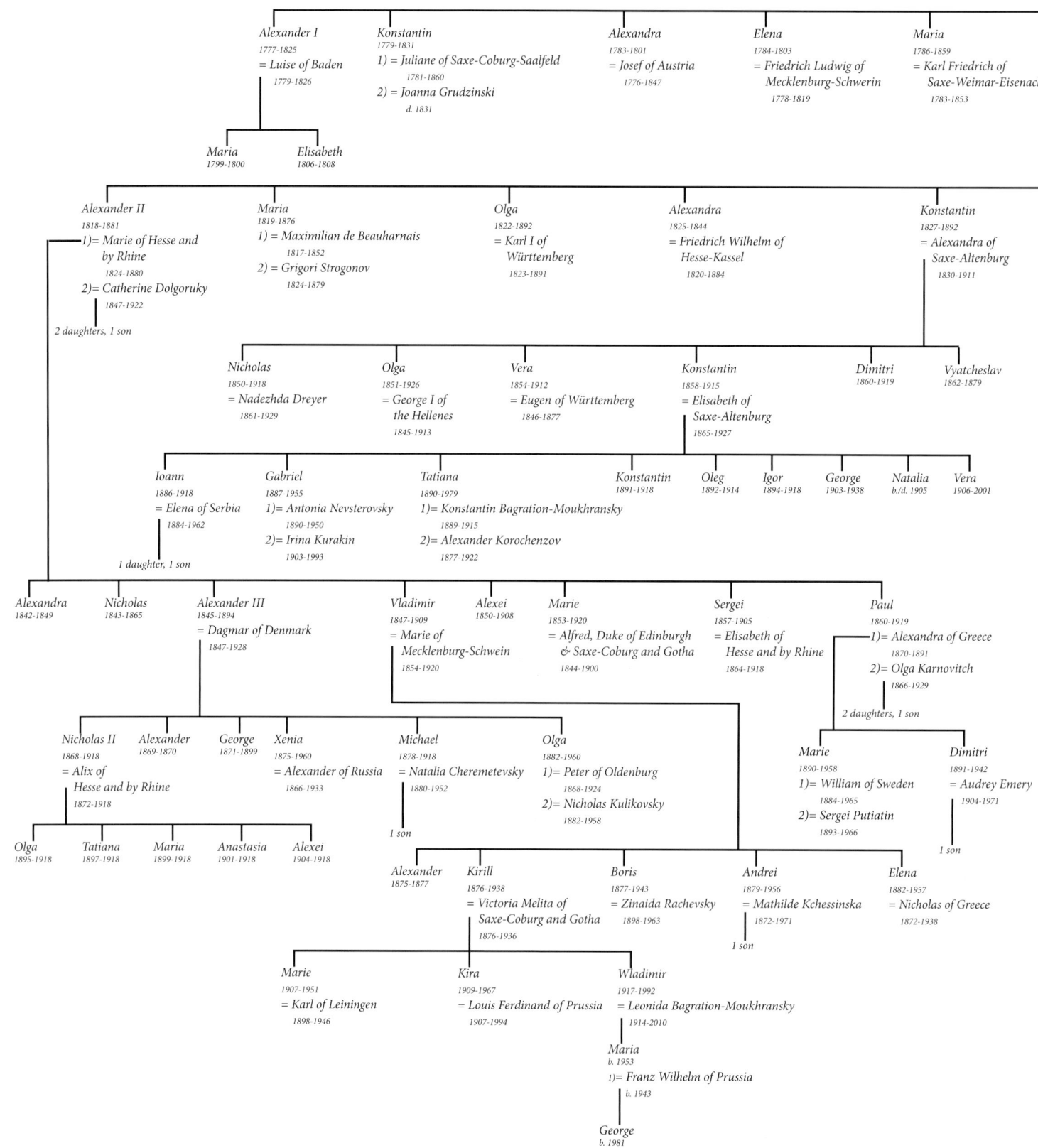

Family Tree

Peter III = Catherine II (née Anhalt-Zerbst)
1728-1762 / 1729-1796

Wilhelmine of Hesse-Darmstadt =(1 Paul I 2)= Sophie of Württemberg
1755-1776 / 1754-1801 / 1759-1828

- **Catherine** 1788-1819
  - 1)= Georg of Oldenburg 1784-1812
  - 2)= Wilhelm I of Württemberg 1781-1864
- **Olga** 1792-1795
- **Anna** 1795-1865 = Willem II of The Netherlands 1792-1849
- **Nicholas I** 1796-1855 = Charlotte of Prussia 1798-1860
- **Michael** 1798-1849 = Charlotte of Württemberg 1807-1873

Children of Nicholas I and Charlotte of Prussia:
- **Nicholas** 1831-1891 = Alexandra of Oldenburg 1838-1900
- **Michael** 1832-1909 = Cecile of Baden 1839-1891

Children of Michael and Charlotte of Württemberg:
- **Maria** 1825-1846
- **Elisabeth** 1826-1845 = Adolf of Nassau 1817-1905
- **Catherine** 1827-1894 = Georg of Mecklenburg-Strelitz 1824-1876
- **Alexander** 1831-1832
- **Anna** 1834-1836

Children of Nicholas (1831-1891) and Alexandra of Oldenburg:
- **Nicholas** 1856-1929 = Anastasia of Montenegro 1868-1929
- **Peter** 1864-1931 = Militza of Montenegro 1866-1951
  - 2 daughters, 1 son

Children of Michael (1832-1909) and Cecile of Baden:
- **Nicholas** 1859-1919
- **Anastasia** 1860-1922 = Friedrich Franz III of Mecklenburg-Schwerin 1851-1897
- **Michael** 1861-1929 = Sophie von Merenberg 1868-1927
  - 2 daughters, 1 son
- **George** 1863-1919 = Marie of Greece 1876-1940
  - **Nina** 1901-1974 = Paul Chavchavadze 1899-1971
  - **Xenia** 1903-1965
    - 1)= William Leeds 1902-1971
    - 2)= Hermann Jud 1911-1987
- **Alexander** 1866-1933 = Xenia of Russia 1875-1960
- **Sergei** 1869-1918
- **Alexei** 1875-1895

Children of Alexander and Xenia of Russia:
- **Irina** 1895-1970 = Felix Yusupov 1887-1967
  - 1 daughter
- **Andrei** 1897-1981
  - 1)= Elisabetha Ruffo 1886-1940
    - 1 daughter, 2 sons
  - 2)= Nadine McDougall 1908-2000
    - 1 daughter
- **Feodor** 1898-1968 = Irina Paley 1903-1990
  - 1 daughter, 1 son
- **Nikita** 1900-1974 = Maria Vorontsov-Dashkov 1903-1997
  - 2 sons
- **Dimitri** 1901-1980
  - 1)= Marina Golenistchev-Kutusov 1912-1969
    - 1 daughter
  - 2)= Sheila Chisholm 1898-1969
- **Rostislav** 1902-1978
  - 1)= Alexandra Galitzine 1905-2006
    - 1 son
  - 2)= Alice Eilken 1923-1996
    - 1 son
  - 3)= Hedwig v. Chapuis 1905-1997
- **Vassili** 1907-1989 = Natalia Galitzine 1907-1989
  - 1 daughter

EUROHISTORY.COM

End Notes

Introduction

1. Prince Nicholas of Greece, 117.
2. See Wortman, 2:2-3.
3. See Krivenko, 7-8; Massie, *Firebird*, 43.
4. Davis, *Year*, 27.
5. Lincoln, 246.
6. Nicholas II's Diary, May 5 (OS), 1896, in GARF, F. 601, Op. 1, D. 36.
7. Quoted in Davis, *Year*, 35-36.
8. Paleologue, Three Critical Years, 78.
9. *Statesman's Handbook for Russia*, 1:7.
10. Fundamental Laws of the Russian Empire, March-April 1903 Revisions, Citing Articles 73 and 100, in Paleologue, *Three Critical Years*, 77.
11. *Moskovskie Vedomosti*, May 6 (OS), 1896.
12. Massie, *Firebird*, 43-44.
13. Buxhoeveden, *Life*, 64; Iroshnikov, Protsai and Shelayev, 38; Wortman, 1:26-28; see also Cherniavsky, 459-476.
14. Wortman, 1:69-74.
15. Wortman, 1:71-75.
16. Wortman, 1:90, 97; de Montclos, in Abate, 19.
17. Wortman, 1:115-118.
18. Wortman, 1:175-76.
19. Taylor, 51.
20. "Iz zapisok imperatora Nikolaia I," in *Byloe*, No. 10, 1907/1910, Volume 77, pages 86-87.
21. Lincoln, 241-42.
22. Wortman, 2:12.
23. Wortman, 1:291-92.
24. Corti, *Downfall*, 87; Tiutcheva, 2:121.
25. Tiutcheva, 2:121-22.
26. *Letopisnyi I Litsevoi Izbornik*, cited in Wortman, 2:447.
27. Wcislo, 173.
28. Logan, 137.
29. Stead, 396.
30. Stanhope, 240.
31. Logan, 67.
32. Davis, *Year*, 28-29.
33. *The New York Times*, May 22, 1896.
34. Hickley, 12.
35. Vorres, 75.
36. Hamilton, 183.
37. Queen Marie of Romania, 1:333, 1:326.
38. *The Times*, London, May 22, 1896.
39. *The New York Times*, May 31, 1896.
40. Logan, 103.
41. Clifton R. Breckinridge to Secretary of State Olney, June 22, 1896, in National Archives, Washington, D.C., cited in von Laue, 354.
42. Prince Sergei Volkonsky, quoted on http://www.vhok.nl/Expo/n&a/home.htm; accessed 2010 but no longer available.
43. Dowager Empress Marie Feodorovna to Queen Louise of Denmark, Letter of May 23/June 4, 1896, in GARF, cited in Krog et al, 172.
44. Nicholas II's Diary, May 18 (OS), 1896, in GARF, F. 601, Op. 1, D. 36.
45. Krivenko, 297.
46. Logan, 183.
47. Habsburg and Lopato, 107; Faberge, Proler, and Skurlov, 47; Timms, 228.
48. Wortman, 2:345-46.
49. Bovey.

Chapter I

1. Gurko, 14.
2. "Death and Burial of Emperor Alexander III" by M. A. Bera, in Berry, 92.
3. Prell, 69.
4. Vassili, *Behind the Veil*, 204.
5. Quoted in Gurko, 19.
6. de Schelking, 103.
7. Quoted in Lowe, *Alexander III*, 342.
8. Nicholas II, Accession Manifesto, quoted in Lowe, *Alexander III*, 356.
9. Paleologue, *Memoirs*, 1:98.
10. Vorres, 12-13.
11. Mossolov, 13.
12. Lambsdorff, 98.
13. Witte, 40, Mossolov, 5, 72.
14. Witte, 40; Verner, 64.
15. Mossolov, 6.
16. Alexander Mikhailovich, 66-67.
17. Witte, 40.
18. Surguchev, 29, 44-49, 87, 84.
19. Mossolov, 6.
20. Alexander Mikhailovich, 59-60.
21. Buxhoeveden, *Before the Storm*, 317.
22. Alexander Mikhailovich, 59-61; Tarsaïdzé, 247-48; Almedingen, Alexander II, 335; Graham, 316; Lowe, *Alexander III*, 46.
23. Lowe, *Alexander III*, 65; Wortman, 2:212.
24. Waddington, 45.
25. Waddington, 40; Tisdall, 182; Alexander Mikhailovich, 71.
26. Waddington, 38.
27. Empress Marie Feodorovna to Queen Louise of Denmark, Letter of May 15/27, 1883, in Krog et al, 149; Waddington, 46.
28. Wortman, 2:13; Wortman, "The Coronation of Alexander III," in Kearney, 288-296.
29. Reade, 12.
30. Taylor, 54.
31. Naryshkina-Kurakina, 75.
32. Lowe, *Alexander III*, 323; Chavchavadze, 92.
33. Cited in Krog et al, 250; cited, Wortman, 2:278; Figes, 16; Perry and Pleshakov, 44; Hall, 155. Recently several revisionists have attempted to dismiss these stories, but their theories, which in some instances rest not on historical evidence but instead on monarchist sentiments, provide no reliable refutation. See Bokhanov, *Imperator Aleksandr III*, 322; Nelipa.
34. Surguchev, 26; S. S. Fabritsky, in "Iz Proshlogo," cited in Lieven, 73.
35. de Schelking, 104; Wortman, 2:311.
36. Shelayev, Shelayeva and Semenov, 13.
37. Wortman, 2:312; Warth, 6; Lieven, 35; Shelayev, Shelayeva and Semenov, 12.
38. Cited in Sorensen, 73.
39. Byrnes, 117.
40. Byrnes, 121.
41. Pobedonostsev, *Pisma Pobjedonostseva k Alekandru III (Letters From Pobedonostsev to Alexander III)*, Moscow, 1925-1926, Volume 1, 315, quoted in Krog et al, 144.
42. Cited in Sorensen, 114.
43. Mossolov, 10-11.
44. Witte, 124-25.
45. V. A. Lambsdorff's Diary, November 4 (OS), 1894, in *Krasnii Arkhiv* No. 46, 1931, 10; see also Alexander Mikhailovich, 168.
46. Grand Duke Konstantin Konstantinovich, Diary of December 7 (OS), 1894, in GARF, F. 660, Op. 1, D. 41.
47. Vorres, 67.
48. Shelayev, Shelayeva and Semenov, 14.
49. Tsesarevich Nicholas's Diary, December 21 (OS), 1891, in GARF, F. 601, Op. 1, D. 27.
50. Tsesarevich Nicholas's Diary, May 2 (OS), 1890, in GARF, F. 601, Op. 1, D. 24.
51. Cited in Wolfe, 72.
52. Gurko, 14.
53. Bing, 36.
54. Cited in Massie, *Nicholas and Alexandra*, 19-20.
55. Empress Marie Feodorovna to Tsesarevich Nicholas, Letter of October 24 (OS), 1890, in Bing, 42.
56. Bing, 42.
57. Witte, 127.
58. Tsesarevich Nicholas's Diary, January 23 (OS), 1893, in GARF, F. 601, Op. 1, D. 54.
59. Tsesarevich Nicholas's Diary, April 1 (OS), 1892, in GARF, F. 601, Op. 1, D. 52.
60. Warwick, 66.
61. Queen Marie of Romania, 1:332.
62. Tsesarevich Nicholas's Diary, May 31 (OS), 1884, in GARF, F. 601, Op. 1, D. 19.
63. Vassili, *Confessions*, 6.
64. Empress Marie Feodorovna's Diary, January 18/30, 1889, cited in Krog et al, 158.
65. de Schelking, 17-18.
66. Obolensky, 61-62.

67. de Schelking, 18.
68. Princess Alix of Hesse to Tsesarevich Nicholas, Letter of November 8 (OS), 1893, in Maylunas and Mironenko, 32-33.
69. Tsesarevich Nicholas to Princess Alix of Hesse, Letter of December 17 (OS), 1893, in Maylunas and Mironenko, 34.
70. Tsesarevich Nicholas to Empress Marie Feodorovna, Letter of April 10 (OS), 1894, in Bing, 75-76.
71. Tsesarevich Nicholas's Diary, April 8 (OS), 1894, in GARF, F. 601, Op. 1, D. 30.
72. Prince Nicholas of Greece, 116.
73. Buxhoeveden, *Before the Storm*, 148; Gilliard, 48.
74. Hickley, 17.
75. *Le Gaulois*, May 26, 1896.
76. Quote in Lowe, *Alexander III*, 345.
77. Quoted in Lowe, *Alexander III*, 350.
78. Lowe, *Alexander III*, 369.
79. Grand Duke Konstantin Konstantinovich's Diary, July 12 (OS), 1896, in GARF, F. 660, Op. 1, D. 43.
80. Paleologue, *Three Critical Years*, 184-85.
81. Witte, 213.
82. de Schelking, 105-06.
83. Grabbe and Grabbe, 21.
84. Vyrubova, 55-56.
85. Tsesarevich Nicholas's Diary, November 21 (OS), 1891, in GARF F 601, Op. 1, D. 28.
86. Izvolsky, 264.
87. Nina Berberova, *The Italics are Mine*, New York: Alfred A. Knopf, 1992, 80, cited in Rowley, 131.
88. Nicholas II to Dowager Empress Marie Feodorovna, Letter of October 20 (OS), 1902, in Bing, 161.
89. Cited in Pipes, 20.
90. See Gurko, 32-33.
91. Kalmykow, 186.
92. Pipes, 27.
93. Warth, 20; Florinsky, 2:1147.
94. Florinsky, 2:1147.
95. Gurko, 19.
96. Pares, 71.
97. See Rodichev, 249-262; Wortman, 2:343.
98. Almedingen, *Empress Alexandra*, 43.
99. Vassili, *Behind the Veil*, 204.
100. Empress Alexandra Feodorovna to Grand Duke Ernst Ludwig, Letter of January 9/21, 1896, in Kleinpenning, 230.
101. Vyrubova, 4.
102. Cantacuzene, 255.
103. Nicholas II to Dowager Empress Marie Feodorovna, Letter of April 27 (OS), 1896, in Bing, 107.

Chapter II

1. Iroshnikov, Protsai and Shelayev, 20.
2. Iroshnikov, Protsai and Shelayev, 21; Demidenko, 18.
3. Polynina, 199-200.
4. Iroshnikov, Protsai and Shelayev, 21.
5. Krivenko, 162; "Remembrances of Kamer Page BA Engelhardt," in Berry, 173.
6. Tillander-Godenhielm, 316.
7. Logan, 145.
8. Salisbury, 52.
9. Maude, 7.
10. Salisbury, 52-53; Suvorin, *Dnevnik*, 223.
11. Salisbury, 52-53.
12. Maude, 15.
13. Zelnik, 37.
14. Maude, 11-13.
15. Hickley, 14.
16. Maude, 12-15.
17. Zelnik, 37.
18. Zelnik, 37; Maude, 12.
19. Zelnik, 40-41.
20. Zelnik, 37.
21. Wortman, 2:348; Davis, *Year*, 40.
22. Wortman, 2:345.
23. Joubert, 223-24. For a full account of Stead's fascination with Russia see Ashton, "Russia," 14-34; also at http://www.directarticle.org/W.T.Stead.pdf and http://www.attackingthedevil.co.uk/worksabout/ashton.php
24. Byrnes, 70.
25. Cited in Rose, 43.
26. See Wortman, Volume 2, passim; King and Wilson, 527-28; and Slater, 128-151.
27. See Ambler for further information.
28. Suvorin, *Dnevnik*, 223.
29. *Le Siècle*, May 29, 1896.
30. Davis, *Adventures*, 181.
31. Davis, *Year*, 43.
32. Stead, 405.
33. Witte, 138.
34. Sykes, 51.
35. Maude, 33-34.
36. Maude, 8-9.
37. Bovey, 32.
38. Davis, *Year*, 43; See Lubow for more information.
39. Davis, *Adventures*, 177.
40. Davis, *Year*, 5.
41. Davis, *Adventures*, 177-78.
42. Davis, *Adventures*, 178-82.
43. http://www.vhok.nl/Expo/n&a/home.htm, Hermitage Amsterdam (accessed 2010, now a dead link); Iroshnikov, Protsai and Shelayev, 22.
44. Wortman, 2:357.
45. Krog et al, 460-62; Timms, 50. For decades after the Revolution it hung in the Palace of Pavlovsk, ogled by groups of grim babushkas and red kerchief-bedecked Soviet Young Pioneers who stared at this fantastic evocation of a world that had vanished.
46. Timms, 72.
47. http://www.vhok.nl/Expo/n&a/home.htm Hermitage Amsterdam.
48. Leyda, 69.
49. Leyda, 18-23.
50. Obolensky, 72.
51. Sykes, 62-64.
52. Sykes, 62; Salisbury, 51; Davis, *Year*, 49.
53. Davis, *Adventures*, 177.
54. Sykes, 62.
55. Wortman, 1:7.
56. Davis, *Year*, 35.
57. Wortman, 1:7.
58. *Zhivopisnoe Obozrenie*, in Koronatsionnyi albom v pamiat sviashchennoi koronvaniia ikh Imperatorskikh Velichestvo, St. Petersburg, 1896, no page given, cited in Wortman, 2:345.
59. *Moskovskie Vedomosti*, May 6 (OS), 1896.
60. Alexander Mikhailovich, 41; Queen Marie of Romania, 1:85-86.
61. Cited in Belyakova, 40.
62. King, 80; Hodgetts, 2:232.
63. Dillon, 12.
64. Ular, 78; Zaionchkovskii, 76, 97; Greenberg, 2:41-42; Dubnow, 2:399-44; Byrnes, 207.
65. Vladimir Lambsdorff's Diary, 1:349, 2:347, cited in Perlmann, 297-323.
66. Paleologue, *Memoirs*, 1:152.
67. Witte, 240.
68. Shelley, 63; Buxhoeveden, *Life*, 109.
69. Grand Duke Konstantin Konstantinovich's Diary, May 29 (OS), 1896, in GARF, F. 660, Op. 1, D. 43.
70. Alexander Mikhailovich, 139.
71. Witte, 156; Radziwill, *Memories*, 250.
72. Davis, *Adventures*, 177.
73. Witte, 242; Mossolov, 106; Obolensky, 70 passim.
74. Ananich and Ganelin, 34-35.
75. Mossolov, 106; Witte, 242, 263; Radziwill, *Sovereigns*, 3.
76. Witte, 263; Vassili, *Behind the Veil*, 131.
77. Samson-Himmelstjerna, 37; Vassili, *Behind the Veil*, 130-31; *Russian Court Memoirs*, 46.
78. Lieven, 66, Radziwill, *Memories*, 250.
79. Naryshkina-Kurakina, 146.
80. Stanhope, 246.
81. Naryshkina-Kurakina, 146.
82. Wortman, 1:75, 1:103.
83. Wortman, 1:294.
84. Ashton, "Coronation," 35.
85. Wortman, 2:45.
86. Ashton, "Coronation," 35.
87. Waddington, 76.
88. Salisbury, 64; Baker, "Monarchy Discredited," 9; Wortman, 2:226-27.
89. Baker, "Monarchy Discredited," 9; Suvorin, *Journal*, 104.
90. Vladimir Dzhunkovsky, "Iz zapisk V. F. Dzhunkoskogo," published in *Otechestvennaia Istoriia*, No. 4, 1997, 15-24, cited in Baker, *Nicholas II and the Khodynka Catastrophe*, 22; also cited in Baker, "Monarchy Discredited," 11.
91. Witte, 241.
92. Vladimir Dzhunkovskii, "*Iz Zapisok Generala V. F. Dzhunkovskogo*," published in Otechestvennaia Istoriia, No. 4, 1997, 22, cited in Baker, "Monarchy Discredited," 11.
93. Ananich and Ganelin, 46.
94. Harcave, 293; Baker, "Monarchy Discredited, 4.
95. Suvorin, *Dnevnik*, 232.
96. Poliakoff, 109.
97. Vladimir Dzhunkovsky, "Iz zapisk V. F. Dzhunkoskogo," published in *Otechestvennaia Istoriia*, No. 4, 1997, 15-24, cited in Baker,

Nicholas II and the Khodynka Catastrophe, 22; also cited in Baker, "Monarchy Discredited," 11.
98. Witte, 241.
99. Report of June 7 (OS), 1896, in *Dokumenty o Khodynskoi katastrofe 1896*, 42-48, cited in Baker, "Monarchy Discredited," 10.
100. Witte, 241; Obolensky, 73.
101. Suvorin, *Dnevnik*, 232.
102. Maude, 81.
103. Suvorin, *Journal*, 104.
104. Obolensky, 73.
105. Suvorin, *Dnevnik*, 235-36.

Chapter III

1. Hickley, 4.
2. Maude, 11.
3. Hickley, 5.
4. Frances and Livermore, 3:471-72.
5. Information from Michael Jones, Director of the John A. Logan Museum, to Greg King.
6. Bovey, ix.
7. For more information see McCullough and Weigold.
8. Logan, 5, 28-30.
9. Logan, 29.
10. Bovey, 1-2; Weigold, 101.
11. Hamilton, 181; de Custine, 393.
12. Hamilton, 181-82; Hickley, 6.
13. Prince Nicholas of Greece, 114.
14. Hickley, 5.
15. Malcolm, 45.
16. Maude, 12-14.
17. Hickley, 4-6.
18. Lewis, 45; Lowe, *Lost Chicago*, 36-38.
19. Bovey, 23.
20. Bovey, 12; Logan, 70-71.
21. Bovey, 10.
22. Logan, 78-79.
23. Bovey, 11; Logan, 78-79.
24. Logan, 72; Bovey, 11.
25. Logan, 72, 81; Bovey, 12.
26. Bovey, 11.
27. Davis, *Adventures*, 176.
28. Davis, *Year*, 14.
29. Logan, 67.
30. Hamilton, 182.
31. Malcolm, 46.
32. Grenfell, 65.
33. Davis, *Year*, 16-17.
34. Bovey, 13 .
35. Zelnik, 40.
36. Maude, 7.
37. Bovey, 32.
38. Maude, 8.
39. Logan, 82.
40. Davis, *Year*, 21.
41. "Remembrances of Kamer Page B. A. Engelhardt," in Berry, 174; Wortman, 2:350; Bovey, 10-12; Logan, 82-83; Grenfell, 28; Davis, *Year*, 21; Maude, 7.
42. Hickley, 11.
43. Maude, 36.
44. Grenfell, 27.
45. Iroshnikov, Protsai, and Shelayev, 22.
46. Hickley, 8.
47. Grenfell, 58.
48. Malcolm, 45.
49. Malcolm, 49.
50. Maude, 67. This jewelers shop was probably the famous Fabergé, whose name Maude took for French, and whose manager was an Englishman named Bowe.
51. Bovey, 11.
52. Weigold, 101.
53. Bovey, 34.
54. Malcolm, 49.
55. Hamilton, 187.
56. Malcolm, 50-51.
57. Logan, 87-88.
58. Hapgood, 179; LaPauze, 82; Ashton, "Coronation," 36; Grenfell, 40; Bovey, 17; Bokhanov et al, 98.
59. Hickley, 9.
60. Shvidkovsky, 126-29; Logan, 110-111.
61. Davis, *Year*, 15.
62. Maclean, 181.
63. Kohl, 132.
64. Massie, *Firebird*, 44; Kohl, 133.
65. Hamilton, 185.
66. Logan, 94-95.
67. Logan, 114; Hickley, 11.
68. Logan, 114.

Chapter IV

1. Maude, 12.
2. Maude, 8.
3. Bovey, 41.
4. Krivenko, 233.
5. Tillander-Godenhielm, 316.
6. Davis, Year, 39.
7. Tillander-Godenhielm, 316.
8. Kaiser Wilhelm II to Nicholas II, Letter of April 7 (OS), 1896, in Maylunas and Mironenko, 139.
9. Buxhoeveden, *Life*, 62.
10. Hough, *Louis and Victoria*, 183.
11. Kaiser Wilhelm II to Nicholas II, Letter of January 20 (OS), 1896 (mistakenly misdated as November 20, 1896), in Levine, 27.
12. Suvorin, Dnevnik, 224; *Le Justice*, Paris, May 30, 1896.
13. Hough, *Louis and Victoria*, 155-56.
14. Sullivan, 136, 182; Elsberry, 61.
15. Hough, *Louis and Victoria*, 97-98; Vickers, 12.
16. Hough, *Louis and Victoria*, 213-14.
17. Buchanan, *Victorian Gallery*, 115.
18. Bovey, 40; Stanhope, 257.
19. Queen Marie of Romania, 1:336.
20. Queen Marie of Romania, 1:327.
21. George, Duke of York to Nicholas II, April 17 (OS), 1896, in Maylunas and Mironenko, 140.
22. Empress Alexandra Feodorovna to Nicholas II, Letter of October 7 (OS), 1915, in Fuhrmann, 266.
23. *Le Temps*, May 29, 1896.
24. Grenfell, 16
25. Grenfell, 16; "Remembrances of Kamer Page B. A. Engelhardt," in Berry, 175.
26. Grenfell, 17.
27. Prince Christopher of Greece, 32.
28. Prince Nicholas of Greece, 114.
29. Davis, *Year*, 51.
30. Aronson, 83.
31. Hough, *Louis and Victoria*, 182.
32. LaPauze, 123.
33. Covert, 213, 243–245.
34. Lutyens, 78; Covert, 221.
35. Davis, *Year*, 49.
36. Creighton, *Historical Essays*, passim.
37. Mansel, 83-85; Arapov, 31.
38. Vianzone, 4; Bovey, 20-21.
39. Finch, 75.
40. Hackett, 171-74.
41. Bovey, 20; Malcolm, 67.
42. Mannix, 130.
43. Mannix, 136-37.
44. Le Justice, May 26, 1896.
45. Logan, 158.
46. Witte, 236.
47. Bernstorff, 33.
48. Lowe, *Alexander III*, 67; *Daily Courier*, London, April 23, 1896; Lutyens, 78.
49. Lutyens, 78; Sykes, 51.
50. Grenfell, 16.
51. Lutyens, 78; Sykes, 51.
52. Malcolm, 54.
53. Logan, 147.
54. Logan, 150.
55. Willis, 16.
56. Logan, 149; Selfridge, 268.
57. Waddington, 83.
58. Bovey, 24.
59. Willis, 24.
60. Willis, 19.
61. Davis, Year, 28.
62. *The New York Times*, January 29, 1896.
63. Radziwill, *Memories*, 306.
64. Hamilton, 189; Salisbury, 52.
65. Maude, 8-9.

Chapter V

1. Krivenko, 198.
2. Maude, 22. Maude's friend Leo Tolstoy coordinated many relief efforts during the 1891-1892 famine, an event infamous for the government's callous response.
3. "Court Service in the Corps des Pages During the Blessed Coronation in 1896: Memoirs of Baron Sergei Roop II," in Berry, 100-03.
4. "Remembrances of Kamer Page B. A. Engelhardt," in Berry, 145).
5. Queen Marie of Romania, 1:329.
6. "Remembrances of Kamer Page B. A. Engelhardt," in Berry, 145-47; Queen Marie of Romania, 1:329.
7. Buxhoeveden, *Life*, 60.
8. Abrikossow, 254.
9. Infanta Eulalia of Spain, 171.
10. Alexander Mikhailovich, 173.

11. Quoted in King, 67.
12. Nicholas II to Grand Duke Vladimir Alexandrovich, Letter of January 29 (OS), 1897, in GARF, F. 652, Op. 1, D. 619.
13. Tsesarevich Nicholas's Diary, April 8 (OS), 1894, in GARF, F. 601, Op. 1, D. 30.
14. Kleinmichel, 201.
15. Vorres, 59.
16. Paleologue, *Memoirs*, 2:138.
17. See, for example, Grand Duke Konstantin Konstantinovich's Diary, September 12 (OS), 1904, in GARF, F. 660, Op. 1, D. 54.
18. Hodgetts 2:148-49, 2:229-30; Tarsaïdzé, 148.
19. Maude, 68.
20. Bovey, 25.
21. Bovey, 8-9.
22. Bovey, 8-9.
23. Maude, 28-29.
24. Tsesarevich Nicholas to Grand Duke George Alexandrovich, Letter of May 9 (OS), 1894, in Maylunas and Mironenko, 73.
25. Nicholas II's Diary, May 6 (OS), 1896, in GARF, F. 601, Op. 1, D. 36; Krivenko, 198.
26. Nicholas II's Diary, May 6 (OS), 1896, in GARF, F. 601, Op. 1, D. 36.
27. Vianzone, 7.
28. Krivenko, 198; Vianzone, 6-7.
29. Maude, 33.
30. Logan, 87.
31. "Remembrances of Kamer Pager B. A. Engelhardt," in Berry, 176.
32. Grenfell, 21.
33. Brumfield, 328; Kirichenko 19; Shvidkovsky, 207-09; Freeman and Burton, 113-15.
34. Maude, 30; Nicholas II's Diary, May 6 (OS), 1896, in GARF, F. 601, Op. 1, D. 36.
35. Maude, 33.
36. Vianzone, 6-7.
37. Suvorin, *Dnevnik*, 223; Maude, 36.
38. Maude, 30.
39. Zeln.ik, 40-41.
40. See U. V. Sobolev, "Khodynka, K tridtsatiletiiu katastrofy," in Krasnaia Niva, No. 22, 1926, 9, cited in Baker, "Monarchy Discredited," 3.
41. LaPauze, 76.
42. Grenfell, 67; Baker, "Monarchy Discredited," 4; Harcave, 293.
43. Decree for Festivities on Khodynka Meadow, May 18 (OS), 1896, in GARF, F. 601, Op. 1, D. 140.
44. Krog et al, 170; Polynina and Rakhmanov, 221; Iroshnikov, Protsai, and Shelayev, 30; Timms, 150, 286; Hancock, 172; Salisbury, 64.
45. Davis, *Year*, 16.
46. Bovey, 13.
47. Hickley, 11.
48. Stanhope, 244-46.
49. Nicholas II's Diary, May 7 (OS), 1896, in GARF, F. 601, Op. 1, D. 36
50. Nicholas II's Diary, May 7 (OS), 1896, in GARF, F. 601, Op. 1, D. 36; Maude, 34-35; Krivenko 198
51. Nicholas II's Diary, May 7-8 (OS), 1896, in GARF, F. 601, Op. 1, D. 36.
52. Grenfell, 21.
53. Vyrubova, 9; Korshunova, 127.
54. Grenfell, 21.
55. Frankland, 200.
56. Grenfell, 21.
57. Nicholas II's Diary, May 8 (OS), 1896, in GARF, F. 601, Op. 1, D. 36.
58. Naryshkina-Kurakina, 147-49.
59. Corti, *Downfall*, 87; Tiutcheva, 2:121-22; Naryshkina-Kurakina, 148; Empress Marie Feodorovna to Queen Louise of Denmark, Letter of May 15/27, 1883, in Krog et al, 150.
60. Naryshkina-Kurakina, 148.
61. Nicholas II's Diary, May 8 (OS), 1896, in GARF, F. 601, Op. 1, D. 36.
62. Mossolov, 95.
63. Dowager Empress Marie Feodorovna to Queen Louise of Denmark, Letter of May 16/28, 1896, cited in Krog et al, 168.
64. Hickley, 9.
65. "Remembrances of Kamer Page B. A. Engelhardt," in Berry, 176; Krivenko, 198.
66. Grand Duke Konstantin Konstantinovich's Diary, May 8 (OS), 1896, in GARF, F. 660, Op. 1, D. 43; Hickley, 9.
67. Hickley, 10.
68. Grand Duke Konstantin Konstantinovich's Diary, May 8 (OS), 1896, in GARF, F. 660, Op. 1, D. 43.
69. Hickley, 10.
70. Grand Duke Konstantin Konstantinovich's Diary, May 8 (OS), 1896, in GARF, F. 660, Op. 1, D. 43.
71. Hickley, 10.
72. Maude, 41.
73. Iroshnikov, Protsai, and Shelayev, 25.

Chapter VI

1. LaPauze, 75.
2. Logan, 98.
3. Kirill, 63.
4. Davis, Year, 21; *The Times*, London, Weekly Edition, May 29, 1896.
5. Suvorin, *Dnevnik*, 233; Maude, 36.
6. LaPauze, 76; Oustimenko, 96; Vernova, 91; Mossolov, 191.
7. Logan, 102-03; Maude, 36.
8. Hickley, 11.
9. Salisbury, 53; Maude, 14, 35.
10. Bovey, 12.
11. Logan, 102; Bovey, 13-14; Suvorin, *Dnevnik*, 223; *Le Temps*, May 24, 1896.
12. Hough, *Louis and Victoria*, 180-81.
13. Bovey, 14.
14. Nicholas II's Diary, May 9 (OS), 1896, in GARF, F. 601, Op. 1, D. 36.
15. Empress Alexandra Feodorovna to Grand Duke Ernst Ludwig of Hesse, Letter of April 22/May 4, 1896, in Kleinpenning, 231.
16. Grenfell, 24; "Remembrances of Kamer Page B. A. Engelhardt," in Berry, 177.
17. Grenfell, 25.
18. Ignatiev, 61.
19. Logan, 98. When Theodore Roosevelt represented America at the funeral of King Edward VII in 1910, his position behind representatives from Greece, Montenegro, Siam, and Coburg was about as far back in the procession as one could get without being a horse. The explanation given was that the Duke of Norfolk, who organized the procession, simply could not allow commoners representing a republic to have precedence over the aristocrats representing monarchies or duchies. See Mott, 168.
20. Maude, 37.
21. Zelnik, 40.
22. "Remembrances of Kamer Page B. A. Engelhardt," in Berry, 178.
23. Hickley, 12; Krivenko, 209.
24. Davis, *Year*, 28.
25. LaPauze, 78.
26. Bovey, 15; Krivenko, 200.
27. *The New York Times*, May 22, 1896; LaPauze, 77; Hickey, 13; Logan, 99; Bovey, 14-15; "Remembrances of Kamer Page B. A. Engelhardt," in Berry, 178; Grenfell, 26.
28. Logan, 99.
29. LaPauze, 77; Hickey, 13; Logan, 99; Bovey, 14-15; Logan, 99.
30. Hickley, 12; Krivenko, 190-98; LaPauze, 77; Maude, 38; Bovey, 14-15; "Remembrances of Kamer Page B. A. Engelhardt," in Berry, 178; Logan, 99-100.
31. Quoted in Iroshnikov, Protsai, and Shelayev, 26).
32. Logan, 99-100; Grenfell, 26; Maude, 38; Bovey, 14-15; *Le Figaro*, May 22, 1896.
33. Hickley, 12-13; Logan, 99-103; Bovey, 15-17; Bokhanov et al, 98; Bovey, 14-15; Ignatiev, 62.
34. *Le Figaro*, May 23, 1896.
35. Suvorin, *Dnevnik*, 223.
36. Logan, 101.
37. Wortman, 1:175; Nicholas II's Diary, May 9 (OS), 1896, in GARF, F. 601, Op. 1, D. 36; Bokhanov et al, 98; Krivenko, 206; Romanovsky-Krassinsky, 58.
38. Krivenko, 206.
39. Vassili, *Confessions*, 37. Radziwill was something of a one-woman industry when it came to penning tomes about European royalty, and wrote under her own name and also under the pseudonym "Count Paul Vassili." Her books, although sometimes filled with gossip and scandalous assertions, also contain much information that, as time has shown, proved to be correct.
40. Romanovsky-Krassinsky 58.
41. Logan, 101; Bovey, 16; Hickley, 13; LaPauze, 79; *Le Figaro*, May 23, 1896.
42. Queen Marie of Romania, 1:330.
43. Davis, *Year*, 32; Hickley, 13.
44. *Le Figaro*, May 22 and May 23, 1896.
45. Bovey, 16.
46. Vianzone, 9-10.
47. Vassili, *Behind the Veil*, 270; Radziwill, *Recollections*, 318.
48. Malcolm, 56; Grenfell, 27.
49. Krivenko, 201.
50. Logan, 103; "Remembrances of Kamer Page B. A. Engelhardt," in Berry, 179.

51. Grenfell, 27-28.
52. Buxhoeveden, *Before*, 150; Hickley, 13; Prince Nicholas of Greece, 115; Maude, 39; LaPauze, 78-80; "Court Service of the Corps des Pages During the Blessed Coronation in 1896, Memoirs of Baron Sergei Roop II," in Berry, 103; "Remembrances of Kamer Page B. A. Engelhardt," in Berry, 179.
53. Maude, 39.
54. "Remembrances of Kamer Page B. A. Engelhardt," in Berry, 179; Alexander Mikhailovich, 157; Nadelhoffer, 187; Twining 535; Meylan, 10; Queen Marie of Romania, 1:331.
55. Radziwill, *Intimate Life*, 89; Radziwill, *Recollections*, 318; Vassili, *Confessions*, 37-38; Davis, *Year*, 32; Suvorin, *Dnevnik*, 223-24; Grenfell, 27; *Le Figaro*, May 23, 1896.
56. Malcolm, 56.
57. Bovey, 17.
58. Grenfell, 27.
59. *Le Matin*, May 22, 1896.
60. Grand Duke Konstantin Konstantinovich's Diary, May 9 (OS), 1896, in GARF, F. 660, Op. 1, D. 43; Bovey, 17.
61. Davis, *Year*, 34; Timms, 172; "Remembrances of Kamer Page B. A. Engelhardt," in Berry, 179
62. Davis, *Year*, 32-34; Pelham-Clinton, 489; Leudet, 220.
63. Davis, *Year*, 33.
64. Ignatiev, 61; Bovey, 17.
65. Radziwill, *Intimate Life*, 90; Vassili, *Confessions*, 38-39.
66. *Le Figaro*, May 23, 1896.
67. Logan, 103.
68. Logan, 103; Nicholas II's Diary, May 9 (OS), 1896, in GARF, F. 601, Op. 1, D. 36.
69. Radziwill, *Recollections*, 318; Vassili, *Behind the Veil*, 271; Vassili, *Confessions*, 38; Radziwill, *Intimate Life*, 89-90. Radziwill first made this claim in a set of memoirs written in 1903 and published in 1904, and thus presumably free of retrospective analysis of Nicholas II's unpopular consort, and the story remained remarkably consistent in all of her numerous works.
70. Maude, 40.
71. There is some doubt about exactly where Grand Duchess Olga Alexandrovna rode. LaPauze, page 80, placed her in the Dowager Empress's carriage, as did Mathilde Kschessinska on page 59 of her memoirs. In a letter written before the actual event, Alexandra recorded that Olga would ride with the Dowager Empress, but this may have changed on the day itself. The official account given in Krivenko, page 203, places Olga in a carriage behind the two Empresses, riding with her cousins Grand Duchesses Elena Vladimirovna and Vera Konstantinovna. Olga's own memoirs, as told to writer Ian Vorres, say on page 75 that she rode in a carriage with Queen Olga of Greece and Crown Princess Marie of Romania. Boris Engelhardt, the Kammer Page assigned to Marie Feodorovna that day, does not mention Olga having been with her mother, in "Remembrances of Kamer Page B. A. Engelhardt," in Berry, page 179. French correspondents for *Le Figaro* on May 22 and *Le Matin* on May 22 both placed Olga in the first carriage with her mother. A photograph, frequently reproduced, has been described as showing the Dowager Empress with Olga as their carriage passed in front of the Kremlin walls; in fact, the carriage depicted lacked the prominent Imperial Crown atop the vehicle in which Marie Feodorovna rode, and the women pictured are almost certainly not the Dowager Empress and her youngest daughter.
72. Vorres, 74-75.
73. Thanks to Penny Wilson for drawing our attention to this image.
74. Ignatiev, 61.
75. Logan, 101.
76. LaPauze, 82; Krivenko, 209.
77. *Le Matin*, May 22, 1896.
78. Maude, 42; Krivenko, 209; Bovey, 17; LaPauze, 83; Maude, 40; Wortman, 2:37.
79. Krivenko, 209.
80. Sykes, 58.
81. Krivenko, 209.
82. *Le Petit Parisien*, May 23, 1896.
83. Bokhanov et al, 96; Iroshnikov, Protsai, and Shelayev, 27.
84. Iroshnikov, 27.
85. Sykes, 58.
86. Krivenko, 206; Logan, 104.
87. Grand Duke Konstantin Konstantinovich's Diary, May 9 (OS), 1896, in GARF, F. 660, Op. 1, D. 43.
88. Grenfell, 30; Logan, 105; Krivenko, 214.
89. Logan, 105; Krivenko, 214; LaPauze, 84-85; Maude, 41; Grenfell, 30; *Le Petit Parisien*, May 23, 1896; *Le Figaro*, May 22, 1896.
90. Maude, 41; Logan, 104-05; Krivenko, 214.
91. Grand Duke Konstantin Konstantinovich's Diary, May 9 (OS), 1896, in GARF, F. 660, Op. 1, D. 43; Suvorin, *Dnevnik*, 224.
92. Krivenko, 214.
93. Grenfell, 31.
94. Krivenko, 214; Grenfell, 32.
95. LaPauze, 85.
96. Maude, 35.
97. Maude, 38-39.
98. *The Times*, London, May 22, 1896.
99. Bernstorff, 32; Davis, *Year*, 28.
100. Prince Christopher of Greece, 54.

Chapter VII

1. Krivenko, 214.
2. Brumfield, 319; Freeman and Burton, 203-05; Floryan, 53, 214.
3. Nicholas II's Diary, May 10-11 (OS), 1896, in GARF, F. 601, Op. 1, D. 36.
4. *Le Temps*, May 22, 1896.
5. LaPauze, 86.
6. Waddington, 50; Rodimezeva, Rahkmanov and Raimann, 196, 200; Odoievsky-Maslov; Raiguel and Huff, 288-90; Stoddard, 331; Logan, 116-17, 169-70; *Le Figaro*, May 23, 1896; *Le Petit Parisien*, May 24, 1896.
7. Rodimezeva, Rahkmanov and Raimann, 202; Krivenko, 219; Waddington, 50.
8. *Le Figaro*, May 23, 1896.
9. Witte, 93, 96.
10. A. N. Kuropatkin's Diary, September 22 (OS), 1899, quoted in Laruelle, 120.
11. Ukhtomskii, K sobytiiam v Kitae, 8, 31, 84 in Laruelle, 127, 133.
12. Ukhtomskii, Puteshestvie, 3:33.
13. A. N. Kuropatkin's Diary, September 22 (OS), 1899, quoted in Laruelle, 120.
14. Mannix, 129.
15. Mannix, 196; Maude, 49; *Le Petit Parisien*, May 19, 1896.
16. Mannix, 135, 199.
17. Mannix, 172.
18. Mannix, 129; Witte, 236-39, see also 756, Note 6 on the payments; Pipes, 13; Gurko, 256; "Perepiska o podkupe kitaiskikh sanovnikov Li-Khun-Chzhana i Chzhan-in-Khuana," in *Krasnii Arkhiv*, 1922, II, pages 287-93.
19. Hackett, 171-74.
20. Finch, 94-95.
21. Finch, 88.
22. Finch, 90-91.
23. Amelekhina and Levykin, 42-3.
24. Grenfell, 35; Vianzone, 12; Maude, 42; LaPauze, 89-90; Krivenko, 219-20; Vernova, 72; Hancock, 174; Logan, 106-07.
25. Amelekhina and Levykin, 42-3; Polynina and Rakhmanov, 200; Logan 106-08; Hancock, 171, 174.
26. Hancock, 171, 174; Logan, 106-08; Polynina and Rakhmanov, 200; Amelekhina and Levykin, 42-43.
27. Logan, 107; also given in Krivenko, 221; LaPauze, 92; and Maude, 43, in variant form.
28. Logan, 108.
29. LaPauze, 93.
30. Logan, 108.
31. LaPauze, 93.
32. Grenfell, 36; Maude, 43-44; Suvorin, *Dnevnik*, 226-27; Malcolm, 55; Stanhope, 247; Sykes, 58.
33. Grenfell, 36; Suvorin, *Dnevnik*, 227; Maude, 44.
34. Maude, 44.
35. Maude, 47-48.
36. Polynina and Rakhmanov, 133, 184; Maude, 45.
37. Maude, 46.
38. Krivenko, 220; Maude, 46.
39. Polynina, 184.
40. Grenfell, 37; Creighton, *Life and Letters*, 155.
41. Nicholas II's Diary, May 12 (OS), 1896, in GARF, F. 601, Op. 1, D. 36.
42. Malcolm, 55; Grenfell, 37; Creighton, *Life and Letters*, 156.
43. Buxhoeveden, *Life*, 64; Iroshnikov, Protsai and Shelayev, 38; Wortman, 1:26.
44. Grand Duke Konstantin Konstantinovich to Queen Olga of Greece, Letter of April 25 (OS),

1896, in Box 3, BAR Ms. Coll./GK Romanov, Bakhmeteff Archive, Rare Book and Manuscript Library. Columbia University.
45. Massie, *Firebird*, 133; Hammer, 227; Prince Michael of Greece, 38; Polynina and Rakhmanov, 144-48; Alexander Mikhailovich, 157.
46. Buxhoeveden, *Life*, 64; Polynina and Rakhmanov, 184.
47. Massie, *Firebird*, 133; Twining, 534; Timms, 112; Alexander Mikhailovich, 157; Nadelhoffer, 187; Meylan, 10; Hammer, 227; Polynina and Rakhmanov, 148.
48. Twining, 55.
49. Hancock, 168; Amelekhina and Levykin, 41; Polynina, 192.
50. Alexander Mikhailovich, 157; Nadelhoffer, 187; Twining 535; Meylan, 10.
51. Alexander Mikhailovich, 157; Nadelhoffer, 187; Twining 535; Meylan, 10; Polynina and Rakhmanov, 184; Essed-Bey, 63; Tillander-Godenhielm, 316; Papi, 36.
52. Krivenko, 230; LaPauze, 96; Logan, 118.
53. Logan, 118.
54. Ignatiev, 61-62; "Remembrances of Kammer Page B. A. Engelhardt," in Berry, 182.
55. Ignatiev, 62.
56. Notes from the Diary of A. N. Mandryk," in Berry, 212.
57. Krivenko, 230; Maude, 49.
58. Nicholas II's Diary, May 13 (OS), 1896, in GARF, F. 601, Op. 1, D. 36.

Chapter VIII

1. Grand Duke Konstantin Konstantinovich, Diary of May 14 (OS), 1896, in GARF, F. 660, Op. 1, D. 43.
2. LaPauze, 98.
3. CB, 231-33; Hickley, 17; Maude, 51.
4. LaPauze, 98.
5. Bovey, 19.
6. Logan, 91.
7. Bovey, 19.
8. *Intimacies of Court*, 114.
9. Weigold, 102.
10. Bovey, 19.
11. Logan, 114; Bovey, 19.
12. Bovey, 19; Logan, 114.
13. Malcolm, 57-58.
14. LaPauze, 99, 103; Vianzone, 16; *Le Petit Parisien*, May 27, 1896; *Le Temps*, May 28, 1896.
15. Logan, 114.
16. Iroshnikov, Protsai, and Shelayev, 27; Krivenko, 233.
17. Creighton, *Historical Essays*, 314.
18. Davis, *Year*, 36.
19. LaPauze, 98; Vianzone, 15.
20. Bovey, 19.
21. *Intimacies of Court*, 114-15.
22. Malcolm, 59.
23. *Intimacies of Court*, 115.
24. Logan, 121; Bokhanov et al, 100.
25. Malcolm, 48.
26. Logan, 121; Bovey, 21; Malcolm, 59; Mossolov, 191.
27. Hickley, 16; LaPauze, 100; Ignatiev, 63; Sykes, 71.
28. Malcolm, 59; Hickley, 16.
29. Bovey, 19-20, 23; Logan, 120.
30. Weigold, 102.
31. Malcolm, 64; Logan, 136.
32. Logan, 113.
33. Bovey, 21-22; LaPauze, 102.
34. Bovey, 21.
35. Hickley, 16.
36. Bovey, 22.
37. Bovey, 22; Hickley, 16; Duff, 245.
38. Bovey, 22.
39. Leyda, 18-23.
40. Davis, *Year*, 49.
41. Vianzone, 16; Sykes, 71; Davis, *Year*, 49.
42. Vianzone, 15-16.
43. Logan, 122.
44. Malcolm, 59; Krivenko, 236.
45. Bovey, 23.
46. Krivenko, 223.
47. Davis, Year, 45.
48. Davis, *Year*, 45; Beable, 83; Krivenko, 233; Massie, *Firebird*, 26, 45; Kohl, 132; Hamilton, 183; Freeman and Burton, 16; Iroshnikov, Protsai, and Shelayev, 40; Timms, 50; Polynina and Rakhmanov, 184.
49. Hamilton, 183.
50. Maude, 51.
51. Krivenko, 233; Iroshnikov, Protsai, and Shelayev, 40; Timms, 50; Polynina and Rakhmanov, 184.
52. Waddington, 51.
53. Waddington, 62.
54. Krivenko, 233; Iroshnikov, Protsai, and Shelayev, 40; Timms, 50; Polynina and Rakhmanov, 98-101, 184, 204; Davis, *Year*, 45; LaPauze, 103; Buxhoeveden, *Life*, 63; Goncharenko and Narozhnaya, 126.
55. Davis, *Year*, 45.
56. Timms, 50; Polynina and Rakhmanov, 98-101, 204; Buxhoeveden, *Life*, 63; Goncharenko and Narozhnaya, 126-28; Krivenko, 233.
57. Grenfell, 44.
58. Duff, 254.
59. *Le Matin*, May 27, 1896; *Le Petit Parisien*, May 27, 1896; *Le Temps*, May 28, 1896.
60. LaPauze, 103; Creighton, *Historical Essays*, 316; Davis, *Year*, 53.
61. Davis, *Year*, 53.
62. *Le Figaro*, May 27, 1896; Krog et al, 460-62; Timms, 50.
63. LaPauze, 103.
64. Hancock, 246, 251; Odom, 36.
65. "Court Service of the Corps des Pages During the Blessed Coronation in 1896: Memoirs of Baron Sergei Roop II," in Berry, 104.
66. Grand Duchess Olga Alexandrovna's Diary, May 14 (OS), 1896, cited in Phenix, 37-38; Vorres, 74.
67. Grand Duchess Olga Alexandrovna's Diary, May 14 (OS), 1896, cited in Phenix, 37.
68. Dowager Empress Marie Feodorovna to Queen Louise of Denmark, Letter of May 16/28, 1896, cited in Krog et al, 168.
69. "Remembrances of Kamer Page B. A. Engelhardt," in Berry, 183; "Notes from the Diary of A. N. Mandryk," in Berry, 209.
70. Bovey, 23; Bariatinsky, 50; "Remembrances of Kamer Page B. A. Engelhardt," in Berry, 183.
71. *Intimacies of Court*, 117.
72. Bariatinsky, 50.
73. "Remembrances of Kamer Page B. A. Engelhardt," in Berry, 183.
74. Dowager Empress Marie Feodorovna to Queen Louise of Denmark, Letter of May 16/28, 1896, cited in Krog et al, 168.
75. Grand Duke Konstantin Konstantinovich's Diary, May 14 (OS), 1896, in GARF, F. 660, Op. 1, D. 43.
76. Bariatinsky, 50.
77. Princess Victoria of Battenberg to Queen Victoria, Letter of May 26, 1896, cited in Hough, *Louis and Victoria*, 182.
78. "Court Service of the Corps des Pages During the Blessed Coronation in 1896: Memoirs of Baron Sergei Roop II," in Berry, 105-106.
79. Grenfell, 44.
80. Malcolm, 59; *Intimacies of Court*, 117; Malcolm, 59; Hickley, 18; LaPauze, 104.
81. *Intimacies of Court*, 117.
82. Malcolm, 59; Logan, 122.
83. Korshunova, 34, 94; Logan, 122; Krivenko, 236.
84. "Court Service of the Corps des Pages During the Blessed Coronation in 1896: Memoirs of Baron Sergei Roop II," in Berry, 106.
85. *Intimacies of Court*, 117; Amelekhina and Levykin, 46; Logan, 135; Bovey, 23-24; Maude, 51.
86. *Intimacies of Court*, 117-118.
87. Logan, 122; Malcolm, 59; Krivenko, 236; Maude, 51.
88. Grenfell, 48; Logan, 122; Vianzone, 16.
89. Grenfell, 48; Krivenko, 236.
90. Bovey, 28.
91. Grenfell, 48.
92. Vorres, 75.
93. Bovey, 28.
94. Buxhoeveden, *Before the Storm*, 153.
95. Buxhoeveden, *Life*, 66-67; Queen Marie of Romania, 1:336
96. Queen Marie of Romania, 1:332-33.
97. Nicholas II's Diary, May 14 (OS), 1896, in GARF, F. 601, Op. 1, D. 36.
98. Hancock, 170; Amelekhina and Levykin, 39.
99. Hancock, 170; Amelekhina and Levykin, 39; Korshunova, 38; GIAR, Hofmarschall Department of the Ministry of the Imperial Court, F. 471, Op. 1, D. 839.
100. Korshunova, 85; Bokhanov et al, 94.
101. Hancock, 168; Amelekhina and Levykin, 41; Polynina and Rakhmanov, 192, 195; Korshunova, 90; Goncharenko and Narozhnaya, 140; Buxhoeveden, *Life*, 64; Wortman, 2:353; Bokhanov et al, 94; Bothmer, 61.
102. Polynina and Rakhmanov, 195; Buxhoeveden, *Life*, 38, 64; Bainbridge, 56.
103. Logan, 122; *Intimacies of Court*, 118.
104. Maude, 52; Logan, 123; Krivenko, 238-39.
105. Maude, 52; Logan, 123; Krivenko, 238-39.
106. Krivenko, 240-41; Maude, 53-54; Logan, 124; LaPauze, 113.
107. Krivenko, 238-40; Maude, 52; Logan, 123-24; Polynina and Rakhmanov, 203-04; Bokhanov et al, 103; *Intimacies of Court*, 118.
108. Marie Pavlovna, 15.
109. Krivenko, 238.
110. Logan, 121.
111. Krivenko, 241; *Intimacies of Court*, 118; Polynina and

Rakhmanov, 203-04; Bokhanov et al, 104.
112. *Intimacies of Court*, 123.
113. Bariatinsky, 51.
114. *Intimacies of Court*, 122.
115. *Intimacies of Court*, 118; Logan, 135; Polynina and Rakhmanov, 203-04; Bokhanov et al, 104; Krivenko, 241-42; Amelekhina and Levykin, 46; Bovey, 23-24; Logan, 135.
116. Maude, 53.
117. Maude, 51; Logan, 122; *Intimacies of Court*, 118; LaPauze, 103.
118. Krivenko, 241.
119. LaPauze, 105.
120. Krivenko, 241.

Chapter IX

1. Grenfell, 43.
2. Maude, 53; Krivenko, 241; Wallace, 199-200.
3. Ignatiev, 62; LaPauze, 105; Prince Nicholas of Greece, 117; Buxhoeveden, *Life*, 63; Krivenko, 241-42; Polynina and Rakhmanov, 204.
4. LaPauze, 105.
5. Dowager Empress Marie Feodorovna to Queen Louise of Denmark, Letter of May 16/28, 1896, cited in Krog et al, 168; Princess Victoria of Battenberg to Queen Victoria, Letter of May 26, 1896, cited in Hough, *Louis and Victoria*, 182.
6. Grand Duke Konstantin Konstantinovich's Diary, May 14 (OS), 1896, in GARF, F. 660, Op. 1, D. 43.
7. LaPauze, 14-15; Davis, *Adventures*, 182.
8. Dowager Empress Marie Feodorovna to Queen Louise of Denmark, Letter of May 16/28, 1896, cited in Krog et al, 168; Princess Victoria of Battenberg to Queen Victoria, Letter of May 26, 1896, cited in Hough, *Louis and Victoria*, 182.
9. Logan, 125.
10. Krivenko, 243-44.
11. Grenfell, 46; Wallace, 199; Malcolm, 62.
12. Maude, 54; Krivenko, 245.
13. Krivenko, 245-46; Grenfell, 46; Woolley, 28.
14. Maude, 58.
15. Maude, 54.
16. Twining, 550.
17. Twining, 524; Timms, 112; Alexander Mikhailovich, 157; Nadelhoffer, 187; Meylan, 10; Grand Duke Konstantin Konstantinovich, Diary, May 14 (OS), 1896, in GARF, F. 660, Op. 1, D. 43; Suvorin, *Dnevnik*, 226; Davis, *Year*, 56. A number of accounts, most second-hand, relate that the chain broke unexpectedly as Nicholas II approached the altar to take communion. Grand Duke Konstantin, Alexei Suvorin, and Richard Harding Davis all saw the chain fall as Grand Duke Vladimir draped it around Nicholas II's neck.
18. Izvolsky, 262.
19. Woolley, 23.
20. Woolley, 22-23.
21. Woolley, 23.
22. Suvorin, *Dnevnik*, 233.
23. Krivenko, 246.
24. Dowager Empress Marie Feodorovna to Queen Louise of Denmark, Letter of May 16/28, 1896, cited in Krog et al, 168.
25. Vorres, 75.
26. Krivenko, 246-47; Stanhope, 241.
27. Stanhope, 241; Krivenko, 248.
28. Davis, *Year*, 55-56.
29. Krivenko, 247.
30. Krivenko, 248; Naryshkina-Kurakina, 149.
31. *Le Figaro*, May 27, 1896.
32. Naryshkina-Kurakina, 149; *Le Matin*, May 27, 1896.
33. Krivenko, 248; Vorres, 76; Princess Victoria of Battenberg to Queen Victoria, Letter of May 26, 1896, cited in Hough, *Louis and Victoria*, 183.
34. Maude, 56.
35. Stanhope, 242.
36. Queen Marie of Romania, 1:332-33.
37. Davis, *Year*, 64-65.
38. Creighton, *Historical Essays*, 318.
39. Krivenko, 248-49. Nicholas II's full title was: "The Lord's Enlightened and Merciful Mediator, the Orthodox and Pious and Christ-Loving, the Absolute Autocrat and Great Lord by the Grace of God, Nicholas Alexandrovich, Emperor and Autocrat of all the Russias, of Moscow, of Kiev, of Vladimir, of Novgorod; Tsar of Kazan, Tsar of Astrakhan, Tsar of Poland, Tsar of Siberia, Tsar of Chersonesus in Taurida, and Tsar of Georgia; Lord of Pskov, Grand Duke of Smolensk, of Lithuania, of Volhynia, of Podolia, and of Finland; Prince of Estland, of Livland, of Courland, of Semigalia, of Somogotia, of Bialostok, of Karelia, of Tver, of Yugoria, of Perm, of Viatka, of Bulgaria, and of other countries; Lord and Grand Duke of Lower Novgorod, of Chernigov, of Riazan, of Polotsk, of Rostov, of Yaroslavl, of Belozero, of Udoria, of Obduria, of Condia, of Vitebsk, of Mstislav, and of all Regions of the North; Lord and Sovereign of the countries of Iveria, Kartalinia, Kardardinia, and the Provinces of Armenia; Hereditary Sovereign Lord of the Circassian Princes and of the Mountain Princes; Lord of Turkestan; Heir of Norway; Duke of Schleswig-Holstein, of Stornmarn, of the Ditmars, and of Oldenburg, et cetera, et cetera, et cetera."
40. Krivenko, 248; LaPauze, 110.
41. *Le Figaro*, May 27, 1896.
42. Krivenko, 248; Logan, 128; Hickley, 18.
43. *Intimacies of Court*, 119.
44. Davis, *Year*, 59.
45. LaPauze, 106; Grenfell, 47; Creighton, *Historical Essays*, 319.
46. Grenfell, 47.
47. Vorres, 76.
48. Davis, *Year*, 59-62.
49. Krivenko, 248-49.
50. Suvorin, Dnevnik, 226.
51. Victoria Milford-Haven, "Reminiscences," cited in Duff, 254; see also LaPauze, 107; *Le Temps*, May 28, 1896; Frankland, 203.
52. Grand Duke Konstantin Konstantinovich's Diary, May 14 (OS), 1896, in GARF, F. Op. 1, D. 43; Suvorin, *Dnevnik*, 226.
53. Empress Alexandra Feodorovna to Nicholas II, Letter of March 3 (OS), 1917, in GARF, F. 601, Op. 1, D. 1151.
54. Grand Duke Konstantin Konstantinovich's Diary, May 14 (OS), 1896, in GARF, F. 660, Op. 1, D. 43.
55. Davis, *Year*, 52-53.
56. Maude, 58.
57. Wallace, 199-200; Oldenburg, 1:59-60; Bokhanov et al, 105; LaPauze, 108.
58. Krivenko, 251.
59. Bokhanov et al, 105; Logan, 126, 132.
60. Logan, 132-33; Bokhanov et al, 105; Twining, 518; Maude, 60; Grenfell, 61.
61. Polynina and Rakhmanov, 210; Bokhanov et al, 105; LaPauze, 109; Maude, 60; Logan, 133.
62. See Empress Alexandra Feodorovna to Nicholas II, Letter of August 22 (OS), 1915, in GARF F. 601, Op. 1, D. 1151.
63. Wortman 2:31, 2:353; LaPauze, 109; Maude, 60.
64. Polynina and Rakhmanov, 156; Krivenko, 254; Wortman, 1:176; Iroshnikov, Protsai and Shelayev, 28.
65. Krivenko, 254.
66. Maude, 60-61.
67. Kirill Vladimirovich, 64.
68. Prince Nicholas of Greece, 117.
69. Kirill Vladimirovich, 64; Bariatinsky, 52.
70. Davis, *Year*, 63.
71. *Pall Mall Gazette*, 29 May 1896.
72. Grenfell, 47. The "dark complexion" may be a description of his appearance, or it may reflect the prejudices of the account's author.
73. Davis, *Year*, 63.
74. Dowager Empress Marie Feodorovna to Queen Louise of Denmark, Letter of May 16/28, 1896, cited in Krog et al, 168.
75. *Le Temps*, May 28, 1896.
76. Krivenko, 256.
77. Logan, 136; Krivenko, 256; Bovey, 25.
78. Hickley, 19.
79. Logan, 134; Krivenko, 256-57.
80. "Notes from the Diary of A. N. Mandryk," in Berry, 210.
81. *Intimacies of Court*, 120.
82. Radziwill, *Recollections*, 321; Vassili, *Behind the Veil*, 271; Vassili, *Confessions*, 40.
83. Vassili, *Behind the Veil*, 271.
84. Logan, 134.
85. Logan, 134; Krivenko, 257.
86. Krivenko, 256.
87. Logan, 135; 119.
88. Prince Nicholas of Greece, 117.
89. Moy, 162-63.
90. Ignatiev, 63.
91. Volkov, 38.
92. Princess Victoria of Battenberg to Queen Victoria, Letter of May 26, 1896, cited in Hough, *Louis and Victoria*, 183.
93. Bovey, 25-26.
94. "Remembrances of Kamer Page B. A. Engelhardt," in Berry, 186.
95. "Court Service of the Corps des Pages

During the Blessed Coronation in 1896: Memoirs of Baron Sergei Roop II," in Berry, 107.
96. Creighton, *Life and Letters*, 156.
97. Weigold, 103.
98. Krivenko, 267.
99. Grand Duke Ernst Ludwig of Hesse, 73.
100. Grenfell, 48.
101. Krivenko, 267.
102. Buxhoeveden, *Life*, 66; Logan, 138.
103. Krivenko, 267.
104. "Remembrances of Kamer Page B. A. Engelhardt," in Berry, 187.
105. Krivenko, 267.
106. LaPauze, 113; Krivenko, 268; Freeman and Burton, 21-22; Wortman, 2:224; Massie, *Firebird*, 46.
107. LaPauze, 112-13; Krivenko, 267-69; Logan, 140-41; Freeman and Burton, 21-22; Wortman, 2:224; Massie, *Firebird*, 46; "Remembrances of Kamer Page B. A. Engelhardt," in Berry, 187; "Notes from the Diary of A. N. Mandryk," in Berry, 209.
108. "Remembrances of Kamer Page B. A. Engelhardt," in Berry, 189.
109. See Empress Marie Feodorovna to Queen Louise of Denmark, Letter of May 15/27, 1883, cited in Krog et al, 152.
110. Krivenko, 267-69; Buxhoeveden, *Before the Storm*, 151; Logan, 141; Mossolov, 183.
111. Krivenko, 267-69.
112. Logan, 140-42; "Remembrances of Kamer Page B. A. Engelhardt," in Berry, 187-188; Krivenko, 267.
113. Lewenhaupt, 11.
114. "Remembrances of Kamer Page B. A. Engelhardt," in Berry, 188.
115. Krivenko, 267; Wortman, 2: 356; Logan, 142; Krog et al, 462.
116. Creighton, *Historical Essays*, 322.
117. Creighton, *Life and Letters*, 157.
118. Buxhoeveden, *Before the Storm*, 151-52.
119. Victoria Milford-Haven, "Reminiscences," cited in Hough, *Louis and Victoria*, 181.
120. Buxhoeveden, *Life*, 66.
121. Bovey, 26; Krog et al, 462; Krivenko, 269.
122. Piper, 9, 12; Odom, 88; Timms, 146; Hancock, 228-29.
123. Demidenko, 24; Timms, 284; Krog et al, 462; Bovey, 26.
124. Odom, 86.
125. Bovey, 26; Krog et al, 462.
126. Grenfell, 49.
127. Mannix, 133.
128. Weigold, 103.
129. Krivenko, 269.
130. Bovey, 29.
131. "Remembrances of Kamer Page B. A. Engelhardt," in Berry, 189.
132. Hickley, 25.
133. "Remembrances of Kamer Page B. A. Engelhardt," in Berry, 173; Merridale, 158.
134. North Eastern Daily Gazette, Middlesbrough, UK, May 5, 1896.
135. LaPauze, 116; Logan, 148.
136. Krivenko, 271; Bariatinsky, 53.
137. Romanovsky-Krassinsky, 59; Krivenko, 272.
138. Krivenko, 271.
139. Davis, *Year*, 21.
140. Logan, 144-46.
141. Krivenko, 271.
142. Grenfell, 50.
143. Hickley, 25.
144. , 65.
145. Sykes, 73.
146. Maude, 68.
147. Nicholas II's Diary, May 14 (OS), 1896, in GARF, F. 601, Op. 1, D. 36.
148. *The Times*, London, May 27, 1896.
149. Creighton, *Historical Essays*, 322.
150. LaPauze, 116.

Chapter X

1. Nicholas II's Diary, May 15 (OS), 1896, in GARF, F. 601, Op. 1, D. 36.
2. Buxhoeveden, *Life*, 62; *The Times*, London, weekly edition, May 29, 1896; *The Times*, London, May 27, 1896; LaPauze, 116-18.
3. Tillander-Godenhielm, 316, 326; Timms, 110; Wortman, 2:346-48.
4. Tillander-Godenhielm, 326.
5. Suvorin, *Dnevnik*, 226.
6. Maude, 64-65.
7. Nicholas II's Diary, May 15 (OS), 1896, in GARF, F. 601, Op. 1, D. 36.
8. Logan, 169; "Remembrances of Kamer Page B. A. Engelhardt," in Berry, 196; Raiguel, 289; Rodimzeva, 200.
9. Maude, 69.
10. Maude, 69; Suvorin, *Dnevnik*, 226.
11. Grand Duke Konstantin Konstantinovich's Diary, May 14 (OS), 1896, in GARF, F. 660, Op. 1, D. 43.
12. Logan, 167-68; Krivenko, 280-81.
13. Suvorin, *Dnevnik*, 226.
14. Nicholas II's Diary, May 15 (OS), 1896, in GARF, F. 601, Op. 1, D. 36; Krivenko, 281.
15. Krivenko, 280-81; LaPauze, 118.
16. Creighton, *Historical Essays*, 323.
17. Nicholas II's Diary, May 15 (OS), 1896, in GARF, F. 601, Op. 1, D. 36.
18. Raiguel, 290; Krivenko, 288.
19. Queen Marie of Romania. 1:335.
20. Grenfell, 54.
21. "Remembrances of Kamer Page B. A. Engelhardt," in Berry, 190.
22. Nicholas II's Diary, May 16 (OS), 1896, in GARF, F. 601, Op. 1, D. 36.
23. Grenfell, 55.
24. *Le Petit Parisien*, May 30, 1896.
25. Krivenko, 289; Mossolov, 191.
26. Logan, 117.
27. Logan, 168-69.
28. Bovey, 40.
29. Logan, 170-71.
30. Krivenko, 288; Logan, 170-72; *Le Petit Parisien*, May 30, 1896; Bovey, 39.
31. Krivenko, 288.
32. Krivenko, 288-89; Logan, 170.
33. "My Last Ball," by P. P. Gudim-Levokovich, in Berry, 73.
34. Buxhoeveden, *Before the Storm*, 153; Bovey, 40.
35. Bovey, 40.
36. Logan, 170; Bovey, 41.
37. "Remembrances of Kamer Page BA Engelhardt," 192; Krivenko, 289-90.
38. Bovey, 41.
39. "Remembrances of Kamer Page B. A. Engelhardt," in Berry, 191-92.
40. See U. V. Sobolev, "Khodynka, K tridtsatiletiiu katastrofy," in *Krasnaia Niva*, No. 22, 1926, 9, cited in Baker, "Monarchy Discredited," 3.
41. Maude, 73-74.
42. Iroshnikov, Protsai, and Shelayev, 25, 30.
43. Polynina and Rakhmanov, 221; Iroshnikov, Protsai and Shelayev, 25, 30.
44. Krog et al, 170; Polynina and Rakhmanov 221; Iroshnikov, Protsai and Shelayev, 30; Timms, 150, 286; Hancock, 172; Salisbury, 64.
45. Vassili Krasnov, quoted in Iroshnikov, Protsai, and Shelayev, 30.
46. Zelnik, 41.
47. Quoted in Salisbury, 54; P. Shostakovsky, in Iroshnikov, Protsai and Shelayev, 30.
48. Police report, in *Krasnii Arkhiv*, 1936, Volume LXXVI, 31-48, cited in Salisbury, 58; Baker, "Monarchy Discredited," 10; Vladimir Giliarovsky, quoted in Iroshnikov, Protsai, and Shelayev, 30; *Illustrated London News*, June 6, 1896; Vianzone, 20; *Le Figaro*, June 1, 1896; *Le Petit Parisien*, June 1, 1896; *La Presse*, June 1, 1896.
49. Quoted in Salisbury, 54; *La Presse*, June 1, 1896; Dillon, 109; Vladimir Dzhunkovsky, "Iz Zapisok Generala V. F. Dzhunkovskogo," in *Otechestvennaia istoriia*, No. 4, 1997, 21, cited in Baker, "Monarchy Discredited," 3.
50. Baker, "Monarchy Discredited," 10; Maude, 87.
51. Baker, "Monarchy Discredited," 10; Harcave, 293-94.
52. Wortman, 1:29.
53. Wortman, 2:45, 2:226.
54. Romanovsky-Krassinsky, 57-58; Wortman, 2:357; Krivenko, 310-11.
55. Romanovsky-Krassinsky, 39.
56. Cited in King, "Glory and Adornment," 36
57. Romanovsky-Krassinsky, 57; Hall, *Imperial Dancer*, 53; Radzinsky, 35; Bobrov and Kirikov, 22.
58. Romanovsky-Krassinsky, 57-58; Bobrov and Kirikov, 22-23.
59. *Le Temps*, May 31, 1896.
60. Logan, 144-46.
61. Freeman and Burton, 113; Salisbury, 52.
62. Krivenko, 308-10; Grenfell, 62.
63. Creighton, *Life and Letters*, 158-59.
64. Logan, 194.
65. LaPauze, 124.
66. *Le Temps*, May 31, 1896; Grenfell, 62; Melgunov, 106.

67. Wortman, 2:358.
68. Grand Duke Konstantin Konstantinovich's Diary, May 17 (OS), 1896, in GARF, F. 660, Op. 1, D. 43. Logan, 195; LaPauze, 124; Krivenko, 308-09; *Le Temps*, May 31, 1896.
69. Logan, 195.
70. Logan, 197.
71. Grenfell, 62.
72. Maude, 81.
73. Obolensky, 72; Vianzone, 20; See report of the first investigation into the catastrophe of 7 June, 1896, in *Dokumenty o Khodynskoi katastrofe 1896*, 42-48, cited in Baker, "Monarchy Discredited," 10; Police report in *Krasnii Arkhiv*, 1936, Volume LXXVI, pages 31-48, cited in Salisbury, 58; Suvorin, *Dnevnik*, 230.
74. See report of the first investigation into the catastrophe of 7 June, 1896, in *Dokumenty o Khodynskoi katastrofe 1896*, 42-48, cited in Baker, "Monarchy Discredited," 10; Police report in *Krasnii Arkhiv*, 1936, Volume LXXVI, pages 31-48, cited in Salisbury, 58; Suvorin, *Dnevnik*, 230.
75. Logan, 197.
76. Selfridge, 265.
Nicholas II's Diary, May 17 (OS), 1896, in GARF, F. 601, Op. 1, D. 36.

Chapter XI

1. *Le Figaro*, May 31, 1896.
2. P. Shostakovsky, in Iroshnikov, Protsai, and Shelayev, 30.
3. Vladimir Giliarovsky, in Iroshnikov, Protsai, and Shelayev, 30.
4. Maude, 81; Suvorin, *Journal*, 104; Suvorin, *Dnevnik*, 232; Maude, 81; Police report, in *Krasnii Arkhiv*, 1936, Volume LXXVI, 31-48, cited in Salisbury, 58.
5. *La Presse*, June 1, 1896.
6. Vladimir Dzhunkovsky, "Iz Zapisok Generala V. F. Dzhunkovskogo," in *Otechestvennaia istoriia*, No. 4, 1997, 21, cited in Baker, "Monarchy Discredited," 3.
7. *Le Matin*, June 1, 1896.
8. *La Presse*, June 1, 1896; Police report in *Krasnii Arkhiv*, 1936, Volume LXXVI, pages 31-48, cited in Salisbury, 58; *Illustrated London News*, June 6, 1896; Suvorin, *Dnevnik*, 229-230; Vianzone, 21; Maude, 81.
9. *La Presse*, June 1, 1896.
10. Stanhope, 249.
11. *La Presse*, June 1, 1896.
12. P. Shostakovsky, in Iroshnikov, Protsai, and Shelayev, 30.
13. *La Croix*, June 2, 1896.
14. Salisbury, 56-57; Harcave, 293-94; Vladimir Giliarovsky, in Iroshnikov, Protsai, and Shelayev, 30.
15. Stanhope, 248.
16. *Le Figaro*, June 1, 1896; Hickley, 31.
17. Suvorin, *Journal*, 93.
18. Stanhope, 248-49.
19. Leyda, 19.
20. Dillon, 110; Vladimir Giliarovsky, in Iroshnikov, Protsai, and Shelayev, 30.
21. Grenfell, 71; Hickley, 30; Warth, 27.
22. Maude, 87.
23. *The Times*, London, June 1, 1896.
24. Grenfell, 71.
25. Iroshnikov, Protsai, and Shelayev. 31; Nemirovich-Danchenko.
26. Iroshnikov, Protsai, and Shelayev, 31.
27. LaPauze, 128.
28. Hickley, 31; *The Times*, London, June 1, 1896
29. Stanhope, 249-51.
30. G. A. Ostrukhov, "Katastrofa na Khodynskom pole," in *Prometei*, No. 7, 1969, 446, cited in Baker, "Monarchy Discredited," 5; Salisbury, 58.
31. Maude, 59.
32. Maude, 89.
33. Leyda, 19.
34. Zelnik, 42.
35. Zelnik, 42.
36. G. A. Ostrukhov, "Katastrofa na Khodynskom pole," in *Prometei*, No. 7, 1969, 446, cited in Baker, "Monarchy Discredited," 5.
37. Suvorin, *Journal*, 96-97.
38. Vladimir von Glazenap, quoted in *Dokumenty o Khodynskoi Katastrofe 1896*, 40, cited in Baker, "Monarchy Discredited," 10; Ananich and Ganelin, 46.
39. Volkov, 39.
40. Izvolsky, 258.
41. Witte, 147.
42. Obolensky, 72.
43. Obolensky, 70-71; Grand Duke Konstantin Konstantinovich's Diary, May 26 (OS), 1896, in GARF, F. 660, Op. 1, D. 43.
44. "Notes from the Diary of A. N. Mandryk," in Berry, 211-12. In his diary, Alexei Suvorin reports what is clearly a piece of second-hand information, suggesting that Nicholas first learned of the disaster when Vorontsov-Dashkov telephoned him at nine that morning. Kammer Page A. N. Mandryk, though, clearly recalled that Sergei Alexandrovich first broke the news when he arrived at the Kremlin that morning, and this is also borne out by Sergei's diary. See Suvorin, *Dnevnik*, 230, and Grand Duke Sergei Alexandrovich's diary, in Efimov and Kovalskaia, 328.
45. Nicholas II's Diary, May 18 (OS), 1896, in GARF, F. 601, Op. 1, D. 36.
46. Izvolsky, *Recollections*, 259.
47. Witte, 239; Ignatiev, 64.
48. Witte, 241.
49. Obolensky, 72.
50. *Le Petit Parisien*, May 26, 1896.
51. *Le Matin*, May 27, 1896.
52. Le Justice, May 29, 1896; *Le Petit Parisien*, May 27, 1896; *Le Gaulois*, May 27, 1896; *Le Temps*, May 27, 1896.
53. *Le Figaro*, June 1, 1896; *Le Temps*, May 29 and June 1, 1896; *Le Petit Parisien*, May 29, 1896; Vorres, 79; Bariatinsky, 56; Hamilton, 189; Salisbury, 52.
54. Radziwill, *Recollections*, 317.
55. *Le Figaro*, June 1, 1896.
56. *Le Petit Parisien*, May 29, 1896.
57. *Le Temps*, May 29, 1896; *Le Petit Parisien*, May 29, 1896.
58. *Le Petit Parisien*, June 1, 1896.
59. *Le Matin*, June 1, 1896
60. Izvolsky, 260.
61. Vorres, 79.
62. Bariatinsky, 56; Buxhoeveden, *Before the Storm*, 154.
63. Queen Marie of Romania, 1:337.
64. Izvolsky, 260.
65. Baker, "Monarchy Discredited," 18.
66. Vorres, 78-79.
67. Grand Duke Konstantin Konstantinovich's Diary, May 26 (OS), 1896, in GARF, F. 660, Op. 1, D. 43; Obolensky, 72.
68. Obolensky, 72.
69. Bariatinsky, 56.
70. Dowager Empress Marie Feodorovna to Queen Louise of Denmark, Letter of May 23/ June 4, 1896, cited in Krog et al, 172.
71. Hall, 181.
72. Alexander Mikhailovich, 146.
73. Buchanan, *Mission*, 1:177.
74. Alexander Mikhailovich, 172.
75. Suvorin, *Journal*, 100-101; Grand Duke Konstantin Konstantinovich's Diary, May 19 (OS), 1896, in GARF, F. 660, Op. 1, D. 43; Grand Duchess Xenia Alexandrovna's Diary, May 18 (OS), 1896, in Maylunas and Mironenko, 146; Empress Alexandra Feodorovna to Gretchen von Fabrice, in von Spreti, 49.
76. Obolensky, 71; Suvorin, *Dnevnik*, 230.
77. Maude, 89.
78. Leyda, 19.
79. Maude, 89.
80. Melgunov, 144; Dillon, 110.
81. Wortman, 2:361.
82. Obolensky, 70-72; Grand Duke Sergei Alexandrovich's diary, May 18 (OS), 1896 in Efimov and Kovalskaia, 328, insists that there were just 400 casualties.
83. Dowager Empress Marie Feodorovna to Queen Louise of Denmark, Letter of May 23/ June 4, 1896, in Krog et al, 172.
84. *Le Figaro*, June 2, 1896; Coryne Hall to authors; Hall, 181-82.
85. Dowager Empress Marie Feodorovna to Queen Louise of Denmark, Letter of May 23/ June 4, 1896, cited in Krog et al, 172.
86. Bovey, 23.
87. *Le Temps*, June 2, 1896.
88. Hickley, 29-30.
89. Grenfell, 68.
90. Hickley, 30.
91. Witte, 240.
92. Lewenhaupt, 12.
93. Stanhope, 252.
94. Vorres, 78.
95. *The Times*, London, June 5, 1896.
96. Krivenko, 311; Hickley, 31.
97. Grenfell, 68; Salisbury, 56; Krivenko, 311;

Witte, 239; *La Croix*, June 2, 1896.
98. Logan, 179.
99. Creighton, *Historical Essays*, 324.
100. Hickley, 31-32; Bovey, 33-34; Vianzone, 21; Grenfell, 69.
101. Grenfell, 69; Stanhope, 253; Nemirovich-Danchenko; Suvorin, Dnevnik, 232.
102. Suvorin, *Dnevnik*, 232.
103. Melgunov, *Nikolai II: Materialy dlia kharakteristiki lichnosti i tsarstvovaniia*, Moscow, 1917, 110, cited in Baker, "Monarchy Discredited," 5; Grand Duke Sergei Alexandrovich's diary, May 18 (OS), 1896, in Efimov and Kovalskaia, 328.
104. General A. N. Kuropatkin's Diary, in Ananich and Ganelin, 53.
105. Suvorin, *Dnevnik*, 235; *Journal*, 97-98; Baker, "Monarchy Discredited," 5.
106. Stanhope, 253; Nemirovich-Danchenko; Grenfell, 69; Suvorin, Dnevnik, 232; Witte, page 765, Note 1.
107. Nemirovich-Danchenko.
108. Grand Duchess Xenia Alexandrovna's Diary, May 18 (OS), 1896, in Maylunas and Mironenko, 145.
109. Cited, Wortman, 2:362.
110. Krivenko, 297.
111. *Moskovskie Vedomosti*, May 19 (OS), 1896.
112. Cited in Wortman, 2:361.
113. Nicholas II's Diary, May 18 (OS), 1896, in GARF, F. 601, Op. 1, D. 36.
114. Krivenko, 311; Suvorin, *Journal*, 89.
115. Bovey, 33-34.
116. Hickley, 32.
117. Salisbury, 56; Vianzone, 22.
118. Salisbury, 57.
119. Wortman, 2:229.
120. Krivenko, 312; Salisbury, 57.
121. Witte, 240.
122. Krivenko, 312.
123. Vorres, 79; Nicholas II's Diary, May 18 (OS), 1896, in GARF, F. 601, Op. 1, D. 36.
124. Obolensky, 70-72; Grand Duke Konstantin Konstantinovich's Diary, May 18 (OS), 1896, in GARF, F. 660, Op. 1, D. 43; Grand Duchess Xenia Alexandrovna's Diary, May 18 (OS), 1896, in Maylunas and Mironenko, 145; Suvorin, *Dnevnik*, 230.
125. Nicholas II's Diary, May 18 (OS), 1896, in GARF, F. 601, Op. 1, D. 36; Grand Duke Konstantin Konstantinovich's Diary, May 18 (OS), 1896, in GARF, F. 660, Op. 1, D. 43; Grand Duchess Xenia Alexandrovna's Diary, May 18 (OS), 1896, in Maylunas and Mironenko, 145; Suvorin, *Journal*, 92.
126. Grand Duke Konstantin Konstantinovich's Diary, May 19 (OS), 1896, in GARF, F. 660, Op. 1, D. 43.
127. Suvorin, *Dnevnik*, 229.
128. *Novoe Vremya*, May 21 (OS), 1896.
129. Grenfell, 66; Krivenko, 317.
130. *Le Figaro*, June 1, 1896; *Le Temps*, June 1, 1896; *Le Petit Parisien*, June 1, 1896.
131. Krivenko, 317; Grenfell, 66-67; Bariatinsky, 57; Davis, *Year*, 50.
132. Witte, 241.
133. Bariatinsky, 57; "Remembrances of Kamer Page B. A. Engelhardt," in Berry, 195.
134. Sir Nicholas O'Conor, quoted in Massie, *Nicholas and Alexandra*, 59.
135. Buxhoeveden, *Before the Storm*, 154.
136. Izwolsky, *Recollections*, 260.
137. "Remembrances of Kamer Page B. A. Engelhardt," in Berry, 195.
138. Ananich and Ganelin, 46.
139. Queen Marie of Romania, 1:337; Pierre d'Alheim, "Khodynskii uzhas, Iz vospominanii," 113, cited in Baker, "Monarchy Discredited," 18-19; see also Salisbury, 58.
140. Alexander Mikhailovich, 172; Grand Duke Sergei Alexandrovich's diary, May 18 (OS), 1896, in Efimov and Kovalskaia, 328.
141. Alexander Mikhailovich, 172.
142. *Le Temps*, May 29 and June 1, 1896; *Le Petit Parisien*, May 29, 1896; *Le Figaro*, May 29, 1896.
143. Grenfell, 66; Krivenko, 317; *Le Temps*, June 1, 1896; *Le Petit Parisien*, June 1, 1896.
144. *Le Figaro*, May 29 and June 1, 1896; Le Temps, June 1, 1896; La Petit Parisien, June 1, 1896.
145. Krivenko, 320; *Le Figaro*, June 1, 1896; *Le Temps*, June 1, 1896.
146. Krivenko, 320; "Remembrances of Kamer Page B. A. Engelhardt," in Berry, 195; *Le Figaro*, June 1, 1896.
147. *Le Siècle*, June 4, 1896.
148. "Remembrances of Kamer Page B. A. Engelhardt," in Berry, 195.
149. Grand Duke Konstantin Konstantinovich's Diary, May 19 (OS), 1896, in GARF, F. 660, Op. 1, D. 43.
150. Suvorin, *Dnevnik*, 237.
151. Grand Duchess Xenia Alexandrovna's Diary, May 18 (OS), 1896, in Maylunas and Mironenko, 146; Grand Duke Konstantin Konstantinovich's Diary, May 19 (OS), 1896, in GARF, F. 660, Op. 1, D. 43; Empress Alexandra Feodorovna to Gretchen von Fabrice, Letter of May 19 (OS), 1896, in von Spreti, 49.
152. *Le Figaro*, June 1, 1896; *Le Temps*, June 1, 1896; *Le Petit Parisien*, June 1, 1896.
153. *Le Figaro*, June 1, 1896; *Le Petit Parisien*, June 1, 1896.
154. Krivenko, 320; Vyrubova, 60.
155. Empress Alexandra Feodorovna to Gretchen von Fabrice, Letter of May 19 (OS), 1896, in von Spreti, 49.
156. Nicholas II, Diary entry of May 18, 1896, in GARF, F. 601, Op. 1, D. 36.
157. *Le Petit Parisien*, June 1, 1896.
158. Nicholas II's Diary, May 18 (OS), 1896, in GARF, F. 601, Op. 1, D. 36.

Chapter XII

1. Suvorin, Dnevnik, 233.
2. Stanhope, 253-56.
3. "Remembrances of Kamer Page B. A. Engelhardt," in Berry, 194.
4. LaPauze, 129.
5. Hickley, 32.
6. Dowager Empress Marie Feodorovna to Queen Louise of Denmark, Letter of May 23/June 4, 1896, cited in Krog et al, 172.
7. Lewenhaupt, 12; Izwolsky, 257, 262.
8. *La Croix*, June 2, 1896.
9. Weigold, 60.
10. LaPauze, 128.
11. Hickley, 35.
12. Malcolm, 68.
13. Logan, 183.
14. Bovey, 33.
15. *Le Figaro*, June 2, 1896.
16. Suvorin, *Journal*, 95.
17. Report from Ivan Goremykin, Minister of the Interior, to St. Petersburg newspaper *Pravitelstvennyi Vestnik*, May 21 (OS), 1896, cited in Baker, "Monarchy Discredited," 6; *The Times*, London, June 8, 1896; Krasnii Arkhiv, LXXXVI, 1936, 38; Timms, 286; Iroshnikov, Protsai, and Shelayev, 31; *Otchet osoboi kommissii, obrazovannoi dlia vyiasneniia lichnosti pogibshikh na Khodynskom Vole 18-go maia 1896 goda*, Moscow, 1896, 5, cited in Baker, "Monarchy Discredited," 5-6.
18. Zelnik, 42-43.
19. *Le Figaro*, May 31, 1896; *Le Petit Parisien*, May 31, 1896.
20. *Le Matin*, June 1, 1896.
21. Le Justice, June 3, 1896; La Croix, June 3, 1896.
22. Maude, 94.
23. Zelnik, 42-43.
24. Zelnik, 45.
25. See GARF, F. 174, Op. 1, D. 21239, cited in Baker, "Monarchy Discredited," 13.
26. *The New York Times*, June 2, 1896.
27. In GARF, F. 102, Op. 3, D. 14, cited in Baker, "Monarchy Discredited," 31-32.
28. Warwick, 189.
29. Dowager Empress Marie Feodorovna to Queen Louise of Denmark, Letter of May 23/June 4, 1896, cited in Krog et al, 172; Grand Duke Konstantin Konstantinovich's Diary, May 19 (OS), 1896, in GARF, F. 660, Op. 1, D. 43; Grand Duchess Xenia Alexandrovna's Diary, May 19 (OS), 1896, in Maylunas and Mironenko, 142.
30. Dowager Empress Marie Feodorovna to Queen Louise of Denmark, Letter of May 23/June 4, 1896, cited in Krog et al, 172.
31. Grand Duke Konstantin Konstantinovich's Diary, May 19 (OS), 1896, in GARF, F. 660, Op. 1, D. 43.
32. Grand Duke Konstantin Konstantinovich's Diary, May 26 (OS), 1896, in GARF, F. 660, Op. 1, D. 43.
33. Grand Duchess Xenia Alexandrovna's Diary, May 19 (OS), 1896, in Maylunas and Mironenko, 142.
34. Queen Marie of Romania, 1:337.
35. Grand Duchess Xenia Alexandrovna's Diary, May 19 (OS), 1896, in Maylunas and Mironenko, 142.

36. Obolensky, 73-75.
37. Suvorin, *Dnevnik*, 235.
38. See Baker, "Monarchy Discredited," 19.
39. *La Presse*, June 1, 1896.
40. *Le Justice*, June 13, 1896; La Croix, June 14, 1896.
41. *L'Universe*, June 16, 1896.
42. Bernstorff, 33.
43. Queen Victoria to Princess Victoria of Battenberg, Letter of June 1, 1896, cited in Hough, *Advice*, 136.
44. Grand Duke Konstantin Konstantinovich's Diary, May 27 (OS), 1896, in GARF. F. 660, Op. 1, D. 43.
45. Nicholas II's Diary, May 19 (OS), 1896, in GARF, F. 601, Op. 1, D. 36; Grand Duke Konstantin Konstantinovich's Diary, May 19 (OS), 1896, in GARF, F. 660, Op. 1, D. 43; Krivenko, 323.
46. Krivenko, 323; Grand Duke Sergei Alexandrovich's dairy, May 19 (OS), 1896, in Efimov and Kovalskaia, 328. Many sources claim that Sergei did not visit any hospitals, but his diary gives the lie to this. His response, however, renders it as empty a gesture as if he had not, perhaps more so.
47. Nicholas II's Diary, May 19 (OS), 1896, in GARF, F. 601, Op. 1, D. 36.
48. Krivenko, 323.
49. Nicholas II's Diary, May 19 (OS), 1896, in GARF, F. 601, Op. 1, D. 36.
50. Krivenko, 327; Nicholas II's Diary, May 20 (OS), 1896, in GARF, F. 601, Op. 1, D. 36.
51. Krivenko, 327; Nicholas II's Diary, May 20 (OS), 1896, in GARF, F. 601, Op. 1, D. 36; Grand Duke Sergei Alexandrovich's diary, May 19 (OS), 1896, in Efimov and Kovalskaia, 330.
52. Nicholas II's Diary, May 20 (OS), 1896, in GARF, F. 601, Op. 1, D. 36.
53. Nicholas II's Diary, May 19-25 (OS), 1896, in GARF, F. 601, Op. 1, D. 36.
54. Grand Duke Konstantin Konstantinovich's Diary, May 19 (OS), 1896, in GARF. F. 660, Op. 1, D. 43.
55. "A Ball at the Moscow Governor-General's," by S. N. Potasky, in Berry, 197.
56. "Remembrances of Kamer Page B. A. Engelhardt," in Berry, 194.
57. Suvorin, *Dnevnik*, 234.
58. Krivenko, 327-38; Nicholas II's Diary, May 20 (OS), 1896, in GARF, F. 601, Op. 1, D. 36; "A Ball at the Moscow Governor-General's," by S. N. Potasky, in Berry, 198.
59. Naryshkina-Kurakina, 149.
60. Grenfell, 71.
61. Krivenko, 327-28; Vernova, 213; "A Ball at the Moscow Governor-General's," by S. N. Potasky, in Berry, 198; Nicholas II's Diary, May 20 (OS), 1896, in GARF, F. 601, Op. 1, D. 36.
62. Nicholas II's Diary, May 21 (OS), 1896, in GARF, F. 601, Op. 1, D. 36.
63. Krivenko, 332; Nicholas II's Diary, May 21 (OS), 1896, in GARF, F. 601, Op. 1, D. 36.
64. *Le Figaro*, June 15, 1896.
65. Nicholas II's Diary, May 21 (OS), 1896, in GARF, F. 601, Op. 1, D. 36.
66. Grenfell, 40; Malcolm, 54.
67. Krivenko, 332.
68. Maude, 34-35.
69. Salisbury, 59; Freeman and Burton, 104; Bovey, 37.
70. Bovey, 38; Malcolm, 54.
71. Bovey, 39; Logan, 172; Krivenko, 333-34.
72. Bovey, 37.
73. Bovey, 38; Logan, 172.
74. Krivenko, 334.
75. Bovey, 38-39; Krivenko, 335-36; Logan, 172.
76. Nicholas II, Diary, May 21, 1896, in GARF, F. 601, Op. 1, D. 36; *Le Siècle*, June 4, 1896.
77. Bovey, 37.
78. Dowager Empress Marie Feodorovna to Alexandra, Princess of Wales, Letter of 28. May/9 June 1896, Hoover Institution, Stanford, Maria Feodorovna, Empress, Box 1, Folder 25, published at http://forum.alexanderpalace.org/index.php?topic=13924.msg496686#msg496686 (accessed October 31, 2011).
79. Krivenko, 338; Nicholas II's Diary, May 22 (OS), 1896, in GARF, F. 601, Op. 1, D. 36; Dowager Empress Marie Feodorovna to Queen Louise of Denmark, Letter of May 23/June 4, 1896, cited in Krog et al, 172; Grenfell, 76.
80. Grenfell, 76.
81. Krivenko, 338; Creighton, *Historical Essays*, 325.
82. Creighton, *Historical Essays*, 325.
83. Grand Duke Sergei Alexandrovich's Diary, May 20 (OS), 1896, in Efimov and Kovalskaia, 330.
84. Grenfell, 77; Krivenko, 338-39; Nicholas II's Diary, May 22 (OS), 1896, in GARF, F. 601, Op. 1, D. 36.
85. Dowager Empress Marie Feodorovna to Queen Louise of Denmark, Letter of May 23/June 4, 1896, cited in Krog et al, 172.
86. Nicholas II's Diary, May 22 (OS), 1896, in GARF, F. 601, Op. 1, D. 36; Krivenko, 338-39.
87. Grenfell, 78.
88. Nicholas II's Diary, May 22 (OS), 1896, in GARF, F. 601, Op. 1, D. 36; Krivenko, 339.
89. Krivenko, 350-52; Nicholas II's Diary, May 23 (OS), 1896, in GARF, F. 601, Op. 1, D. 36.
90. Nicholas II, Diary, May 23 (OS), 1896, in GARF, F. 601, Op. 1, D. 36.
91. Nicholas II's Diary, May 23 (OS), 1896, in GARF, F. 601, Op. 1, D. 36; Krivenko, 354-55; Malcolm, 54.
92. Dowager Empress Marie Feodorovna to Queen Louise of Denmark, Letter of May 23/June 4, 1896, cited in Krog et al, 172.
93. Krivenko, 352-55.
94. Bariatinsky, 53.
95. Krivenko, 352-55; Nicholas II Diary, May 23 (OS), 1896, in GARF, F. 601, Op. 1, D. 36.
96. Nicholas II's Diary, May 24 (OS), 1896, in GARF, F. 601, Op. 1, D. 36.
97. Bernstorff, 33.
98. Salisbury, 52.
99. Logan, 111; Krivenko, 363.
100. Bernstorff, 33; Maude, 49.
101. "Notes from the Diary of A. N. Mandryk," in Berry, 209.
102. Bernstorff, 33-34.
103. Ignatiev, 63.
104. "Notes from the Diary of A. N. Mandryk," in Berry, 209; Nicholas II, Diary, May 24 (OS), 1896, GARF, F. 601, Op. 1, D. 36.
105. Nicholas II's Diary, May 25 (OS), 1896, in GARF, F. 601, Op. 1, D. 36.
106. Krivenko, 364.
107. Nicholas II's Diary, May 25 (OS), 1896, in GARF, F. 601, Op. 1, D. 36.
108. Nicholas II's Diary, May 25 (OS), 1896, in GARF, F. 601, Op. 1, D. 36; Finch, 94; Krivenko, 364.
109. Krivenko, 364-65.
110. Bovey, 42.
111. Nicholas II's Diary, May 26 (OS), 1896, in GARF, F. 601, Op. 1, D. 36.
112. Hickley, 33.
113. Nicholas II's Diary, May 26 (OS), 1896, in GARF, F. 601, Op. 1, D. 36; Krivenko, 370.
114. Grenfell, 81.
115. Krivenko, 370.
116. Hickley, 33.
117. Nicholas II's Diary, May 26 (OS), 1896, in GARF, F. 601, Op. 1, D. 36.
118. Hickley, 34.
119, Mannix, 134-35.
120. Mannix, 201.
121. Krivenko, 371-72.
122. Krivenko, 372; Nicholas II's Diary, May 26 (OS), 1896, in GARF, F. 601, Op. 1, D. 36.
123. Krivenko, 373 .
124. Maude, 24; Diary of S.D. Sheremetiev, May 26 (OS), in Efimov and Kovalskaia, 332.
125. Nicholas II's Diary, May 26 (OS), 1896, in GARF, F. 601, Op. 1, D. 36.

Epilogue

1. Nicholas II's Diary, May 27 (OS), 1896, in GARF, F. 601, Op. 1, D. 36.
2. Nicholas II's Diary, May 28 (OS), 1896, in GARF, F. 601, Op. 1, D. 36.
3. Nicholas II to Dowager Empress Marie Feodorovna, Letter of May 31 (OS), 1896, in Maylunas and Mironenko, 150.
4. Witte, 247.
5. Nicholas II to Grand Duke George Alexandrovich, Letter of July 29 (OS), 1896, in Maylunas and Mironenko, 151.
6. Baker, "Monarchy Discredited," 21.
7. Suvorin, *Dnevnik*, 230.
8. Maude, 43-44.
9. Witte, 147, 242; Baker, "Monarchy Discredited," 13.
10. Grand Duke Konstantin Konstantinovich's Diary, June 8 (OS), 1896, in GARF, F. 660, Op. 1, D. 43.
11. See Baker, "Monarchy Discredited," 11; Suvorin, *Dnevnik*, 232.
12. Witte, 242.
13. Baker, "Monarchy Discredited," 13; Witte, 242; Suvorin, *Journal*, 104.

14. Witte, 242; Baker, "Monarchy Discredited," 13; Suvorin, *Journal*, 103-05.
15. Suvorin, *Journal*, 103.
16. See Baker, "Monarchy Discredited," 15.
17. Ukase of Nicholas II, July 15 (OS), 1896, published in *Pravitel'stvennyi Vestnik*, July 17 (OS), 1896, cited in Baker, "Monarchy Discredited," 15.
18. Witte, Chapter 25, 766, Note 6.
19. Baker, "Monarchy Discredited," 15-16.
20. Grand Duke Sergei Alexandrovich's Diary, May 23 (OS), 1896, in Efimov and Kovalskaia, 330.
21. Grand Duke Sergei Alexandrovich's diary, May 23, 1896 (OS), in Efimov and Kovalskaia, 330; Obolensky, 73-74.
22. Obolensky, 74; Grand Duke Konstantin Konstantinovich's Diary, May 26 (OS), 1896, in GARF, F. 660, Op. 1, D. 43.
23. Witte, 242; Izwolsky, 261.
24. Obolensky, 73-74.
25. See Grand Duke Konstantin Konstantinovich's Diary, May 26 (OS), 1896; May 29 (OS), 1896; and June 8 (OS), 1896, in GARF, F. 660, Op. 1, D. 43; Volkov, 39; Warwick, 190; Grand Duchess Xenia Alexandrovna's Diary, May 26 (OS), 1896, in Maylunas and Mironenko, 149; Naryshkina-Kurakina, 151.
26. Volkov, 39; Izwolsky, 260.
27. Nicholas II's Diary, May 25 (OS), 1896, in GARF, F. 601, Op. 1, D. 36.
28. Grand Duke Konstantin Konstantinovich's Diary, June 8 (OS), 1896, in GARF. F. 660, Op. 1, D. 43.
29. Grand Duke Konstantin Konstantinovich's Diary, May 29 (OS), 1896, in GARF. F. 660, Op. 1, D. 43.
30. See Baker, "Monarchy Discredited," 14; Volkov, 39; Witte, 241-42.
31. See Obolensky, 74; Mossolov, 106; Volkov, 39; Witte, 242.
32. Izwolsky, 259-61.
33. Witte, 242.
34. Witte, Chapter 25, 766, Note 5.
35. Grand Duchess Xenia Alexandrovna's Diary, July 29 (OS), 1896, in Maylunas and Mironenko, 151.
36. Obolensky, 74.
37. Obolensky, 74-75; File in GARF, F. 102, Op. 3, D. 1422, cited in Baker, *Nicholas II and the Khodynka Catastrophe*, 122.
38. Obolensky, 74.
39. It is generally unwise to take Alexander Mikhailovich's memoirs at face value, but in this instance his account of the culmination of his battle with Alexei is fully corroborated in letters written by Grand Duke Konstantin Konstantinovich to Queen Olga of Greece held in the Bakhmeteff Archive at Columbia University. It is worth noting, however, that the battle of wills between these two Naval cousins began some time before Khodynka, and as early as April 1896 Sergei was complaining in his diary about "ce villain Sandro" and his "cochonneries" vis-a-vis Alexei. See Efimov and Kovalskaia, 321. It was yet another symptom of the factionalism and battles for power within the Romanov family. Khodynka to an extent permitted them to further such battles, rather than creating any that did not exist in the first place.
40. Grand Duke George Alexandrovich to Nicholas II, Letter of August 5 (OS), 1896, in Maylunas and Mironenko, 151.
41. Nicholas II to Grand Duke Vladimir Alexandrovich, Letter of November 26 (OS), 1896, in GARF, F. 652, Op. 1, D. 619.
42. Salisbury, 65; Melgunov, 60).
43. Diary of Count S. D. Sheremetev, June 15, 1896 (OS), in Efimov and Kovalskaia, 342-3; Grand Duke Konstantin Konstantinovich's Diary, July 2 (OS), 1896, in GARF. F. 660, Op. 1, D. 43.
44. Grand Duchess Elisabeth Feodorovna to Queen Victoria, Letter of November 3 (OS), 1896, cited in Warwick, 193-94.
45. Grand Duchess Elisabeth Feodorovna to Nicholas II, Letter of December 22 (OS), 1896, in Maylunas and Mironenko, 156.
46. Grand Duke Sergei Alexandrovich's Diary, September 28 (OS), 1896, in Efimov and Kovalskaia, 347.
47. Obolensky, 73-75.
48. Witte, 242.
49. Izwolsky, *No Time*, 44.
50. Witte, 242-43; Obolensky, 73-74.
51. Witte, 262-63; Mossolov, 106.
52. Witte, 263; Mossolov, 106.
53. Radziwill, *Nicholas II*, 78-79).
54. Dillon, 110.
55. See Baker, "Monarchy Discredited," 6.
56. Suvorin, *Journal*, 89.
57. *Le Figaro*, May 31, 1896; *Le Petit Parisien*, May 31, 1896.
58. Suvorin, *Dnevnik*, 233; *Le Figaro*, June 1, 1896; *La Croix*, June 2, 1896; *Le Matin*, June 1, 1896; *Le Petit Parisien*, June 2, 1896.
59. *Le Matin*, June 1, 1896.
60. *Le Justice*, June 3, 1896; La Croix, June 3, 1896.
61. Grenfell, 70; LaPauze, 127; Bovey, 33; Hickley, 30.
62. *The Illustrated London News*, June 6, 1896; *The New York Times*, June 7, 1896.
63. Witte, 239; Izwolsky, *Recollections*, 259.
64. Maude, 90; Alexander Mikhailovich, 143.
65. Logan, 182; Hickley, 34.
66. Report from Ivan Goremykin, Minister of the Interior, to St. Petersburg newspaper *Pravitelstvennyi Vestnik*, May 21 (OS), 1896, cited in Baker, "Monarchy Discredited," 6; *The Times*, London, June 8, 1896; *Krasnii Arkhiv*, LXXXVI, 1936, 38; Timms, 286; Iroshnikov, 31; *Otchet osoboi kommissii, obrazovannoi dlia vyiasneniia lichnosti pogibshikh na Khodynskom Vole 18-go maia 1896 goda*, Moscow, 1896, 5, cited in Baker, Monarchy Discredited, 5-6); *Otchet osoboi kommissii, obrazovannoi dlia vyiasneniia lichnosti pogibshikh na Khodynskom Vole 18-go maia 1896 goda*, Moscow, 1896, cited in Baker, "Monarchy Discredited," 6.
67. Cited in Baker, "Monarchy Discredited," 6-7
68. Stanhope, 259.
69. See *Otchet osoboi kommissii, obrazovannoi dlia vyiasneniia lichnosti pogibshikh na Khodynsom Pole 18-go maia 1896 goda*, Moscow, 1896, 5, cited in Baker, "Monarchy Discredited," 6.
70. Baker, "Monarchy Discredited," 30.
71. See GARF, F. 102, Op. 2, D. 126, cited in Baker, "Monarchy Discredited," 24-25, 30; Baker, *Nicholas II and the Khodynka Catastrophe*, 144.
72. Baker, *Nicholas II and the Khodynka Catastrophe*, 113; Baker, "Monarchy Discredited," 25.
73. Baker, *Nicholas II and the Khodynka Catastrophe*, 117.
74. Baker, *Nicholas II and the Khodynka Catastrophe*, 115.
75. Cited in Baker, "Monarchy Discredited," 26.
76. See GARF, F. 102, D. 2, Op. 126, cited in Baker, "Monarchy Discredited," 25.
77. Baker, "Monarchy Discredited," 23.
78. Vorres, 79.
79. Baker, "Monarchy Discredited," 23.
80. See GARF, F. 1741, Op. 21239, D. 1, cited in Baker, "Monarchy Discredited," 32.
81. See D. N. Shakhovskoi, Khodynka, Geneva: Ukrainskaia tipografiia, 1896, cited in Baker, "Monarchy Discredited," 32.
82. Iroshnikov, Protsai, and Shelayev, 33.
83. Zelnik, 45.
84. Oldenburg, 1:81; Baker, "Monarchy Discredited," 35-36.
85. Zelnik, 45.
86. Baker, "Monarchy Discredited," 38-39.
87. Warth, 28.
88. See Nicholas II's Diary, May 10-26 (OS), 1896, in GARF, F. 601, Op. 1, D. 36.
89. Wortman, 2:358.
90. Wortman, 2:362.
91. Suvorin, French, 121.
92. *Sheffield Independent*, December 17, 1896; see also Izwolsky, 262.
93. Cited, Wortman, 2:345.
94. Buxhoeveden, *Life*, 64.
95. See Verner, 239-41, 299-300.
96. Ascher, 351-57; Wortman, 2:504-07.
97. Elchaninov, 1-2.
98. Empress Alexandra Feodorovna to Nicholas II, Letter of December 14 (OS), 1916, in GARF, F. 601, Op. 1, D. 1151.
99. Nicholas II's Abdication Manifesto, March 2 (OS), 1917, in GARF, F. 601, Op. 1, D. 2100.

Bibliography

Archival Sources

Materials utilized in this book draw on both published and unpublished sources. Archives and abbreviations used within the Source Notes are listed below.

Bakhmeteff Archive, Rare Book and Manuscript Library, Columbia University, New York City.
Eurohistory Royal Photographic Archive, Eurohistory, East Richmond Heights, California.
GARF: Gosudarstvennyi Arkhiv Rossisskii Federatsii (State Archives of the Russian Federation), Moscow.
GIAR: Gosudarstvennyi Istoricheskii Arkhiv Rossisskii (State Historical Archives of the Russian Federation), St. Petersburg.

Books

Abate, Michele, Editor. *Moscow: Splendours of the Romanovs*. Monte Carlo: Skira/Grimaldi Forum Monaco, 2009.
Abrikossow, Dmitri Ivanovich. *Revelations of a Russian Diplomat*. Seattle: University of Washington Press, 1964.
Alexander Mikhailovich, Grand Duke of Russia. *Once a Grand Duke*. New York: Farrar & Rinehart, 1932.
Almedingen, E. M. *The Empress Alexandra*. London: Hutchinson, 1961.
___ *The Emperor Alexander II*. London: The Bodley Head, 1962.
Ambler, Effie. *The Career of Aleksei S. Suvorin: Russian Journalism and Politics, 1861–1881*. Detroit: Wayne State University, 1972.
Amelekhina, Svetlana A., and Alexey K. Levykin. *Magnificence of the Tsars: Ceremonial Men's Dress of the Russian Imperial Court, 1721-1917*. London: Victoria and Albert Museum, 2009.
Ananich, B.V. and R. Sh. Ganelin, Editors. *Nikolai Vtoroi: Vospominaniia, Dnevniki*. St Petersburg: Pushkinskii Fond, 1994.
Arapov, Dmitriy Yu. *Bukhara: Caught in Time*. Reading, UK: Garnet Publishing Ltd., 1993.
Aronson, Theo. *Crowns in Conflict*. London: John Murray, 1986.
Ascher, Abraham. *The Revolution of 1905*. Stanford: Stanford University Press, 2004.
Bainbridge, Henry Charles. *Peter Carl Fabergé: Goldsmith and Jeweler to the Russian Imperial Court*. London: Hamlyn Publishing Group, 1949.
Bariatinsky, Princess Anatole. *My Russian Life*. London: Hutchinson, 1923.
Beable, William. *Russian Gazetter and Guide*. London: Russian Outlook, 1919.
Beéche, Arturo E. and Coryne Hall. *APAPA: King Christian IX and His Descendants*. East Richmond Heights, California: Eurohistory, 2014.
Belyakova, Zoia. *The Romanovs: The Way It Was*. St. Petersburg: Ego Publishers, 2000.
Bernstorff, Count Johann von. *The Memoirs of Count Bernstorff*. London: Heinemann, 1936.
Berry, Thomas E., Editor. *Memoirs of the Pages to the Tsars*. Mississauga, Ontario: Gilbert's Royal Books, 2001.
Bing, Edward, Editor. *The Secret Letters of the Last Tsar*. London: Ivor Nicholson and Watson, 1937.
Bobrov, V. D., and B. M. Kirikov. *Osobnyak Kschessinskoi*. St. Petersburg: Beloe i Chernoe, 1996.
Bokhanov, Alexander, Dr. Manfred Knodt, Vladimir Oustimenko, Zinaida Peregudova, and Lyubov Tyutyunnik. *The Romanovs: Love, Power, and Tragedy*. London: Leppi Publications, 1993.
Bokhanov, Aleksandr. *Imperator Aleksandr III*. Moscow: Russkoe Slovo, 2001.
Bothmer, Countess A. von. *The Sovereign Ladies of Europe*. London: Hutchinson, 1899.

Bovey, Kate Koon. *Russian Coronation, 1896.* Minneapolis, Minnesota: Privately Published, 1942.
Brumfield, William Craft. *A History of Russian Architecture.* Cambridge: Cambridge University Press, 1993.
Buchanan, Sir George. *My Mission to Russia.* Boston: Little, Brown, and Company, 1923.
Buchanan, Meriel. *Victorian Gallery.* London: Cassell, 1956.
Buxhoeveden, Baroness Sophie. *The Life and Tragedy of Alexandra Feodorovna, Empress of Russia.* London: Longmans, Green and Co., 1929.
___ *Before the Storm.* London: Macmillan, 1938.
Byrnes, Robert F. *Pobedonostsev: His Life and Thought.* Bloomington, Indiana: Indiana University Press, 1968.
Cantacuzene, Julia. *My Life Here and There.* New York: Charles Scribner's Sons, 1921
Chavchavadze, Prince David. *The Grand Dukes.* New York: Atlantic International Publications, 1990.
Cockfield, Jamie H. *White Crow: The Life and Times of the Grand Duke Nicholas Mikhailovich Romanov, 1859-1919.* Westport, CT: Praeger, 2002.
Corti, Count Egan. *Downfall of Three Dynasties.* London: Methuen & Co., 1934.
___ *Alexander von Battenberg.* London: Cassell, 1954.
Covert, James. *A Victorian Marriage: Mandell and Louise Creighton.* London: Hambledon, 2000.
Creighton, Louise. *Life and Letters of Mandell Creighton.* London: Longmans, Green & Co., 1904.
Creighton, Mandell. *Historical essays and reviews.* London: Longman, Green & Co., 1902.
de Custine, Astolphe, Marquis de. *Empire of the Czar: A Journey Through Eternal Russia.* New York: Doubleday, 1989.
Davis, Richard Harding. *A Year From a Correspondent's Note Book.* London: Harper and Brothers, 1898.
___ *Adventures and Letters of Richard Harding Davis.* New York: Charles Scribner's Sons, 1918.
Demidenko, Julia. *Reveling St. Petersburg: An Artistic Chronicle of High Society Life.* St. Petersburg: Palace Editions, 1994.
Dillon, E. J. *The Eclipse of Russia.* London: J. M. Dent, 1918.
Dubnow, S. M. *The History of the Jews in Russia and Poland.* New York: Jewish Publishing Society, 1916.
Duff, David. *Hessian Tapestry.* London: Frederick Muller, 1967.
Efimov, A.B. and E. Iu. Kovalskaia, Editors. *Velikaia Kniaginia Elizaveta Feodorovna i Imperator Nikolai II. Dokumenty i materialy (1884-1909 gg.).* St Petersburg: Aleteia, 2009.
Elchaninov, Major-General Andrei. *The Tsar and His People.* London: Hutchinson, 1914.
Elsbery, Terence. *Marie of Romania: The Intimate Life of a Twentieth Century Queen.* London: Cassell, 1937.
Essed-Bey, Mohammed. *Nicholas II: Prisoner of the Purple.* London: Hutchinson, 1936.
Faberge, Tatiana, Lynette G. Proler, and Valentin V. Skurlov. *The Fabergé Imperial Easter Eggs.* London: Christie, Manson, and Woods, 1997.
Federov, Vyacheslav, and Marlies Kleiterp, Editors. *At the Russian Court: Palace and Protocol in the 19th Century.* Amsterdam: Hermitage Amsterdam, 2009.
Figes, Orlando. *A People's Tragedy: The Russian Revolution, 1891-1924.* London: Random House, 1996.
Finch, Michael. *Min-Yong-hwan: A Political Biography.* Honolulu: University of Hawaii Press, 2002.
Florinsky, Michael. *Russia: A History and an Interpretation. Two Volumes.* New York: Macmillan, 1953.
Floryan, Margrethe. *Gardens of the Tsars: A Study of the Aesthetics, Semantics, and Uses of Late 18th Century Russian Gardens.* Portland, OR: Sagapress, 1996.
Frances, Willard, and Mary A. Livermore, Editors. *A Woman of the Century: Fourteen Hundred Seventy Biographical Sketches Accompanied by Portraits of Leading American Women in All Walks of Life.* Buffalo, NY: Charles Wells Moulton, 1993.
Frankland, Noble. *Witness of a Century: The Life and Times of Prince Arthur, Duke of Connaught.* London: Shepheard-Walwyn, 1993.
Freeman, John, and Kathleen Burton. *Moscow Revealed.* New York: Abbeville, 1991.
Fuhrmann, Joseph T., Editor. *The Complete Wartime Correspondence of Nicholas and Alexandra.* Westport, CT: Greenwood Press, 1999.
Gilliard, Pierre. *Thirteen Years at the Russian Court.* New York: George H. Doran, 1923.

Goncharenko, Valentina, and Valentina Narozhnaya. *The Armory Chamber*. Moscow: Progress, 1979.

Grabbe, Paul, and Beatrice Grabbe. *The Private World of the Last Tsar: In the Photographs and Notes of General Count Alexander Grabbe*. Boston: Little, Brown, and Company, 1994.

Graham, Stephen. *The Life of Alexander II, Emperor of All the Russias*. London: W. H. Allen, 1935.

Greece, Prince Christopher of. *Memoirs*. London: The Right Book Club, 1934.

Greece, Prince Michael of. *Crown Jewels of Europe*. New York: Crescent Books, 1986.

Greece, Prince Nicholas of. *My Fifty Years: The Memoirs of Prince Nicholas of Greece*. Oakland, CA: Eurohistory.com, 2006.

Greenberg, Louis. *The Jews in Russia*. New Haven, CT: Yale University Press, 1944.

Grenfell, Sir Francis. *Three Weeks in Moscow*. London: Harrison & Sons, 1896.

Gurko, Vladimir. *Features and Figures of the Past: Government and Opinion in the Reign of Nicholas II*. New York: Russell & Russell, 1936.

Habsburg, Geza von, and Marina Lopato. *Fabergé: Imperial Jeweler*. New York: Harry N. Abrams, 1993.

Hackett, Roger F. *Yamagata Aritomo and the Rise of Modern Japan, 1838-1922*. Cambridge, MA: Harvard University Press, 1971.

Hall, Coryne. *Little Mother of Russia: A Biography of the Empress Marie Feodorovna*. London: Shepheard-Walwyn, 1999.

___ *Imperial Dancer*. Stroud, Gloucestershire: Sutton, 2002

Hamilton, Lord Frederic. *The Vanished Pomps of Yesterday*. Garden City, NY: Doubleday, 1934.

Hammer, Armand. *The Quest of the Romanoff Treasure*. New York: William Farquhar, Payson, 1934.

Hancock, Ralph, Editor. *Treasures of the Czars*. London: Booth-Clibborn Editions, 1995.

Hapgood, Isabel F. *Russian Rambles*. Boston: Houghton, Mifflin, 1895.

Harcave, Sidney. *Years of the Golden Cockerel*. New York: Macmillan, 1968.

Hesse, Grand Duke Ernst Ludwig of. *Erinnertes: Aufzeichnungen des Letzten Grossherzogs Ernst Ludwig von Hesse und Bei Rhein*. Darmstadt: Eduard Roether Verlag, 1983.

Hickley, Mary. *Gold, Glitter, and Gloom*. Devon: Brenda Marsault, 1997.

Hodgetts, E.A. Brayley. *The Court of Russia in the Nineteenth Century*. London: Methuen, 1908.

Hough, Richard. *Louis and Victoria, the First Mountbattens*. London: Hutchinson, 1974.

___ Editor. *Advice to My Granddaughter: Letters from Queen Victoria to Princess Victoria of Hesse*. New York: Simon & Schuster, 1976.

Ignatiev, Alexei. *A Subaltern in Old Russia*. London: Hutchinson, 1944.

Intimacies of Court and Society: An Unconventional Narrative of Unofficial Days, by the Widow of an American Diplomat. New York: Dodd, Mead, 1912.

Iroshnikov, Mikhail, Lyudmila Protsai, and Yuri Shelayev. *Sunset of the Romanov Dynasty*. Moscow: Terra, 1992.

Izwolsky, Alexander. *Recollections of a Foreign Minister*. New York: Doubleday, 1921.

Izwolsky, Helene. *No Time to Grieve*. Philadelphia: Winchell, 1985.

Joubert, Carl. *The Truth about the Tsar*. London: Eveleigh Nash, 1905.

Kalmykow, Andrei Dmitrievich. *Memoirs of a Russian Diplomat*. London and New Haven: Yale UP, 1971.

Kearney, Leslie, Editor. *Tchaikovsky and His World*. Princeton: Princeton University Press, 1998.

King, Greg. *The Court of the Last Tsar*. Hoboken, N. J.: John Wiley & Sons, 2006.

King, Greg and Penny Wilson. *The Fate of the Romanovs*. Hoboken: N. J.: John Wiley & Sons, 2003.

Kirichenko, Eugenia. *Russian Design and the Fine Arts, 1750-1917*. New York: Harry N. Abrams, 1991.

Kirill Vladimirovich, Grand Duke of Russia. *My Life in Russia's Service, Then and Now*. London: Selwyn & Blount, 1939.

Kleimichel, Countess Marie. *Memories of a Shipwrecked World*. London: Brentano's, 1923.

Kleinpenning, Petra H., Editor. *The Correspondence of the Empress Alexandra of Russia with Ernst Ludwig and Eleonore, Grand Duke and Duchess of Hesse, 1878-1916*. Norderstedt: Books on Demand, 2010.

Kohl, J. G. *Russia: St. Petersburg, Moscow, Kharkoff, Riga, Odessa, the German Provinces on the Baltic, the Steppes, the Crimea, and the Interior of the Empire*. London: Chapman and Hall, 1842.

Korneva, Galina and Tatiana Cheboksarova. (Expanded and Edited by Arturo E. Beéche) *Russia & Europe – Dynastic Ties*. East Richmond Heights: Eurohistory. 2014.

___ *Grand Duchess Marie Pavlovna*. East Richmond Heights: Eurohistory. 2014.

Korshunova, Tamara, Editor. *Russian Style, 1700-1920: Court and Country Dress from the Hermitage*. London: Barbican Editions, 1987.

Krivenko, V. S., Editor. *Les Solennites du Saint Couronnement: Ouvrage Publie avec l'autorisation de Sa Majesté l'Empereur par le Ministere de la Maison Imperiale*. St. Petersburg: Ministerstvo Imperatorskago Dvora i Udielov, 1899.

Krog, Ole Villumsen, and Dominic Lieven, Yulia Kudrina, Vladimir Dmitriev, Aliya Barkovetz, Preben Ulstrup, Bent Jensen, Alexander Golubev, Andrey Larianov, Andrey Yanovsky, Pastor Gennady Belovolov, Sergei Gontar, Mogens Bencard, Tatiana Muntian, William Clarke and Alexander Sokolov. *Marie Feodorovna, Empress of Russia: An Exhibition about the Danish Princess who Became Empress of Russia*. Exhibit catalogue. Copenhagen: Christiansborg Palace-der Kongelige Udstillingsfond, 1997.

Lambsdorff, Vladimir. *Dnevnik, 1892-1894*. Moscow: Central State Publishing, 1961.

LaPauze, Henry. *De Paris au Volga*. Paris: Lemerre 1896.

Letin, Sergei. *Rossiiskaia imperatorskaia gvardiia*. St Petersburg: Slaviia, 2005.

Leudet, Maurice. *Nicolas II Intime*. Paris: F. Juven, 1898.

Levine, Issac Don, Editor. *Letters from the Kaiser to the Czar*. New York: Frederick Stokes, 1920.

Lewenhaupt, Count Eric, Editor. *The Memoirs of Marshal Mannerheim*. London: Cassell, 1953.

Lewis, Arnold. *American Country Houses of the Gilded Age*. New York: Dover Publications, 1982.

Leyda, Jay. *Kino: A History of the Russian and Soviet Film*. London: Allen & Unwin, 1983.

Lieven, Dominic. *Nicholas II: Twilight of the Empire*. New York: St. Martin's Press, 1993.

Lincoln, W. Bruce. *Nicholas I: Emperor and Autocrat of all the Russias*. London: Allen Lane, 1978.

Logan, John A. *In Joyful Russia*. New York: Appleton and Company, 1897.

Lowe, Charles. *Alexander III of Russia*. New York: Macmillan, 1895.

Lowe, David Garrard. *Lost Chicago*. New York: Watson-Gutpill Publications, 2000.

Lubow, Arthur. *The Reporter Who Would Be King: A Biography of Richard Harding Davis*. New York: Charles Scribner's Sons, 1992.

Lutyens, Mary, Editor. *Lady Lytton's Court Diary*. London: Rupert Hart-Davis, 1961.

Maclean, Fitzroy. *Holy Russia*. London: Smithmark, 1983.

Malcolm, Ian. *Trodden Ways, 1895-1930*. London: Macmillan, 1930.

Mannix, William F., Editor. *The Memoirs of Li-Hung Chang: His Life and Times*. Boston: Houghton Mifflin, 1923.

Mansel, Philip. *Sultans in Splendour*. London: Andre Deutsche, 1988.

Marie Pavlovna, Grand Duchess of Russia. *Education of a Princess*. New York: Viking, 1931.

Markova, G. *The Great Palace of the Moscow Kremlin*. Leningrad: Aurora Art Publishers, 1981.

Massie, Robert K. *Nicholas and Alexandra*. New York: Athenaeum, 1967.

Massie, Suzanne. *Land of the Firebird: The Beauty of Old Russia*. New York: Simon & Schuster, 1980.

Maude, Aylmer (writing as de Monte Alto). *The Tsar's Coronation, as Seen by de Monte Alto*. London: Brotherhood Publishing Company, 1896.

Maylunas, Andrei, and Sergei Mironenko. *A Lifelong Passion: Nicholas & Alexandra, Their Own Story*. London: Weidenfeld & Nicolson, 1996.

McCullough, David. *The Great Bridge: The Epic Story of the Building of the Brooklyn Bridge*. New York: Simon & Schuster, 1983.

Melgunov, SP. *Nikolai II: Materialy dlia kharateristiki lichnosti i charstvovaniia*. Moscow: Izdanie zhurnala "Golos Minuvschago", 1917.

Merridale, Catherine. *Red Fortress: the Secret Heart of Russia's History*. London: Allen Lane, 2013.

Meylan, Vincent. *Queen's Jewels*. New York: Assouline, 2002.

Mossolov, Alexander. *At the Court of the Last Tsar*. London: Methuen, 1935.

Mott, Thomas Bentley. *Twenty Years as Military Attaché*. New York: Arno Press, 1979.

Moy, Carl, Graf von. *Als Diplomat am Zarenhof.* Munich: Prestel-Verlag, 1971.
Nadelhoffer, Hans. *Cartier: Jewelers Extraordinary.* New York: Harry N. Abrams, 1984.
Naryshkina-Kurakina, Princess Elizabeth. *Under Three Tsars.* New York: Dutton, 1931.
Norman, John Henry. *Norman's Universal Cambist: a ready reckoner of the world's foreign and colonial exchanges.* London: Effingham Wilson, 1897.
Obolensky, Dimitri. *Bread of Exile: A Russian Family.* London: Harvill, 1999.
Odom, Anne. *What Became of Peter's Dream? Court Culture in the Reign of Nicholas II.* Exhibition catalogue, Middlebury College Museum of Art, Middlebury Vermont/Hillwood Museum and Gardens, Washington, DC. Seattle: University of Washington Press, 2003.
Oldenburg, Sergei S. *Last Tsar: Nicholas II, His Reign and His Russia. Four volumes.* Gulf Breeze, FL: Academic International Press, 1975.
Paleologue, Maurice. *An Ambassador's Memoirs. Three volumes.* New York: Doran, 1925.
Paleologue, Maurice. *Three Critical Years.* New York: Robert Speller, 1957.
Paoli, Xavier. *My Royal Clients.* London: Hodder and Stoughton, 1910.
Papi, Stefano. *Jewels of the Romanovs: Family & Court.* London: Thames & Hudson, 2010.
Pares, Bernard. *Russia and Reform.* London: Archibald Constable, 1907.
Perry, John Curtis, and Constantine Pleshakov. *The Flight of the Romanovs.* New York: Konecky & Konecky, 2002.
Phenix, Patricia. *Olga Romanov: Russia's Last Grand Duchess.* Toronto: Viking, 1999.
Piper, Raymond. *Russian Imperial Porcelain from the Raymond F Piper Collection.* Privately Printed, 1995.
Pipes, Richard. *The Russian Revolution.* New York: Random House, 1990.
Poliakoff, Vladimir. *The Tragic Bride: The Story of The Empress Alexandra of Russia.* New York: Appleton and Company, 1927.
Polynina, Irina, and Nikolai Rakhmanov. *The Regalia of the Russian Empire.* Moscow: Red Square, 1994.
Prall, William, Editor. *The Court of Alexander III: letters of Mrs Lothrop.* Philadelphia: The John C. Winston Company, 1910.
Radzinsky, Edvard. *The Last Tsar: The Life and Death of Nicholas II.* New York: Doubleday, 1992.
Radziwill, Princess Catherine. *The Intimate Life of the Last Tsarina.* London: Cassell, 1929.
____*My Recollections.* London. Isbister & Company, 1904.
____*My Memories of Forty Years.* New York: Funk & Wagnalls, 1915.
____*Nicholas II, The Last of the Tsars.* London: Cassell, 1931.
____*Sovereigns and Statesmen of Europe.* New York: Funk & Wagnalls, 1916.
Raiguel, George Earle, and William Kistler Huff. *This is Russia.* Philadelphia: Pennsylvania Publishing, 1932.
Reade, Arthur. *Russia under Nicholas II.* London: Thomas Nelson, 1915.
Rice, Christopher and Melanie. *Moscow: Eyewitness Guide.* New York: DK Publishing, 1998.
Rodimezeva, Irina, Nikolai Rahkmanov, and Alfons Raimann. *The Kremlin and its Treasures.* New York: Rizzoli, 1987.
Romanovsky-Krassinsky, Princess (Mathilde Kschessinska). *Dancing in Petersburg: The Memoirs of Kschessinska.* London: Victor Gollancz, 1960.
Rose, Andreas. *Zwischen Empire und Kontinent: Britische Außenpolitik vor dem Ersten Weltkrieg.* Munich: Oldenbourg Wissenschaftsverlag, 2011
Romania, Queen Marie of. *The Story of My Life.* New York: Charles Scribner's Sons, 1934.
Russian Court Memoirs, 1914-1916. New York: E. P. Dutton, 1916.
Salisbury, Harrison E. *Black Night, White Snow: Russia's Revolutions, 1905-1917.* New York: Doubleday, 1977.
Samson-Himmelstjerna, Hermann von. *Russia under Alexander III.* London: Fisher Unwin, 1893.
Schelking, Eugene de. *Suicide of Monarchy: Recollections of a Diplomat.* Toronto: Macmillan, 1918.
Selfridge, Thomas O. *Memoirs of Thomas O. Selfridge Jr., Rear Admiral U.S.N.* New York: G. Putnam's Sons, 1924.
Shelley, Gerard. *The Speckled Domes.* London: Duckworth, 1925.
Shvidkovsky, Dmitry. *Russian Architecture and the West.* New Haven, CT: Yale University Press, 2007.
Slater, Wendy. *The Many Deaths of Tsar Nicholas II.* London: Routledge, 2007.

Spain, Infanta Eulalia of. *Court Life from Within*. New York: Dodd, Mead, 1916.

von Spreti, Heinrich, Graf (editor). *Alix an Gretchen, Briefe der Zarin Alexandra Feodorovna an Freiin Margarethe v. Fabrice aus den Jahren 1891-1914*. Germany: Privately Published, 2003.

Stanhope, Aubrey. *On the Track of the Great: Recollections of a Special Correspondent*. London: Eveleigh Nash, 1914.

Statesman's Handbook for Russia. Edited by the Imperial Council of Ministers. St. Petersburg: Eugene Thiele, 1896.

Stoddard, John L. *John L. Stoddard's Lectures: Berlin, Vienna, St. Petersburg and Moscow*. Chicago: George L. Shuman, 1911.

de Stoeckl, Baroness Agnes. My Dear Marquis. London: John Murray, 1952.

Sullivan, Michael John. *A Fatal Passion: The Story of the Uncrowned Last Empress of Russia*. London: Random House, 1997.

Suvorin, Alexei. *Journal Intime d'Alexis Souvorine*. Paris: Privately Published, 1926.

___ *Dnevnik Alekseia Sergeevicha Suvorina: tekstologicheskaia rasshifrovka N. A. Rosinskoi, podgotovka teksta D. Reifilda i O. E. Makarovoi*. London: Garnett Press, 1999.

Surguchev, I. *Detstvo Imperatora Nikolaia II*. Paris: Payot, 1953.

Sykes, Arthur Alkin. *The Coronation Cruise of the Midnight Sun to Russia, Whitsuntide 1896, A Record*. London: Private Published, 1896.

Tarsaïdzé, Alexandre. *Katia: Wife Before God*. New York: Macmillan, 1970.

Taylor, Edmond. *The Fall of the Dynasties and the Collapse of the Old Order, 1905-1922*. Garden City: New York, 1963.

Tillander-Godenhielm, Ulla. *The Russian Imperial Award System during the Reign of Nicholas II, 1894-1917*. Helsinki: Finnish Antiquarian Society, 2005.

Timms, Robert, Editor. *Nicholas & Alexandra: The Last Imperial Family of Tsarist Russia*. New York: Harry N. Abrams, 1998.

Tisdall, E. E. P. T*he Dowager Empress*. London: Stanley Paul, 1957.

Tiutcheva, Anna. *Pri Dvore Dvukh Imperatorov*. Moscow: Mysl, 1990.

Twining, Edward Francis, Baron. *A History of the Crown Jewels of Europe*. London: Batsford, 1960.

Ukhtomskii, Esper Esperovich. *Puteshestvie na Vostok' Ego Imperatorskago Vysochestva Gosudaria Nasliednika Tsesarevicha, 1890-1 (Puteshestvie Gosudaria Imperatora Nikolaia II na Vostok)*. St. Petersburg: Brokgauz, 1893-97.

Ular, Alexander. *Russia From Within*. London: Heinemann, 1905.

Valkovich, A. M., and A. P. Kapitonov, Editors. *Rossiiskaia gvardiia, 1700-1918: spravochnik*. Moscow: Novyi khronograf, 2005.

Vassili, Count Paul (Princess Catherine Radziwill). *Behind the Veil of the Russian Court*. London: Cassell, 1913.

___ *Confessions of the Czarina*. New York: Harper & Brothers, 1918.

Verner, Andrew. *The Crisis of Russian Autocracy: Nicholas II and the 1905 Revolution*. Princeton, NJ: Princeton University Press, 1990.

Vernova, Nina. *Treasures of Russia: From the Peterhof Palaces of the Tsars*. New York: Forbes Custom, 1999.

Vianzone, Therese de. *Lettres sur Couronnement de l'Empereur Nicolas II et de l'Imperatrice Alexandra, et de Leur Sejour en France*. Paris: Privately Published, 1896.

Vickers, Hugo. *Alice, Princess Andrew of Greece*. London, Hamish Hamilton, 2000

Volkov, Alexei. *Souvenirs d'Alexis Volkov*. Payot: Paris, 1928.

Vorres, Ian. *The Last Grand Duchess*. London: Hutchinson, 1964.

Vyrubova, Anna. *Memories of the Russian Court*. New York: Macmillan, 1923.

Waddington, Mary King. *Letters of a Diplomat's Wife*. New York: Charles Scribner's Sons, 1903.

Wallace, Sir Donald Mackenzie. *Russia*. New York: Vintage Books, 1962.

Warth, Robert D. *Nicholas II*. Westport, CT: Praeger, 1997.

Warwick, Christopher. *Ella: Princess, Saint, and Martyr*. Chichester, UK: John Wiley & Sons, 2006.

Wcislo, Francis W. *Tales of Imperial Russia: The Life and Times of Sergei Witte, 1849-1915*. Oxford: OUP, 2011.

Weigold, Marilyn. *Silent Builder: Emily Warren Roebling and the Brooklyn Bridge*. New York: Associated Faculty Press, 1984.

Witte, Count Serge. *The Memoirs of Count Witte*. Edited by Sidney Harcave. Armonk, NY: M. E. Sharpe, 1990.

Wolfe, Bertram. *Revolution and Reality: Essays on the Origin and Fate of the Soviet System*. Chapel Hill: North Carolina University Press, 1981.

Woolley, Reginald Maxwell. *Coronation Rites*. Cambridge: Cambridge University Press, 1915.

Wortman, Richard S. *Scenarios of Power: Myth and Ceremony in the Russian Monarchy. Volume I*. Princeton, NJ: Princeton University Press, 1995.

___ *Scenarios of Power: Myth and Ceremony in Russian Monarchy. Volume II*. Princeton, NJ: Princeton University Press, 2000.

Zaionchkovskii, Peter. *Krizis samoderhavia na ribezhe*. Moscow: Moscow University Press, 1964.

Zelnik, Reginald E., Editor. *A Radical Worker in Tsarist Russia: The Autobiography of Semen Ivanovich Kanatchikov*. Stanford: Stanford University Press, 1986.

Articles

Ashton, Janet, "The coronation of Tsar Alexander II: a translation from a book by Joachim Murat [Duc de Morny]." In *European Royal History Journal (Eurohistory)*, Volume 9, Issue 4, and Volume 9, Issue 5, 2006.

Ashton, Janet. "'Russia owes a great deal to Mr. Stead:' Tsarism's unlikely champion and the international press". In *Atlantis Magazine*, Volume 5, No. 2, 2004, 14-34.

Baker, Helen. "Monarchy Discredited? Reactions to the Khodynka Coronation Catastrophe of 1896." In *Revolutionary Russia*, Volume 16, No. 1, June 2003, 1-46.

Cherniavsky, Michael. "Khan or Basileus: An Aspect of Russian Medieval Political Theory." In *The Journal of the History of Ideas*, Volume 20, No. 4, 1959, 459-476.

"Iz zapisok imperatora Nikolaia I." In *Byloe*, Volume 77, No. 10, 1907/1910, 86-87.

King, Greg. "Glory and Adornment: Kschessinska, the Romanov Men and a Mansion." In *Atlantis Magazine*, Volume 4, No. 3, 2003, 24-52.

von Laue, Theodore. "Imperial Russia at the Turn of the Century: The Cultural Slope and the Revolution from Without." In *Comparative Studies in Society and History*, Volume 3, No. 4, July 1961. Cambridge: Cambridge University Press, 1961.

Lamsdorff, Vladimir. "Dnevnik V.A. Lamzdorfa". In *Krasnyi Arkhiv*, 46 (1931): 10.

Nemirovich-Danchenko, V. I. "Moskva v Mae 1896 goda: Pisma o Koronatsii." In *Niva*, No. 22, 1896.

Pelham-Clinton, Charles. "The Russian Coronation." In *Strand*, Volume 11, 1897, 482-96.

"Perepiska o podkupe kitaiskikh sanovnikov Li-Khun-Chzhana i Chzhan-in-Khuana," In *Krasnyi Arkhiv*, 2 (1922): 287-93.

Perlmann, Moshe. "The British Embassy in St. Petersburg on Russian Jewry, 1890-92." In *Proceedings of the American Academy for Jewish Research*, Volume 48, 1981, 297-323.

Rodichev, F. "The Liberal Movement in Russia, 1891-1905." In *The Slavonic Review*, December 1923, 249-262.

Rowley, Alison. "Monarchy and the Mundane: Picture Postcards and Images of the Romanovs, 1890-1917." In *Revolutionary Russia*, Volume 22, No. 2, December 2009.

Stead, W. T. "Character Sketch: Nicholas II, the Tsar of Russia." In *Review of Reviews*, 1896, 396-407.

Willis, James F. "An Arkansan in St. Petersburg: Clifton Rhodes Breckinridge, Minister to Russia, 1894–1897." In *Arkansas Historical Quarterly*, Volume 38, Spring 1979, 3–31.

Newspapers and Periodicals

Individual issues are cited within the notes by date

La Croix, Paris
Daily Courier, London
Le Figaro, Paris
Le Gaulois, Paris
Illustrated London News
Le Justice, Paris
Krasnii Arkhiv, Moscow
Le Matin, Paris
Moskovkie Vedomosti
New York Times
Niva, St. Petersburg
North Eastern Daily Gazette, Middlesbrough, UK
Novoe Vremia, St. Petersburg
Pall Mall Gazette, London
Le Petit Parisien, Paris
La Presse, Paris
Sheffield Independent, UK
Le Siècle, Paris
Le Temps, Paris
The Times of London
The Times of London, Weekly Edition
L'Universe, Paris

Other Media

Baker, Helen Samantha. *Nicholas II and the Khodynka Catastrophe, May 1896: A Study of Contemporary Responses*. Unpublished PhD Thesis. University of Leeds, 2002.
Sorenson, Thomas C. *The Thought and Policies of Konstantin Pobedonostsev*. Unpublished PhD Thesis. Seattle: University of Washington, 1977.

Websites

http://forum.alexanderpalace.org/index.php?topic=13924.msg496686#msg496686 [accessed October 31, 2011]
http://www.vhok.nl/Expo/n&a/home.htm, Hermitage Amsterdam [accessed 2010, dead link]
Laruelle, Marlène. *The White Tsar": Romantic imperialism in Russia's legitimizing of conquering the Far East*. Acta Slavica Iaponica, 25, 113-134, at http://src-h.slav.hokudai.ac.jp/publictn/acta/25/laruelle.pdf [accessed January 3, 2011]
Nelipa, Margarita. *Alexander III: An Imperial Death Surrounded by Myth*. http://www.facebook.com/note.php?note_id=143898655625916 [accessed April 30, 2013]
Odoievsky-Maslov, Prince. *The Kremlin*. Moscow: Russian Orthodox Synod Press, 1912, at http://www.alexanderpalace.org, http://216.30.130.50/kremlin1912 [accessed February 16, 2011]

Index

A
Agliardi, Cardinal Antonio   vii, 52, 130, 137
Alexander, Harriet   37, 38, 42, 62
Alheim, Pierre d'   22, 152, 157
Apraxin, Kammer Page   x
Aritomo, Marquis Yamagata   54, 82
Arnold, Edwin   22
Arthur, Chester A. (US President)   36
Astor, Mrs Caroline   37
AUSTRIA
Franz Josef, Emperor of 66
Karl Ludwig, Archduke of 66, 168

B
Baker, Helen   176, 179
Bakunin, Michael   xv
BATTENBERG
Beatrice, Princess of (née UK) 49
Henry, Prince of   49
Julie, Princess of (née von Hauke)   vii
Louis, Prince of (later Louis Mountbatten, Marquess of Milford Haven)   vii, 48, 49, 51, 68, 164, 187
Victoria, Princess of (née Hesse and by Rhine – later Marchioness of Milford Haven)   vii, 10, 48, 49, 68, 86, 98, 107, 114, 117, 124, 164

Bariatinsky, Princess Anatole   97, 171
Basil II, Byzantine Emperor xiii
BAVARIA
Ludwig, Prince of (future King Ludwig III)   51, 124, 172

BELGIUM
Albert, Prince of (future King Albert I)   51

Benois, Albert   25
Benson, Edward White   52
Bernstorff, Count Johann von   55, 163, 172
Berr, General N.N.   viii, 32, 33
Bokhara, Sayed Abd al-Ahad Bakhadur-Khan, Emir of viii, 53, 54, 55, 70, 94, 130, 167

Bovey, Charles C.   187
Breckinridge, Katherine Carson   vii, 24, 56, 57, 62, 70, 133
Breckinridge, Clifton R.   vii, xvii, 56, 57, 61, 70, 90, 186
Breckinridge, John (US Vice President)   56
Budberg, Colonel   33
Bulbenkova, Olga   87, 102
BULGARIA
Ferdinand, Prince of (later King Ferdinand)   52
Boris, Crown Prince of (later King Boris III)   52

Bulygin, Alexander   183

C
Cerf, Camille   26
Chang, Li-Hung   ii, vii, xix, 54, 55, 81, 94, 125, 152, 173, 186
Cherkesov, Sergei   x, 59
Chikhachev, N.M.   8
Chira, Prince of Siam   54
Ci-Xi, Empress of China   54, 81
Cleveland, Grover (US President)   56
Creighton, Dr. Mandell   vii, 52, 53, 121, 123, 127, 137
Crocker, Charles   37

D
Dargomyzhsky, Alexander   67
Davidson, Randall   52
Davis, Richard Harding   viii, xix, 23, 25, 27, 30, 39, 44, 46, 52, 65, 70, 72, 73, 77, 92, 94, 96, 97, 107, 113, 114, 116, 117, 118, 126, 186
DENMARK
Christian IX, King of   v, vii, 51
Frederick, Crown Prince of (later King Frederick VIII) vii, 51, 98
Louise, Queen of (née Hesse-Kassel)   67, 97, 150

Deruzhinsky, Kammer Page   x, 97, 98
Dillon, E.J.   182

Index

Dolgoruky, Prince Alexander Sergeievich   x, 71, 79, 89
Doublier, François   viii, 26, 94, 140, 143, 144, 150
Drigo, Riccardo   135

E

Egorov, Ivan   102
Engelhardt, Boris   x, 74, 89, 97, 98, 122, 157

F

Fabergé, Peter Karl   xviii, 42, 85, 103
Faure, Felix   147, 168, 186
Flourence, Emile   13

FRANCE
Bonaparte
Napoleon, Emperor of the French   xiv, 45, 63, 76, 170
Bourbon
Louis XVI, King   xi, 64, 161
Marie Antoinette, Queen (née Austria)   xii, 147, 161

Freedericksz, Baron (later Count) Vladimir   x

G

Gerveux, Henri   25, 97
Giliarovsky, Vladimir   22, 140
Glavatch, V.I.   92
Glazunov, Alexander   123
Glinka, Michael   xiii, xix, 135
Godunov, Boris   xiii, 44, 170
Gojong, King of Korea   54
Golitsyn, Princess Marie   66
Golitsyn, Prince   70
Gounod, Charles   67

GREECE
Constantine, Crown Prince of (future King Constantine I)   52
George I, King (né Denmark)   vii, 52
George, Prince of   52
Nicholas, Prince of   52, 118
Olga, Queen (née Russia)   v, vii, 52, 87, 99, 116, 132

Grenfell, Major-General Sir Francis   vii, xix, 51, 63, 66, 68, 72, 73, 77, 84, 96, 99, 116, 118, 122, 124, 126, 138, 143, 152, 167, 169, 173, 182, 186

H

Hahn, Kurt   88
Harrison, Benjamin (US President)   35
Hearst, William Randolph   25

HESSE AND BY RHINE
Alexander, prince of   vii
Alice, Grand Duchess of (née UK)   10
Ernst Ludwig, Grand Duke of   v, vii, 10, 11, 48, 121
Friedrich, Prince of   10
Ludwig IV, Grand Duke of   10
Victoria Melita, Grand Duchess of (née Edinburgh)   v, 11, 48, 50, 59, 101, 173

Hickley, Mary   viii, xix, 35, 36, 37, 40, 41, 65, 67, 68, 70, 72, 93, 94, 116, 119, 125, 126, 152, 153, 155, 161, 173, 182, 187

I

Ignatiev, Alexei   x, 76, 89, 120
Ioannikius, Metropolitan of Kiev   x, 99, 104, 105, 128
Izwolsky, Alexander   x, 107, 146, 157, 180, 182

K

Kanatchikov, Semen Ivanovich   viii, 64, 70, 134, 144, 162, 183, 186, 187
Karamzin, Nicholas   5
Keller, General Count Feodor   x, 59, 89
Khiva, Khan of   70
Klyuchevsky, Vassili   5
Koon, Katherine   viii, xix, 35, 36, 38, 40, 49, 61, 62, 65, 72, 73, 90, 92, 93, 94, 95, 99, 120, 124, 125, 131, 133, 152, 154, 162, 168, 169, 172, 182, 187
Koon, Marilla Louise   viii, 35, 36, 38, 62, 90, 92, 187
Koon, Martin Buren   viii, 35
Krasnov, Vassili   133
Krivenko, Vassili   x, 27
Kronstadt, Father John of   123
Kschessinska, Mathilde (later Princess Romanovsky-Krassinsky)   viii, 9, 11, 72, 135, 138
Kuropatkin, General Alexei   154

L

Ladow, (Musician) 67
Langtry, Jeanne Marie 49, 51, 187
Langtry, Lilie 49, 187
Lambsdorff, Count Vladimir 29
LaPauze, Henry viii, 22, 64, 70, 77, 79, 92, 95, 116, 127, 137, 161, 182
Launitz, General Von der 167
Le Mouton de Boisdeffre, General Raoul 79, 157, 158
Legnani, Pierrina 135
Lehr, Mrs. 42
Lenin, Vladimir Ilych Ulianov xviii, 4
Leonowens, Anna 54
Liechtenstein, Prince Franz of 168
Lobanov-Rostovsky, Prince Andrei 82
Logan, Edith 35
Logan, Captain John A. vii, viii, 35, 38, 39, 40, 43, 45, 56, 63, 68, 70, 71, 72, 74, 84, 90, 92, 93, 104, 120, 126, 131, 133, 137, 138, 153, 155, 161, 182, 187
Logan, Senator John A. vii, viii, 35, 36
Logan, Mary Cunningham vii, viii, 35, 36, 38, 62, 187
Lobanov-Rostovsky, Prince Andrei 147
Lvovich, Captain 134, 138

M

Malcolm, Ian vii, 39, 42, 51, 72, 73, 92, 93, 161, 187
Mandryk, Alexander x, 76, 89, 119
Mannerheim, Gustav 123, 153
Mark, Karl xviii
Maude, Aylmer viii, xix, 23, 24, 35, 40, 41, 46, 57, 59, 63, 64, 73, 74, 76, 85, 95, 105, 107, 114, 118, 126, 143, 162, 168, 182, 186
Maude, Louise 186
MECKLENBURG-SCHWERIN
Friedrich Franz II, Grand Duke of v

Meiji, Emperor of Japan 54
Mendelssohn, Felix 67
Min, Yŏng-hwan 54, 82, 83
MONACO
Louis, Prince of 51

Mongkut, King of Siam 54
MONTENEGRO
Jelena, Princess of 167
Nicholas, Prince of (later King) 51, 167

Moisson, Charles viii, 26, 94, 140, 143, 144, 150
Montebello, Count Louis Gustave de viii, 57, 79, 92, 146, 147, 157, 158, 163, 169, 186
Montebello, Countess Madeleine de (née Guillemin) viii, 57, 157, 158
Mossolov, Alexander 181
Moy, Baron Carl 120
Muraviev, Nicholas x, 145, 178, 179, 180, 182

N

Nabokov, Dimitri 111
Nabokov, Vladimir 111
Naryshkina-Kurakina, Princess Elisabeth x, 66
Nemirovich-Danchenko, Vladimir viii, 22, 134, 154, 157
Nesterov, Michael 25
Nikolia, Vladimir 32

O

O'Conor, Sir Nicholas viii, 51, 53, 56, 57, 86, 96, 171, 186
Orelov-Davidov, Count (Ober-Stallmeister) 73
Ostrukhov, Alexei 143

P

Pahlen, Count Konstantin von der x, 77, 179, 180, 181, 182
Palladius, of St. Petersburg x, 99, 105, 107, 108, 111, 113, 116, 117, 118, 119, 120, 128
Palmer, Bertha Honoré viii, 37, 38, 42, 62, 187
Palmer, Potter viii, 37, 38, 42
Pasha, Zia Husny 92, 132
Perault, Charles 83
Peterborough, Bishop of 87, 92, 96, 118, 121, 123, 137, 153, 170
Petipa, Marius 135
Petrov-Ropet, Ivan 84
Piasetsky, Paul 26
Pobedonostsev, Konstantin x, 5, 6, 8, 15, 21, 53, 103, 121, 123, 128, 147, 170, 180
Posier, Jérémie 87
PRUSSIA
Frederick the Great, King of 88

Heinrich (Henry), Prince of   vii, 48, 171, 172
Irene, Princess of (née Hesse and by Rhine)   vii, 10, 48
Wilhelm II, German Kaiser   vii, 46, 48, 172

R

Radolin, Hugo, Prince von   viii, 171, 172
Radonezh, St. Sergei of   170
Radziwill, Princess Catherine   30, 72, 74, 119
Rasputin, Gregory   xi, 188, 189
Repin, Ilya   25, 79
Roebling, Emily Warren   viii, 35, 36, 37, 38, 42, 62, 90, 93, 121, 125, 161, 187
Roebling, Washington   36

ROMANIA
Ferdinand, Crown Prince of (later King Ferdinand)   vii, 49, 50
Marie, Crown Princess (née Edinburgh and Saxe-Coburg and Gotha)   vii, x, xvi, xix, 10, 49, 50, 59, 101, 114, 130, 132, 147, 163, 173

Roop, Sergei   x, 59, 98
Roosevelt, Theodore (US President)   186
Rothschild, Baron Alphonse   128

RUSSIA
Alexander I, Tsar   xiv, 18
Alexander II, Tsar   v, vii, xv, 3, 4, 22, 31, 49, 60, 66, 87, 135, 171, 178
Alexander III, Tsar   I, v, vii, x, xv, 1, 2, 3, 4, 5, 7, 10, 11, 12, 13, 16, 18, 21, 22, 28, 30, 31, 33, 37, 52, 60, 61, 67, 79, 80, 88, 96, 103, 124, 135, 149, 156, 179, 181
Alexander Mikhailovich, Grand Duke v, 29, 60, 62, 149, 157, 180
Alexandra Feodorovna, Empress (née Prussia)   xv
Alexandra Feodorovna, Empress (née Hesse and by Rhine)   i, v, vii, x, xi, xii, xvi, xvii, xviii, xix, 9, 10, 11, 12, 13, 16, 17, 18, 24, 26, 29, 46, 48, 49, 50, 51, 55, 56, 60, 61, 62, 63, 64, 65, 66, 67, 68, 72, 73, 74, 76, 77, 79, 81, 84, 86, 87, 88, 89, 96, 98, 101, 102, 103, 104, 105, 107, 113, 114, 116, 117, 118, 119, 120, 121, 122, 124, 125, 126, 127, 128, 130, 131, 132, 135, 137, 146, 148, 153, 154, 155, 157, 158, 161, 163, 164, 165, 166, 168, 169, 170, 171, 172, 173, 175, 176, 180, 181, 182, 185, 186, 187, 188, 189
Alexandra Iosifovna, Grand Duchess (née Saxe-Altenburg)   v, vii, 60, 99, 180
Alexei, Tsar   15, 87, 96
Alexei Alexandrovich, Grand Duke   v, 60, 61, 98, 133, 148, 157, 158, 180, 185
Alexei Nikolaievich, Tsesarevich   v, 188
Anastasia, Grand Princess of Moscow (née Romanoav)   xiii
Andrei Vladimirovich, Grand Duke   viii
Boris Vladimirovich, Grand Duke   50
Catherine I, Empress   xiii, xiv, 83
Catherine the Great   xiv, xvii, 1, 18, 63, 73, 87
Dimitri Ivanovich, Prince of Moscow   xiii, 44
Elisabeth, Empress   xiv, 107
Elisabeth Feodorovna, Grand Duchess (née Hesse and by Rhine)   v, 10, 11, 29, 62, 101, 131, 133, 148, 163, 164, 175, 176, 181, 186
George Alexandrovich, Grand Duke   i, v, 2, 60, 176, 180
George Mikhailovich, Grand Duke of   149
Ivan III, Grand Prince of Moscow   xii, xiii, 95, 96
Ivan IV, Tsar (the Terrible)   xiii, 1, 44, 45, 96, 117, 189
Kirill Vladimirovich, Grand Duke   v, vii, 50, 68, 118, 165
Konstantin Nikolaievich, Grand Duke   v, vii
Konstantin Konstantinovich, Grand Duke   v, 29, 61, 67, 87, 90, 98, 107, 117, 130, 162, 163, 164, 166, 178, 180, 181
Marie Alexandrovna, Empress (née Hesse and by Rhine)   vii, xv, 10, 66
Marie Feodorovna, Empress (née Denmark) v, vii, x, xvii, 2, 4, 5, 8, 9, 10, 11, 13, 16, 18, 30, 51, 52, 55, 61, 66, 67, 73, 74, 76, 77, 82, 87, 88, 89, 96, 97, 98, 99, 101, 102, 103, 111, 116, 119, 122, 125, 126, 127, 130, 135, 137, 138, 148, 149, 150, 152, 156, 161, 162, 165, 166, 168, 169, 170, 171, 180, 187
Marie Pavlovna, Grand Duchess (née Mecklenburg-Schwerin)   v, 61, 96, 121
Marie Pavlovna Jr., Grand Duchess   i
Michael I, Tsar   xiii, xvi, 96, 107, 124, 138, 170
Michael Alexandrovich, Grand Duke   v, 2, 67, 97, 104, 105, 107
Michael Mikhailovich, Grand Duke of 60
Michael Nikolaievich, Grand Duke   v, 130
Nicholas I, Tsar   I, v, vii, xiv, xv, 5, 21, 31, 45, 52, 60, 120, 124, 135, 175, 178, 180
Nicholas II, Tsar   I, ii, v, vii, viii, x, xi, xii, xv, xvi, xvii, xviii, xix, 1, 2, 3, 4, 5, 6, 7, 8, 9, 10, 11, 12, 13, 14, 15, 16, 17, 18, 21, 22, 23, 24, 25, 26, 27, 28, 29, 30, 31, 35, 37, 43, 46, 48, 49, 50, 52, 53, 54, 56, 59, 60, 61, 62, 63, 64, 65, 66, 67, 68, 70, 71, 72, 73, 74, 76, 77, 79, 80, 81, 84, 85, 86, 87, 88, 89, 90, 96, 101, 102, 103, 104, 105, 107, 108, 111, 113, 114, 116, 117, 118, 119, 120, 121, 122, 124, 125, 126, 127, 128, 130, 131, 132, 133, 135, 137,

138, 139, 146, 147, 148, 149, 150, 153, 154, 155, 156, 157, 158, 161, 162, 163, 164, 165, 166, 167, 168, 169, 170, 171, 172, 173, 175, 176, 178, 179, 180, 181, 182, 183, 184, 185, 186, 187, 188
Nicholas Konstantinovich, Grand Duke of 60
Nicholas Mikhailovich, Grand Duke v, 149, 182
Olga Alexandrovna, Grand Duchess v, xvii, 2, 7, 67, 74, 97, 98, 113, 116, 147, 148, 153, 156, 183
Olga Nikolaievna, Grand Duchess v, 17, 62, 64, 104
Paul, Tsar i, xiv, 18, 60, 71, 88, 101, 189
Paul Alexandrovich, Grand Duke i, v, x, 51, 60, 61, 104, 107, 148, 158, 163, 185
Peter the Great i, ii, xiii, xiv, 1, 15, 18, 45, 83, 189
Sergei Alexandrovich, Grand Duke v, x, 10, 11, 28, 29, 30, 31, 32, 33, 51, 59, 60, 63, 68, 76, 104, 107, 117, 145, 146, 148, 149, 150, 153, 156, 157, 158, 162, 163, 164, 165, 166, 167, 169, 170, 175, 176, 178, 179, 180, 181, 183, 185, 186
Sergei Mikhailovich, Grand Duke of 149
Sophie, Regent 45
Vladimir, Grand Prince of Moscow xiii
Vladimir Alexandrovich, Grand Duke v, viii, 33, 50, 51, 60, 61, 76, 96, 104, 107, 119, 121, 123, 135, 148, 158, 163, 165, 185
Xenia Alexandrovna, Grand Duchess v, 2, 11, 62, 154, 163, 180
Zoe, Grand Princess of Moscow (née Paleologue) xiii, 96

Rublev, Andrei 44, 170
Ryabushkin, Andrei 25

Sergei, Metropolitan of Moscow x, 76, 99, 104, 105, 128
Serov, Valentin 25
Shishkova, Maria 162
Shuvalov, Count Paul x, 145, 150, 156, 181
Stalin, Joseph xviii
Stanhope, Aubrey viii, 23, 65, 113, 114, 140, 143, 153, 161, 183
Stackelberg, Baron 70
Stead, W.T. xvi, 21, 23, 37
Susanin, Ivan xiii, 138, 189
Suvorin, Alexei viii, 22, 117, 128, 144, 145, 153, 154, 156, 163, 167, 176-178, 182, 186
SWEDEN
Gustaf, Crown Prince of (future King Gustaf V) 52
Victoria, Crown Princess of (née Baden) 52

Sykes, Arthur Alkin viii, 23, 27

T

Tchaikovsky, Peter 67, 104
Tokijuro, Nishi 54
Tolstoy, Count Leo 23, 37, 186
Ton, Konstantin 45
Trombitsky, A. 87
Trowbridge, Augustus 24
Trubetskoy, Prince Peter x, 70, 169
Trubetskoy, Princess 169
Tuxen, Laurits Regner 25, 97

S

Sadanaru, Prince Fushimi 54, 82, 171
Safonov, V.A. 153
SAVOY
Victor Emanuel, Prince of Naples (future King of Italy) 51, 116, 167

SAXE-COBURG and GOTHA
Alfred, Duke of (also Duke of Edinburgh) vii, 49, 55, 86
Ernst II, Duke of vii
Marie Alexandrovna, Duchess of (née Russia) vii, 49, 171

Selfridge, Admiral Thomas 56

U

Ukhtomskii, Prince Esper 80, 81
Ulyanov, Alexander Ilych 4
UNITED KINGDOM
Alexandra, Princess of Wales (née Denmark) 169
Arthur, Duke of Connaught vii, 50, 51, 66, 86, 116, 132-133, 165
Charles I xi
George V 15, 50
Louise Margaret, Duchess of Connaught (née Prussia) vii, 50, 51, 66, 165
Victoria, Queen vii, xvi, 10, 16, 48, 50, 51, 52, 66, 83, 86, 98, 114, 164, 172, 181

V

Vasnetsov, Viktor   25, 124
VATICAN
Leo XIII, Pope   vii, 52, 130

Vianzone, Therese   viii, 22, 64, 72, 95
Vlassovsky, Colonel A.A.   x, 32, 33, 70, 138, 145, 178, 179
Volkonsky, Prince Sergei   xvii
Volkov, Alexei   x, 120
Vorontsov-Dashkov, Countess Alexandra Hilarionovna   x
Vorontsov-Dashkov, Count Hilarion Ivanovich   x, 29, 30, 31, 32, 33, 104, 128, 138, 145, 146, 148, 150, 156, 162, 163, 164, 178, 179, 180, 181, 182, 185
Vsevelozsky, Ivan   135

W

Wagner, Richard   172
Wallace, Sir Donald Mackenzie   viii, xix, 23, 127, 143
Warth, Robert   185
Winterhalter, Franz Zavier   25
Witte, Count Sergei   x, 7, 14, 23, 30, 32, 55, 152, 156, 157, 176, 179, 180, 181, 182
Worth, Charles Frederick   102
Wortman, Richard   21, 25, 27, 118, 185
WURTTEMBERG
Olga, Queen of (née Russia)   2

Y

Yanishev, Father Ioann   x, 85, 89

Z

Zaguliaev, Michael   22

APAPA

King Christian IX of Denmark and His Descendants

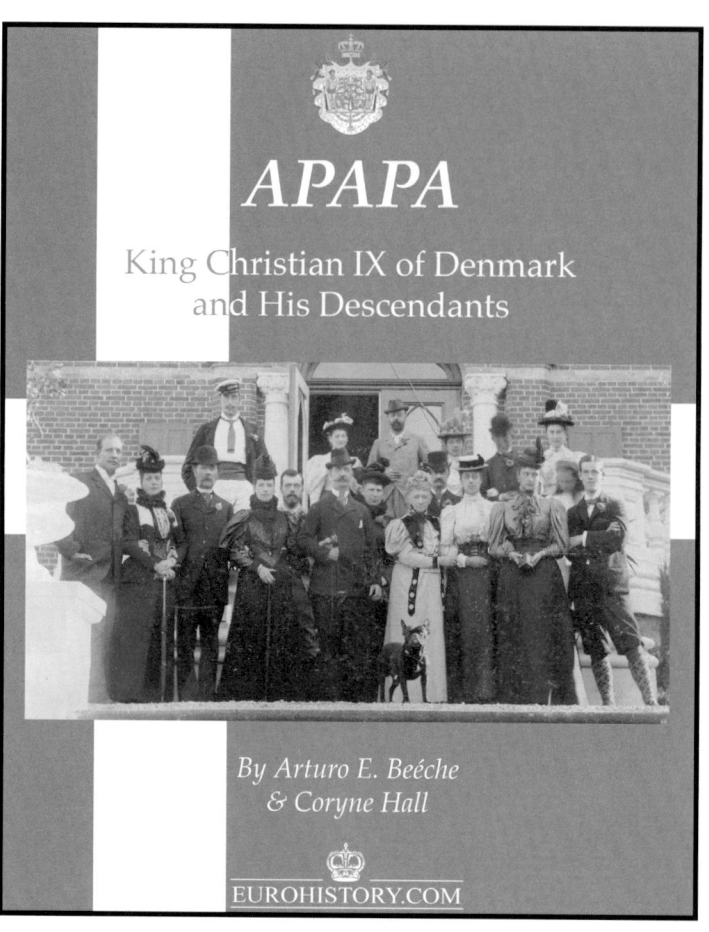

The history of King Christian IX of Denmark, the Father-in-law of Europe, and his descendants. Covering the last 150 years of the royal and imperial houses of: Denmark, Norway, Great Britain, Greece, Romania, Russia, Hanover, Baden, Mecklenburg-Schwerin and many other related dynasties and princely houses.

The authors have handsomely documented their writings with nearly 450 exquisite and rare photos of King Christian IX and his wife Louise and their descendants.

USA price: $48.95 plus shipping ($8.00 in the USA – $35.00 overseas).

Russia and Europe – Dynastic Ties

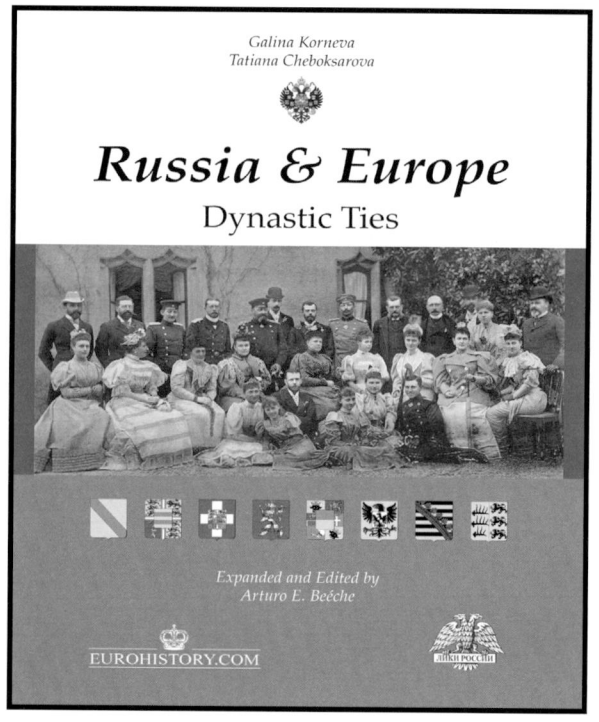

Authored by Galina Korneva and Tatiana Cheboksarova, it includes nearly 600 photos, an overwhelming majority among them collected from the main archives of Russia and several European countries. The moment captured by these original photos is able, often times, to tell the reader far more about the unique world of royalty and aristocracy than countless pages of text. The authors also relied on important information obtained from Russian and foreign periodicals, memoirs and scientific literature. The English-language version of this book was expanded with contributions written by Arturo Beéche, founder and publisher of Eurohistory.

The price of this hardback book is: USA price: $49.95 + shipping ($8 in the USA – $35.00 overseas).

WE SHIP WORLDWIDE!

To order by phone: (510) 236-1730 or email: books@eurohistory.com

The Grand Dukes
Sons and Grandsons of Russia's Tsars

Included in this unique work, the First Volume in a two-volume series, are biographies of Russian grand dukes who were sons of Tsars or Claimants. These grand dukes came from the senior lines of the Russian Imperial Family at the time of the Revolution in 1917. The book is illustrated with exquisite and rare photographs of these intriguing men, their families and descendants. It also includes several family trees. The chapters were authored by some of today's most recognized authors and scholars on the Romanov Dynasty.

The price of this hardback book is: USA price: $43.95 plus $8 shipping and handling. International shipping and handling: $35.00 – WE SHIP WORLDWIDE! To order by phone: (510) 236-1730 or email: books@eurohistory.com

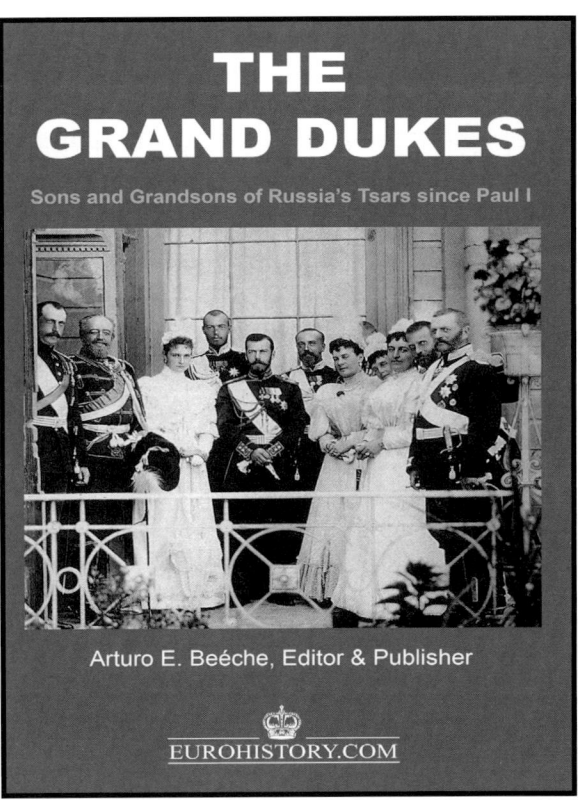

The Other Grand Dukes
Sons and Grandsons of Russia's Grand Dukes

Included in this unique work, the Second Volume in a two-volume series, are 18 biographies of Russian grand dukes. These grand dukes came from the junior lines of the Russian Imperial Family at the time of the Revolution in 1917: Vladimirovichi, Konstantinovichi, Nikolaevichi and Mikhailovichi. The book is illustrated with exquisite and rare photographs of these intriguing men, their families and descendants. It also includes several family trees. The chapters were authored by some of today's most recognized authors and scholars on the Romanov Dynasty. With a foreword by HRH Prince Michael of Kent.

The price of this hardback book is: USA price: $43.95 + shipping ($8 in the USA – $35.00 overseas). WE SHIP WORLDWIDE! To order by phone: (510) 236-1730 or email: books@eurohistory.com

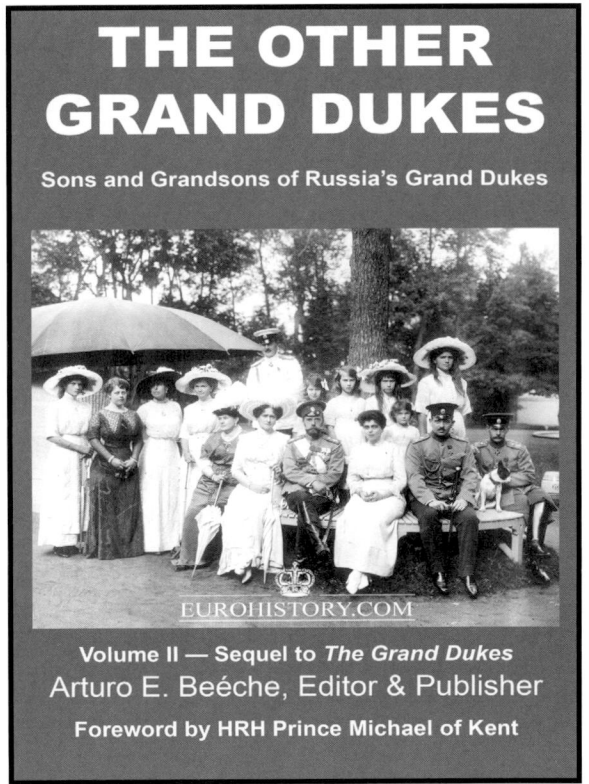

The Grand Duchesses

Eurohistory presents to you an amazing book about the daughters and granddaughters of Russia's Tsars from the time of Paul I.

Included in this unique work, are 26 biographies of Romanov women, along with exquisite and rare photographs — many of them from the private collections of Russia's Imperial Family.

The book also includes eight family trees, 36 glossy pages of beautiful photos of these women and their families — 73 photos in total, as well as contributions from many of today's most distinguished royalty authors.

The price of this paperback book is: USA price: $43.95 plus $8 shipping and handling. International shipping and handling: $35.00.

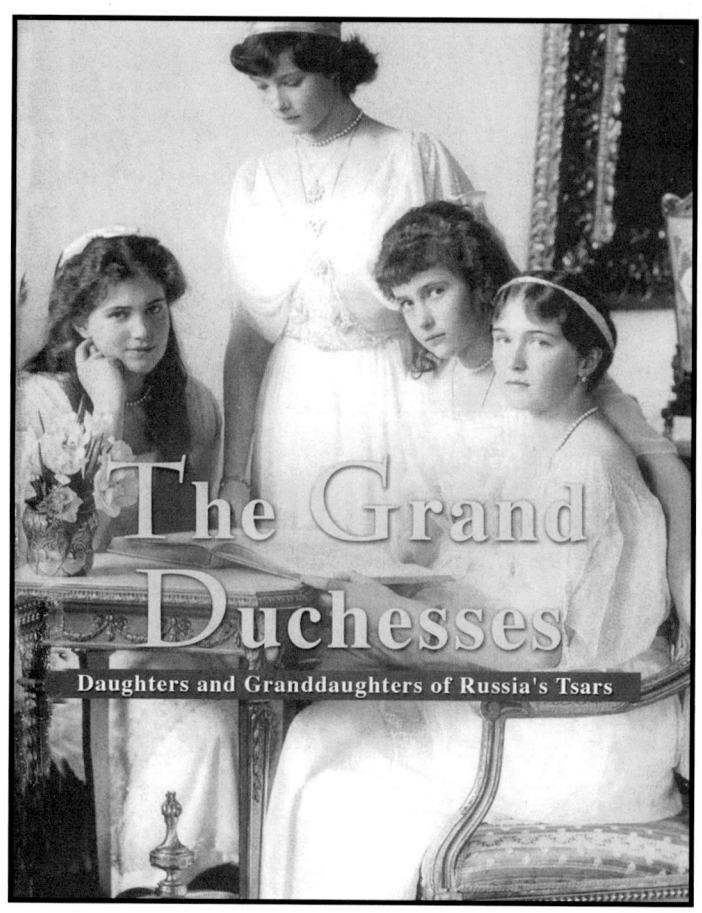

Gilded Prism

Eurohistory is proud to present to you *GILDED PRISM:* The Konstantinovichi Grand Dukes and the Last Years of the Romanov Dynasty, by renowned royalty authors Greg King and Penny Wilson.

It brings to life the story of the Konstantinovich line of the Russian Imperial Family, beginning with Grand Duke Konstantin Nicholaevich (1827-1892) and following the lives of his six children (Nicholas Konstantinovich, Queen Olga of Greece, Vera of Württemberg, Konstantin Konstantinovich (the famed poet KR), Dimitri Konstantinovich and Vyacheslav Konstantinovich) and many of this grandchildren and great-grandchildren. 238 pages, 3 photo sections!

The book sells for $43.95 plus shipping ($8.00 in the USA – $35.00 overseas).

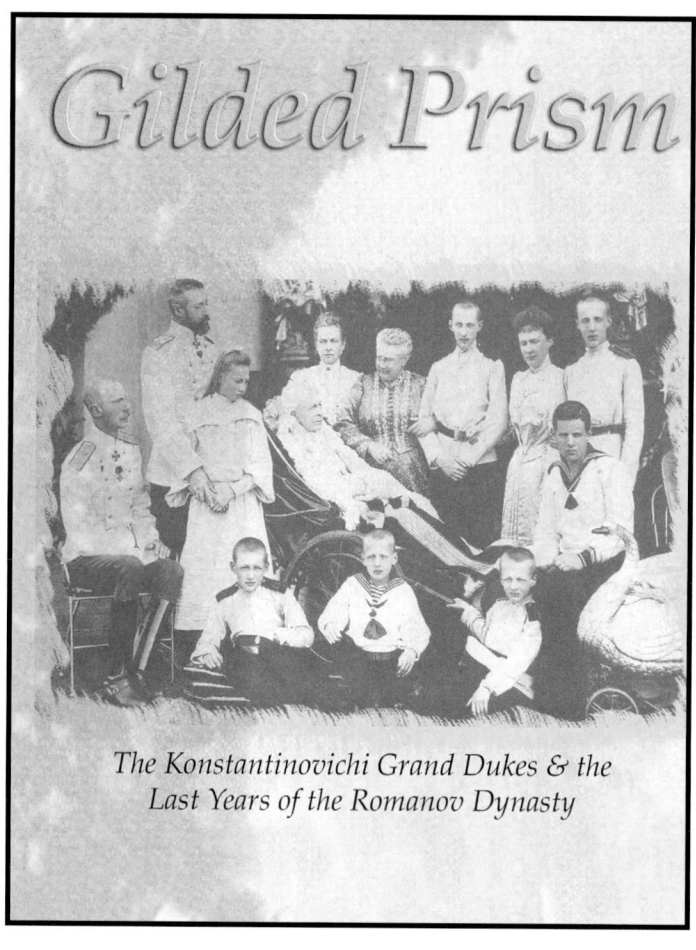

The Konstantinovichi Grand Dukes & the Last Years of the Romanov Dynasty